Palgrave Historical Studies in Witchcraft and Magic

Series Editors
Jonathan Barry
Department of History
University of Exeter
Exeter, United Kingdom

Willem de Blécourt
Sicklehatch
Maynards Green, United Kingdom

Owen Davies
University of Hertfordshire
School of Humanities
Hertfordshire, United Kingdom

The history of European witchcraft and magic continues to fascinate and challenge students and scholars. There is certainly no shortage of books on the subject. Several general surveys of the witch trials and numerous regional and micro studies have been published for an English-speaking readership. While the quality of publications on witchcraft has been high, some regions and topics have received less attention over the years. The aim of this series is to help illuminate these lesser known or little studied aspects of the history of witchcraft and magic. It will also encourage the development of a broader corpus of work in other related areas of magic and the supernatural: such as angels, devils, spirits, ghosts, folk healing and divination. To help further our understanding and interest in this wider history of beliefs and practices, the series will include research that looks beyond the usual focus on Western Europe and that also explores their relevance and influence from the medieval to the modern period.

More information about this series at
http://www.springer.com/series/14693

Francis Young

A History of Exorcism in Catholic Christianity

Francis Young
Cambridge Theological Federation
Cambridge
United Kingdom

Palgrave Historical Studies in Witchcraft and Magic
ISBN 978-3-319-80491-0   ISBN 978-3-319-29112-3 (eBook)
DOI 10.1007/978-3-319-29112-3

© The Editor(s) (if applicable) and The Author(s) 2016
Softcover reprint of the hardcover 1st edition 2016
This work is subject to copyright. All rights are reserved by the Publisher, whether the whole or part of the material is concerned, specifically the rights of translation, reprinting, reuse of illustrations, recitation, broadcasting, reproduction on microfilms or in any other physical way, and transmission or information storage and retrieval, electronic adaptation, computer software, or by similar or dissimilar methodology now known or hereafter developed.
The use of general descriptive names, registered names, trademarks, service marks, etc. in this publication does not imply, even in the absence of a specific statement, that such names are exempt from the relevant protective laws and regulations and therefore free for general use.
The publisher, the authors and the editors are safe to assume that the advice and information in this book are believed to be true and accurate at the date of publication. Neither the publisher nor the authors or the editors give a warranty, express or implied, with respect to the material contained herein or for any errors or omissions that may have been made.

Printed on acid-free paper

This Palgrave Macmillan imprint is published by Springer Nature
The registered company is Springer International Publishing AG, Switzerland

For Abigail

PREFACE

The last three decades have seen an explosion of interest amongst historians in the phenomenon of demonic possession. A large number of studies have dealt with individual cases or collections of cases, most of them from the Reformation era. Most of these studies have focused on the behaviour of the people supposed to have been possessed; some of them have focused on the behaviour of the exorcists. Virtually none of them have dealt with exorcism from a 'procedural' point of view, examining the texts and rituals of exorcism itself. This book aims to supply that deficit, offering an account of the evolution of rites of exorcism. It appears as part of a series dedicated to magic and witchcraft for two reasons. In the first place, exorcism was one possible response to witchcraft. Secondly, exorcism has a complicated relationship with ritual magic, furnishing magicians with many of their texts from the late Middle Ages onwards. The history of magic cannot be properly understood without an appreciation of the history of exorcism.

I first began to work on exorcism in 2009 in the context of English Catholic history, and dealt with the subject in the final chapter of my *English Catholics and the Supernatural, 1553–1829* (2013). However, during the course of research I became acutely aware of the need for a book that defines the boundaries of what can be considered exorcism, and which sets the much-studied early modern exorcisms in their broader historical context. In particular, a book was needed that addressed the textual, ritual and canonical evolution of exorcism. Furthermore, the resurgence of exorcism within twenty-first-century Catholicism is a phenomenon that demands some kind of historical analysis. Do late twentieth- and twenty-first-century exorcisms really hark back to the Middle Ages, or are they a distinctly modern phenomenon whose roots lie in recent history? This book aims to provide that analysis and offer answers to this question and others.

Many people have contributed to this book in more or less significant ways over the last few years. My wife, Rachel Hilditch, has patiently tolerated my preoccupation with all things exorcism-related, and deserves my first and lasting thanks. I am grateful to Dr Bridget Nichols and Dr James Noyes for reading and commenting on portions of my draft manuscript, as well as the anonymous readers appointed by Palgrave Macmillan who contributed such helpful and constructive suggestions. I thank Tim Roe and Annaïck Kisby for their help whenever I have got stuck on translations from Latin and French, and Emily Russell and the staff at Palgrave Macmillan for shepherding this book toward publication. The staff of the Rare Books and Manuscript Rooms at the British Library and Cambridge University Library have been unfailingly helpful, as have the staff of the Kent History and Library Centre. I am grateful to Abbot Geoffrey Scott for allowing me the use of the monastic library at Douai Abbey, which gave me access to some otherwise obscure and inaccessible texts.

Finally, I owe a special debt of gratitude to Fr Jeremy Davies, a founder member of the International Association of Exorcists and exorcist of the Archdiocese of Westminster, for being prepared to read and comment on this book's final chapter from the perspective of a practising exorcist.

All translations from works in languages other than English are my own, unless otherwise stated. Naturally, I take responsibility for any and all errors that may remain in the text.

Francis Young
Ely, Cambridgeshire, UK
November 2015

Contents

1 Introduction   1

2 Exorcism in the Early Christian West, 300–900   27

3 Exorcism in Crisis: The Middle Ages, 900–1500   61

4 Exorcism in Counter-Reformation Europe   99

5 Catholic Exorcism Beyond Catholic Europe   131

6 Exorcism in the Age of Reason   155

7 Exorcism in an Age of Doubt:
   The Nineteenth and Twentieth Centuries   181

8 The Return of Exorcism   209

Bibliography   245

Index   265

Abbreviations

BL   British Library, London
CCCM   *Corpus Christianorum Continuatio Mediaevalis* (Turnhout: Brepols, 1966–2014), 316 vols
CCSL   *Corpus Christianorum Series Latina* (Turnhout: Brepols, 1953–2014), 201 vols
CSEL   *Corpus Scriptorum Ecclesiasticorum Latinorum* (Salzburg: University of Salzburg, 1866–2011), 99 vols
CUL   Cambridge University Library, Cambridge
DESQ   *De Exorcismis et Supplicationibus Quibusdam*, 2nd edn (Vatican City: Typis Vaticanis, 2004)
KHLC   Kent History and Library Centre, Maidstone
OR   *Les Ordines Romani du Haut Moyen Âge*, ed. M. Andrieu (Louvain: Spicilegium Sacrum Lovaniense, 1931–61), 5 vols
PG   *Patrologia Graeca*, ed. J.-P. Migne (Paris, 1857–66), 161 vols
PL   *Patrologia Latina*, ed. J.-P. Migne (Paris, 1844–64), 221 vols
RR   *Rituale Romanum editio princeps (1614)*, ed. M. Sodi and J. J. Flores Arcas (Vatican City: Libreria Editrice Vaticana, 2004)
SG   *Liber sacramentorum Gellonensis, textus*, ed. A. Dumas, *CCSL* 159, 159A (Turnhout: Brepols, 1981), 2 vols
ST   Aquinas, Thomas (ed. P. Caramello), *S. Thomae Aquinatis Summa theologiae* (Turin, 1963), 3 vols

LIST OF TABLES

2.1 Similarities between the rites of exorcism in the
Rituale Romanum (1614) and the Gellone Sacramentary 49
2.2 Similarities between the rites of exorcism in the
Rituale Romanum (1614) and the Paris Supplement 51
8.1 Comparison of the 1614 and 1999 rites of exorcism 235

CHAPTER 1

Introduction

It is likely that there are now more books in print on the subject of Catholic exorcism than at any time in history. They range from journalistic investigations, both sympathetic and hostile, to warnings about the power of the devil and instructions on how the laity can participate in casting out Satan and his demonic servants. Exorcism is widely and freely discussed by twenty-first-century Catholics, and the secular media's appetite for exorcists and stories of exorcism is seemingly insatiable. If the sixteenth and seventeenth centuries were 'the golden age of the demoniac',[1] the twenty-first century is a second golden age of the exorcist. After three centuries of sustained scrutiny and suspicion from within and without the church, exorcism has proved to be a dark yet enduring feature of Catholic culture. Exorcism is in demand as never before, from Catholics and non-Catholics alike, and thanks to the global impact of cinema, the figure of the priest-exorcist has come to be recognized throughout the world.

The contemporary popularity of exorcism raises a historical question. How did exorcism, marginalized for so long, manage a rebirth at the end of the twentieth century? Media events of the last forty years, such as William Friedkin's 1973 film *The Exorcist* and the Satanic abuse panic of the 1980s, do not adequately explain the thorough resurgence of an ancient and controversial practice. The historical roots of exorcism are as

---

[1] Monter, E. W., *Witchcraft in France and Switzerland: The Borderlands during the Reformation* (Ithaca, NY: Cornell University Press, 1976), p. 60.

deep as those of any Christian rite, yet the renewal of interest in exorcism does not so much represent the antiquarian resurrection of a long-dead custom as the re-emergence of an organic, adaptive tradition. The origins of contemporary exorcism lie as much in the apocalyptic spirituality of Pope Leo XIII (1878–1903) and the charismatic exorcisms of Johann-Joseph Gassner in eighteenth-century Germany as they do in twentieth-century events.

To answer thoroughly the question of why exorcism has made a successful come-back, the entire history of exorcism within Catholic Christianity needs to be examined. Many historians are still apologetic when they approach 'an aspect of Catholic religious culture that has long been considered hopelessly superstitious',[2] but while it is certainly not for the historian to determine what is and what is not superstitious, 'superstition' is undoubtedly a subject of historical interest. This book approaches exorcism from the perspective of church history as an aspect of Catholic religious behaviour, concentrating on the development of the theological, liturgical and legal foundations of exorcism rather than the physical phenomena of possession. Sarah Ferber saw religious war, fear of witches and a concern to regulate new spirituality as the 'predisposing conditions' of an explosion in exorcism in sixteenth-century France.[3] This book endorses that thesis, and applies it in more general terms to the entire history of exorcism. In fact, Ferber's conditions can be broken down to just two ingredients essential for a flourishing of exorcism: division within the church and fear of an external spiritual enemy. These factors are almost invariably accompanied by an apocalyptic sensibility, as threats to the church are often construed within a Christian religious outlook as signs of the imminent end of the world. Where one or more of these factors have been absent, the practice of exorcism has undergone a crisis, leading eventually to a transformation to suit better the needs of the time.

Periods in which exorcism has flourished include late antiquity, the early medieval era, the late Middle Ages, the sixteenth and seventeenth centuries and the present day (1980s onwards). Whilst no period of church history has ever been without division, the instigation of reform has produced particularly acute questions of identity for Catholics. This occurred in the

---

[2] Midelfort, H. C. E., *Exorcism and Enlightenment: Johann Joseph Gassner and the Demons of Eighteenth-Century Germany* (New Haven, CT: Yale University Press, 2005), p. 7.

[3] Ferber, S., *Demonic Possession and Exorcism in Early Modern France* (London: Routledge, 2004), p. 4.

sixteenth century, before and after the Council of Trent (1545–63), and again in the twentieth century, when Catholics were divided by interpretation of the Second Vatican Council (1962–65). The threat of paganism in late antiquity and the early Middle Ages eventually passed, producing a crisis for exorcism between the eleventh and thirteenth centuries. A revival of demonology in the thirteenth century, in response to the theological threat to traditional doctrines of evil by the Cathars, formed the background to the late medieval revival of exorcism, aided by an increased awareness of a new threat in the form of witchcraft. The Reformation and a continuing obsession with witchcraft produced perfect conditions for the growth of exorcism in the sixteenth and seventeenth centuries. However, embarrassed by exorcism in an age when the church's relations with secular governments were seen as paramount in importance, church authorities discouraged exorcism in the eighteenth and nineteenth centuries. In other words, exorcism declined as the spiritual threats of heresy and witchcraft were perceived as less important, at least by elites. The roots of the contemporary revival of exorcism lie in Pope Leo XIII's conviction that a new spiritual threat, a Satanist global conspiracy directed by Freemasons, menaced the church in the late nineteenth century.

The story of exorcism can be told in many ways other than as church history. Histories of exorcism could also be written from the perspectives of medical history, the history of mental illness, gender studies, religious anthropology and the sociology of religion, to name just a few.[4]

---

[4] For an approach to exorcism as an aspect of medical history see Clarke, B., *Mental Disorder in Earlier Britain: Exploratory Studies* (Cardiff: University of Wales Press, 1975); on exorcism and gender studies, see Blackwell, J., 'German Narratives of Women's Divine and Demonic Possession and Supernatural Visions 1555–1800: A Bibliography', *Women in German Yearbook* 16 (2000), pp. 241–57; Caciola, N., *Discerning Spirits: Divine and Demonic Possession in the Middle Ages* (Ithaca, NY: Cornell University Press, 2003); for anthropological studies of exorcism see Goodman (1988); Kapferer, B., *A Celebration of Demons: Exorcism and the Aesthetics of Healing in Sri Lanka* (Providence, RI: Berg, 1991); Stirrat, R. L., 'Demonic Possession in Roman Catholic Sri Lanka', *Journal of Anthropological Research* 33 (1977), pp. 133–57; Stirrat, R. L., *Power and Religiosity in a Post-Colonial Setting: Sinhala Catholics in Contemporary Sri Lanka* (Cambridge: Cambridge University Press, 1992); Solomon, R. M., *Living in Two Worlds: Pastoral Responses to Possession in Singapore* (Frankfurt-am-Main: P. Lang, 1994); Carrin-Bouez, M. (ed.), *Managing Distress: Possession and Therapeutic Cults in South Asia* (New Delhi: Manohar, 1999); Chohan, S. S., 'The Exorcist: Personification of Human Wickedness or Upholder of Religious Duties?' in Hamilton, R. P. and Breen, M. S. (eds), *This Thing of Darkness: Perspectives on Evil and Human Wickedness* (Amsterdam: Rodopi, 2004), pp. 103–14.

These histories are undoubtedly needed, but this volume confines itself to the consideration of exorcism as part of the history of the Catholic church. Exorcism in the New Testament and the very earliest centuries of Christianity lies beyond its scope, since its purpose is not to address the ultimate biblical or theological origins of exorcism, but to trace the evolution of exorcism as a practice of the Catholic church. Any attempt to deal with Christian exorcisms before around 150 CE runs into the debate about when Christianity became differentiated from Judaism as a distinct religion. Before the fourth century, when the concept of 'orthodoxy' was established, it is all too easy for the historian to impose 'anachronistic conceptual limitations' on the material.[5] Likewise this study makes no attempt to survey the traditions that emerged from the Protestant Reformation, which have been ably treated elsewhere.[6]

It is by no means uncontroversial to speak of the Catholic church as a single organization with a continuous history from the fourth century.[7] A history of 'the Catholic church' is really a history of 'the Catholic tradition', and in Chap. 2, I use the term 'Latin West', conscious of the ambiguous meaning of the word 'Catholic' in the early centuries of Christianity. This book traces the history of a ritual tradition within Latin Christianity, and is thus more than a history of the institutions and regulations of a

---

[5] Nicolotti, A., *Esorcismo Cristiano e Possessione Diabolica tra II e III Secolo* (Turnhout: Brepols, 2011), pp. 17–8.

[6] On the Reformers' rejection of exorcism see Cameron, E., *Enchanted Europe: Superstition, Reason, and Religion, 1250–1750* (Oxford: Oxford University Press, 2010), pp. 205–8. On the Protestant reform of baptismal exorcism see Kelly, H. A., *The Devil at Baptism: Ritual, Theology and Drama* (Ithaca, NY: Cornell University Press, 1985), pp. 254–71; Nischan, B., 'The Exorcism Controversy and Baptism in the Late Reformation', *Sixteenth Century Journal* 18 (1987), pp. 31–52. On Protestant exorcists see Freeman, T. S., 'Demons, Deviance and Defiance: John Darrell and the Politics of Exorcism in Late Elizabethan England' in Lake, P. and Questier, M. (eds), *Conformity and Orthodoxy in the English Church, c. 1560–1660* (Woodbridge: Boydell, 2000), pp. 34–63; Almond, P. C., *Demonic Possession and Exorcism in Early Modern England: Contemporary Texts and their Cultural Contexts* (Cambridge: Cambridge University Press, 2004); Gibson, M., *Possession, Puritanism and Print: Darrell, Harsnett, Shakespeare and the Elizabethan Exorcism Controversy* (London: Pickering and Chatto, 2006). On contemporary Protestant exorcism and deliverance see Collins, J. M., *Exorcism and Deliverance Ministry in the Twentieth Century: An Analysis of the Practice and Theology of Exorcism in Modern Western Christianity* (Bletchley: Paternoster, 2009).

[7] On this issue see Macy, G., 'Was there a "The Church" in the Middle Ages?' in Swanson, R. (ed.), *Unity and Diversity in the Church* (Cambridge: Cambridge University Press, 1996), pp. 107–16.

reified church. The practice of exorcism is as old as the church, and older than most of the institutions within the church that have tried to regulate it throughout the centuries. Failure to appreciate the antiquity and enduring nature of exorcism is a feature of much contemporary scholarship on exorcism in specific historical eras, and a shortcoming this book is intended to address.

Exorcism and Its Histories

An exorcist speaks with the authority of God to cast out demons. Whether or not this invisible drama really takes place behind the outward words and actions of exorcist and demoniac, the Catholic exorcist's pretensions to authority are grounded not in personal self-assurance but in legal fact. In contemporary Catholicism, exorcists claim to confront the devil not only with the authority of God, but also with that of the church, which they themselves have received by an explicit licence from a diocesan bishop within the strictures of Canon Law. Catholic theology presents exorcism as a political act in the invisible polity, in which the kingdom of Jesus Christ confronts and overthrows the devil's kingdom of darkness. However, exorcism is also a political act on the human level of church history. The entire canonical process of exorcism, beginning with the authorization of the exorcist and ending in the spoken rite, dramatically brings into focus questions of authority and legitimacy, to a greater extent than any other rite of the church. Furthermore, the exorcist is not the only participant in the drama of exorcism: by means of exorcism the demons speak and are bound to tell the truth, so that their words become 'suitable and versatile weapons in inner-church conflicts, theological controversies, and church politics'.[8] Exorcism defines the 'other', that which is opposed to God's church, and it has been exploited both by the defenders of Catholic 'orthodoxy' and dissidents seeking to establish their own claims to authority and authenticity. Individual cases of exorcism, and indeed the question of whether exorcisms should be performed at all, have polarized Catholics for centuries.

For many contemporary Europeans and Americans, including Catholics, the practice of exorcism seems an unaccountable 'medieval' survival whose intrusion into the modern world is discomforting and bizarre. However,

---

[8] Goodman, F. D., *How about Demons? Possession and Exorcism in the Modern World* (Bloomington, IN: Indiana University Press, 1988), p. 97.

the origins of exorcism as practised in the Catholic church today, with its diagnostic criteria and attempted safeguards, lie in the early modern period. Indeed, the Middle Ages were a period of crisis and transition for exorcism, in which it was transformed from the charismatic, saint-focused practice of late antiquity into a liturgical rite invoking priestly authority. For many centuries, a strong tension existed between the idea that exorcism was the preserve of especially holy men and women (or their relics after death) and the notion that any priest could command a demon. By the late Middle Ages exorcism was identified as a sacramental rather than a sacrament: unlike the regenerative grace of baptism or the transubstantiation of bread and wine in the mass, the success of a priestly exorcism was not guaranteed, and depended at least partly on the piety and holiness of the exorcist.

Exorcism as officially practised in the contemporary Catholic church is an adaptation of a seventeenth-century rite liturgically rooted in the early church but applied according to early modern criteria of diagnosis and canonical legitimacy. The intense, confrontational and dramatic exorcisms that captured popular imagination in films such as *The Exorcist*, placing great emphasis on the power of words uttered by a priest, are a distinctly modern phenomenon. The intensity of Counter-Reformation theology imbued the liberation of demoniacs with a new significance in a perceived apocalyptic conflict between the church of God and the synagogue of Satan, in the form of the Protestant Reformation. From the sixteenth century onwards debates about exorcism and possession provided the occasion for discussions of the relationship between mind and body that paved the way for modern psychology. Exorcism, like every other aspect of Catholic liturgy and practice, has evolved and changed over the centuries, but in its present form it is best described as a legacy of the early modern rather than the medieval world.

The purpose of the earliest historical accounts of exorcism by Catholics was to argue for the rite's continuing importance as part of the practice of the church.[9] The German priest Anton Joseph Binterim (1779–1855) began the systematic study of the ancient sources for the rite of exorcism in 1831,[10] and later in the nineteenth century, Ferdinand Probst and

---

[9] Nicolotti (2011), p. 23. See pp. 24–9 for Nicolotti's helpful overview of the literature on exorcism.

[10] Binterim, A. J., *Über die Besessenen (Energumenen) und ihre Behandlung in der alten Kirche* (Munich: Arbeitsgemeinschaft für Religions, 1979), originally published 1831.

Franz Wieland examined the history of exorcism in the context of a discussion of the status of sacramentals and the development of the office of exorcist as a minor order of the clergy.[11] Another German priest, Franz Joseph Dölger, produced the first dedicated modern study of the Patristic and textual sources of baptismal exorcism in 1909.[12] This has only recently been surpassed as an authoritative treatment by the work of Henry Ansgar Kelly and Andrea Nicolotti.[13]

In spite of the extensive historical literature on exorcism, no scholarly work dedicated to the entire history of exorcism exists in English.[14] The contribution that a systematic history of developing attitudes to exorcism could make to Catholic church history has largely been overlooked. Fears of possession, and consequently the practice of exorcism, have tended to surface at times of crisis in the history of the church. At such times exorcism (or the control of exorcism) has served as an important means of establishing authority and identity. The Reformation was not the only period of crisis in the history of the Catholic church when this was true. The recent concentration of historical work on Counter-Reformation exorcisms carries with it a danger that the type of exorcisms practised at that time are projected back onto the medieval past and forward onto the present, when in fact exorcism is a complex and evolving Christian tradition.

---

[11] Probst, F., *Sakramente und Sakramentalien in den drei ersten christlichen Jahrhunderten* (Tübingen: H. Laupp'schen, 1872); Wieland, F., *Die genetische Entwicklung der sog Ordines Minores in den drei erstern Jahrhunderten* (Rome: Herder, 1897).

[12] Dölger, F. J., *Der Exorzismus im altchristlichen Taufritual*, Studien zur Geschichte und Kultur des Altertums 3.1–2 (Paderborn: F. Schöningh, 1909).

[13] The two best short accounts of the history of exorcism in English are Kelly, H. A., *Towards the Death of Satan: The Growth and Decline of Christian Demonology* (London: Geoffrey Chapman, 1968), pp. 77–95; De Waardt, H., 'Demonic Possession: An Introductory Note' in De Waardt, H., Schmidt, J. M., Midelfort, H. C. E. and Bauer, D. R. (eds), *Dämonische Besessenheit: zur Interpretation eines kulturhistorischen Phänomens* (Bielefeld: Verlag für Regionalgeschichte, 2005), pp. 20–35.

[14] As observed by Nicolotti (2011), p. 25. Monika Scala's study in German, *Der Exorzismus in der Katholischen Kirche: Ein liturgisches Ritual zwischen Film, Mythos und Realität* (Hamburg: Friedrich Pustet, 2012) is a fairly comprehensive history of exorcism. Scala sets her analysis of the film *The Exorcist* and reactions to it (pp. 25–143) in the context of an examination of the Biblical and Patristic origins of exorcism (pp. 145–222, 223–311), the early evolution of the Gelasian Sacramentary (pp. 312–49), the *Rituale Romanum* of 1614 (pp. 350–86), the Exorcism of Leo XIII (pp. 387–94) and the revised liturgy of 1999 (pp. 395–424). The essay collection in German and English edited by De Waardt, Schmidt, Midelfort, Lorenz and Bauer, *Dämonische Besessenheit* (2005) also deserves a mention.

The literature on Catholic exorcism produced over the last hundred years can be divided into three broad categories. The first consists of theological reflections by theologians or liturgists on the theory and practice of exorcism, often including its relationship with contemporary understandings of mental health and/or parapsychology.[15] In the second category are collections of exorcism accounts and the personal testimonies of exorcists,[16] while the third category consists of critical historical studies of exorcism from the perspective of religious history. These three categories leave aside the vast popular literature on exorcism and demonology, whether Catholic religious works or the products of sensationalist journalism.

Historical interest in exorcism has tended to focus on certain periods of Christian history whilst neglecting others. So, for instance, the first, second and third centuries have received a great deal of attention from biblical and Patristic scholars,[17] but the period between the fourth and tenth centuries remains comparatively neglected, except where exorcism has been treated as one form of miraculous healing among many.[18] Florence Chave-Mahir's study of exorcism in Western Europe between the tenth and fourteenth centuries is by far the most thorough study of medieval exorcism and, indeed, the only one that tackles directly the period of the High Middle Ages.[19] In addition to her detailed analysis of a wide

---

[15] See Balducci, C., 'Parapsychology and Diabolic Possession', *International Journal of Parapsychology* 8 (1966), pp. 193–212; Suenens, L.-J., *Renewal and the Powers of Darkness* (London: Darton, Longmann and Todd, 1983); Triacca, A., 'Esorcismo: un sacramentale discusso', *Ecclesia Orans* 4 (1987), pp. 285–300.

[16] An early collection of this kind was Traugott K. Österreich's *Possession, Demoniacal and Other, among Primitive Races, in Antiquity, the Middle Ages, and Modern Times* (New York: Routledge and Kegan Paul, 1930). More recently, works of personal testimony by Vatican exorcists have achieved considerable popularity and have reached an audience well beyond the Vatican and Italy by being translated into English (Balducci, C. (trans. J. Aumann), *The Devil: Alive and Active in our World* (Alba House, 1990); Amorth, G., *An Exorcist Tells his Story* (San Francisco, CA: Ignatius Press, 1999); Amorth, G., *An Exorcist: More Stories* (San Francisco, CA: Ignatius Press, 2002); Baglio, M., *The Rite: The Making of a Modern Exorcist* (London: Simon and Schuster, 2009)).

[17] Sorensen, E., *Possession and Exorcism in the New Testament and Early Christianity* (Tübingen: Mohr Siebeck, 2002); Twelftree, G. H., *In the Name of Jesus: Exorcism among the Early Christians* (Grand Rapids, MN: Baker Academic, 2007); Nicolotti (2011).

[18] See, for instance, Gentilcore, D., *Healers and Healing in Early Modern Italy* (Manchester: Manchester University Press, 1998); Porterfield, A., *Healing in the History of Christianity* (Oxford: Oxford University Press, 2005).

[19] Chave-Mahir, F., *L'Exorcisme des Possédés dans l'Eglise d'Occident (Xe–XIVe siècle)* (Turnhout: Brepols, 2011), p. 22. One of the few articles in English on this period is

variety of hagiographical and liturgical sources, Chave-Mahir identified every surviving liturgical book produced between the ninth and fifteenth centuries containing a rite of exorcism,[20] *exempla* of exorcisms most commonly employed in medieval and early modern texts,[21] and every instance of exorcism mentioned in the *Golden Legend* of Jacques de Voragine.[22]

Contemporary historical study of exorcism has its roots in the historiography of witchcraft, and foundational studies such as Keith Thomas's *Religion and the Decline of Magic* (1971), D. P. Walker's *Unclean Spirits* (1981) and Stuart Clark's *Thinking with Demons* (1997) emphasized the links between exorcism, eschatology and the drive to extirpate witchcraft.[23] However, as Armando Maggi observed, one shortcoming of these witchcraft-focused studies was that they did not address exorcism as an important theme in its own right, concentrating instead on deviant exorcists who were thought to have misused the church's rites.[24] In the early 2000s two complementary approaches to exorcism emerged. Maggi and Hilaire Kallendorff developed the study of exorcism as a literary genre and emphasized the formative role of language in early modern exorcisms,[25] with Maggi arguing that the performative voice of the exorcist imposed order on disordered language, while Kallendorff drew attention to the rhetorical nature of exorcism.[26] Nancy Caciola, Moshe Sluhovsky and Sarah Ferber advanced the thesis that late medieval and early modern exorcism developed as a response to anxieties about mysticism and the

---

Goddu, A., 'The Failure of Exorcism in the Middle Ages' in Zimmerman, A. (ed.), *Soziale Ordnungen im Selbstverständnis des Mittelalters*, Miscellanea Mediaevalia 12/2 (Berlin: Walter de Gruyter, 1980), pp. 540–57. On medieval exorcism see also Newman, B., 'Possessed by the Spirit: Devout Women, Demoniacs and the Apostolic Life in the Thirteenth Century', *Speculum* 73 (1998), pp. 733–70; Boureau, A. (trans. T. L. Fagan), *Satan the Heretic: The Birth of Demonology in the Medieval West* (Chicago, IL: University of Chicago Press, 2006).

[20] Chave-Mahir (2011), pp. 343–59.
[21] Ibid. pp. 385–94.
[22] Ibid. pp. 395–9.
[23] Thomas, K., *Religion and the Decline of Magic*, 4th edn (London: Penguin, 1991); Walker, D. P., *Unclean Spirits: Possession and Exorcism in France and England in the late Sixteenth and early Seventeenth Centuries* (London: Scolar, 1981); Clark, S., *Thinking with Demons* (Oxford: Clarendon, 1997).
[24] Maggi, A., *Satan's Rhetoric: A Study of Renaissance Demonology* (Chicago, IL: University of Chicago Press, 2001), p. 104.
[25] Maggi (2001), pp. 96–136; Kallendorf, H., *Exorcism and its Texts: Subjectivity in Early Modern Literature of England and Spain* (Toronto: University of Toronto Press, 2003); Kallendorf, H., 'The Rhetoric of Exorcism', *Rhetorica* 23 (2005), pp. 209–37.
[26] Maggi (2001), p. 106.

need to distinguish between good and evil spirits. Caciola's *Discerning Spirits* (2003) included a detailed study of exorcism and exorcism manuals in the fifteenth century,[27] and this remains one of the few studies of medieval exorcism in English.[28] Sluhovsky's *Believe not Every Spirit* (2007) examined the later development of the 1614 rite of exorcism within a similar historiographical framework,[29] while Ferber's *Demonic Possession and Exorcism in Early Modern France* (2004) approaches its theme through case studies.

The historical literature on early modern possession, exorcism and demonology, by English-speaking and European scholars alike, is vast and growing. The classic studies of Michel de Certeau, Jonathan L. Pearl, Giovanni Levi and David Gentilcore have been complemented by Euan Cameron's significant *Enchanted Europe* (2010) and a plethora of books and articles.[30] However, the majority of studies of early modern 'exorcism' have, in reality, focused on possession. Sluhovsky, for instance, was primarily concerned with exorcists as interpreters of possessed behaviour, and controversies concerning the process of exorcism itself were of secondary interest to him. Brian Levack's recent *The Devil Within* (2013), although subtitled 'Possession and Exorcism in the Christian West', is in reality a history of possession and demoniacs. Just one chapter, 'Expelling

---

[27] Caciola (2003), pp. 225–73; see also Caciola, N., 'Mystics, Demoniacs and the Physiology of Spirit Possession in Medieval Europe', *Comparative Studies in Society and History* 42 (2000), pp. 268–306.

[28] Marek Tamm provided a brief overview of medieval exorcism in 'Saints and Demoniacs: Exorcistic Rites in Medieval Europe (11th–13th Century)', *Folklore: Electronic Journal of Folklore* 23 (2003), pp. 7–24.

[29] Sluhovsky, M., *Believe not Every Spirit: Possession, Mysticism and Discernment in Early Modern Catholicism* (Chicago, IL: University of Chicago Press, 2007).

[30] De Certeau, M., *La Possession de Loudun*, 2nd edn (Paris: Archives Gallimard Juliard, 1980); Pearl, J. L., 'Demons and Politics in France, 1560–1630', *Historical Reflections* 12 (1985), pp. 241–51; Levi, G., *Inheriting Power: The Story of an Exorcist* (Chicago, IL: University of Chicago Press, 1988); Gentilcore, D., *From Bishop to Witch: The System of the Sacred in Early Modern Terra d'Otranto* (Manchester: Manchester University Press, 1992); Pearl, J. L., *The Crime of Crimes: Demonology and Politics in France, 1560–1620* (Waterloo, Ont: Wilfrid Laurier University Press, 1999), pp. 41–58. Other notable studies of early modern exorcism include Weber, H., 'L'Exorcisme à la fin du XVIe siècle: Instrument de la Contre Réforme et Spectacle Baroque', *Nouvelle Revue du Seizième Siècle* 1 (1983), pp. 79–101; Tolosana, C. L., *Demonios y Exorcismos en los Siglos de Oro* (Madrid: Akal, 1990); Romeo, G., *Inquisitori, Esorcisti e Streghe nell'Italia della Controriforma* (Florence: Sansoni, 2003); Ferber (2004); Lederer, D., *Madness, Religion and the State in Early Modern Europe: A Bavarian Beacon* (Cambridge: Cambridge University Press, 2006).

the Demon', addresses exorcism directly, and even here the focus is on the purposes of exorcism. Levack devotes fewer than ten pages to the techniques of exorcism themselves.[31]

Although no study has ever been devoted to exorcism in the early modern Americas, numerous historians have written on demonology and the relationship between exorcism and the Inquisition in the Spanish and Portuguese Americas.[32] The work of Hans de Waardt and Marc Wingens on Catholic exorcisms in the Protestant Dutch Republic is complemented by Alexandra Walsham's investigations into Catholic exorcisms as miraculous healing in England, as well as my own extensive analysis of exorcism as part of the Counter-Reformation Catholic mission in England.[33] Possessions and bewitchment became almost synonymous in many countries in the eighteenth century, and the history of exorcism at this period has tended to be subsumed within studies of European witchcraft and a large body of literature concerning the history of belief in the devil.[34]

---

[31] Levack, B., *The Devil Within: Possession and Exorcism in the Christian West* (New Haven, CT: Yale University Press, 2013), pp. 100–10.

[32] Cervantes, F., *The Devil in the New World: The Impact of Diabolism in New Spain* (New Haven, CT: Yale University Press, 1994); De Mello e Souza, L. (trans. D. Grosklaus Whitty), *The Devil and the Land of the Holy Cross: Witchcraft, Slavery, and Popular Religion in Colonial Brazil* (Austin, TX: University of Texas Press, 2003); Ebright, M. and Hendricks, R., *The Witches of Abiquiu: the Governor, the Priest, the Genizaro Indians, and the Devil* (Albuquerque, NM: University of New Mexico Press, 2006); Mills, K., 'Demonios within and without: Hieronymites and the Devil in the early modern Hispanic world' in Cervantes, F. and Redden, A. (eds), *Angels, Demons and the New World* (Cambridge: Cambridge University Press, 2013), pp. 40–68, at pp. 53–5.

[33] Wingens, M., 'Political Change and Demon Possession in the South of the Dutch Republic: The Confrontation of a Protestant Bailiff and a Catholic Priest in 1650' in De Waardt et al. (2005), pp. 249–62; De Waardt, H., 'Jesuits, Propaganda and Faith Healing in the Dutch Republic', *History* 94 (2009), pp. 344–59; Walsham, A., 'Miracles and the Counter-Reformation Mission to England', *The Historical Journal* 46 (2003), pp. 779–815; Young, F., 'Catholic Exorcism in Early Modern England: Polemic, Propaganda and Folklore', *Recusant History* 29 (2009), pp. 487–507; Young, F., *English Catholics and the Supernatural, 1553–1829* (Farnham: Ashgate, 2013), pp. 189–230.

[34] For discussions of exorcism as a remedy for witchcraft see Davies, O., *Witchcraft, Magic and Culture 1736–1951* (Manchester: Manchester University Press, 1999), pp. 23–6; Seitz, J., *Witchcraft and Inquisition in Early Modern Venice* (Cambridge: Cambridge University Press, 2011), pp. 97–103. On the devil see Russell, J. B., *The Devil: Perceptions of Evil from Antiquity to Primitive Christianity* (Ithaca, NY: Cornell University Press, 1977); Nugent, C., *Masks of Satan: The Demonic in History* (London: Sheed and Ward, 1983); Russell, J. B., *Lucifer, The Devil in the Middle Ages* (Ithaca, NY: Cornell University Press, 1984); Russell, J. B., *Mephistopheles: the Devil in the Modern World* (Ithaca, NY: Cornell University

Of course, there are exceptions, notably Erik Midelfort's work on Johann-Joseph Gassner and Elena Brambilla's important study of the relationship between exorcism, medicine and the church in eighteenth-century Italy.[35] Historical studies of possession and exorcism in the nineteenth and early twentieth centuries are scarce,[36] yet this is a period that deserves attention. In the nineteenth century, for the first time since the Middle Ages, the laity (and sometimes demoniacs themselves) became the driving force behind exorcism, rather than the clergy.

The Catholic church's strict secrecy regarding exorcisms presents an obvious obstacle to the historian seeking to give an account of exorcism in the twentieth century when, in theory, records of exorcisms and their authorization were kept by diocesan chanceries. Fr Jeremy Davies, exorcist of the Archdiocese of Westminster, was kind enough to share with me his views on contemporary exorcism, but it would have been unreasonable of me to expect him to reveal any specific details of his work, given the strictures of Canon Law. However, a couple of high-profile exorcisms have been extensively documented in the public domain, notably those of the Bavarian student Anneliese Michel in 1976 and the American boy known as 'Robbie Mannheim' or 'Roland Doe' in 1949. Michel's death during an ongoing exorcism led to the trial of her parents and two exorcists and, consequently, the public release of all papers relating to the exorcism. Felicitas Goodman's analysis of this case from the perspective of religious anthropology and comparative psychology is a valuable contribution to the

---

Press, 1986); Forsyth, N., *The Old Enemy: Satan and the Combat Myth* (Princeton, NJ: Princeton University Press, 1987); O'Grady, J., *The Prince of Darkness: The Devil in History, Religion and the Human Psyche* (Longmead: Element Books, 1989); Messadié, G. (trans. M. Romano), *The History of the Devil* (London: Newleaf, 1996); Pagels, E., *The Origin of Satan* (London: Allen Lane, 1996); Muchembled, R. (trans. J. Birrell), *A History of the Devil from the Middle Ages to the Present* (Cambridge: Polity Press, 2003); Johnstone, N., *The Devil and Demonism in Early Modern England* (Cambridge: Cambridge University Press, 2006); Kelly, H. A., *Satan: A Biography* (Cambridge: Cambridge University Press, 2006); Oldridge, D., *The Devil in Tudor and Stuart England*, 3rd edn (Stroud: History Press, 2010).

[35] Midelfort (2005a); Brambilla, E., *Corpi Invasi e Viaggi dell'Anima: santita, possessione, esorcismo dalla teologia barocca alla medicina illuminista* (Rome: Viella, 2010).

[36] Two important studies are Harris, R., 'Possession on the Borders: The "Mal de Morzine" in Nineteenth-Century France', *Journal of Modern History* 69 (1997), pp. 451–78; Tausiet, M., 'The Possessed of Tosos (1812–1814): Witchcraft and Popular Justice during the Spanish Revolution' in De Waardt et al. (2005), pp. 263–80. Brian Levack devotes a chapter to comparison of twentieth-century and early modern possessions (Levack (2013), pp. 240–53).

history of twentieth-century exorcism, while Thomas B. Allen's detailed study of the exorcism of 'Robbie Mannheim' shows more concern for critical analysis of the historical material than most journalistic accounts of exorcism.[37]

In spite of the small number of documented twentieth-century exorcisms, the papacies of John Paul II (1978–2005) and Benedict XVI (2005–13) fostered a revival of conservative theological thought on the devil, creating an environment conducive to practising exorcists sharing their own and others' experiences. Gabriele Amorth's two books about his mentor Candido Amantini, and José Antonio Fortea's *Summa Demoniaca* (2008), a latter-day manual for exorcists, offer considerable insight into the beliefs and practices of twenty-first-century Catholic exorcists. However, sceptical voices of dissent from within the Catholic community, such as the Jesuits Henry Ansgar Kelly and Juan B. Cortés, cannot be overlooked.[38] The resurgence of exorcism from the 1970s onwards has been the subject of Michael Cuneo's *American Exorcism* (2001) and James Collins's comparative study of 'charismatic' twentieth-century exorcists of all backgrounds, from Pentecostal to Catholic.[39] However, both Cuneo and Collins concentrated on America, and there has been little consideration of contemporary European exorcists in their historical context.

Defining Exorcism, Possession and Demons

Exorcism, possession and demonology each have a distinct and separable history, albeit the history of each has mingled and intersected with that of the others.[40] Demonology in the abstract need not involve any reference to exorcism at all, and likewise possession has not always resulted in exorcism. However, there is no exorcism without possession, and demonological theory, to a greater or lesser extent, underlies every exorcism.

---

[37] Goodman, F. D., *The Exorcism of Anneliese Michel*, 2nd edn (Eugene, OR: Resource Publications, 2005); Allen, T. B., *Possessed: The True Story of an Exorcism*, 2nd edn (Lincoln, NE: iUniverse, 2000).

[38] Kelly, H. A., *Towards the Death of Satan: The Growth and Decline of Christian Demonology* (London: Geoffrey Chapman, 1968); Cortés, J. B. and Gatti, F., *The Case against Possessions and Exorcisms: A Historical, Biblical and Psychological Analysis of Demons, Devils and Demoniacs* (New York: Vantage, 1975).

[39] Cuneo, M. W., *American Exorcism: Expelling Demons in the Land of Plenty*, 2nd edn (London: Bantam, 2002); Collins (2009).

[40] Chave-Mahir (2011), p. 15.

Historians have adopted a variety of different approaches to the problem of the 'reality' of possession. Brian Levack, whilst rejecting all previous interpretations of 'what is really going on' in possessions, nevertheless insists that the historian must offer some sort of answer, and chooses to interpret possessions as conscious or unconscious 'theatrical productions' following a religious script.[41] Moshe Sluhovsky was critical of 'psychopathological', 'sociological feminist' and 'communicative-performative' explanations of demoniac behaviour,[42] and Sarah Ferber has likewise rejected attempts to 'pathologise' the possessed, on the grounds that we might as well do the same to the exorcists.[43] Ramsay MacMullen argued that the historian who doubts the reality of what ancient people believed they saw is engaged in theology, not history.[44]

For the greater part of the sixteen centuries covered by this study, possession was a reality for those who believed that they or their loved ones experienced it, and the effects of exorcism were equally real to them. The starting point for a historical study of exorcism must be to treat possession and the effectiveness of exorcism as experiential realities for the individuals and communities who believed they were subject to demonic attack. Attempts at 'historical diagnosis', such as Richard Raiswell and Peter Dendle's suggestion that most of the demoniacs in Anglo-Saxon England were suffering from epilepsy,[45] create difficulties. If possession was mental or physical illness, why was exorcism thought to work? Speculation concerning the reasons for the effectiveness or ineffectiveness of exorcism may have a place in medical history, but in a history of the practice of exorcism it is an unwelcome distraction. At the same time, however, it must be recognized that neither possession nor exorcism have ever been stable categories unaffected by their historical context. As Raiswell points out,

> ... just as the devil lacks a fixed and wholly coherent identity, as his nature and significance vary according to the time and place in which he is perceived, so the strategies employed to redress his incursions shift according

---

[41] Levack (2013), pp. 29–31.
[42] Sluhovsky (2007), pp. 2–6.
[43] Ferber (2004), p. 49.
[44] MacMullen, R., *Christianizing the Roman Empire (A.D. 100–400)* (New Haven, CT: Yale University Press, 1984), p. 24.
[45] Raiswell, R. and Dendle, P., 'Demon Possession in Anglo-Saxon and Early Modern England: Continuity and Evolution in Social Context', *Journal of British Studies* 47 (2008), 738–67, at p. 745.

to the social and cultural context in which he is detected ... the methods people used were as varied as the guises of the devil himself.[46]

Consequently, to assume—or even to entertain—the reality of spiritual phenomena in a historical work makes the business of history all but impossible, because behaviours and practices need to be evaluated within their historical context rather than as expressions of timeless religious truths. The question of the real existence of demonic personalities needs to be set aside in order to permit historical judgements, but so also do alternative explanations that run the risk of imposing contemporary frameworks of thought on pre-modern and early modern people. As Raiswell and Dendle have noted in relation to the devil, 'imposing a single, universalist definition on an imaginary concept ... that is a reflection of people's lived experience only as it is refracted through contemporary theological, natural philosophical and legal paradigms' carries with it numerous difficulties, and the same is equally true of exorcism.[47]

Theologians, anthropologists and historians under anthropological influence have a tendency to define exorcism very differently. J. Forget's theological definition has proved influential, forming the basis of Edward Gratsch's definition in the *New Catholic Encyclopedia* (1967) as well as the definition adopted by Nicolotti: 'The means employed to expel a real or alleged demon, by casting it out from one place, body or object, especially a human body, which it occupies, possesses, haunts or invades'.[48] Gratsch modified this to 'The act of driving out or warding off demons or evil spirits from persons, places, or things that are, or are believed to be, possessed or infested by them or are liable to become instruments of their malice'.[49] Gratsch thus took account of the possibility that exorcism may be deployed as an apotropaic or preventative measure as well as a literal driving out of demons. However, apotropaic practices guarding against

---

[46] Raiswell, R., 'Introduction: Conceptualising the Devil in Society' in Raiswell, R. and Dendle, R. (eds), *The Devil in Society in Pre-Modern Europe* (Toronto: Centre for Reformation Studies, 2012), pp. 23–68, at pp. 58–9.

[47] Raiswell, R. and Dendle, P., 'Epilogue: Inscribing the Devil in Cultural Contexts' in Raiswell, R. and Dendle, P. (eds), *The Devil in Society in Pre-Modern Europe* (Toronto: Centre for Reformation and Renaissance Studies, 2012), pp. 537–51, at p. 537.

[48] Forget, J., 'Exorcisme' in Vacant, A. et al. (eds), *Dictionnaire de Théologie Catholique* (Paris, 1903–50), vol. 5:2, pp. 1762–80.

[49] Gratsch, E. J., 'Exorcism' in *The New Catholic Encyclopedia*, 2nd edn (Washington, DC: Catholic University of America, 2003), vol. 5, pp. 551–3, at p. 551.

evil are technically distinct from exorcism itself, even though apotropaic words and gestures such as the sign of the cross form part of the rites of exorcism. Apotropaic words and gestures, whilst not exorcistic in themselves, can easily become exorcistic through adaptation for the purpose of expelling evil.

Whereas theologians argue that exorcism is a manifestation of God's grace, entrusted to the church and performed through the exorcist,[50] many anthropologists view exorcism, Christian or otherwise, as a practice 'of a decisively magical character'.[51] One interpretative issue facing the historian of exorcism is whether exorcism should be defined by an underlying human need to cast out evil, or whether it should be defined in terms of specific religious beliefs and therefore by religious leaders. Another is whether the activity of exorcism should be defined in relation to the exorcist, as a 'commander of demons' claiming special powers for himself, or whether it should be defined in relation to the victim of possession as a therapeutic activity. This study, which is confined to the practice of exorcism within one form of Christianity, cannot consider the broader anthropological question of whether 'exorcism' is a phenomenon present in all or most human cultures. However, historians who treat exorcism primarily as a cross-cultural anthropological category run the risk of losing sight of the profound controversies that the practice of exorcism has created in Catholic history. If exorcism is seen as 'commanding demons', then it is clear that it cannot be distinguished in any meaningful way from magic, especially Western European ritual magic inspired by stories of Solomon's power over demons: the priest exorcizing a demoniac was no more and no less an exorcist than the magician conjuring and dismissing demons. The official exorcistic practice of the contemporary Catholic church emphasizes the therapeutic aspect of exorcism, but historically the main difference between exorcism and ritual magic has been one of authorization rather than form or function. Ritual magic is unauthorized exorcism.

The separation of exorcism and magic is a difficult—if not impossible—historical exercise, and reiterated 'official' statements from the church that

---

[50] See, for instance, Elmer, L. J., 'Exorcism: Theology' in *New Catholic Encyclopedia* (2003), vol. 5, p. 553: 'It is always the Church that prays through the instrumentality of the exorcist, so that the efficacy of the rite is analogous to that of the sacramentals'.

[51] Nicolotti (2011), p. 32. An influential anthropological treatment of exorcism was Favret-Saada, J., *Les Mots, la Mort, les Sorts* (Paris: Gallimard, 1977). See also the summary of the anthropological literature in Boddy, J., 'Spirit Possession Revisited: Beyond Instrumentality', *Annual Review of Anthropology* 23 (1994), pp. 407–34.

exorcism has nothing to do with magic do not change the fact that rites of exorcism share profoundly similar structural features with ritual magic. The abiding relationship between exorcism and magic raises a 'chicken and egg' question that is, perhaps, unanswerable: did magicians draw on the church's exorcisms before exorcists drew on magical material, or vice versa? On the basis that magicians tend to draw on any source of sacred power available within their cultural context, it seems likely that the church's rites of exorcism were put to magical use as soon as they came into being. The extent to which the church's rites were influenced by magical texts is a great deal more difficult to determine, although it is certainly possible to argue that exorcisms are by their very nature a form of magic. Exorcism formed part of every procedure of ritual magic, and as Maijastina Kahlos has observed, 'The label of magic is a marginalizing strategy that reveals the presence of contest over religious authority'.[52] What is a solemn religious rite for one person may be a superstitious magical operation to another. Even if we endeavour to distinguish exorcism and magic by means of authority, this is complicated by the fact that exorcists authorized by the church might act just like magicians and introduce elements into the rite that did not have official approval: yet until 1614, there was no such thing as an official rite of exorcism anyway.

The conflict between Catholic lay exorcists, charismatic clerical exorcists and a centralizing church was an important feature of the history of exorcism in the late Middle Ages and early modern period. Catholicism is and has been for many centuries a global and multifaceted religious culture, and a history of Catholic exorcism cannot confine itself to the institutional history of exorcism by approved clergy. If Catholic exorcism is defined as 'exorcism as practised by Catholics', rather than 'exorcism as defined by the Catholic church', then it embraces the phenomena of lay exorcism and exorcism by means of objects, as well as unauthorized exorcisms by Catholic clergy, not to mention the baptismal exorcism performed by all priests and exorcisms that form part of magical rituals. Throughout history, Catholic laypeople have attempted exorcisms, consciously invoking the church's power and often making use of objects believed to be imbued with sacred power such as relics and sacramentals. Furthermore, enterprising clergy promoted the exorcistic power of particular shrines and relics

---

[52] Kahlos, M., 'The Early Church' in Collins, D. J. (ed.), *The Cambridge History of Magic and Witchcraft in the West* (Cambridge: Cambridge University Press, 2015), pp. 148–82, at p. 152.

and developed elaborate exorcistic procedures that went far beyond the authorized liturgies. The extent to which these practices were condoned by church authorities varied from age to age, but lay exorcism became especially important during the Reformation period for Catholics isolated within Protestant societies.

Christian exorcism, like Christian prayer, is founded on an underlying belief in the power of an omnipotent God. Unlike prayer, however, exorcism involves an adjuration or direct imperative speech directed towards spiritual beings other than God, saints and angels. Where prayer is supplicatory, exorcism is imperative. Differentiating exorcism from magic is notoriously difficult, and depends to a large extent on the definition of magic adopted.[53] In Graham Twelftree's view, early Christian exorcism was distinguishable from magic only in form rather than function. The early Christians did not follow the 'magico-charismatic' approach of Jesus himself and 'resorted to a more magical method, which depended not so much on their own personal force as on explicitly engaging an outside power-authority to evict the demons'. On the other hand, Christians' high level of confidence that the exorcism would work and the 'extreme brevity of their method' distinguished them from the magicians of the era.[54] Assurances from the church that exorcism is not magic cannot be taken at face value.

The Latin word *exorcizo*, a direct borrowing from the Greek, originated in legal terminology; its ultimate root was the Greek *horkos*, 'an oath'. To exorcize, in its Greek and Latin legal meanings, meant 'to swear an oath',[55] and in Latin became almost synonymous with *coniuro*, 'to take an oath together'. However, over time the compound verb *coniuro* was used as an intensified form of the verb *iuro*, 'I swear', and in late Latin it came to have the sense of 'beg' or 'implore'. The medieval Latin *coniuro* produced the English word 'conjure', whose original legal and religious sense has now been replaced almost completely by its magical sense (which always existed alongside the other meanings). The difficulty of separating exorcism from magic therefore occurs at the linguistic level; 'conjuration' is an activity of the magician and exorcist alike. Eusebius, bishop of

---

[53] On the relationship between magic and Christian exorcism see Amirav, H., 'The Application of Magical Formulas of Invocation in Christian Contexts' in Vos, N. and Otten, W., *Demons and the Devil in Ancient and Mediaeval Christianity* (Leiden: Brill, 2011), pp. 117–27.

[54] Twelftree (2007), p. 280.

[55] For a detailed discussion of the etymology see Nicolotti (2011), pp. 33–8.

Dorylaeum, addressed the Council of Chalcedon in 451 as if invoking a magical formula: 'I adjure you by the Holy Trinity' (*per sanctam trinitatem vos adiuro*).[56] Amirav has argued that this demonstrated the extent to which early Christianity was suffused with the vocabulary of magic. Christians claimed that the religious identity of the exorcist, rather than his or her skill, was the determining factor in the exorcism's success,[57] but this is true of much ritual magic as well: many medieval and early modern grimoires require the operator to be a priest, a cleric or at the very least a baptized Christian. For Amirav, the earliest Christians 'embraced magic and were familiar with its technicalities', and it was only in the fourth century, when 'a sense of embarrassment crept into the psyche of the patristic Fathers', that sustained attempts were made to differentiate Christian practices from magic.[58]

Amirav's interpretation is based on a controversial reading of Acts 19:13–20 as advocating revision of the way in which magical formulas should be used, rather than a rejection of all magic. The 'official' view of the contemporary church is that exorcism does not work via the intrinsic power of specific words which have the capacity to restrain or expel an evil spirit, but attachment to specific words does not necessarily define magic. At the opposite extreme to Amirav, Elmar Bartsch argued that the original sense of *exorcizo* in the liturgy had nothing to do with driving out demons; it had the sense of 'command the attention of' or 'address solemnly by way of apostrophe'. Only later did the Fathers interpret it as meaning a driving out of demons.[59] This interpretation of the original meaning of exorcism, coinciding with the bias of twentieth-century liberal theology, was broadly endorsed by Kelly,[60] but it risks imposing the intellectual values of the late twentieth century on early Christians, and such a complete rejection of a magical worldview seems improbable in late antiquity.

Nicolotti distinguished four Latin terms describing different kinds of possession phenomena: *circumsessio*, *infestatio*, *obsessio*, *possessio*

---

[56] According to the Latin translation of Rusticus (Schwartz, E. (ed.), *Acta Conciliorum Oecumenicorum. Concilium Oecumenicum Chalcedonense*, 3.1 (Berlin: De Gruyter, 1935), p. 41).

[57] Amirav (2011), pp. 120–1.

[58] Ibid. pp. 126–7.

[59] Bartsch, E., *Die Sachbeschwörungen der römischen Liturgie: eine liturgiegeschichtliche und liturgietheologische Studie* (Münster: Aschendorff, 1967), pp. 387–91.

[60] Kelly (1985), p. 226.

and *insessio*.⁶¹ *Circumsessio* denotes 'a vexation and a persistent negative action against a person which manifests itself as a true and proper siege', whilst *infestatio* is 'vexatious activity explained with reference to persons or things', for instance witchcraft or cursed objects. *Obsessio* and *possessio* are so often used interchangeably in the theological sources that defining their meaning is very difficult indeed, and therefore Nicolotti resorts to the word *insessio* to mean the bodily possession of a human body by an evil spirit. This approach, whilst admirably precise, forces Nicolotti to coin a new word in the vernacular inaccessible to all but the specialist, and for this reason I use the word 'possession' throughout to refer to people whose bodies were allegedly under the control of an evil spirit.

Matters are further complicated by the fact that 'possession' is not, in every case, a negative term. Frankfurter has argued that 'divine possession' or possession by angelic spirits was also a feature of early Christianity, and that every case of 'possession' underwent a process of performance, negotiation and interpretation.⁶² In late fourth-century Nola, demoniacs claimed to be afflicted by St Felix.⁶³ 'Divine possession' has, indeed, been a feature of the Western Christian mystical tradition throughout history, and was a particularly prominent feature of some late medieval and early modern spiritualities.⁶⁴ In Frankfurter's view, 'possession' is a neutral term in itself and a perennial form taken by religious experience, and the interpretation of specific cases of possession as evil in origin has more to do with power relations generating the 'polarized classifications' of good and evil than with the original religious experience. 'Possession' may be a manifestation of the supernatural or a source of prophecy, and is not merely a negative state to be exorcized as soon as possible. Michael Cuneo offers a more modern interpretation of the same issue, arguing that exorcism in contemporary America serves a double function as a way of designating moral behaviour (and the consequences of immorality) and a

---

⁶¹ Nicolotti (2011), p. 31.

⁶² Frankfurter (2010), pp. 27–46. On divine possession see also Ericson, G., 'The Enigmatic Metamorphosis: From Divine Possession to Demonic Possession', *Journal of Popular Culture* 11 (1977), pp. 656–81.

⁶³ Paulinus of Nola, *Carmen* 14.25–33 in Walsh, P. G. (trans.), *The Poems of St. Paulinus of Nola* (New York: Newman Press, 1975), p. 78.

⁶⁴ On divine possession see Caciola (2000), pp. 268–306 and idem (2003), pp. 54–72. Divine possession was not confined to women; in 1616 the English priest Everard Hands claimed to be divinely possessed (Gee, J., *New Shreds of the Old Snare, containing the Apparitions of two new Female Ghosts* (London, 1624), pp. 54–7).

means of partially exculpating the demoniac: 'getting rid of [demons] is the key to moral and psychological redemption'. Cuneo goes so far as to describe exorcism as 'Personal engineering through demon-expulsion'.[65] If exorcism is instant and straightforward these purposes are not necessarily achieved, and the state of possession and what it reveals are at least as important as the act of exorcism itself.

There is no exact English equivalent for the Italian adjective *indemoniato* that Nicolotti chose as the best term to describe the possessed, following the usage of demonologist Corrado Balducci.[66] The English word 'demonized' is ambiguous, and could denote both a possessed person and someone or somewhere tormented by demonic activity, as well as someone or something associated with evil by others. However, in Latin texts of late antiquity and the early Middle Ages *daemoniacus* was the noun most commonly used to describe victims of evil spirits, followed by *energumenus* and then *arrepticus*.[67] There were slight differences of meaning between these terms. 'Demoniac' signified someone completely under the domination of a demon, whereas a demoniac who manifested the powers (*energeia*) of the demon possessing him or her was an *energumenus*.[68] The term *arrepticus*, which was taken from the Latin Vulgate's description of the Gerasene demoniac (Luke 8:29), had the sense of a person 'torn away' from his or her right mind. In order to avoid both ambiguity and the use of excessively specialized terms, I use the word 'demoniac' throughout this book to refer to supposed victims of possession in the true sense.

A further linguistic difficulty thrown up by possession is the belief that more than one personality can be present in a single body. Rather than attributing words and actions done by demoniacs solely to the possessed individual, for the sake of convenience, to avoid confusion and to match the historical sources themselves I refer to the demonic personalities within the possessed individual as subjects in their own right on the understanding that this reflects the probable perception of exorcists and witnesses at the time. I often use the term 'demoniac' to designate the subject because it is ambiguous: 'The demoniac said ...' could mean either that the victim

---

[65] Cuneo, M. W., *American Exorcism: Expelling Demons in the Land of Plenty*, 2nd edn (London: Bantam, 2002), pp. 1–4.

[66] In his book *Gli indemoniati* (Rome: Coletti Editore, 1959), Balducci set out criteria for distinguishing genuine possession from mental illness which will be examined in more detail in Chap. 7.

[67] Chave-Mahir (2011), p. 35.

[68] Nicolotti (2011), p. 638.

spoke or the real or imagined possessing demon spoke. Either way, the words came out of the demoniac's mouth. Even exorcists themselves faced uncertainty in this regard, and this ambiguity must be reflected in the historical language used for the study of exorcism.

Beliefs concerning the mechanics of possession are undoubtedly a significant influence in determining the form of exorcism, and the precise demonology underlying such possession-beliefs has been considered less important. A number of scholars have argued that the fluid religious environment of the late Roman Mediterranean was such that it is historically inappropriate to adopt fixed assumptions, such as the unambiguously evil character of possessing spirits.[69] Raiswell noted that 'angels, devils, demons, unclean, lying or vile spirits were not necessarily seen as distinct by pre-modern people and scripture made no sharp distinctions between them'.[70] A. K. Petersen went a step further by arguing that the concept of 'demon' in early Christian thought was too open and diffuse for 'substantive definition' of a demon to be possible at all. Petersen therefore adopted a functionalist approach, defining the demon as whatever required exorcism. On this interpretation the act of exorcism becomes much more significant than the finer points of theories about the nature of the entity being exorcized. In Greek thought, a *daimōn* represented a form of mediation between the gods and human beings, yet in early Christian thought 'the daimon came to mediate between the concepts of good and evil'.[71] Speculation about the nature of demons is discouraged in the contemporary Catholic church.[72]

In contrast to Petersen's functionalism, Nienke Vos was critical of the tendency of some authors, notably Peter Brown, to see demons as a psychological 'extension of the self', rather than characters with a significant

---

[69] Smith, J. Z., 'Towards interpreting Demonic Powers in Hellenistic and Roman Antiquity', *Aufstieg und Niedergang der römischen Welt* 2.16.1 (Berlin: De Gruyter, 1978), pp. 425–39; Caciola, N., *Discerning Spirits: Divine and Demonic Possession in the Middle Ages* (Ithaca, NY: Cornell University Press, 2003), p. xli; Frankfurter (2010), p. 29.

[70] Raiswell (2012), p. 33.

[71] Petersen, A. K., 'The Notion of Demon: Open Questions to a Diffuse Concept' in Lange, A. and Lichtenberger, H. (eds), *Die Dämonen: die Dämonologie der israelitisch-jüdischen und frühchristlichen Literatur im Kontext ihrer Umwelt (Demons: the Demonology of Israelite-Jewish and Early Christian Literature in Context of their Environment)* (Tübingen: Mohr Siebeck, 2003), pp. 23–41, at p. 27. On early Christian demonology see also Nicolotti (2011), pp. 38–42.

[72] *DESQ*, p. 10.

role to play in the story.⁷³ For Vos, demons are an essential ingredient in saints' lives because they personify evil.⁷⁴ Frankfurter argued that exorcists did not merely respond to anxieties that they themselves saw no need to define: 'we should regard [exorcists] as *shapers* of demonic possession, authorities in the definition of spirits that laypeople initially construct themselves'.⁷⁵ Frankfurter saw exorcists as demonologists whose task was to take the fears of ordinary people and explain them. However, there is insufficient evidence to suggest that exorcists were always interested in the nature of the beings they cast out. The vast number of cases in which exorcists seem to show no interest at all in the technicalities of demonology count against Frankfurter's view, which is based primarily on famous cases such as the possessions of Loudun, in which the exorcists also engaged in demonology.⁷⁶ The ability to perform effective exorcisms has not always been accompanied by demonological knowledge or an ability to define the exact nature of possession and demons. Furthermore, in many cases the presence of the exorcist alone has acted as a catalyst for 'demoniac' behaviour, suggesting that the presence of the exorcist, and his holiness, was thought to provoke demons into revealing their presence.

A functionalist approach to demons themselves permits a relatively uncomplicated focus on the practice of exorcism as an historical phenomenon, but it is clear that beliefs about demons have influenced the conduct of exorcists through the ages. Debates about demonic physicality, especially in the late Middle Ages and the early modern period, contributed to the contrasting approaches of Counter-Reformation exorcists and demonologists (notably Girolamo Menghi and Martin Delrio). More recently, it is likely that the revised rite of exorcism promulgated in 1999 reminded exorcists of the purely spiritual nature of the devil and demons in reaction to the markedly physical depiction of exorcisms in twentieth-century popular culture.⁷⁷

---

⁷³ Brown, P., *The Making of Late Antiquity* (Cambridge, MA: Harvard University Press, 1978), p. 90.

⁷⁴ Vos, N., 'Demons Without and Within: The Representation of Demons, the Saint, and the Soul in Early Christian Lives, Letters and Sayings' in Vos and Otten (2011), pp. 159–82, at p. 181.

⁷⁵ Frankfurter (2010), p. 41.

⁷⁶ Frankfurter, D., *Evil Incarnate: Rumors of Satanic Conspiracy and Satanic Abuse in History* (Princeton, NJ: Princeton University Press, 2008), pp. 27–8.

⁷⁷ *DESQ*, p. 5.

Gender and Status

An influential thesis advanced by Nancy Caciola interprets Catholic exorcism in the medieval and early modern periods as a gendered activity that involved the male-led church designating women as demonic. The evidence from late antiquity and the twentieth century indicates that women do not necessarily constitute the overwhelming majority of demoniacs at all periods in history. However, it is undeniable that for at least a thousand years, between the ninth and nineteenth centuries, most recorded exorcisms were performed on women. The question of whether exorcism, by its very nature, functioned to subjugate women and demonize their spiritual experiences is one that a history of exorcism must address.

Caciola has argued, on the basis of the frequent use of feminine grammatical endings in late medieval exorcism manuals, that women were thought of as the exclusive subjects of exorcism. The aim of exorcism was a 'demonic convergence' in which, by being made to respond as a demon, the female demoniac was fully conflated with the demon possessing her.[78] This approach seems to assume that the female demoniac was aware of what she said to the exorcist, which is something of which the historian cannot be sure. The medieval exorcist believed that he was addressing a demon, not a woman. Caciola argues that female demoniacs were 'forced into collusion' with the exorcist's interpretation of demonic possession, but such collusion may not always have been conscious. Caciola is undoubtedly right that women who claimed to be 'divinely possessed' or in touch with folk entities such as the fairies were coerced into an exorcistic dialogue, but some women believed themselves to be possessed by the devil.

It is certainly true that women were frequently blamed for the Fall and associated with the devil by medieval theologians, but interpretations other than active hatred of women can be applied to the overwhelming number of exorcisms performed on women. For instance, the widespread assumption that women were morally weaker than men meant that they were thought to be more vulnerable to possession and therefore in need of exorcism. Exorcism of female demoniacs was thus a consequence of gendered assumptions, but not necessarily always associated with the subjugation of women or the conflation of women with the demonic. Indeed, as beliefs shifted in the late Middle Ages and possession was seen as not just the consequence of sin, exorcism became a charitable act towards the unfortunate.

---

[78] Caciola (2003), pp. 251–4.

Scholars of medieval religion are divided on the extent to which women were seen as the obvious targets of demonic attack. Rudolph Bell and Donald Weinstein argued, on the basis of an analysis of the *vitae* of female saints, that women were more likely than men to engage in spiritual struggles with the devil.[79] Caciola accepted Bell and Weinstein's view.[80] However, Carolyn Walker Bynum has noted that medieval women's spirituality contained elements of personal responsibility and did not always emphasize attacks from the devil and cosmic spiritual warfare, and David Keck has noted that women were less likely to call upon the protection of spiritual figures such as St Michael.[81] It is the argument of this book that exorcism always involves an exercise of power. Throughout history, the subjects of exorcism have often been among those then perceived as the weakest members of society: women, children and those who failed to meet cultural standards of rationality. Levack argues that neither gender nor social subordination can be used as exclusive determinants of who was likely to become possessed.[82] The determining factor in exorcism was a power relationship between the authoritative exorcist and the helpless demoniac, and gender, although one determinant of 'weakness', was not the only one. The greater gender balance amongst demoniacs in late antiquity and the twentieth century may reflect the different perceptions of 'weakness' in those societies. Women could enjoy considerable spiritual status in the pagan world of late antiquity and, some have argued, in the early church as well.[83] Furthermore, the fact that individuals were subjected to exorcism does not necessarily mean that they were demonized; indeed, quite the opposite was sometimes true, and 'demoniac saints' form a small sub-category of individuals either officially or unofficially venerated for their holiness.

This study aims to avoid a functionalist interpretation, seeking instead an understanding of exorcism in its own terms, whatever those have been throughout the centuries. It aims to privilege neither 'official' accounts

---

[79] Bell, R. and Weinstein, D., *Saints and Society: Christendom, 1000–1700* (Chicago, IL: University of Chicago Press, 1982), pp. 228–9.

[80] Caciola (2003), p. 70.

[81] Bynum, C. W., *Jesus as Mother: Studies in the Spirituality of the High Middle Ages* (Berkeley, CA: University of California Press, 1982), p. 88; Keck, D., *Angels and Angelology in the Middle Ages* (Oxford: Oxford University Press, 1998), pp. 187–8.

[82] Levack (2013), pp. 184–90.

[83] On the status of women in the early church see DeConick, A. D., *Holy Misogyny: Why the Sex and Gender Conflicts in the Early Church still matter* (London: Continuum, 2011).

of churchmen and theologians nor hostile deconstructions of exorcism as superstitious or abusive. To lay claim to objectivity in an area so fraught with hermeneutical difficulties would be presumptuous. However, by paying attention to both the proponents and opponents of exorcism throughout the centuries, as well as the many cautious voices in between, the historian can attempt to tell the story of exorcism in Catholic Christianity without privileging either the perspective of the exorcist or the demoniac.

CHAPTER 2

Exorcism in the Early Christian West, 300–900

At the beginning of the fourth century, the early Christian author Lactantius blamed the suffering of Christians in the Roman Empire on evil spirits possessing the bodies of the persecutors[1]:

> The men themselves do not persecute, who do not have a reason why they should be angry with the innocent; but those unclean, abandoned spirits to whom the truth is both known and unwanted, insinuate themselves into their minds and incite them, unwitting, to fury. These spirits, for as long as there is peace in the people of God, flee the just and are terrified; and when they occupy the bodies of men and torment their souls, they are adjured by these men, and flee in the name of the true God. At hearing this name they tremble, cry out, and testify that they are branded and beaten; and asked who they are and when they came, and how they possess a man, they confess it. Thus tormented and tortured by the power of the divine name, they are eased away.

---

[1] Lactantius, *Divinae Institutiones* 22 (*PL* 6.633A–623B): *Non enim ipsi homines persequuntur, qui causam cur irascantur innocentibus non habent: sed illi spiritus contaminati ac perditi, quibus veritas et nota est, et invisa, insinuant se mentibus eorum, et instigant nescios in furorem. Hi enim quamdiu pax est in populo Dei, fugitant justos, et pavent; et cum corpora hominum occupant, animasque divexant, adjurantur ab his, et nomine Dei veri fugantur. Quo audito tremunt, exclamant, et uri se verberarique testantur; et interroganti, qui sint quando venerint, quomodo in hominem irrepserint, confitentur. Sic extorti et excruciati virtute divini nominis, exsolantur.*

Many of the themes that recur repeatedly in the history of exorcism are encapsulated in these words. In the first place, Lactantius suggested that evil spirits will not try to possess someone's body 'for as long as there is peace in the people of God', implying that the prevalence of demonic activity is a sign of theological and political division between Christians. By the same token, the effectiveness of exorcism was a vindication of 'the just', proof that God is on the side of those who can cast out evil spirits in the name of God. Lactantius stressed the quasi-magical power of the name of God, a theme picked up by later exorcists, as well as the violence, spiritual or otherwise, inherent in the process of exorcism. These four themes—the link between exorcism and disunity, exorcism as vindication, the ambiguous relationship between exorcism and magic, and the link between exorcism and violence—remained (and still remain) significant themes throughout the history of exorcism.

Exorcism was a defining feature of early Christianity. Peter Brown described exorcism, without exaggeration, as 'possibly the most highly rated activity of the early Christian church'.[2] Whilst exorcism was not unique to Christianity, it found an unprecedented flowering in the new faith.[3] However, as the church became established as a legitimate and powerful institution of Roman and post-Roman society between the fourth and ninth centuries, exorcism in the Latin church underwent a multilayered and complex transformation. Neglect of the history of exorcism from the third century onwards has obscured this change and created the impression that the pattern of exorcism was laid in the first two centuries of Christianity.[4] From the fourth century onwards, Latin Christian authors (most notably Augustine) began to downplay or reinterpret in non-exorcistic terms the dramatic rituals of pre-baptismal exorcism established as part of the liturgy in the third century. Meanwhile, exorcism of demoniacs outside the rites of baptism was gradually transformed from a lay charism and a form of spiritual healing into a miracle that was the preserve of holy individuals, living or dead. It was also during this period that 'indirect exorcism' through the use of exorcized objects like salt, oil and water laid the foundations of medieval exorcistic practices. These are generalizations, and exorcism did

---

[2] Brown, P., *The Cult of the Saints: Its Rise and Function in Latin Christianity* (Chicago, IL: University of Chicago Press, 1981), p. 108.
[3] MacMullen (1984), p. 28.
[4] See for instance Levack (2013), pp. 32–55 who makes a direct transition from the Antenicene period to the thirteenth century.

not always move in these directions. However, changing attitudes to exorcism reflected changes in the church's relationship with a Christianized society in which the practice of infant baptism became increasingly common and spiritual conflict with pagan religion less marked. Furthermore, progressively greater reliance on the exceptional holiness of the saints and their shrines was reflected in the development of exorcism as a holy miracle rather than a ministry of lay Christians.

The theology of early Christian exorcism was underpinned by the belief that God imparted to believers the charism of casting out demons, both to demonstrate the assimilation of the believer to Jesus through baptism, and to demonstrate Christ's victory over the devil. Although demons remained in the world, Christ's victory was nevertheless complete and God permitted them to continue their work at least partly so that Christians could demonstrate their adherence to the true faith by exorcizing them.[5] Between the middle of the second century and the middle of the third, exorcism became a critical mechanism of Christian self-definition. Christian demonology transformed the gods of the ancient world into beings of evil, and required their systematic renunciation as a prerequisite of baptism; believers who lapsed back into paganism were portrayed as falling under the dominion of these demons, and were often possessed by them.

From the fourth century onwards, the church extended its authority over exorcism and took care to differentiate exorcism from magic, drawing upon earlier texts such as Origen's classic account of the difference between Christian exorcism and magic in *Contra Celsum*.[6] Thus the miracle of exorcism, performed by believers, transformed any wonders done by rival believers into magic accomplished by the agency of demons. Any activity that involved a 'technique' of capturing the divine was magic: 'Magicians cast spells of an illusory or ephemeral nature in cooperation with diabolic forces enslaved through material formulas', in contrast to the faithful who could use simple prayers and petitions to invoke divine aid.[7]

---

[5] Nicolotti (2011), p. 637.
[6] Origen, *Contra Celsum* 1.24 (*PG* 9.342); 2.51 (*PG* 9.425–7); 6.41 (*PG* 9.662–3); 7.69 (*PG* 9.753). On Origen's views on magic see Nicolotti (2011), pp. 453–9.
[7] Nicolotti (2011), pp. 632–4.

Exorcism and Baptism

At the beginning of the third century, the once simple rite of baptism underwent a liturgical transformation that turned it into 'a drama of resolute and sometimes fierce struggle against the devil'.[8] There are three broad views as to how exorcism became part of the baptismal or, more precisely, pre-baptismal liturgy. Kelly, following Dölger, believed that the origins of the exorcisms lay in the doctrine of 'sin demons', evil spirits corresponding to sins who took up residence in the unbaptized.[9] For Toon Bastiaensen, the beginnings of pre-baptismal exorcism were to be found in the Donatist controversy in North Africa, where the idea of exorcizing objects like oil, water and salt gradually came to be applied to the catechumens themselves.[10] The Donatist controversy was concerned with whether Christians who had succumbed to apostasy during periods of persecution could be readmitted to the church, but also included discussion of whether church goods confiscated by pagans required exorcism. Finally, Elizabeth Leeper has argued that pre-baptismal exorcism, whose original purpose was a renunciation of evil powers, was imported from Alexandria to Rome by the heretic Valentinus in the mid-second century.[11] Whatever the truth, exorcism was established as part of the baptismal rite in Rome by around 250.[12]

The liturgy of exorcism practised at Rome was that found in the *Traditio apostolica*, a collection of canons and liturgical regulations relating primarily to the Roman church, whose earliest Latin text dates from between 375 and 400. Although its original attribution to Hippolytus of Rome (170–235) is now questionable, the *Traditio* does contain elements that predate the fourth century.[13] The first stage of pre-baptismal exorcism in the *Traditio apostolica* consisted of daily exorcisms performed early in the morning by exorcists who may have been either presbyters, deacons,

---

[8] Kelly (1985), p. 10.

[9] Ibid. pp. 45–56.

[10] Bastiaensen, A. A. R., 'Exorcism: Tackling the Devil by Word of Mouth' in Vos and Otten (2011), pp. 129–44, at p. 136.

[11] Leeper, E. A., 'From Alexandria to Rome: The Valentinian Connection to the Incorporation of Exorcism as a Prebaptismal Rite', *Vigiliae Christianae* 44 (1990), pp. 6–24. Kelly (2006), pp. 209–14 later subscribed to the Valentinian hypothesis.

[12] Nicolotti (2011), p. 19.

[13] Bradshaw, P. F., Johnson, M. E. and Phillips, L. E., *The Apostolic Tradition: A Commentary* (Minneapolis, MN: Fortress Press, 2002), p. 14; Nicolotti (2011), pp. 586–7.

ordained exorcists or lay exorcists. The first mention of the office of exorcist as an order bestowed by the laying on of hands occurs in a fragment of a letter of Cyprian of Carthage.[14] A well-known letter of Pope Cornelius quoted by Eusebius in his *Church History* noted that, in the middle of the third century, the Roman church counted fifty-two exorcists, readers and doorkeepers in addition to its priests, deacons, sub-deacons and acolytes.[15] In the fourth century, Pseudo-Ambrose made clear that 'exorcist' was a minor order of the clergy, 'for a priest and the deacons enact the office of both exorcist and reader'.[16] Furthermore, in her description of the liturgy of the church of Jerusalem, the late fourth-century Gaulish pilgrim Egeria noted that catechumens were exorcized daily, early in the morning by 'clerics' during Lent.[17]

The second stage of the exorcism described in the *Traditio apostolica* was the exsufflation. On the day of their baptism the catechumens would be exorcized by the bishop who 'blew out' evil influences. Thirdly, a presbyter anointed those who were about to be baptized with oil previously exorcized by the bishop (the Oil of Catechumens), with the words 'Let every spirit depart from you' in what amounted to an indirect exorcism.[18] In Nicolotti's view, the requirement of absolute nudity for the baptized, who were also to eat only exorcized bread, reflected their separation from all possible demonic influence.[19] The *Traditio apostolica* was the first text to establish the significance of anointing and the sign of the cross in exorcism.[20]

One way in which the pre-baptismal exorcism of catechumens may be understood is by analogy with the exorcism of salt, water and oil. These materials were not so much exorcized on the grounds that they were

---

[14] Cyprian, *Epistula* 16 (*PL* 4.269A). On Cyprian and exorcism see Nicolotti (2011), pp. 62–3.

[15] Eusebius, *Historia Ecclesiastica* 6.43 (*PG* 20.244).

[16] Ambrosiaster, *Quaestiones veteris et novi testamenti* 101.4 (*PL* 35.2302): *presbyter enim et diaconi agit officium et exorcistae et lectoris*.

[17] Egeria, *Itinerarium Egeriae* 46.1 (ed. O. Prinz) (Carl Winter: Heidelberg, 1960), pp. 53–4: *Consuetudo est ... hic talis, ut qui accedunt ad baptismum per ipsos dies quadraginta, quibus ieiunatur, primum mature a clericis exorcizentur.*

[18] On the role of oils in the *Apostolica Traditio* see Segelberg, E., 'The Benedictio Olei in the Apostolic Tradition of Hippolytus', *Oriens Christianas* 48 (1964), pp. 268–81; Nicolotti (2011), pp. 609–14, 681.

[19] Nicolotti (2011), p. 681.

[20] Augustine argued for the apotropaic use of the sign of the cross in *Tractatus in Iohannis Evangelium* 50.2 (*CCL* 36.433–4); 118.5 (*CCL* 36.657).

inhabited by evil spirits but in order to restore them to their pristine condition as God's creatures. The original purpose of pre-baptismal exorcism was similarly positive, and the repeated early morning exorcisms performed on catechumens during Lent also functioned as a test of commitment. However, one particular fourth-century doctrinal dispute brought about a reappraisal of the meaning and significance of the pre-baptismal exorcisms. Optatus of Mileve (fl. c. 375) asserted that every unbaptized human being was possessed by an evil spirit.[21] Claims of this kind misled an earlier generation of scholars to assume that the development of pre-baptismal exorcism was a consequence of the appearance of the doctrine of Original Sin. This disregarded the fact that the exorcisms considerably pre-dated Augustine's controversy with the followers of Pelagius.[22] However, the opponents of Pelagianism did recruit the existence of the rites of exorcism as evidence that all human beings were under the dominion of the devil, and this was the orthodoxy of the Roman church.

Augustine's emphasis on Original Sin redefined the purpose of pre-baptismal exorcism. Whereas in the earlier rites the catechumen was considered vulnerable to attack by evil spirits, perhaps because he or she had chosen the Christian path, by the middle of the fourth century many Roman and North African Christians believed that an evil spirit was expelled from the body of the catechumen prior to baptism. In Kelly's view, Augustine's own belief was more nuanced, and not quite so literal. He regarded the eviction of demons from the unbaptized as 'a dramatic metaphor for the redemption of souls from their diabolical oppressor'.[23] For Augustine, the rites of pre-baptismal exorcism were 'sacred and manifest signs of hidden things by which the candidates are shown to pass from their evil captor to the good redeemer who took on infirmity for us and bound the strong one in order to snatch away his vessels'.[24] His emphasis on baptism as a war against Satan had the consequence that exorcism became a preparation for the formal renunciation of Satan, in which 'the

---

[21] Optatus of Mileve, *Libri VII* 4.6 (*CSEL* 26.110).
[22] Nicolotti (2011), p. 86; Kelly (1985), pp. 112–15.
[23] Kelly (1985), p. 113.
[24] Augustine, *De Gratia Christi et de Peccato Originali* 2.40 (*PL* 44.408): *Quibus omnibus rerum occultarum sacratis et evidentibus signis, a captivatore pessimo ad optimum redemptorem transire monstrantur; qui pro nobis infirmitate suscepta, alligavit fortem, ut vasa ejus eriperet.*

candidate was to find in himself the repentance and moral courage necessary to make the formal renunciation of Satan meaningful and lasting'.[25]

Between the writings of Augustine and Leo the Great in the fourth century and the writings of John the Deacon at the end of the fifth, there are very few references to pre-baptismal exorcism in the west.[26] However, it can be safely assumed that the baptismal liturgy became progressively more elaborate. John the Deacon described baptism in late fifth-century North Africa as consisting of eleven stages:

1. Catechesis
2. Exsufflation
3. Reception of salt
4. Renunciation of the devil's snares and pomps
5. Reception of the Apostles' Creed
6. Scrutiny
7. The first anointing (on the ears and nostrils)
8. The second anointing (on the breast)
9. Unclothing
10. Baptism
11. Clothing and the final anointing

John's interpretation of these rites was not explicitly exorcistic. For instance, he interpreted the exsufflation as an insult to the devil rather than his literal casting out. Likewise, the reception of salt was given an allegorical meaning as a symbol of the spiritual preservation of the soul. Neither the scrutiny (which was described by Leo as a series of exorcisms) nor the anointings were described in exorcistic terms; the scrutiny was an examination of the candidate's faith, the first anointing (on the ears and nostrils) was intended to prevent the entry of an unclean spirit rather than to cast one out, and the second anointing on the breast symbolized purity of heart. The final, post-baptismal anointing represented the priestly status of the new believer.[27] For John, it was not so much the anointing or scrutiny, but rather the renunciation that involved a direct

---

[25] Kelly (1985), p. 115.

[26] Leo, *Epistola* 16.6 (*PL* 54.702); Siricius, *Epistola ad Himerium Tarraconensem* 2.3 (*PL* 13.1135); *Canones ad Gallos* 8; Celestine, *Epistola* 21.13 (*PL* 50.536).

[27] John the Deacon, *Epistle to Senarius* 3 in Wilmart, A. (ed.), *Auteurs Spirituels et Textes dévots du Moyen Âge latin* (Paris: Etudes Augustiniennes, 1971), pp. 171–5. On John's description see Kelly (1985), pp. 116–18.

confrontation with Satan. Kelly suggests that John failed to mention exorcisms because it was understood by the late fifth century that exorcisms were embedded in the scrutinies. Furthermore, the fourth-century Illyrian author Nicetas of Remesiana suggested that exorcistic language was integrated into the renunciation of Satan itself.[28] The baptismal exorcism had come to mean both a voluntary renunciation of evil and a cleansing spiritual fire: 'the exorcism was not literally a demon-expelling rite but a symbolic service dramatizing the devil's hold over men and the need to purify oneself of his influence by divine aid'.[29]

The earliest extant liturgy for pre-baptismal exorcism in the west is known as *Ordo Romanus XI* (henceforth *Ordo XI*), which dates from the seventh century or possibly the end of the sixth century. The rite included the involvement of a *pontifex*, suggesting that it was the rite performed in the churches and baptisteries of Rome at which the Pope himself assisted.[30] *Ordo XI* formed the basis for the liturgies in the eighth-century Romano-Frankish Gelasian Sacramentary that went on to dominate medieval Europe.[31] The liturgy consisted of seven dramatic scrutinies which began on the Wednesday after the Third Sunday of Lent. Kelly argued that the scrutinies were deliberately designed to reflect the liturgical drama of Holy Week, culminating in Christ's defeat of Satan.

The first exorcism in *Ordo XI* was an exorcism of salt to be used as 'a salutary sacrament for putting the enemy to flight' (*salutare sacramentum ad effugandum inimicum*).[32] The catechumens were subsequently sent outside the church and then summoned back in, where they were signed with the cross by their godparents and then by an acolyte, who recited a prayer over the male and female catechumens (*Deus Abraham, Deus Isaac, Deus Iacob ...*) that ended with a rebuke to the devil and a demand for him to withdraw (*recede*), although Kelly did not regard this as an exorcism in the true sense[33]:

---

[28] Nicetas, *Instructio ad Competentes* 1.1.7 in Gamber, K. (ed.), *Instructio ad Competentes: frühchristliche Katechesen aus Dacien* (Regensburg: F. Pustet, 1964), p. 17.
[29] Kelly (1985), p. 120.
[30] On the origins and date of *Ordo XI* see *OR*, vol. 2, pp. 409–13.
[31] On the *Ordo XI* see Kelly (1985), pp. 201–7.
[32] *Ordo XI* 4–5 (*OR* vol. 2, pp. 418–19).
[33] *Ordo XI* 14 (*OR* vol. 2, p. 421): ... *Ergo, maledicte diabole, recognosce sentenciam tuam et da honorem Deo vivo et vero, da honorem Iesu Christo filio eius et spiritui sancto, recede ab his famulis Dei, quia istos sibi Deus et dominus noster Iesus Christus ad suam sanctam gratiam et*

Therefore, accursed devil, recognise your sentence and give honour to the living and true God, give honour to Jesus Christ his Son, draw back from this servant of God, because God himself and our Lord Jesus Christ deigns to call these [catechumens] to his holy grace and blessing, the font, and the gift of baptism; by this sign of the cross on their foreheads, which we give, and which you, accursed devil, may never dare to violate.

The formula *Ergo maledicte diabole* ('Therefore, accursed devil ...') was repeated at the end of the prayer beginning *Deus caeli, Deus terrae* ('God of heaven, God of earth ...').[34] An exorcism was then pronounced by a second acolyte, laying hands on the male catechumens after signing them with the cross, although it did not explicitly command the devil to depart from the bodies of the candidates[35]:

Hear, accursed Satan, adjured by the name of the eternal God and our Saviour, the Son of God, depart having been defeated, trembling and groaning, with your envy. Let there be nothing in common between you and the servants of God, now contemplating heavenly things, about to renounce you and your world, and about to win a blessed immortality. Therefore give honour to the coming Holy Spirit ...

The third acolyte, after laying hands on the male candidates and signing them with the cross, pronounced a second, more explicit exorcism: 'I exorcize you, unclean spirit, so that in the name of the Father, of the Son, and of the Holy Spirit, you should go out and draw back from these servants of God. For he himself commands you, accursed [and] damned one, who opened the eyes of the man born blind and raised Lazarus from the tomb on the fourth day'.[36] The formula of exorcism for the male candidates referred instead to Jesus saving Peter from the waves. As Kelly has

---

benediccionem fontemque baptismatis donum vocare dignum est; per hoc signum sancte crucis frontibus eorum, quem nos damus, tu, maledicte diabole, nunquam audeas violare.

[34] *Ordo XI* 16 (*OR* vol. 2, p. 421).

[35] *Ordo XI* 18 (*OR* vol. 2, p. 422): *Audi maledicte Satanas, adiuratus per nomen eterni Dei et salvatoris nostri filii Dei cum tua victus invidia tremens gemensque discede, nihil tibi sit commune cum servis Dei iam celestia cogitantibus, renunciatoribus tibi ac secolo tuo et beate inmortalitatis victuris. Da igitur honorem advenientis spiritu sancto ...*

[36] *Ordo XI* 21-2 (*OR* vol. 2, p. 423): *Exorcizo te, inmunde spiritus, ut in nomine patris et filii et spiritus sancti ut exeas et recedas ab his famulabus Dei. Ipse aenim tibi imperat, maledicte dampnate, qui cecu nato oculos aperuit et quatriduanum Lazarum de monumento suscitavit. Ergo maledicte diabole ...*

observed, none of the incidents recalled from the life of Christ were themselves exorcisms, and he argued that 'they seem to have been meant originally as prototypes of the saving grace of baptism rather than as reminders of Christ's ability to control evil spirits'.[37] Furthermore, the multiplication of scrutinies from three in the fifth century to seven in the seventh century was not 'demonologically motivated', but rather came out of a desire for the symbolism of the scrutinies to correspond with the seven gifts of the Holy Spirit.[38]

The seventh and final scrutiny of *Ordo XI*, on the morning of Holy Saturday, was oddly described as a catechization of the catechumens, but clearly had the character of an exorcism[39]:

> Nor does it escape you, Satan, that punishments threaten you, torments threaten you, the day of judgement threatens you, the day of punishment, the day that is to come like a burning furnace, in which eternal perdition will come for you and all your angels. Therefore, damned one, give honour to the living and true God, give honour to Jesus Christ his Son, and to the Holy Spirit, in whose name and power I command you to go out and depart from this servant of God, whom today the Lord our God Jesus Christ has deigned to call by his gift to his holy grace and to the blessing and font of baptism, that he may become his temple by the water of regeneration for the remission of all sins.

The 'exorcistic' formula (more properly a rhetorical apostrophe) *Ergo maledicte diabole* occurred four times during the course of the baptismal liturgy in *Ordo XI*, usually embedded in other prayers. The frequent repetition of the formula, its adaptation to *Audi maledicte Satanas* ('Hear, o accursed Satan') and the ease with which it became embedded in other prayers suggests that it was the oldest part of the exorcistic liturgy.

---

[37] Kelly (1985), p. 209.

[38] Ibid. p. 210.

[39] *Ordo XI* 83–4: *Nec te lateat, satanas, inminere tibi poenas, inminere tibi tormenta, inminere tibi diem iudicii, diem supplicii, diem qui venturus est velut clibanus ardens, in quo tibi atque universis angelis tuis aeternus veniet interitus. Proinde, damnate, da honorem deo vivo et vero, da honorem iesu christo filio eius et spiritu sancto, in cuius nomine atque virtute precipio tibi, quicumque es spiritus inmundus, ut exias et recedas ab hoc famulo dei quem hodie dominus Deus noster iesus christus ad suam sanctam gratiam et benedictionem fontemque baptismatis donum vocare dignatus est, et fiant eius templum per aquam regenerationis in remissionem omnium peccatorum in nomine domini nostri iesu christi qui venturus est iudicare vivos et mortuos et seculum per ignem.*

However, the imperative command accompanying the *Ergo maledicte, recede* ('draw back') casts doubt on whether the *Ergo maledicte* was an exorcism proper. Although Kelly translates *recede* as 'depart' it is better translated as 'draw back', conveying an image of the devil as a tempter lurking in the vicinity of the catechumen rather than any notion that the devil is within the baptismal candidates.

Although the ritual of *Ordo XI* was intended for infants, it was clearly derived from a formula for the baptism of adults. However, as Christianity advanced into pagan northern Europe, the baptism of adults became once more an urgent necessity. The Gelasian Sacramentary (*SG* 2387–90) contained a rite *Ad catechumenum ex pagano faciendum* ('for making a catechumen from a pagan') in which the catechumen was instructed to 'be in horror of idols [and] despise images' (*horresce idola[m], respue simulacra*).[40] In a letter to Oduin and another to monks in Septimania, the English monk and Carolingian scholar Alcuin (c. 735–804) described baptismal rites suitable for a pagan in the last decade of the eighth century.[41] In contrast to Augustine's reluctance to interpret pre-baptismal exorcism as a literal expulsion of the devil, Alcuin did not hesitate to assert that the exsufflation put the devil to flight and that the adjuration commanded the devil to depart and give way to Christ. Furthermore, the anointings denied the devil entry to the catechumen's body. As a monk from the fringe of Christendom, Alcuin may have reasserted the earlier literal understanding of pre-baptismal exorcism as a response to the challenge of evangelizing northern Europe. However, there is little evidence to support Chave-Mahir's view that, up to the turn of the second millennium, pagans were considered to be possessed by the devil and, as a consequence, 'exorcism of the possessed separated itself from its baptismal roots' only after 1000.[42]

In the Gelasian Sacramentary, as in *Ordo XI*, a slightly different form of words was adopted for men and women,[43] and the exorcisms used on the font during the vigil of Easter give a vivid impression of the fears connected with demons. The priest prayed that an evil spirit 'should not fly around, laying an ambush, should not steal anything away by lying hidden,

---

[40] *SG* 2388.
[41] Alcuin, *Epistula* 134, 137 in Dümmler, E. (ed.), *Epistulae Karolini Aevi* 2, Monumenta Germaniae Historia 4 (Berlin, 1895), pp. 202–3, 210–16.
[42] Chave-Mahir (2011), p. 17.
[43] *SG* 2238, 2240.

and not corrupt anything by infection'.[44] The catechumen was anointed with oil on the breast and back, and the exorcist touched the candidate's nose and ears with saliva in a ceremony known as the Effeta, a corruption of the Aramaic word *ephphatha* spoken by Jesus when he opened the ears and mouth of the deaf-mute man (Mark 7:32–5).[45] This ceremony appears to have been the successor of the first anointing described by John the Deacon in the fifth century, and the fact that an anointing with consecrated oil was replaced by a ceremony derived from a biblical healing suggests that the Effeta was not primarily exorcistic.

Kelly argued that the pre-baptismal exorcisms in the Roman rite were not only exorcistic in the true sense, but also apotropaic 'in the ad hoc sense of protecting [the candidate] here and now while he is undergoing the ceremonies of baptism'. This was particularly true of the anointing with the exorcized Oil of Catechumens. However, the Roman rite never made explicit that the exorcisms offered any 'long range' protection of the baptismal candidate from evil influence (unlike the Byzantine rite), although interpreters such as Alcuin inferred this.[46] However, the ultimate success of the Roman rite as the principal rite of the west ensured that the peculiar features of its exorcisms, such as the exorcistic formulas addressed to water, salt and oil, were perpetuated and expanded.

EXORCISMS, ADJURATIONS AND BLESSINGS

In the second century, Cyprian of Carthage wrote in response to a group of orthodox bishops from Numidia and suggested that heretics were unable to perform post-baptismal unction because they could not 'sanctify the creature of oil' (*sanctificare ... non potuit olei creaturam*).[47] Bastiaensen argued that use of the term 'creature of oil' was an indication that third-century Christians believed that any object used in the sacraments needed to be freed from the potential influence of evil spirits in order to become God's creature in the original, prelapsarian sense.[48] By the fourth century, Ambrose attested to similar beliefs about the water used for baptism

---

[44] SG 2317c: *... non insidiando circumvolet, non latendo subripiat, non inficiendo corrumpat*. On the exorcism of the font in the Easter Vigil see Kelly (1985), pp. 225–6.
[45] SG 2999–300. On the Effeta in the Gelasian Sacramentary see Kelly (1985), p. 222.
[46] Kelly (1985), pp. 230–1.
[47] Cyprian, *Epistula* 70.2 (*PL* 3.408A).
[48] Bastiaensen (2011), p. 136.

by referring to it as *creatura aquae* ('creature of water').[49] Theologically speaking, driving away evil influences from a physical object and thereby restoring it to its nature as 'the unspoilt product of God's hand' made it unnecessary to call down God's blessing upon it thereafter.

Elmar Bartsch argued that exorcism of objects was a peculiarly Roman practice, and that its prominence within the Gelasian Sacramentary reflected a combination of Byzantine influences and the dualistic tendencies of the peoples of northern Europe amongst whom the Gallican liturgy originated.[50] Kelly has argued, however, that the origination of such ideas in Rome was just as likely.[51] Bridget Nichols has drawn attention to the early medieval mentality that 'objects cannot have a cultic use unless they have first been withdrawn from profane use',[52] and exorcism accomplished this 'withdrawal' which was then enhanced and completed by consecration or blessing. However, it is clear that the line between exorcism and blessing was blurred early on. In Kelly's view, the exorcism of the water of baptism was older than the blessing of water that replaced it in the Gelasian Sacramentary. He argued that the original form, preserved in the Irish *Stowe Missal*, was merged clumsily with the blessing of water in the post-Tridentine formula.[53]

Richard Kieckhefer distinguished exorcisms from adjurations. Whereas an adjuration takes the form of a command and is directed against a sickness, worm, demon or other invisible agent, an exorcism is 'an extended ritual expressly directed against demons'.[54] This distinction is inevitably a fluid one, and the use of the words *adiuro* or *exorcizo* is not a sufficient condition to distinguish adjurations from exorcisms, since *adiuro* was sometimes used in extended exorcistic rituals whilst *exorcizo* was sometimes used in the most mundane of contexts. Kieckhefer's distinction between adjuration and exorcism proper

---

[49] Ambrose, *De Sacramentis* 5 (*PL* 16.422C–423A): *nam ubi primum ingreditur sacerdos, exorcismum facit secundum creaturam aquae, invocationem postea et precem defert; ut sanctificetur fons, et adsit praesentia Trinitatis aeternae: Christus autem ante descendit, secutus est Spiritus.*
[50] Bartsch (1967), pp. 139–47.
[51] Kelly (1985), p. 212.
[52] Nichols, B., 'Introduction' in Nichols, B. and MacGregor, A. (eds), *Deliver us from Evil: Medieval Blessings and Exorcisms of the Latin West* (Durham: Ushaw College Library, 2003), p. 6.
[53] Kelly (1985), pp. 226–7.
[54] Kieckhefer, R., *Magic in the Middle Ages* (Cambridge: Cambridge University Press, 1990), p. 69.

is comparable to the distinction in contemporary Catholic theology between minor and major exorcism, with the important difference that in late antiquity and the Middle Ages, adjurations were often used in contexts of healing and illness that few in the modern west would regard as the work of evil spirits.

Exorcism Beyond Baptism

Augustine produced the classic definition of exorcism of demoniacs in the Latin west in *De beata vita* ('On the Blessed Life'): 'an extrinsic unclean spirit invades the soul and disturbs the senses, and brings fury into certain men; those who take charge of shutting him out are said to lay on hands or exorcize, that is to expel him by adjuring the divine [name]'.[55] The very earliest references to exorcism as an activity conducted outside of baptism are to be found in apologetic literature. For Nicolotti, extra-baptismal exorcism in the early church was inherently missionary in purpose; so much so, in fact, that Christian authors saw no need to adduce evidence for the effectiveness of exorcisms and incorporated conventional, anonymous tales of exorcisms into their apologetic works as a literary *topos*.[56] There is no sign in these early sources that exorcism of demoniacs was a liturgical act, nor that it was conducted by the clergy.

The *Traditio apostolica* prohibited the imposition of hands (i.e. ordination) on anyone who had received the gift of healing by a special revelation,[57] suggesting that lay exorcists who dealt with demoniacs were considered distinct from the ordained clergy who carried out pre-baptismal exorcisms. This reflected the provision of the *Constitutiones apostolorum* that exorcists were not to be ordained, since the success of their exorcisms depended on their personal faith and integrity.[58] The exclusion of charismatic exorcists from ordination served a dual purpose; on the one hand, it allowed the hierarchy of the church to distance itself from their activities if they deviated from orthodox practice, and on the other it ensured that

---

[55] Augustine, *De Beata Vita* 3 (*PL* 32.968): ... *spiritus immundus ... extrinsecus invadit animam sensusque conturbat et quemdam hominibus infert furorem; cui excludendo qui praesunt, manum imponere vel exorcizare dicuntur, hoc est per divina eum adiurando expellere.*

[56] Nicolotti (2011), pp. 634–5.

[57] *Traditio Apostolica* 15 in Hippolytus of Rome (ed. B. Botte), *La Tradition Apostolique* (Paris: Cerf, 1946), p. 43.

[58] *Constitutiones Apostolorum* 8.25–6, ed. P. A. Lagarde (London: Williams and Norgate, 1862), p. 265.

the church maintained control of exorcists' activities by granting them implicit recognition.[59]

The *Traditio* indicates an awareness of the distinction between pre-baptismal exorcism and exorcism of energumens by specifying that a candidate who was also a demoniac had to be exorcized before baptism.[60] Since exorcism was part of the baptismal rite anyway, this suggests that baptismal exorcism was not considered adequate to deal with actual demoniacs, and a separate rite was performed. Nicolotti has speculated that this may have been the responsibility of the bishop or clergy appointed by him,[61] but it is also possible that it was a task undertaken by charismatic lay exorcists. No liturgical rite of extra-baptismal exorcism survives from the earliest centuries of the church, and it is a considerable leap to suggest that magical texts such as the *Testament of Solomon* were used for this purpose.[62] This assumes that Christian exorcism was essentially a magical rite, which is the very point at issue in attempts to define exorcism and differentiate it from magic. It is more likely that extra-baptismal rites of exorcism were 'charismatic' and extempore in the fourth and fifth centuries, although it is also possible that they drew on elements of the baptismal rite. Peter Brown's assumption that 'the great prayers of exorcism … in liturgical form' liberated demoniacs at the basilicas of fifth-century Gaul is not altogether justified by the evidence.[63]

Bastiaensen noted that, in contrast to the suggestion in Acts 19:11–16 that exorcism might involve a corporeal struggle between the exorcist and the demoniac, Christian sources from the fourth century presented a different picture: 'The duel was rather a contest in words; the exorcist gave a command and the evil spirit felt compelled to obey and to leave his victim in peace'.[64] Exorcism was a 'word-to-word fight'. This assessment is in contrast to Dyan Elliott's view that there was general agreement on the corporeal nature of demons in the first three centuries of Christianity,[65] albeit a belief in the corporeality of demons does not, *ipso facto*, mean that exorcisms will be violent affairs. However, Bastiaensen's analysis

---

[59] Nicolotti (2011), p. 593.
[60] *Traditio Apostolica* 16 (p. 44).
[61] Nicolotti (2011), p. 594.
[62] Frankfurter (2010), n. p. 41.
[63] Brown (1981), p. 112.
[64] Bastiaensen (2011), pp. 129–44, at p. 134.
[65] Elliott, D., *Fallen Bodies: Pollution, Sexuality and Demonology in the High Middle Ages* (Philadelphia, PA: University of Pennsylvania Press, 1999), p. 128.

does suggest that the 'twelfth century tendency to present demons as disembodied' may have originated much earlier,[66] even before the fourth century. The physicality of biblical representations of possession should not be allowed to mislead the historian on what early Christians actually believed. As Graham Twelftree noted, the early Christians did not model their exorcisms directly on those of Christ.[67]

Pseudo-Ambrose, in the late fourth-century *Epistula ad Ephesos* ('Letter to the Ephesians'), picked up on Cyprian and Lactantius' vocabulary of exorcistic violence towards demons, suggesting that 'the exorcists in the church bridle and flog the restless',[68] while Hilary of Poitiers (c. 300–68) used similarly violent descriptions to describe the fate of demons at the hands of the faithful.[69] Augustine used the metaphor 'fire of exorcism' to describe the experience of the catechumen, noting that unclean spirits often claimed that the words and actions of the exorcists caused them the pain of burning.[70] The first reference to 'commands' (*imperia*) given by exorcists to a demon to depart occurs in a sermon of Pope Leo the Great, in the context of a warning against the ineffectiveness of commands alone, unaccompanied by prayer and fasting.[71] However, in his treatise on holy orders Isidore of Seville (c. 560–636) defined exorcism as 'a speech of reproof' against the devil, and referred neither to the casting out of demons nor to the torment suffered by them.[72] This hints at an alternative

---

[66] Otten, W., 'Overshadowing or Foreshadowing Return: The Role of Demons in Eriugena's *Periphyseon*' in Vos and Otten (2011), pp. 211–30, at p. 213.

[67] Twelftree (2007), p. 280.

[68] Ambrosiaster, *In Epistulam Pauli ad Ephesios* 4.12 (*PL* 17.387D): *Exorcistae ... in ecclesia ... compescunt et verberant inquietos.*

[69] Hilary of Poitiers, *Tractatus super Psalmos* 64.10 (ed. A. Zingerle), *CSEL* 22 (Vienna: F. Tempsky, 1891), p. 242: *Credentium verbis torquentur, laniantur, uruntur ... continentur, puniuntur, abiguntur, et invisibiles nobis atque incomprehensibiles naturae verbo continentur, puniuntur, abiguntur.*

[70] Augustine, *Ennarrationes in psalmos* 65.17 (*PL* 36.797): *Propterea et in Sacramentis, et in catechizando, et in exorcizando, adhibetur prius ignis. Nam unde plerumque immundi spiritus clamant, Ardeo, si ille ignis non est? Post ignem autem exorcismi venitur ad Baptismum; ut ab igne ad aquam, ab aqua in refrigerium.*

[71] Leo the Great, *Sermo* 87[=85].2 (*PL* 54.439B): *Nam in omni agone certaminis Christiani, utilitas continentiae plurimum valet, ita ut quidam saevissimorum spiritus daemonum, qui obsessis corporibus nullis exorcizantium fugantur imperiis, sola jejuniorum et orationum virtute pellantur.*

[72] Isidore of Seville (ed. M. Lawson), *Sancti Isidori Episcopi Hispalensis De Ecclesiasticis Officiis*, *CCSL* 113 (Turnhout: Brepols, 1989), p. 96: *Exorcismus autem sermo increpationis est.*

interpretation of exorcism grounded in the baptismal liturgy, in which the devil was cursed and rebuked but there was no clear idea of 'casting out' an evil spirit.

In the fourth century, the use of the term 'energumen' distinguished the possessed from unbelievers who had yet to receive baptism and were therefore under the dominion of the devil. The late fifth-century compilation of early ecclesiastical decrees known as the *Statuta ecclesiae antiqua*, usually attributed to Gennadius of Marseilles, ordered that 'the exorcists should lay their hands on the energumens every day', that 'the energumens should sweep the floors of the houses of God', and that 'with the energumens working assiduously in the house of God, defeated [i.e. exorcized] every day, they should be ministered to by the exorcists at an opportune time'.[73] These canons demonstrate that fifth- and sixth-century exorcism was a long drawn-out process that might require the demoniacs to live in the church and make themselves useful by performing tasks within it, which also seems to presuppose an understanding of possession in which the activity of the demon was intermittent rather than continuous. Brown suggested that the canons are evidence that some deliberately came to the basilicas of the saints in order to become possessed,[74] although this interpretation is not necessarily supported by the evidence.

The earliest representation of a demoniac in the west to portray the demon leaving the demoniac's body is to be found on the ivory cover of the Murano Gospel, produced at the end of the fifth century and now in Ravenna.[75] This, like most early depictions, is an image of the Gerasene demoniac. The demoniac's ankles are tied together and both of his wrists are chained to his neck; the demon is shown leaving from his head. The motif of the demon leaving from the demoniac's mouth, so frequently found in the Middle Ages, first occurred in a Syriac Gospel of the late sixth century and had spread to the west via Byzantine influence on Ottonian

---

[73] *Statuta Ecclesiae Antiqua* (*Concilia Galliae*) 62–4, ed. C. Munier and C. De Clerq (Turnhout: Brepols, 1963), p. 176: *Omni die exorcistae energumenis manis imponant … Pauimenta domorum Dei energumeni euerrant … Energumenis in domo Dei assidentibus uictus quotidianus per exorcistas opportune tempore ministretur.*

[74] Brown (1981), p. 111.

[75] Chave-Mahir (2011), p. 30; reproduced in Mandouze, A., *Histoire des Saints et de la Sainteté chrétienne* 2 (Paris: Hachette, 1986), p. 20. See also Lunn-Rockliffe, S., 'Visualizing the Demonic: The Gadarene Exorcism in Early Christian Art and Literature' in Raiswell, R. and Dendle, P. (eds), *The Devil in Society in Pre-Modern Europe* (Toronto: Centre for Reformation and Renaissance Studies, 2012), pp. 439–58.

art by the ninth century.⁷⁶ To the extent that portrayals in art influenced the way in which viewers, and especially illiterate viewers, conceptualized exorcism, the foundations of medieval representations of possession were laid as early as the fifth century. Visual portrayals of the invisible process of exorcism inevitably strengthened the belief that it involved the literal casting out of an evil spirit inhabiting the limits of the physical body, and as Raiswell has observed, 'endowing the devil with a physical form was a way to constrain and control him'.⁷⁷

Origins of Liturgical Exorcism

The earliest reference to a written rite of extra-baptismal exorcism occurs in the Gregorian Sacramentary, where during the service of ordination of an exorcist, a *libellus* ('little book') is placed in the hands of the exorcist with the words: 'Receive this and commit it to memory, and have the power of laying hands upon an energumen, whether baptized or catechumen'.⁷⁸ This form of words implies that, in addition to the pre-baptismal rites, the *libellus* also contained a rite for exorcizing the baptized. The Gregorian Sacramentary's formula derived from the seventh canon of the fourth Council of Carthage (398) and the *Statuta ecclesiae antiqua*, in which the ordination of exorcists was mentioned without reference to a *libellus*.⁷⁹ A letter of Pope Innocent I (d. 417) to the Bishop of Gubbio may be interpreted as evidence that any priest or deacon could be designated an exorcist, setting the precedent for episcopal jurisdiction over exorcisms that became so important at the Counter-Reformation. Alternatively, however, it may mean that a priest or bishop could identify a person as possessed only with the bishop's authority⁸⁰:

---

⁷⁶ Chave-Mahir (2011), pp. 30–1.
⁷⁷ Raiswell (2012), p. 59.
⁷⁸ 'Ordinatio exorcistae' in Deshusses, J. (ed.), *Le Sacramentaire Grégorien: ses principales formes d'après les plus anciens manuscrits*, 3rd edn (Fribourg: Editions Universitaires, 1992), p. 601: *Accipe et commenda memoriae et habeto potestatem imponendi manum super energuminum sive baptizatum sive catecuminum.* See also Van Slyke, D. G., 'The Ancestry and Theology of the Rite of Major Exorcism', *Antiphon* 10 (2006), pp. 70–116, at p. 74.
⁷⁹ *Concilia Galliae*, pp. 95–8. On the *libelli* see Chave-Mahir (2011), pp. 67–70, 313–18.
⁸⁰ *PL* 20.557–8: *De his vero baptizatis, qui postea a demonio, vitio aliquo aut peccato interveniente, arripiuntur, est sollicita dilectio tua, si a presbytero vel diacono possint aut debeant designari. Quod hoc, nisi episcopus praeceperit non licet.*

You must have a loving concern for those baptized persons, who are afterwards possessed by a demon on account of some vice or intervening sin, if they are able or ought to be designated by a priest or deacon. This thing is not permitted unless the bishop orders it.

Brown and Chave-Mahir both assumed that the liturgy for the exorcism of a demoniac, the earliest form of which is to be found in a late eighth-century text of the Gelasian Sacramentary compiled at the Abbey of Gellone (Saint Guillaume-le-Desert) in southern France, was essentially an adaptation of the earlier rites of pre-baptismal exorcism. Exorcism of demoniacs was thus, liturgically, the descendent of the pre-baptismal exorcisms and an adjustment of an already established liturgy to new conditions. However, a comparison of the exorcism of demoniacs in the Gellone Sacramentary with *Ordo XI* reveals comparatively few linguistic similarities. Robert Van Slyke has undertaken a detailed analysis of the Gellone Sacramentary's rite of exorcism in the course of a study of the liturgical history of exorcism.[81] However, the purpose of Van Slyke's study was to compare the Gellone Sacramentary with twentieth-century rites rather than to elucidate the particular characteristics of the earliest extant liturgy of exorcism.[82]

The liturgy in the Gellone Sacramentary began with the priest laying hands on the energumen and the prayer *Omnipotens sempiterne deus a cuis faciae celi distillant* ('Almighty and eternal God, before whose face the heavens flee').[83] An alternative form of the prayer was provided for an infant energumen; this referred to the 'sins of the parents' (*parentum delecta*), suggesting that an infant might be possessed before baptism on account of ancestral sin.[84] The next part of the liturgy, entitled 'Prayer over a Christian man vexed by a demon' (*Oratio super hominem Christianum qui a demonio vexatur*), began with the short prayer *Repelle Domine* ('Repel, o Lord') for the energumen, and then the first of the exorcisms. This began with the prayer *Deus angelorum, deus arcangelorum* ('God of angels, God of archangels...') for the exorcist, 'that you would deign to grant me help against this most wicked spirit, so that wherever he may hide, having heard your name, he should quickly go out and draw

---

[81] Van Slyke (2006), pp. 74–7.
[82] Kelly (1968), pp. 82–3 followed the view of Franz (1909), vol. 2, p. 579 who believed that the earliest form of exorcism was contained in the *Missale Gallicanum Vetus*.
[83] *SG* 2400.
[84] *SG* 2401.

back'.[85] The exorcist then addressed the devil directly, reminding him of the power of Christ to command: 'He himself commands you, devil, who commanded the wind and the sea or the tempests. He himself commands you who ordered you to be sunk in the lower earth. He himself commands you who ordered you to go back'.[86] The first imperative command follows: 'Hear therefore and be afraid, Satan, defeated and prostrate, depart in the name of our Lord Jesus Christ'.[87] The exorcist then insults the devil with a number of titles, 'enemy of the faith of the human race, plunderer of death, avoider of justice, root of evils, touchwood of vices, seducer of men, betrayer of peoples, inciter of envy, origin of greed, cause of discord, arouser of griefs, master of demons'.[88] The exorcist demands of the devil, 'Why do you stand and resist, when you know that you have lost your powers?' (*quid stas et resistis, cum scis eum tuas perdere vires?*) and encourages him to fear Christ. A second imperative command is given, accompanied by the sign of the cross: 'Draw back in the name of the Father, the Son and the Holy Spirit, and give place to the Holy Spirit'.[89]

Another prayer for the energumen follows (*Deus, conditur et defensor generis humani*), appealing to God to liberate a human being made in his image.[90] Then, after a prayer that God would strike terror into the devil, (*Domine sancte pater omnipotens eterne deus, osanna in excelsis*), the exorcist moved to the three 'great adjurations'[91]:

1. 'I adjure you, therefore, ancient serpent' (*Adiuro ergo te serpens antique*)
2. 'I adjure you, not by my weakness but in the power of the Holy Spirit' (*Adiuro te, non mea infirmitate sed in virtute spiritus sancti*)
3. 'I adjure you, therefore, most wicked dragon' (*Adiuro ergo te, draco quiessime* [sic. for *nequissime*])

---

[85] SG 2403: *ut mihi auxilium praestare digneris adversus hunc nequissimum spiritum, ut ubicumque latet, audito nomini tuo, velociter exiat et recedat.*

[86] *Ipse tibi imperat, diabule, qui ventus et mare vel tempestatibus imperavit. Ipse tibi imperat qui te de superna celorum in inferiora terre demergi precepit. Ipse tibi imperat qui te retrorsum redire precepit.*

[87] *Audi ergo et time satanas, victus et prostratus, abscede in nomine domini nostri iesu christi.*

[88] *... inimicus fidei generis humani, mortis raptur, iustitiae declinatur, malorum radix, fomis vitiorum, sedoctor hominum, perditur gentium, incitatur invidiae, origo avaritiae, causa discordiae, excitatur dolorum, demonum magister.*

[89] *Recede in nomine patris et filii et spiritus sancti, et da locum spiritu<i> sancto.*

[90] SG 2404.

[91] SG 2405.

Each of these adjurations has a slightly different emphasis. The first adjuration calls upon God as judge of the living and the dead, maker of the world, and as the one who condemned the devil to hell, and reminds the devil that he should depart in fear from an individual who has sought the aid of the church. The second adjuration makes clear that the exorcist does not seek to command the devil by his own power but by the power of God, and increases the pressure on the devil by means of imperative commands—*cede* (yield) and *contremisce* (tremble). The human body itself is presented as an object of terror to the devil in a clear expression of the implications of the Incarnation: 'Let the body of man be a terror to you, let the image of God be an object of dread to you, and do not resist or delay in departing from this man, since it pleased Christ to dwell in man'.[92] The exorcist then returns to the theme of his own unworthiness, calling instead upon the Lord, the majesty of Christ, the Trinity, the faith of Peter and Paul and the apostles, the indulgence of confessors, the blood of martyrs, the cross and the power of the mysteries (i.e. the sacraments).

The second great adjuration concludes with the dramatic imperatives *exi* (go out), repeated twice, and *da locum* (give place to …), repeated three times, contrasting the devil as 'seducer, full of every trick and falsehood, the enemy of truth, the persecutor of the innocent' with Christ 'in whom you have found none of your works, who despoiled you, who destroyed your kingdom, who bound you, defeated and disrupted your security, who cast you into outer darkness …'. The exorcist then switches to the terminology of the law courts, taunting the devil with his inability to respond to the accusations made against him and the demand that he depart, 'But what now do you consider, in confusion? Why do you blindly draw back?' (*Sed qui nunc, turbulente recogitas? Quid, temerariae, retractas?*). The exorcist reminds the devil of his legal position: 'You are bound by almighty God whose statutes you have transgressed; you are bound by his Son Jesus Christ whom you dared to tempt and whom you presumed to crucify; you are bound by the human race to whom death came by your persuasion'.[93] The word used to express the devil's obligation, *reus*, is a legal one, with the sense that the devil is accused, condemned and bound to answer for his crimes.

---

[92] *Sit tibi terror corpus hominis, sit tibi formido imago dei, nec resistas nec moreris discedere ab homine, quoniam complacuit christo ut in homine habitaret.*

[93] *Reus omnipotenti deo cuius statuta transgressus es, reus filio eius iesu christo quem temptare ausus es et crucifigere presumpsisti, reus humani generi[s] cui mors tuis persuasionis venit.*

The third great adjuration commands the devil to 'depart from this man, depart from the church of God' (*discedas ab homine, discedas ab ecclesia dei*). The devil is commanded to 'tremble and flee' (*contremisce et effuge*) while the angelic hierarchies of the Powers, Dominions, Cherubim and Seraphim are invoked. The devil is reminded once more who commands him: the Word made flesh, the one born of a virgin, Jesus Christ who cast him out of the Gerasene demoniac into a herd of pigs (this is the first reference to a biblical exorcism). Finally, the exorcist makes a rhetorical argument to the devil: 'It is hard for you to kick against the goad, since the later you depart your punishment increases, since you do not hold a man in contempt but he who is the Lord of the living and the dead, who is coming to judge the world by fire'.[94]

The exorcism continues from *SG* 2406 onwards with a liturgy hereafter peculiar to the Gellone Sacramentary that was not, therefore, the ancestor of all subsequent rites of exorcism (albeit this material was influential on English pontificals, for which see Chap. 3 below). However, the first five sections of the Gellone exorcism described above are not obviously derived from the ancient pre-baptismal exorcisms. Most strikingly, no form of words in the Gellone exorcism echoes the *Ergo maledicte diabole*, the most frequently repeated and perhaps the most ancient part of the pre-baptismal exorcism. The *Audi maledicte Satanas* of *Ordo XI* bears some similarity to the *Audi ergo et time satanas* of *SG* 2403:

> Hear, accursed Satan, adjured by the name of the eternal God and our Saviour, the Son of God, depart having been defeated, trembling and groaning, with your envy. (*Ordo XI*)
> Hear therefore and be afraid, Satan, defeated and prostrate, depart in the name of our Lord Jesus Christ. (*SG* 2403)

However, it is by no means obvious that the second text is an adaptation of the first. The formula *Ipse enim tibi imperat* ('for he himself commands you') appears frequently in the Gellone exorcism as *imperat te* ('He commands you'), followed by a divine or angelic name, but the formula *Exorcizo te, inmunde spiritus* ('I exorcize you, unclean spirit …'), although it appears in very many later rites of exorcism, does not feature in the

---

[94] *Durum tibi est contra stimulum calcitrare, quia quicquid tardius exis supplicium tuum crescit, quoniam non hominem contempnis sed illum qui dominatur vivorum et mortuorum est, qui venturus est iudicare <seculum per ignem.>*

Gellone Sacramentary. Crucially, the intent of the demonic exhortations in the pre-baptismal exorcisms and the Gellone exorcism seems to be different: in *Ordo XI*, the devil is commanded to give honour (*da honorem*) to God. This is never demanded of the devil in the Gellone exorcism, who is accused of holding God in contempt but never told to honour him.

Table 2.1 uses the *Rituale Romanum* of 1614, the final form of the medieval exorcism liturgies, as a point of comparison for the Gellone Sacramentary. The *Rituale* followed the Gellone Sacramentary insofar as it generally avoided the language of the baptismal exorcisms. Seven sections of the 1614 liturgy corresponded to the liturgy in the Gellone Sacramentary.

Table 2.1 Similarities between the rites of exorcism in the *Rituale Romanum* (1614) and the Gellone Sacramentary

Rituale Romanum (1614)	Sacramentarium Gellonensis
RR 886: Holy Lord, omnipotent Father, eternal God, Father of Our Lord Jesus Christ …	SG 2405: Holy Lord, omnipotent Father, eternal God, hosanna in the highest, Father of Our Lord Jesus Christ …
RR 896: … He himself commands you, who commanded the sea, the winds and the storms …	SG 2403 … He himself commands you, devil, who commanded the winds and the sea or the storms …
RR 897: Draw back therefore in the name of the Father + and of the Son and of the Holy Spirit + give place to the Holy Spirit …	SG 2403: Draw back in the name of the Father and of the Son and of the Holy Spirit, and give place to the Holy Spirit …
RR 898: O God, creator and defender of the human race, who formed man in your image …	SG 2404: O God, creator and defender of the human race, who formed man by your mouth in your image and likeness by your holy hands and the providence of your divinity …
RR 899: Guard + the inner breast of this man. Rule + his inward parts …	SG 2404: Guard what belongs to this sinner [*peccatoris*, probably a scribal error for *pectoris*] forever, rule his inward parts …
RR 900: I adjure you, ancient serpent, by the judge of the living and the dead, by the maker of the world … I adjure you again + not by my weakness, but by the strength of the Holy Spirit …	SG 2405 : I adjure you, therefore, ancient serpent, by the judge of the living and the dead, by the maker of the world … I adjure you, not by my weakness but in the strength of the Holy Spirit …
RR 901: I adjure you, therefore, most evil dragon, in the name of the Lamb + unblemished …	SG 2405: I adjure you, therefore, most quiet [*quiessime*, probably a scribal error for *nequissime*] dragon, in the name of the Lamb unblemished …

A manuscript of the Gelasian Sacramentary of around the same period as the Gellone manuscript is the so-called 'Paris Supplement' to Vatican MS Reginensis 316.[95] In the Paris Supplement, a long exorcism containing ten adjurations precedes a version of *Domine sancte Pater omnipotens* almost identical to *SG* 2405. Unlike the Gellone Sacramentary, the Paris Supplement makes extensive use of language derived from the baptismal exorcisms of *Ordo XI*, including *Ergo maledicte Satana*. The exorcism that follows *Domine sancte pater omnipotens* is the *Nec te lateat*[96]:

> Nor does it escape you, Satan, that punishments threaten you, torments threaten you, the day of judgement threatens you, the day of eternal punishment, the day that is to come like a burning furnace, in which destruction has been prepared for you and your angels forever. And therefore on account of your wickedness, who are damned and being damned, give honour to the living God, give honour to Jesus Christ his Son, give honour to the Holy Spirit, the holy Paraclete in whose power I command you, whoever you are, unclean spirit, to go out and depart from this servant of God, and give him back to his God, since our Lord Jesus Christ has deigned to call him to his grace and blessing.

As a comparison of the Paris Supplement to the *Rituale* of 1614 shows (Table 2.2), five of the corresponding sections are shared between the Gellone and Paris liturgies. However, the Paris liturgy supplies the words *Praecipio tibi* from *Ordo XI*.[97] However, whereas *Ipse tibi imperat* (*SG* 2403) is relatively unchanged in the *Rituale* (*RR* 896), the corresponding words in the Paris Supplement are significantly different, as are the words of the exorcism *Recede ergo*, substantially the same in the *Rituale* and the

---

[95] Paris, Bibliothèque Nationale, MS Lat. 7193, fols 41–56, edited text in Lowe, E. A., 'The Vatican MS of the Gelasian Sacramentary and its Supplement at Paris', *Journal of Theological Studies* 27 (108) (1926), pp. 357–73, at pp. 360–5.

[96] Lowe (1926), p. 364: *Nec te lateat satanas inmineri tibi poenas inmineri tibi tormenta diem iudicii. diem supplicii sempiterni diem qui uenturus est uelut clybanus ardens in quo tibi atque angelis tuis sempiternus est praeparatus interitus et ideo pro tua nequicia damnate atque damnandae Da honore deo uiuo da honore iesu christo filio eius Da honore spiritui. sancto paraclyto In cuius uirtute praecipio tibi quicumque es spiritus inmundi Ut exias et recidas ab hoc famulo dei illo et eum deo suo reddas quoniam dominus noster iesus christus eum ad suam graciam et benedictionem uocare dignatus es.*

[97] Although the phrase *praecipio tibi* appears in both the Paris Supplement and the *Rituale Romanum*, in the latter it is used to command the spirit to reveal its name and the time of its departure; in the ancient liturgies it is simply a command to depart.

Table 2.2 Similarities between the rites of exorcism in the *Rituale Romanum* (1614) and the Paris Supplement

Rituale Romanum (1614)	*Paris Supplement*
RR 886: Holy Lord, omnipotent Father, eternal God, Father of Our Lord Jesus Christ ...	Holy Lord, omnipotent Father, eternal God, hosanna in the highest, Father of Our Lord Jesus Christ ...
RR 887: I command you, whoever you are, unclean spirit ...	... In whose strength I command you, whoever you are, unclean spirit, that you should go out and draw back from this servant of God ...
RR 896: ... He himself commands you, who commanded the sea, the winds and the storms ...	He commands you, not by flesh and blood nor by the pomp of the world; God commands you, the Father, the Son and the Holy Spirit ...
RR 897: Draw back, therefore, in the name of the Father + and of the Son, and of the Holy Spirit + give place to the Holy Spirit ...	Draw back, therefore, having been adjured, in his name from the man whom he himself formed ...
RR 900: I adjure you, ancient serpent, by the judge of the living and the dead, by the maker of the world ... I adjure you again + not by my weakness, but by the strength of the Holy Spirit ...	I adjure you, therefore, ancient serpent, by the judge of the living and the dead, by the maker of the world ...
RR 901: I adjure you, most evil dragon, in the name of the Lamb + unblemished ...	I adjure you, therefore, most evil dragon, in the name of the Lamb unblemished ...
RR 903: God of heaven, God of earth, God of angels, God of archangels, God of prophets, God of apostles, God of martyrs, God of virgins, God who has power to give life after death ...	God of the heavens, God of angels, God of archangels, God of patriarchs, God of prophets, God of martyrs, God of confessors, God of virgins, God of all the saints, God of Abraham, God of Isaac, God of Jacob, God who has given life after death ...

Gellone Sacramentary. The Paris Supplement supplies the earliest version of the prayer *Deus caeli, Deus terrae*, absent in the Gellone Sacramentary.

Whilst the texts shared between the Tridentine liturgy and the Gellone Sacramentary were picked up in a form scarcely altered in the passage of nine centuries, the Gellone Sacramentary nevertheless lacks key texts that were included in 1614. The most important of these, the *Praecipio tibi*, was derived from *Ordo XI*. It is possible to discern in the Paris Supplement and the Gellone Sacramentary two distinct liturgical traditions regarding the exorcism of demoniacs: the one made use of baptismal exorcisms while the other did not. It would be a mistake, therefore, to view all exorcisms of demoniacs as an adaptation of baptismal rites, and later sacramentaries give a clue as to why the Paris Supplement may have included baptismal exorcisms. In the St Amand Sacramentary (c. 1170) the 'laying of hands on an energumen' (*Inpositio manus energuminum*) was expected to take place on the Saturday after Pentecost.[98] This liturgy included two prayers matching those in the Gellone Sacramentary, *Omnipotens sempiterne deus a cuius facie celi distillant* (*SG* 2400, St Amand 333) and the prayer for an infant energumen (*SG* 2401, St Amand 334). However, in the St Amand Sacramentary, as in the Paris Supplement, the *Nec te lateat* follows (St Amand 336), but the major prayer pronounced over the energumen is not an exorcism at all (St Amand 337)[99]:

> We suppliants implore you, Lord, that by your holy visitation that you would raise this your servant to you, and that the adversary should not be permitted to arrive at temptation of his soul. But as in Job, set a limit, lest the enemy should begin to triumph concerning this soul without the redemption of baptism. Bear away, Lord, the doom of death, you who judge concerning things to come and extend the space of his life. Reveal whom you lead to the sacrament of baptism and do not bring damnation to your redemption. Take away the occasion of the devil's triumph, and preserve those who are assimilated to Christ, in whom you triumph, that he may be reborn, made well in your church by your grace of baptism, all which we ask to be done.

The liturgy in the St Amand Sacramentary is not an exorcism of a demoniac but the preparation of an energumen for baptism. It is possible that the liturgy in the Paris Supplement developed from a specialized liturgy for the exorcism of energumens, but in the case of the Gellone Sacramentary this cannot be asserted with any certainty.

The Gelasian Sacramentary contained a variety of distinct forms of exorcism: the ancient pre-baptismal exorcisms for adults and infants,

---

[98] *Sacramentarium Gelasianum mixtum von Saint-Amand*, ed. K. Gamber, Textus Patristici et Liturgici 10 (Regensburg: F. Pustet, 1973), p. 76.

[99] *Te domine supplices exoramus, ut visitatione tua sancta erigas ad te hunc famulum tuum ne adversario liceat usque ad temptationem animae pervenire. sed sicut in iob terminum pone. ne inimicus de anima huius sine redemptione baptismatis incipiat triumphare. Differ domine exitum mortis qui iudicas de futuris. et spatium vitae distendere. revela quem perducas ad baptismi sacramentum. ne redemptioni tuae inferas damnum. Tolle occasionem diabulo triumphandi. et reserva in quem triumphes conpares xpi. ut sanus tibi in ecclesia tua gratia baptismatis renascatur. facturus cuncta quae petimus.*

special exorcisms for possessed and sick catechumens, exorcism of energumens and an implicit post-baptismal exorcism by Oil of Chrism.[100] To see all of these forms of exorcism as outgrowths of the original liturgical exorcism that took place before baptism would be erroneous. The absence of a surviving liturgy of exorcism of demoniacs earlier than the eighth century does not alter the important differences in form and intent between pre-baptismal exorcism and exorcism of demoniacs in the Gellone Sacramentary. Whilst the theological idea of formally rebuking the devil may well have originated in the early Roman liturgy of baptism, there is no convincing evidence that the ancestry of the most important component of the liturgy of exorcism of energumens lies in pre-baptismal rites. This component was *Domine sancte Pater* (*SG* 2405), shared by both the Gellone and Paris liturgies. It is likely that this exorcism, containing the three 'great adjurations', had its own distinct history, perhaps stretching back as far as the *libelli* of the Council of Carthage. The view that the exorcism of energumens was an adaptation of pre-baptismal exorcism seems to have arisen from the mistaken assumption, rightly questioned by Kelly, that pre-baptismal exorcism was originally intended as a literal casting out of the devil. Once this error is removed from the picture, it becomes clear that pre-baptismal exorcism and exorcism of energumens were parallel yet interpenetrating liturgical developments.

SAINTS AND EXORCISTS

During the course of the fourth century and thereafter, exorcism became ever more closely associated with the cult of the saints. Liberation from demons was linked to holy places and with the 'special' power of holy individuals, rather than with a specific rite of the church and the church's exercise of divine power. The arrival of monasticism in Gaul with John Cassian (c. 360–435) brought with it the Egyptian monks' emphasis on combat with the devil. The Gaulish monastic tradition, exemplified by Sulpicius Severus' *Life of St Martin of Tours*, emphasized 'the monk's fervent opposition to paganism, backed up by miraculous deeds', including confrontations with demons.[101] However, Cassian argued that the Gaulish monks should cultivate perfection of life rather than seeking after wonders, and

---

[100] See *SG* 2344–86, 384.
[101] Brakke, D., *Demons and the Making of the Monk: Spiritual Combat in Early Christianity* (Cambridge, MA: Harvard University Press, 2006), p. 242.

observed that the deceits of the devil in Gaul were less dramatic than they had been in the Egyptian desert for the likes of St Anthony, perhaps because Western European monks were not prepared to fight the devil with the same intensity. Although Cassian emphasized demonic combat to a lesser extent than some Egyptian authors, he nevertheless left his mark on Western monasticism and the demonology of the Latin church in general.[102]

Frankfurter has argued that the process of creating sacred places within early Christianity represented an accommodation and transformation of local pantheons.[103] Exorcism simultaneously rid the landscape of the old gods and transformed its practitioners—the saints—into a new and heroic pantheon. This was vividly demonstrated when Martin of Tours (316–97) compelled spirits to name themselves as 'Jupiter' and 'Mercury'.[104] Recognition of the Christian God and the saints who served him by demoniacs possessed by local spirits served to articulate the shift in pantheons.[105] Shrines became the site of a form of 'demonic theatre' where the possessed would congregate and the faithful would gather to witness remarkable sights, like a man dangling upside-down from a balcony at the shrine of St Felix of Nola in fourth-century Italy.[106] In MacMullen's view, these new religious phenomena filled a religious vacuum left by Christian persecution of non-Christian practices.[107]

Nicetius of Trier upheld the presence of demoniacs at the shrines of basilicas in Gaul as a sign of the superiority of the Catholic faith compared with Arianism.[108] In an influential thesis, Peter Brown argued that non-believers were more likely to be moved to belief in the truth of the Christian faith by exorcism than by anything else; it constituted proof of the *praesentia* and *potestas* (presence and power) of Catholic saints. Exorcism at the shrines of the saints had 'heavy judicial overtones';

---

[102] Ibid. p. 245.
[103] Frankfurter (2010), pp. 29, 36–7.
[104] Sulpicius Severus, *Gallus* 6.4 in Fontaine, J. (ed. and trans.), *Scriptores Christianae* 510 (Paris: Editions du Cerf, 2006), pp. 311–13. The principal deity of the Gauls was usually called Mercury. On Martin's exorcisms see Donaldson, C., *Martin of Tours: Parish Priest, Mystic and Exorcist* (London: Routledge and Kegan Paul, 1980), pp. 99–102.
[105] Frankfurter (2010), p. 39.
[106] Paulinus of Nola, *Carmina* 23.82–95 in Walsh, *Poems*, p. 212. Jerome reported that a similar scene was witnessed by the pilgrim Paula in the Holy Land (Brown (1981), p. 106).
[107] MacMullen (1984), p. 152.
[108] Brown (1981), pp. 106–7.

the demons were tormented like criminal suspects in their encounter with the saint, and forced to confess the truth.[109] As Victricius of Rouen put it, 'A torturer bends over the unclean spirit, but is not seen. There are no chains here now, but the being who suffers is bound. God's anger has other hooks to tear the flesh and other racks to stretch invisible limbs'.[110] Unlike the pagan shrines of Gaul, the shrines of the saints modelled 'vertical dependence' between saint and worshipper and the saint's complete jurisdictional domination. These up-to-date religious themes carried a greater popular appeal in the late Empire than the impersonal deities of the ancient Gaulish healing shrines,[111] and exorcisms produced a 'special loyalty' to the saint and to Christianity from witnesses and beneficiaries.[112] The relationship of saint to believer reflected the relationship between the Emperor and Roman citizens in the autocratic polity of the late Empire. Christians, recognizing a single divine authority, made good citizens of the Empire. Brown's argument that exorcism was essentially a judicial process is supported by the occurrence of judicial language in the eighth-century liturgy of exorcism, already noted. However, in the absence of an extant textual tradition for this liturgy, the idea that this legal terminology was applied to demons as early as the fifth century must be speculation.

As the effectiveness of the ancient system of public penance came under strain as Christianity gained social acceptance, Brown argued, the dramatic dialogue of exorcism came to enact 'the old ideal of public penance and forgiveness'. The exorcisms of the saints reassured people in a changing world by mirroring Roman justice and preserving early Christian values.[113] Over time, the emphasis on the saints' and martyrs' victory over demons led to a transformation of the relationship between saints and demons; so complete was the victory, that the saints had the power to make use of the possessed for other purposes before exorcizing them. The possessed defended the honour of the saint and even abused bishops.[114] At the shrine of St Felix, the possession of the demoniacs was prolonged rather than alleviated, supposedly so that their sins could be more completely expiated

---

[109] Ibid. p. 108.
[110] Victricius of Rouen, *De laude sanctorum* 11 (*PL* 20, 453D–454A): *Ecce incumbit immundi pollutique spiritus tortor, nec venit sub aspectu ille, qui torquet. Nulla sunt vincula, et ligatur ille qui patitur. Equuleum aeris habet ira coelestis.*
[111] Brown (1981), p. 118.
[112] MacMullen (1984), p. 28. See also Sorensen (2002), pp. 168–221.
[113] Brown (1981), pp. 110–11.
[114] Ibid. p. 111.

and the glory of God thereby demonstrated.[115] One legend described how St Martin had a demoniac brought before him in church and forced a demon to confess that he had spread panic amongst the population of Trier by convincing them that a barbarian attack was imminent.[116] On another occasion, a demoniac announced in the middle of the church that the general Aegidius had triumphed in battle owing to Martin's assistance.[117]

Exorcism in Carolingian Europe

The Gelasian Sacramentary, in copies of which the earliest liturgies for exorcisms of demoniacs are to be found, originated in the late eighth century at a time when the Frankish leader Charlemagne, soon to be crowned the first Holy Roman Emperor, was concerned that the liturgy of the Frankish church should follow that of Rome. The Gelasian Sacramentary is, therefore, usually described as Romano-Frankish, since it was produced in Frankish territories following Roman models. Liturgical material presents a difficulty to the historian for two main reasons. Firstly, liturgical compilations tend to be conservative, sometimes including rites that are either obsolete or culturally irrelevant to the immediate context of their production. Secondly, liturgical texts cannot in themselves tell us anything about the frequency with which a given rite was performed, and usually they tell us little about the gestures used, the people present or the place where the ritual took place. As we have seen, it cannot be assumed that the liturgy found in the late eighth-century Gellone Sacramentary was created in an eighth-century context, and much of the material is likely to be far older.

It is possible that the Gelasian liturgy of exorcism of an energumen was rarely if ever used. However, the inventiveness of the latter half of the liturgy in the Gellone Sacramentary makes this unlikely. An exorcism beginning *Exorcizo te, inimice diabule* ('I exorcize you, enemy the devil ...') specifies in great detail the parts of the body from which the devil is to be excluded,[118] suggesting that the authors of the liturgy had begun to adapt it to a context of healing appropriate for a northern European culture in

---

[115] Frankfurter (2010), p. 40.

[116] Sulpicius Severus, *De Vita Martini* 18 (*PL* 20.170B).

[117] Sulpicius Severus, *De Virtutibus Martini* 1.2 in *Scriptores Rerum Merovingicarum*, ed. B. Krusch (Hanover: Hahn, 1969), pp. 136–7. On Martin's exorcisms see Frankfurter (2010), p. 33.

[118] *SG* 2406.

which physical illnesses such as headaches were often attributed to malign spiritual forces. Furthermore, the use of multiple titles for God, associating him with the rest of the company of heaven, may be an indication that the compilers of the liturgy were keen to associate a successful exorcism not just with God himself but also with local cults of angels, virgins, martyrs and so on, as Frankfurter has argued. Van Slyke has noted that the multiplication of titles of God disappeared over the centuries, suggesting it was a peculiar feature produced by the Frankish context of the Gelasian Sacramentary.[119]

Only one source attests to the theological context in which the Gelasian Sacramentary was composed. The only example of developed demonology from the Carolingian period is to be found in the *Periphyseon* of the Irish Neoplatonist philosopher John Scotus Eriugena, although it is of a level of theological abstraction that makes its implications for exorcism difficult to gauge.[120] Eriugena was troubled by the doctrine of the eternal damnation or annihilation of demons. Their eternal damnation meant that evil would continue to exist somewhere in God's creation even at the end of time, whilst their annihilation would mean that God would destroy their being. Eriugena (following Augustine) believed that being was intrinsically good *qua* being, and therefore God could not annihilate what was good. Eriugena's solution was to argue that God would damn the demons not by annihilating or punishing them eternally but by stripping them of their evil natures: 'Indeed [Christ] extinguishes their evil and the power of their harmful impiety. And perhaps their eternal damnation will be the universal abolition of their evil and impiety'.[121] Willemien Otten has convincingly argued that this radical solution to the problem of demons, far from deriving from Origen's universalism, was deeply Augustinian in origin.[122] Eriugena revealed a paradox at the heart of Augustine's analysis of evil as *deprivatio boni*; if the demons are good

---

[119] Van Slyke (2006), p. 75.

[120] Carolingian demonology was also reflected in the multiplicity of titles bestowed on the devil in sacramentaries such as the *Missale Gothicum*, composed in Luxeuil in around 700 (Bartelink, G., 'Denominations of the Devil and Demons in the *Missale Gothicum*' in Vos and Otten (2011), pp. 195–209).

[121] Eriugena, *Periphyseon* V 923C in *CCCM* 165 (Turnhout: Brepols, 2003), p. 89: *Illorum vero malitiam et impietatemque nocivamque potentiam ... extinguet. Et fortassis illorum erit aeterna damnatio suae malitiae impietatisque universalis abolitio.*

[122] Otten (2011), pp. 226–9. For Augustine's original argument see *Contra Epistulam Manichaei* 35 (PL 42.201).

in their essence and evil in their nature, then there remains something in them to be redeemed, but the Bible and the reality of possession seem to dictate the opposite. As Henry Chadwick expressed it, 'Biblical language about the devil and personal experience ensured that Christian theology must recognize evil as a positive force, a *depravatio* rather than only a *deprivatio*'.[123]

However, although Augustine was responsible for placing a renewed emphasis on the potential of evil to corrupt the good in the fourth century, Eriugena's willingness in the ninth century to entertain the possibility that the demons might be redeemed demonstrates that more than one interpretation of Augustine was at work in early medieval demonology. Eriugena's theology, deeply influenced by the theology of Maximus the Confessor, foreshadowed the twelfth century's increasingly positive view of the human body and emphasis on bodily resurrection.[124] Eriugena's suggestion that the defeat of the demons could take the form of their radical disempowerment has implications for exorcism, which could be viewed either as confronting the demons with the disempowering truth, or engaging in combat with Satan. Read in the context of this debate, the liturgy of exorcism in the Gellone Sacramentary swings from one extreme to the other. On the one hand, the prayers or 'deprecatory exorcisms' beseech God to engage in conflict with the devil: 'hurry so that you may tear this man formed by your hands from ruin and from the noontime demon'.[125] On the other hand, there are times when the devil is simply confronted with the truth and expected to depart without an intervention from God, such as when the exorcist tells him to tremble at the human body, chosen by Christ for the Incarnation. This part of the exorcism is redolent, accidentally or otherwise, of the theology of Maximus the Confessor transmitted to the Latin West by Eriugena, who wrote that '[God] leaves nothing of humanity, which he took completely upon himself, to perpetual punishment and the bonds of insoluble evil'.[126] Although he made no reference to exorcism, Eriugena's conception of

---

[123] Chadwick, H., 'Origen' in Armstrong, A. H. (ed.), *The Cambridge History of Later Greek and Early Mediaeval Theology*, 7th edn (Cambridge: Cambridge University Press, 2007), pp. 182–94, at p. 188.

[124] Elliott (1999), p. 27.

[125] SG 2405: *adcelera ut eripias hominem tuis formatum manibus a ruina et demonio meridiano.*

[126] ... *et nihil humanitatis, quam totam accepit, perpetuis poenis insolubilibusque malitiae ... nexibus obnoxium reliquit.*

demons as bodiless beings disempowered by their encounter with God made it harder to imagine the need for a dramatic struggle between God and the devil. Indeed, Eriugena's thought was an early sign that exorcism would face a crisis in the medieval period that began amongst theologians before spreading to the rest of the church.

CHAPTER 3

Exorcism in Crisis: The Middle Ages, 900–1500

Far from being the 'golden age' of exorcisms, the Middle Ages were a period in which the practice of priestly liturgical exorcism underwent a profound crisis. In the absence of effective centralized church government at the fringes of Europe, especially before the eleventh century, the theological and liturgical foundations for exorcism laid in late antiquity and the Carolingian era were in perpetual danger of dissolving as the diverse cultures of Christian Europe either adapted liturgical exorcism for their own purposes or ignored it altogether. Medieval exorcism made use of ancient liturgical formulas as ubiquitous solutions to spiritual and medical problems, from sexual temptation to toothache, and was at times a 'trivial' process.[1] Yet exorcism was also a subject of interest to medieval theologians (rarely practising exorcists themselves) who explored philosophical problems associated with it. How could the devil take possession of a human body without compromising free will? How could an exorcist tell the difference between a madman and a demon speaking through the mouth of a demoniac? The diagnostic criteria for possession that took centre stage in the early modern period were underpinned by the speculations of medieval theologians.

Between the beginning of the 'renaissance' of the High Middle Ages in the twelfth century and the end of the fifteenth, exorcism underwent

---

[1] For the argument that late medieval and early modern exorcism was trivialized see Sluhovsky (2007), pp. 13–6.

© The Editor(s) (if applicable) and The Author(s) 2016
F. Young, *A History of Exorcism in Catholic Christianity*,
DOI 10.1007/978-3-319-29112-3_3

two distinct transformations.[2] At the start of the era in question, exorcism remained, as it did in late antiquity, an activity associated with the saints. Demoniacs sought refuge at shrines or in monasteries presided over by holy men and women, as in the famous case of the woman Sigewize, exorcized by Hildegard of Bingen after an unsuccessful appeal to the intercession of St Nicholas.[3] These were 'charismatic' as opposed to clerical exorcisms, underpinned by a view of saints as powerful spiritual beings engaged in a contest with demons, who sometimes claimed that they could only be exorcized by a particular saint.[4] By the thirteenth century, exorcism of demoniacs had disappeared almost completely from liturgical books. However, the threat of Catharism, the dualist heresy that emerged in the Pyrenees in the late twelfth century, eventually produced a transformation of Catholic demonology. The Cathar heresy challenged orthodox Christian teaching on the origin of evil, forcing theologians to return to the question of Satan, his agents and how to deal with him. By the beginning of the fourteenth century a new kind of exorcism had emerged, embodied in distinct exorcism books and often going beyond the ancient ritual to include components drawn from magic. This 'magicalized' and materialistic form of exorcism featured in the earliest printed works on the subject and became the foundation for early modern debates on the meaning, purpose and appropriateness of exorcism.

The 'crisis of exorcism' in the Middle Ages was first identified by André Goddu, who observed a decline in the number of exorcisms in saints' lives from the twelfth century onwards. Whilst the same basic narrative of the history of medieval exorcism has been accepted by both Nancy Caciola and Florence Chave-Mahir (whose studies are the foundation of contemporary scholarship in this area), differences of detail and emphasis remain. Kieckhefer has argued that the fifteenth-century 'failure of exorcism' identified by Goddu led not to the abandonment of exorcism, but rather to an increased emphasis on exorcism as liturgical and therapeutic instead of on a saint's definitive defeat of the devil.[5] However, perhaps as a consequence of their concentration on the high and late medieval periods, Caciola and

---

[2] On the transformations of medieval exorcism see Chave-Mahir (2011), p. 334.
[3] *Vita Sanctae Hildegardis* (ed. M. Klaes), *CCCM* 126 (Turnhout: Brepols, 1993), pp. 208–30. On this case see Maggi (2001), pp. 101–2; Porterfield (2005), pp. 86–7; Chave-Mahir (2011), pp. 13–4.
[4] Tamm (2003), p. 8.
[5] Kieckhefer, R., *Forbidden Rites: A Necromancer's Manual of the Fifteenth Century* (Stroud: Sutton, 1997), p. 149.

Chave-Mahir's studies lack a thorough exploration of the early Christian and Carolingian origins of medieval exorcism. This chapter examines the argument for the medieval crisis of exorcism, with a detailed concentration on the evidence from England. The English material received little attention from Chave-Mahir and Caciola, yet medieval England experienced the crisis of exorcism particularly acutely. The failure of liturgical exorcism to take root in England can be attributed, at least in part, to the absence of a coherent political reason for confronting the devil. Exorcism requires a human subject, and whereas in some parts of Europe demonologists provided suitable subjects in the form of witches, this development did not take place in England until after the Reformation.

CHARACTERISTICS OF MEDIEVAL EXORCISM

The evidence for exorcism in the Middle Ages is of two kinds: liturgical and historical-hagiographical. Given the conservatism of the textual tradition of medieval pontificals, the existence of exorcisms in liturgical books tells us little about how they were used, or even if they were used at all.[6] On the other hand, exorcistic liturgies did not by any means stand still, and when they changed it was for a reason. Historical-hagiographical accounts of exorcisms can be found in sources as diverse as sermons, hagiographies, theological summas, personal correspondence and autobiographies,[7] but these pose their own evidential problems. Such sources rarely make clear whether a person exorcized was actually possessed or suffering from some other illness,[8] since exorcism was regularly used as a quasi-medical treatment for physical illnesses.[9] Hagiographical accounts offer few details, usually focusing on the success of a saint's exorcisms rather than the methods employed.

Chave-Mahir discerned two chronological poles in the medieval attitude to exorcism: in the High Middle Ages, exorcism was associated with the conversion of pagans, while at the end of the period it was part of the campaign against magicians.[10] In the 1000s the Romano-Germanic Pontifical rearranged the liturgy of pre-baptismal exorcism so that it

---

[6] On the evidential problems of liturgical exorcisms see Caciola (2003), p. 243.
[7] Chave-Mahir (2011), p. 25.
[8] Ibid. p. 23.
[9] Sluhovsky (2007), p. 14.
[10] Chave-Mahir (2011), p. 17.

could be used for exorcism of demoniacs. An independent liturgical book devoted to exorcism of demoniacs appeared for the first time in the fourteenth century. Thereafter, exorcism became the church's response to theological deviants, such as magicians and heretics who were accused of dealing with the devil. This analysis has its shortcomings. As I have demonstrated in Chap. 2, whilst some liturgical exorcisms of demoniacs drew on older baptismal liturgies, others did not. Baptismal exorcism undoubtedly declined in significance as the Christianization of Western Europe was completed, but it does not follow that the increased significance of exorcism of demoniacs in the eleventh century was a consequence of this decline. Furthermore, some influential late medieval texts such as the *Malleus maleficarum* ('Hammer of Witches') downplayed the significance and effectiveness of exorcism as a remedy against witchcraft. Witchcraft was a new challenge that demanded new remedies.

The liturgy of baptismal exorcism used in the Latin West for the first six hundred years of the second millennium was the work of a monk of the Abbey of St Alban at Mainz in the mid-tenth century. This was the Roman Pontifical, which remained virtually unaltered until the late sixteenth century.[11] However, the dramatic ritual of pre-baptismal exorcism was relegated to the liturgical background,[12] and in the twelfth century Petrus Cantor (d. 1197), Professor of Theology at the cathedral school of Notre Dame de Paris, raised theological doubts concerning the importance and effectiveness of pre-baptismal exorcism. Some exorcized children died before baptism, whilst many unexorcized ones lived, so there was little sign that God automatically gave his grace to exorcized children so that they were prepared for baptism. Petrus went on to argue that the exorcisms of the present day were less effective than those of Solomon,[13] an argument that paved the way for the classification of exorcism as a sacramental dependent on God's grace at a particular moment rather than as a sacrament, an effectual sign of God's grace whose effectiveness

---

[11] Kelly (1985), p. 261. On the decline of the ancient baptismal liturgy in the medieval West see Fisher, J. D. C., *Christian Initiation: Baptism in the Medieval West: A Study in the Disintegration of the Primitive Rite of Initiation* (London: SPCK, 1965).

[12] This did not prevent exorcistic additions to the baptismal liturgy; a 1539 manual of the English Sarum rite recommended that the priest should read the casting out of the dumb spirit in Mark 9 over the newly baptized infant to prevent epilepsy (Duffy, E., *The Stripping of the Altars* (New Haven, CT: Yale University Press, 1992), p. 281).

[13] Petrus Cantor (ed. J.-A. Dugauquier), *Summa de Sacramentis* 21, Analecta Mediaevalia Namuracensia 4 (Lille: Löwen, 1954), pp. 60–4.

was guaranteed by Christ himself. Adolph Franz defined a sacramental by three essential characteristics: cultic usage, apotropaic function, and contribution to the well-being of believers.[14]

Caciola has argued that the order of exorcist was in terminal decline by the tenth century, since pre-baptismal exorcisms were generally performed by the same priests who performed the baptisms. However, one ordination prayer for an exorcist from this time suggests that the order of exorcist could be considered to confer authority to exorcize demoniacs, since it prayed 'that he may be a spiritual commander for casting out demons from possessed bodies'.[15] Chave-Mahir was critical of Caciola's interpretation of the twelfth, thirteenth and fourteenth centuries as an era of 'improvised exorcism',[16] and has demonstrated that Caciola ignored key thirteenth-century liturgical texts that were grounded in the tradition of the Gelasian Sacramentary.[17] According to Caciola, twelfth-century Christians faced with demonic possession were unsure what to do, and made use of a mixture of relics, communion and baptismal exorcism to drive out the devil. Chave-Mahir, by contrast, has suggested that twelfth-century authors rarely mentioned actual encounters with demoniacs because sufferers may have been hidden within their communities in a pre-urban society.[18]

The idea that exorcism underwent a period of transition and crisis between 1100 and 1300, during which time the connection between exorcism and the saints weakened, is supported by the evidence of hagiographies. Goddu demonstrated that references to exorcism in lives of the saints peaked in the fourteenth century.[19] He connected the tendency of some medieval theologians such as William of Auxerre (d. 1237) to deny the possibility of full bodily possession (in favour of demonic 'suggestion' or 'influence') with a blurring of the distinction between possession, in which the demoniac was the victim, and witchcraft where the witch was

---

[14] Franz, A., *Die Kirchlichen Benediktionen im Mittelalter* (Freiburg-im-Breslau: Herdersche Verlagshandlung, 1909), vol. 1, p. 14.

[15] Vatican MS Vat. Lat. 7701, quoted in Caciola (2003), n. p. 230: ... *ut sit spiritualis imperator ad abiciendos demones de corporibus obsessis.*

[16] Caciola (2003), pp. 231–5.

[17] Chave-Mahir (2011), p. 328. Transcriptions of the four exorcism texts (Vatican MS Vat. Lat. 7701, fols 74–9; Paris, Bibliothèque Nationale MS Lat. 14833, fols 31v–42v; Munich, Bayerische Staatsbibliothek, Clm 100, fols 110–16; Clm 3909, fols 250–3) are to be found in Chave-Mahir (2011), pp. 362–84.

[18] Chave-Mahir (2011), p. 27.

[19] Goddu (1980), pp. 552–7.

guilty of traffic with the devil.[20] However, Caciola criticized Goddu's conclusion that exorcism declined significantly in the fifteenth century, on the grounds that he considered only hagiographical sources.[21] This criticism is more than justified by Caciola and Chave-Mahir's analyses of the proliferation of fifteenth-century exorcism manuals, as well as the seamless transition of these manuals into the print age at the end of the century,[22] and the claim that the decline of exorcism continued into the fifteenth century throughout Europe is now unsustainable.

In 1215 the Fourth Lateran Council produced the first dogmatic definition of demons in response to the theological threat from the Cathars, who held that evil was uncreated.[23] Caciola has argued that the threat of Catharism and the need to respond to the millenarianism of the Cistercian abbot Joachim of Fiore meant that the pontificate of Innocent III (1198–1216) marked a decisive shift in attitudes to the supernatural. The miraculous was to be tested rather than accepted uncritically as the product of divine grace.[24] However, an interest in demonology and the need to combat heresy did not immediately result in more exorcisms. Alain Boureau, Kieckhefer and Chave-Mahir have all argued that the pontificate of John XXII (1316–34) was the turning point in Western European attitudes to magic as the work of demonic powers.[25] However, greater awareness of the devil did not mean that exorcism was primarily deployed on the victims of magic and witchcraft rather than demoniacs suffering the consequences of their sins. Just because witchcraft became a matter of interest to the church in the fourteenth century, it does not follow that exorcism was used as a weapon against witchcraft.

Another factor singled out by Caciola as a cause of the revival of liturgical exorcism in the fourteenth century was the Papal Schism of 1378–1417, which challenged faith in the unity and authority of the church. In order to bolster the church's authority over dissident groups, 'exorcism

---

[20] William of Auxerre (ed. P. Pigouchet), *Summa Aurea* (Frankfurt-am-Main: Minerva, 1964), fol. 253, col. 4; Goddu (1980), p. 551.
[21] Caciola (2003), p. 236.
[22] Ibid. pp. 236–51; Chave-Mahir (2011), pp. 327–34.
[23] On Lateran IV's definition of demons see Quay, P., 'Angels and Demons: The Teaching of IV Lateran', *Theological Studies* 42 (1981), pp. 20–45.
[24] Caciola (2003), pp. 12–14.
[25] Boureau (2006), pp. 22–7; Kieckhefer, R., *European Witch Trials: Their Foundation in Popular and Learned Culture, 1300–1500* (Berkeley, CA: University of California Press, 1976), pp. 12–13; Chave-Mahir (2011), pp. 322–3.

was appropriated from the realm of saints' cults and transformed into a discourse of clerical authority and power'.[26] However, as Goddu demonstrated, by the fourteenth century the association between exorcism and shrines of the saints was much less prominent than it had been, and Chave-Mahir has argued for a much less rapid evolution of exorcism than Caciola describes. The liturgies of exorcism were more than relics lingering in the pages of twelfth- and thirteenth-century pontificals. In reality, the liturgy was both used and adapted before the fourteenth century, and the widespread appearance of exorcism manuals in the fourteenth century was a consequence of the decline of monumental pontificals as the principal source of liturgical material. There is much evidence to suggest that exorcism was 'a discourse of clerical authority and power' long before the fourteenth century, and indeed it is difficult to imagine how exorcism, which calls upon the power of God to defeat the devil, could be anything else.

Medieval exorcism could assume the proportions of a cosmic battle between the forces of good (angels) and evil (demons), and the view of exorcism as active spiritual warfare (rather than a sign of Christ's victory) was closely associated with apocalyptic and millenarian rhetoric.[27] Peter Abelard connected the fact that Satan still had the power to attack human beings with the need to seek the help of St Michael, the devil's adversary,[28] and Michael was inevitably linked with apocalypticism owing to his role in the Book of the Apocalypse (Revelation).[29] Specific orders of angels were associated with the fight against Satan; in representations of the nine angelic hierarchies of Pseudo-Dionysius, the Powers were often shown with swords, as it was their function to oppose hostile spiritual powers.[30] One of the early followers of St Francis of Assisi, Brother Benintende, discovered that a demon he was exorcizing was unable to name any of the celestial hierarchies beyond the first three because it caused him too much pain to do so.[31]

The symptoms of possession described by medieval authors were diverse and often contradictory, including shouting and swearing, dumbness, impossible bodily contortions, and paralysis. Most victims of possession

---

[26] Caciola (2003), pp. 236–7.
[27] On exorcism and apocalypticism see ibid. pp. 264–7.
[28] Keck (1998), p. 181.
[29] Ibid. p. 45.
[30] Ibid. pp. 65–6.
[31] Salimbene de Adam (ed. G. Scalia), *Cronica* (Bari: Laterza, 1966), vol. 2, pp. 828–9.

were women, but some were men and the clergy were no less likely to fall victim to the devil.[32] Chave-Mahir has argued that until the very end of the Middle Ages, 'possession, which is the mark of sin, places an individual, their family or their community completely under the stamp of suspicion because the evil manifested has received God's consent'. Exorcism constituted a rite of purification of sin as well as liberation from demonic influence.[33] However, medieval demoniacs also shared certain characteristics with the shamans described by some medieval travellers in Asia, since they were capable of revealing secrets and communicating with another world, and sometimes played a prophetic role.[34] Nevertheless, in Europe possession was seen as a punishment on society at large rather than a matter of choice, as it was for the shaman, and it was only in the fifteenth century that possession came to be interpreted as a potential sign of holiness.

Exorcism was just one of several remedies against witches, who became a major concern of the clergy in the fifteenth century. The Dominican Johannes Nider's *Formicarius* ('Ant Hill') of 1431 was among the first texts to deal with witchcraft, which Nider presented as the inverse of genuine inspiration from God, labelling inspired women such as Joan of Arc as witches.[35] Nider's *Formicarius* was a precursor of the *Malleus maleficarum* (1486), largely authored by the German Dominican inquisitor Heinrich Kramer (otherwise known as Institoris). Kramer insisted that 'the only possible way for [witchcraft] to be remedied is for the judges who are responsible for the sorceresses to get rid of them',[36] and noted in the case of a nun afflicted by an incubus, 'it was not possible for her to be freed ... through talent, effort or art or by the Sign of the Cross or Holy Water, things specifically ordained for putting demons to flight'.[37] In other words, sacramentals might not be effective against demonic attack caused by witchcraft; Kramer was critical of Nider's view that confession, the sign of the cross, the saying of Hail Marys, exorcism, a change of location and 'cautious excommunication on the part of saintly men' were all sure

---

[32] Lahaire, M., *La Folie au Moyen Age, XIe–XIIIe siècles* (Paris: Léopard d'Or, 1991), pp. 29–32; Boureau (2006), pp. 143–62.
[33] Chave-Mahir (2011), p. 16.
[34] Ibid. pp. 15–16; Caciola (2003), p. 49.
[35] For Nider's views on exorcism see *Formicarius* (Strasbourg, 1517), fols 76r–80r, 87v. On Nider see Maggi (2001), pp. 98–9; Caciola (2003), pp. 314–19.
[36] Institoris, H. (trans. C. S. Mackay), *The Hammer of Witches: a complete translation of the Malleus maleficarum* (Cambridge: Cambridge University Press, 2009), p. 413.
[37] Ibid. p. 415.

methods of unbewitchment, warning that 'It does not follow that just because a remedy helps one person, it helps another'.[38]

Kramer portrayed exorcism as a last resort to free someone from bewitchment, but even then success was not guaranteed:

> ... when none of the lawful remedies ... helps, recourse should be had to lawful forms of exorcism ... But if these are not sufficient to put the demon's evil to flight, then this harassment on the demon's part is in fact a penalty in satisfaction of a sin, if, as is necessary, the harassment is endured in charity, just like the other evils of this world, which oppress us in such a way as to force us to go to God.[39]

Because it was a sacramental, no theologian believed that exorcism worked automatically, but Kramer has an evident agenda to underplay the effectiveness of exorcism in favour of judicial remedies against witches. The inquisitor was determined to make witchcraft a judicial rather than a mere pastoral problem; exorcism was a secondary weapon (at best) in the war against witches, and Kramer repeatedly pointed out that judicial execution was preferable.[40] For many inquisitors, exorcism was a mere 'verbal remedy' for witchcraft on a par with herbal remedies.[41]

Both Caciola and Sluhovsky have argued that the prominence of the devil in the theology of salvation and the lives of the saints rendered exorcism an all-pervasive and relatively trivial *topos* of the Middle Ages.[42] Caciola described this as the 'domestication' of exorcism, in which formulas ultimately derived from the ancient baptismal liturgy were adapted for such purposes as preventing bees from swarming and worm infections in horses.[43] Many late medieval examples of exorcisms of this sort were recorded by Franz, and more recently Catherine Chène made a study of exorcisms used against pests and troublesome animals in the Diocese of Lausanne

---

[38] Ibid. p. 416.
[39] Ibid. pp. 419–20.
[40] There is some evidence that exorcism was used during early modern witch trials; see De Waardt, H. and De Blécourt, W., '"It is no Sin to put an Evil Person to Death", Judicial Proceedings concerning Witchcraft during the Reign of Duke Charles of Gelderland' in Gijswijt-Hofstra, M. and Frijhoff, W. (eds), *Witchcraft in the Netherlands from the Fourteenth to the Twentieth Century* (Rotterdam: Universitaire Pers, 1991), pp. 66–78, at pp. 71–4.
[41] Maggi (2001), pp. 99–101.
[42] Sluhovsky (2007), pp. 13–32.
[43] Caciola (2003), pp. 231, 237–8.

in Switzerland in the fifteenth and sixteenth centuries.[44] However, whilst Franz and Chène maintained that exorcism of animals was a fairly late import from Eastern Christianity, there is much evidence for the creative and 'trivial' use of exorcistic formulas much earlier, especially in northern Europe. The 'trivialization' of exorcism in medieval England will be considered later in this chapter.

THEOLOGICAL FOUNDATIONS

It may be an exaggeration to claim that possession was 'at the very margins of theological discourse' before the fifteenth century,[45] but it was never a significant topic of study. Demonology, the branch of theology dealing with the devil, demons and, by extension, exorcism took its origin from the study of angels. While demonology was a rather more specialized study, angelology was a central component of medieval Scholastic philosophy. Discussions of angels featured in virtually every theological *summa*, which began with God and subsequently moved to the angels, the most perfect of God's creatures. Furthermore, Scholastic philosophers applied Aristotle's discussion of 'separated substances' in his *Metaphysics* to angels, and the separated substances or 'intelligences' were a crucial part of the Aristotelian cosmos. Since demons were fallen angels, philosophical discussions of angels naturally gave rise to demonological speculations.

Thomas Aquinas (1225–74) dealt with exorcism directly only twice in his extensive works. In the *Summa Theologica*, Aquinas addressed the question 'Whether it is licit to adjure demons?' (*utrum liceat adiurare Daemones*) as part of a broader discussion of 'the assumption of the name of God by means of adjuration' (*de assumptione divini nominis per modum adiurationis*).[46] Elsewhere Aquinas addressed four related questions concerning baptismal exorcism: 'Firstly, whether the catechization should precede baptism; secondly, whether baptism should precede exorcism; thirdly, whether those things that act in the catechization and exorcism effect anything, or are only symbolic; fourthly, whether the baptized

---

[44] Chène, C., *Juger les Vers: Exorcismes et Procès d'Animaux dans le Diocèse de Lausanne (XVe–XVIe s.)*, Cahiers Lausannois d'Histoire Médiévale (Lausanne: Université de Lausanne, 1995).
[45] Sluhovsky (2007), p. 1.
[46] *ST* 2a 2ae q. 90 col. 42929.

should be catechized or exorcized by priests?'.⁴⁷ In his treatise on evil, *De malo*, Aquinas addressed two questions which, whilst not directly addressing exorcism, were of profound importance to the exorcist: 'Whether demons know the future?' (*utrum demones cognoscant futura*) and 'Whether demons know the thoughts of our hearts?' (*utrum demones cognoscant cogitationes cordium nostrorum*).⁴⁸ Furthermore, Aquinas also dealt with questions of importance to the psychology of possession, such as 'Whether demons can move bodies locally?' and 'Whether demons are able to change the human intellect?'⁴⁹

Aquinas distinguished between two modes of adjuration. On the one hand, it was forbidden to Christians to entreat demons for anything, but it was permissible for them to compel demons by adjuration, since this power was given by Christ to the church. Even then, it was not permissible to adjure demons in order to gain knowledge or obtain anything by them; this, for Aquinas, was the crucial difference between true religion and magic.⁵⁰ Aquinas's view contrasted with Petrus Cantor's in the twelfth century, who was happy to consider Solomon the father of exorcism; Solomon was also universally accepted as the father of ritual magic. Aquinas was in a difficult position: on the one hand, he was inclined to argue that the exorcisms of Christ rather than the exorcisms of Solomon should be the pattern for Christian exorcisms, but on the other hand the liturgical exorcisms of the church did not resemble Christ's straightforward dispossessions in the Gospel, and took a highly ritualized form.

Aquinas's approach to baptismal exorcism was twofold: on the one hand, he justified it on the grounds that the devil was the enemy of salvation, and therefore became the enemy of the baptized, who would

---

⁴⁷ *ST* 3a q. 71 col. 50277: *Primo, utrum catechismus debeat praecedere Baptismum. Secundo, utrum Baptismum debeat praecedere exorcismus. Tertio, utrum ea quae aguntur in catechismo et exorcismo aliquid efficiant, vel solum significent. Quarto, utrum baptizandi debeant catechizari vel exorcizari per sacerdotes.*

⁴⁸ Aquinas (cd. B. Davies), *The De Malo of Thomas Aquinas* (Oxford: Oxford University Press, 2001), qs. 7, 8 (pp. 896–923).

⁴⁹ Aquinas, *De Malo* qs. 10, 12 (pp. 932–9, 950–9). Aquinas's only direct reference to possession is in *De malo* q. 16 (p. 948): 'Therefore we must say that demons are able to disturb the imagination by virtue of their nature and completely impede human cognition of intelligibles, as appears in the possessed; however they are not always able to do this' (*Dicendum est ergo quod demones possunt virtute sue nature fantasmata perturbando totaliter intelligibilem cognitionem hominis impedire, sicut patet in arrepticiis; non tamen semper hoc facere permittuntur*).

⁵⁰ *ST* 2a 2ae q. 90 a. 2 col. 42942.

need protection from him. On the other hand, Aquinas reaffirmed the Augustinian view that 'all the unbaptized are subjected to the power of the devil' (*omnes ... non baptizati potestati Daemonum subiiciuntur*).[51] Aquinas appealed again to Augustine to justify the genuine effectiveness of baptismal exorcism, as well as to the liturgy: the church would not use imperative commands in exorcism, he argued, unless they had some real effect.[52] As might be expected, Aquinas denied that it was possible for demons to know 'the future as the future' (*futura prout futura*), as this was a power of God alone. However, he maintained that it was possible for demons to have an understanding of natural causes beyond the capacity of human beings that gave them intuition about the future and allowed them to deceive humans into thinking that their knowledge of the future was certain. Likewise, it was possible for demons to have knowledge of human thoughts as theirs was a higher intellect than that of humans. On the other hand, demons could have no knowledge of 'voluntary thoughts', thoughts bringing about the exercise of human will, as the devil was unable to interfere directly with human freedom.

The most controversial of Aquinas's demonological claims was his view that both angels and demons were pure spirit, with no kind of body at all. Aquinas adapted Aristotle's theory of separated substances in the light of the theology of Pseudo-Dionysius. However, the Franciscan philosophers, beginning with Aquinas's contemporary Bonaventure (1221–74), were inspired by their reading of the Jewish philosopher Avicebron to treat angels as composed of form in combination with 'spiritual matter'.[53] In other words, angels and demons were just like human beings, composed of matter (the body) and form (the soul), except that in the case of angels and demons the body was of a different kind. Aquinas's approach, since it treated angels as purely spiritual, had the consequence that the sin of the fallen angels could not alter their essential nature as spirit. The rebellion of the angels was an act of will.[54]

Aquinas's position on the angels was condemned by the University of Paris in 1277,[55] and the Bonaventurean position subsequently gained widespread acceptance until it was rejected by Duns Scotus and William

---

[51] *ST* 3a q. 71 a. 2 cols. 50290–1.
[52] *ST* 3a q. 71 a. 2 cols. 50299–300.
[53] On this dispute see Keck (1998), pp. 93–114; Boureau (2006), pp. 93–118.
[54] On demonic incorporeality see Aquinas, *De malo* q. 16, pp. 803–1.
[55] Keck (1998), p. 94.

of Ockham in the fourteenth century. By treating angels as both matter and form, the Franciscans opened the possibility that by rebelling against God, the fallen angels retained their spiritual form but forfeited their 'spiritual matter' in return for a grosser material nature. This was in fact merely a return to an earlier view: Isidore of Seville argued that the fallen angels were imprisoned in aerial bodies when they fell from heaven,[56] and Augustine alluded to an 'aerial [body], like that of the devil or of the demonic spirits'.[57] Bonaventure argued that only one angel could occupy any one space at a given time.[58]

Caciola has demonstrated that medieval possession was understood more often than not in terms of physical ingestion and ejection.[59] This had the consequence that exorcism became an increasingly physical activity, in spite of Aquinas' best efforts to portray demons as non-physical beings. By the fifteenth century exorcists regularly exorcized individual body parts, including the heart, the seat of the soul; this was a nod to Aquinas's claim that demons could not know or affect the seat of the will. Aquinas's clear statement that possession could not affect human free will liberated the demoniac from any suspicion of collusion with demons, at least during possession, and rendered the demoniac an object of pity rather than censure.

Exorcism, Liturgy and Magic

In Chave-Mahir's view, the liturgy of exorcism provided a resource upon which the medieval clergy could draw, rather than a strict liturgical framework for the practice of exorcism.[60] Exorcism was associated with books and with reading; it was not only the words themselves that had force, but also the written formulas.[61] Thus the emergence of a rite of exorcism as a distinct liturgical book in the fourteenth century was an important

---

[56] Isidore, *Etymologia* 8.11 (*PL* 82.316A).

[57] Augustine, *De Genesi ad litteram* 11.13 (*PL* 34.436): *In spiritu rationalis creaturae bonum est hoc ipsum quod vivit et vivificat corpus, sive aereum sicut ipsius diaboli vel daemonum spiritus, sive terrenum sicut hominis anima.*

[58] Bonaventure, *Opera omnia* (Rome: Quaracchi, 1882–1902), vol. 2, pp. 75–7. On Franciscan demonology see Boureau (2006), pp. 111–18.

[59] Caciola (2003), pp. 41–4. On representations of demoniacs in medieval art see Chave-Mahir (2011), pp. 27–35.

[60] Chave-Mahir (2011), p. 14.

[61] Ibid. p. 313.

moment.[62] However, the liturgy in these exorcism books was little different from that which had been appearing in sacramentaries and pontificals since the eighth century. The appearance of distinctive exorcism books was not so much a milestone in liturgical history as a reflection of the greater awareness of the demonic in fourteenth-century Europe. Rites of exorcism from the thirteenth century are rare and fragmentary, and most of those that survive have been collated by Chave-Mahir.

The first distinct exorcism book, a manuscript of around 1400 now in the Bäyerische Staatsbibliothek in Munich, strongly resembled the Carolingian sacramentaries. However, in a seemingly new development, the priest was instructed to make use of quasi-magical words and gestures towards the demoniac: 'Take the head of the possessed in your left hand and place your thumb in the mouth of the possessed, saying the following words to both ears: "Rise up again from here *abrya*, rise up again from here, things consecrated together *ypar ytumba opote alacent alaphie*"'.[63] These *nomina ignota* are not only magical; they also constitute a primitive diagnostic test before the exorcism proper begins. Furthermore, the Munich exorcism employed Greek and Hebrew names for God such as *Agla*, *Tetragrammaton*, *Ysiton* and *Pneumaton* that were also used commonly used by magicians.[64]

It may be that the medieval association between magic and the clergy was down to nothing more than the fact that the clergy were literate, but it is also possible that developing theological understanding of sacramentals led magicians to the view, by the late Middle Ages, that only a priest (or at least a deacon) could make exorcisms efficacious.[65] When it came to talking to demons, the boundary between legitimate exorcism and magic was more easily blurred than theologians like Aquinas, who distinguished between licit and illicit adjuration, would have cared to admit. It was possible to argue convincingly that the more the demon was made to confess, the more greatly God was glorified through the exorcist, to the edification of the faithful. Furthermore, there were historical precedents for using

---

[62] Ibid. pp. 320–34.

[63] Munich, Bayerische Staatsbibliothek, MS Clm 10085, fol. 3v, quoted in Chave-Mahir (2011), n. p. 325: *Recipe caput obsessi in sinistra manu et pone pollicem dextere manus in os obsessi, dicendo sibi verba sequencia ad ambas aures: 'Abremonte abrya, abremonte consacramentaria ypar ytumba opote alacent alaphie'*.

[64] Chave-Mahir (2011), pp. 325–6.

[65] For examples of the use of exorcisms in magical formulas see Kieckhefer (1997), pp. 126–69.

demoniacs as prophets in lives of saints such as Martin of Tours. Magical adjurations in garbled or imaginary languages and *nomina ignota* began to creep into exorcisms in the fourteenth century, probably because someone had found them useful. Exorcism was a practical business, and exorcists learnt from experience. Whilst Chave-Mahir identified the Munich manuscript as the first to add such formulas to an exorcism of a demoniac, she ignored exorcisms of objects and animals and exorcisms used against illness that already manifested these features in the thirteenth century. A barely comprehensible thirteenth-century exorcism of holy water from England used the formula: 'I exorcize you *bessio bessala grega tumio* initiated *auditom* of enemies. The angel announced, Christ touched. Indeed they belonged. Indeed they had been touched. Spare with all your works *agi + agi est + agi + sens + sens + sens +* gathering gathering gathering those pigs and those cattle'.[66] Since the rest of the liturgy from which this was drawn makes grammatical sense, the peculiar language of this exorcism was deliberate. It may be that barbarous names began in exorcisms of objects and later made their way into exorcisms of people.

Also existing in the grey area between magic and exorcism were apotropaic amulets, often consisting of verses of scripture written on strips of parchment.[67] Indeed, amulets influenced the liturgy of exorcism itself. According to a 1367 life of Anthony of Padua, a woman who had almost been deceived into committing suicide by the devil masquerading as Christ received a dream-vision of the saint, in which he gave her an amulet on parchment inscribed in gold with the words 'Behold the cross of Christ! Flee, hostile powers! The lion from the tribe of Judah and the root of David vanquishes! Alleluia! Alleluia!'[68] These words were later incorporated into the 1614 rite of exorcism as well as remaining part of a still popular apotropaic amulet, the Medal of St Benedict.[69]

The interplay between illicit magic and the church's exorcisms is clearly evident in many surviving magical manuscripts, for example a sixteenth-century English grimoire in Cambridge University Library which contains

---

[66] This is a conjectural translation of BL MS Add. 34652, fol. 14r: *[E]xorcizo te bessio. bessala. grega. tumio auditom inimicorum iniciavit. angle nunciavit Christus libavit. quin tactici. quin tac[ti] fuit. pepicis cum omnibus operibus agi + agi est + agi + sens + sens + sens + congregans. congregans. congregans. illos porcos illa pecora.*

[67] On the development of exorcistic amulets see Skemer (2006), pp. 47–9, 175.

[68] *De Sancto Antonio Patavii Liber Miraculorum, AASS*, June 3:736: *Ecce crucem Christi! Fugite partes adversae! Vincit leo de tribu Iuda et radix David! Alleluia! Alleluia!*

[69] Caciola (2003), p. 250. On the Medal of St Benedict see Lederer (2005), pp. 226, 232.

a combination of Solomonic ceremonial magic and image magic of Arabic origin.[70] The exorcisms, always beginning 'I conjure' (*coniuro*) rather than 'I exorcize', are recognizably influenced by the late fifteenth-century *Coniuratio malignorum spirituum in corporibus hominum prout Sancto Petro* (1477), first printed in Rome by Johannes Bulle. One spell to harm and kill enemies, known as the 'Trojan Revenge', is followed by an incongruous conjuration of Satan to make the spell effective in the name of Christ's love for God the Father, the martyrs and confessors, Mary the Mother of God, the virgins, patriarchs and prophets and each of the instruments of Christ's passion.[71] Exorcisms in both Latin and English are also used for binding and dismissing spirits raised in the circle.[72] As Frank Klaassen has demonstrated, ritual magic survived the Reformation (at least in England) with the most superficial changes.[73] The Protestants John Dee and Elias Ashmole continued to use exorcisms that were closely based on medieval originals, especially *SG* 2407, 'I confound you ... by the living God, I confound you ... by the true God'.[74]

In the period after 1400 there was a rapid growth in the number of exorcism books available. Exorcism was not entirely 'an unregulated and trivial profession',[75] and in 1384 a Florentine magician was pursued by the city's secular authorities for exorcizing a girl without proper authorization.[76] In his exorcism he made use of magical 'demonic' language whispered into the girl's ear. Chave-Mahir's judgement that the fifteenth century was 'the century of controlled exorcism' may seem exaggerated when compared with the draconian restrictions placed on exorcists in the eighteenth century,[77]

---

[70] Another instance of magical use of the exorcisms of the church, almost word for word, occurs in a conjuration of a mirage of Satan in the Munich handbook, edited in Kieckhefer (1997), pp. 276–86 and discussed by him at pp. 144–9.

[71] Foreman, P. (trans. F. Young), *The Cambridge Book of Magic: A Tudor Necromancer's Manual* (Cambridge: Texts in Early Modern Magic, 2015), pp. 82–5 (an edition of CUL MS Add. 3544).

[72] Ibid. pp. 19–21.

[73] Klaassen, F., *The Transformations of Magic: Illicit Learned Magic in the Later Middle Ages and Renaissance* (University Park, PA: Pennsylvania State University Press, 2013), pp. 164–7.

[74] See for instance the English exorcism against witches collected by Ashmole in BL MS Sloane 3846 fol. 95r.

[75] Sluhovsky (2007), p. 2.

[76] Brucker, G., 'Sorcery in Renaissance Florence', *Studies in the Renaissance* 10 (1963), pp. 7–23.

[77] Chave-Mahir (2011), p. 333. See also Caciola (2003), pp. 238–9.

and it might be more accurate to say that exorcism was refined by specialists during this period rather than rigorously controlled. The physical size of exorcism manuals meant that they were ideally suited for the mendicant orders.[78] Fifteenth-century exorcism texts were characterized by their great diversity, and the ancient exorcisms from the pontificals were supplemented with prayers against witchcraft, litanies of the saints and pharmaceutical recipes.[79] The recommendation that the demoniac should confess his sins also appears in texts of this period, and the *Coniuratio malignorum spirituum* was prefaced with instructions for confessors (the *Coniuratio* will be examined in Chap. 4). Chave-Mahir has argued that a new era in which the exorcist and his book replaced the power of the saints and their tombs began before the advent of printing, which merely made more widely available new exorcistic texts.[80] In their emphasis on proving the possession of the demoniac and elaborate questioning of demons, late medieval exorcism liturgies anticipated the preoccupations of early modern exorcists.

Adaptations of Exorcism

The casting out of demons from the possessed and magic were not the only purposes to which exorcism was put in the Middle Ages. Sluhovsky's description of medieval exorcists as 'mere health practitioners' may be exaggerated,[81] but medieval exorcisms were sometimes ambiguous in intent, having more to do with restoring psychological wholeness or even protecting individuals against moral temptation. It would be going beyond the historical evidence to suggest that some medieval Christians did not believe that exorcism literally expelled demons, but accounts of exorcisms did not always stress the presence of a demonic personality. In an analysis of three thousand miracles attributed to saints in thirteenth- and fourteenth-century France and England, Ronald Finucane observed that 'the intrusion of demons was quite limited. They were normally only associated with mental aberrations, when the victim was said to have become possessed, and they seldom appeared in other forms of illness'.[82]

---

[78] Caciola (2003), pp. 239–41.
[79] Chave-Mahir (2011), p. 330.
[80] Ibid. p. 328.
[81] Sluhovsky (2007), p. 2.
[82] Finucane, R., *Miracles and Pilgrims: Popular Beliefs in Medieval England* (London: Dent, 1977), p. 72.

Exorcism narratives of the early Middle Ages rarely described the personality of the afflicting demon in any detail. The detailed account of Hildegard's exorcism of Sigewize in the saint's *Vita* placed little emphasis on the demon itself; instead, it concentrated on Hildegard's treatment of Sigewize by means of an unusual improvised exorcism received in a vision.[83] Although the exorcism was initially successful, the demon returned to Sigewize's body almost immediately, and thereafter Hildegard resorted to fasting and prayer. Amanda Porterfield has drawn attention to the contrast between Hildegard's subtle treatment of Sigewize and an exorcism performed by St Hospicius in the sixth century. Whereas Hospicius 'seized the patient's hair and tongue and made the demon leave by pouring oil on the patient's head and down his throat', and the demoniac showed no consciousness of his own possession, 'Hildegard healed by inserting her interpretations of God and the Devil into Sigewize's subjectivity'. Instead of offering violence to the possessed and adhering slavishly to prescribed ritual, 'Hildegard employed elements of empirical observation and strategic analysis that pointed in the direction of psychological thinking'.[84] On the other hand, Hildegard was a visionary who might have been expected to respond to observation and inspiration, and her approach may say more about her confidence in her relationship with God than her 'psychological' insight.

For Porterfield, the age of the witch hunts in late medieval Europe was also, paradoxically, the age of the birth of psychology: 'The tendency to anthropomorphize evil and become fascinated with personal relationships between people and demons or Satan contributed to the witch hunts of the late Middle Ages and early modern period. It also became a means of exploring and describing subjectivity and its torments and modes of relief'. The witchfinders' and exorcists' 'Fascination with the personal relationships between demons and their victims opened human subjectivity to new inspection and analysis and perhaps laid some of the preliminary groundwork for modern psychological thinking'.[85] It is certainly true that the challenge of witchcraft stretched the theological framework established for possession in the thirteenth century, and the distinction drawn early on between bewitchment and possession demonstrated that medieval demonologists were prepared to respond to experience as well as imposing

---

[83] *Vita Sanctae Hildegardis*, pp. 212–14.
[84] Porterfield (2005), pp. 86–7; Chave-Mahir (2011), pp. 13–14.
[85] Porterfield (2005), p. 85.

pre-existing theological categories. Not all individuals whose behaviour suggested mental aberration were treated as possessed, and naturalistic explanations for mental illness from antiquity survived and flourished in the Middle Ages.[86]

The most obvious signs of a more sophisticated understanding of possession were the diagnostic criteria that began to be employed from the fourteenth century onwards. One manual suggested that a pyx containing the sacrament should be secretly placed on the head of the demoniac; if the demoniac, when asked, was able to say what he had on his head then he was genuinely possessed. Other tests involved blowing or spitting into the demoniac's mouth, displaying an image of St Jerome, and making use of 'demonic language'. This latter practice was virtually indistinguishable from the techniques of magicians who claimed to possess secret knowledge of the languages of demons. For Caciola, 'the demonic tongue is an intentional ordering device that graphically represents—and thereby subordinates—demonic disorder'.[87] Another exorcistic tradition that emerged in the fourteenth-century manuals, of greater and more lasting significance than demonic language, was the systematic interrogation of demons. Although the devil was directly addressed and renounced in early Christian baptismal liturgies, he was never questioned (except rhetorically). Exorcists began to ask demons to identify themselves and the order to which they belonged.[88] Thus an increasingly elaborate epistemological framework for possession was established; demoniacs were distinguished from lunatics and the insane, even if the latter were also, indirectly, victims of the devil's malice.

In the late Middle Ages prayers resembling exorcisms were also adopted as a form of personal devotion, like those found in a tiny yet dense book of devotions compiled by the fifteenth-century Franciscan friar William Turnout of Coblenz. This included two 'exorcisms' 'against temptations of the flesh' (*contra temptationes carnis*) prefixed by a story about how St Edmund of Abingdon warded off temptation by contemplating an image of the Virgin Mary breastfeeding the infant Jesus. The exorcism begins with an address to a spirit of impurity: 'The Lord is my helper, I shall not fear you, wherefore go unclean spirit, go; uncleanness is your work.

---

[86] See Van Arsdall, A., *Medieval Herbal Remedies: The Old English Herbarium and Anglo-Saxon Medicine* (London: Routledge, 2002), p. 178.
[87] Caciola (2003), pp. 244–8.
[88] Ibid. pp. 248–9.

Therefore I do not fear you or yours, whose strength and virtue is in the God of the living and the dead, and I have his Son as my defender.'[89] The second exorcism begins with the familiar words 'Go, unclean spirit' (*Vade immunde spiritus*). However, the remainder of the text is a largely invented form of 'self-exorcism'[90]:

> Depart from me, worst seducer, you will not have any part in me as a strong warrior, and you will stand and submit to every penalty which is due to you. Be quiet and be silent. I will not hear you anymore .... The Lord is my light and my salvation who then stands as a fortress to my use. My heart will not fear, my Lord and my redeemer. Glory be to the Father, etc.

It seems highly unlikely from the context of this 'exorcism' in a book of personal devotion that Turnout believed himself to be possessed by an evil spirit. Rather, Turnout personified his unclean thoughts and made use of the metaphor of exorcism as a means of dismissing them. The conscious or unconscious use of formulas of exorcism in a manner that a contemporary reader might regard as metaphorical was nothing unusual, given that priests pronouncing exorcisms on a daily basis over infants or water did not believe that they were casting out demons. The conflation of exorcism and blessing in the late Middle Ages contributed to its trivialization, and allowed Turnout's personal prayers against impurity to assume the language of exorcism.

Exorcism in Crisis: The Case of Medieval England

The conversion of Anglo-Saxon England to Christianity began in 597 when Augustine and his companions landed in Kent. Within a century the rulers of the Anglo-Saxon kingdoms were nominally Christian, and England was beginning to play a part in the conversion of the rest of the northern Germanic world. The laws and customs of Anglo-Saxon England were pagan and Germanic in origin, and the rites of the church were super-

---

[89] BL MS Royal 2 A II, fol. 141r: *dominus mihi adiutor est non te timebo quia ve immundus spiritus ve immunditia est opus tuum[.] Itaque tuo nec tuos non timeo qui vimque virtusque est in deum vivorum et mortuorum et filium eius me defensore habeo.*

[90] *Discede a me seductor pessimus[,] non habebis in me partem ullam tamque bellator fortis et tu stabis et omnem penam subire qui tibi constitus[.] tace et obtumesce[.] non audiam te amplius ... dominus illuminatio mea et salus mea qui tum [illeg.] adsistat ad usu me castra[.] non timebit cor meum dominus meus et redemptor meus.*

imposed on this framework and adapted to suit the needs of Anglo-Saxon society. The earliest evidence of a Christian exorcism of a demoniac in England is the story of the priest Tydi, who at some time between 687 and 700 attempted (unsuccessfully) to free a boy from a demon. Tydi advised the boy's father to take him to Lindisfarne, where a man took dirt from the ditch in which the water used to wash St Cuthbert's body after death had been thrown and mixed it with some holy water, which cured the boy.[91]

Tydi's failure typifies the early medieval tendency to rely on the exorcistic power of the saints and their relics rather than the rites of the church. Commenting on the exorcism of the Gerasene demoniac in Luke's Gospel, Bede (c. 673–735) portrayed some of the challenges affecting the exorcists of his day, insisting that exorcism could only be effective if the demoniac was completely honest about what he had experienced. Bede assumed that demonic attack would take the form of what would later become known as incubi and succubi, and made an early reference to the idea of a pact (*foedus*) between demons and their victims (although in this case it was a promise made to a lover who was really a demon in disguise). Furthermore, Bede insisted on the importance of identifying the name of the molesting demon[92]:

> But the priests of our time, who know how to eject demons by the grace of exorcism, are accustomed to say that sufferers are not able to be cured [and] made well otherwise, unless they are able to acquire wisdom concerning everything they endured from the unclean spirits by sight, by hearing, by taste, by touch, and by any other sense of the body or soul whatsoever, waking or sleeping, and expose it by openly confessing. And especially, whether appearing as men in female form, or as women in male dress, which demons the Gauls call Dusi, by an unspeakable miracle incorporeal spirits contrive to seek and desire to sleep with a human body. And they command that the name of the demon, which they would say to be forbidden, and the means of swearing oaths by which each pledged a pact of love to the other should be produced.

---

[91] Raiswell and Dendle (2008), p. 738.
[92] Bede, *In Lucae evangelium expositio* (*PL* 92.438B): *Sed et nostri temporis sacerdotes, qui per exorcismi gratiam daemones ejicere norunt, solent dicere patientes non aliter valere curari nisi quantum sapere possunt omne quod ab immundis spiritibus visu, auditu, gustu, tactu, et alio quolibet corporis vel animi sensu, vigilantes dormientesve pertulerint, confitendo patenter exponant. Et maxime, quando vel viris in specie feminea, vel in virili habitu feminis apparentes, quos daemones Galli Dusios vocant, infando miraculo spiritus incorporei corporis humani concubitum petere se ac patrare confingunt. Et nomen daemonis, quo se censeri dixerit, et dejerandi modos, quibus amoris sui foedus alterutrum pepigerint, prodendos esse praecipiunt.*

Bede acknowledged that his readers might find this hard to believe, but insisted that he spoke from personal testimony[93]:

> A certain priest, a neighbour to me, related that he began to cure a certain holy nun from a demon, but for as long as the matter lay hidden, there was nothing that he was able to accomplish for her. But with her confession that she was molested by phantasms, soon it fled by means of prayers and other kinds of purifications which were necessary, and he cured the body of the same woman of the ulcers, which she had contracted by the touch of the demon, by his medical zeal joined with blessed salt.

Whether 'the other purifications which were necessary' included the rite of exorcism itself we cannot know, but the combination of a sexual component to possession and the association of demonic touch with physical illnesses was peculiarly English.[94] However, when the exorcism was unable to remove one of the ulcers, the exorcist was prepared to accept the nun's advice on how to proceed; she told him to anoint her with the oil of the sick, and this finally cured the ulcer.

Exorcisms of demoniacs were not particularly significant or common in Anglo-Saxon England. Richard Raiswell and Peter Dendle have observed that, whilst demoniacs are sometimes mentioned amongst visitors to the tombs of the saints, the vague nature of the evidence makes it difficult to evaluate how common demonic possession was.[95] Furthermore, works such as the *Life of St Cuthbert* and Bede's *Ecclesiastical History* tended to denigrate the power of priestly exorcism.[96] In some cases the authorities did not dare to exorcize and even ejected the demoniac from church, such as a woman who arrived at the shrine of St Frideswide in Oxford[97]:

---

[93] *Quidam vicinus mihi presbyter retulerit se quamdam sanctimonialem feminam a daemonio curare coepisse, sed quandiu res latebat, nihil apud eam proficere potuisse. Confesso autem quo molestabatur phantasmate, mox et ipsum orationibus caeterisque quae oportebat purificationum generibus effugasse, et ejusdem feminae corpus ab ulceribus, quae daemonis tactu contraxerat, medicinali studio adjuncto sale benedicto curasse.*

[94] Raiswell and Dendle (2008), pp. 741–2.

[95] Ibid. p. 742.

[96] Ibid. p. 747.

[97] *Miracula S. Frideswidae* 25, *AASS*, October 7:573: *Nam et lignorum maxima robora circa ipsum posita sine aliqua difficultate a se rejiciebat, et horrendis gestibus turbam circumstantem arcebat, quandoque etiam ab ecclesia expellabat: nullus etenim vel expectare eum audebat vel contingere. Cogit furoris rabies terribiles vocem emittere, clamoribus ecclesiam implere, nec Creatorem a creatura sinit agnosci, talis ac tanti mali vehementia.*

For she threw off without any difficulty the great strength of the restraints placed around her, and she warded off the crowd standing around with horrible gestures, so that she was even expelled from the church: for none dared to hope for her or to touch her. The terrible madness of her fury forced her to cry out and fill the church with her shouts, nor did it allow the Creator to be acknowledged by the creature, so much and so great is the force of evil.

Eventually it was the *virtus* of St Frideswide, and not any actions by the shrine authorities, that healed the woman.

However, the fact that liturgical exorcism was practised in Anglo-Saxon England is confirmed by the survival of exorcism texts, the earliest of which is found in the 'Royal Prayer Book' produced in Mercia (probably at Worcester) in the late eighth or early ninth century. This contains a prayer invoking the holy cross to guard against all the wiles of the enemy (*ab omnibus insidiis inimici*), followed by a garbled Greek invocation of the persons of the Trinity and then an adjuration: 'I adjure you demon of Satan/of an elf (*diabulus aelfae*) by the living and true God and by the tremendous day of judgement that you should take flight from that man ...'.[98] The form of this exorcism suggests some knowledge of the great adjurations of the Gelasian Sacramentary (*SG* 2405) on the part of the compiler, although the exorcism's most striking feature is the reference to elves. Alaric Hall interpreted *aelfae* as a feminine genitive, suggesting that a demon might belong either to Satan or to an elf. Neither elves nor other beings of early English folklore were unambiguously evil, and this may be why exorcism was not always effective against them.[99] The term *diabulus aelfae* could imply an alternative source of spiritual attack separate from the devil. The mention of elves, who were associated in the

---

[98] BL MS Royal 2 A XX, fol. 45v: *Eulogumen patera cae yo cae agion pneuma cae nym cae ia cae iseonas nenon amin. Adiuro te satanae diabulus aelfae per deum vivum ac verum et per trementem diem iudicii ut refugiatur ab homine illo* ... On the Royal Prayer Book see Hall, A., *Elves in Anglo-Saxon England: Matters of Belief, Health, Gender and Identity* (Woodbridge: Boydell, 2007), pp. 71–2. Another possible translation is 'I adjure you devil, elf of Satan ...'

[99] Gervase of Tilbury noted that 'follets', who threw sticks and stones and kitchen utensils, were not deterred by holy water or exorcism (Gervase of Tilbury (ed. S. E. Banks and J. W. Binns), *Otia Imperialia: Recreation for an Emperor* (Oxford: Oxford University Press, 2002), p. 99). Both Gervase and Gerald of Wales were forced to concede that there were 'categories of morally neutral spirit' (Watkins, C. S., *History and the Supernatural in Medieval England* (Cambridge: Cambridge University Press, 2007), p. 61). In some Anglo-Saxon sources *ælfe* ('elves') was Latinized to *Castalides*, an alternative name for nymphs or muses (Hall (2006), p. 106).

Lacnunga Manuscript with many diseases but distinguished from demons, suggests that the exorcism was not intended for the possessed but to deal with a mental or physical illness. Not only the purpose of the exorcism, but also the identity of the entity being exorcized, was adapted to the Anglo-Saxon cultural context.

The trend of cultural adaptation was to continue. Eleventh-century English pontificals contained the exorcism of energumens from the Gelasian Sacramentary, but usually in a truncated form, almost as an afterthought to the much more elaborate exorcism of holy water.[100] For instance, the Lanalet Pontifical, produced for the use of the Bishop of Crediton in Devon in the mid-eleventh century, contains an 'exorcism against a demon' that requires the bishop or priest to fast for three days and give alms before pronouncing two exorcisms over the water. Whilst the second is the standard exorcism of water from the Gelasian Sacramentary that remained part of the Roman liturgy until 1962, the first is distinctive[101]:

> I adjure you, creature of water, in the name of Jesus Christ of Nazareth the Son of the living God, our king and our judge, that you may be purged for the sanctification of all things, and that you should not transmit any unclean spirit, but will give honour to the living and reigning Father, Son and Holy Spirit, to the ages of ages.

This adjuration, in its assumption that an evil spirit might lurk in water, is distinctively Anglo-Saxon. Furthermore, it treats the water as a conscious being, demanding that it should honour God. The demand that the devil should honour God is found in the early baptismal liturgies but not in the Gelasian Sacramentary's exorcism of demoniacs. This may point to an origin for this distinctive prayer of exorcism in the baptism of pagan Anglo-Saxons, when clergy who were conscious of local beliefs about

---

[100] One exception to this was the eleventh-century Leofric Missal, which contained a liturgy similar to the Paris Supplement's version of the Gelasian rite (*The Leofric Missal, as used in the Cathedral of Exeter*, ed. F. E. Warren (Oxford: Clarendon, 1883), pp. 233–5). On the Leofric Missal see Chave-Mahir (2011), pp. 96–7.

[101] *Pontificale Lanaletense: (Bibliothèque de la ville de Rouen A. 27. cat. 368.) A Pontifical formerly in use at St. Germans, Cornwall*, ed. G. H. Doble, Henry Bradshaw Society 74 (London: Harrison and Sons, 1937), p. 111: *Adiuro te creatura aque in nomine ihesu christi nazareni filii dei uiui regis et iudicis nostri ut sis purgata in sanctificationem omnibus et ne communiceris ullo spiritui immundo sed dabis honorem uiuenti atque regnanti patri et filio et spiritui sancto in secula seculorum.*

water sprites took care to exorcize it before performing outdoor baptisms. The Old English word for exorcism, *halsung*, was a direct borrowing from pagan religion. *Halsung* or *hælsung* could also mean 'a diviner', and derived from *hæl*, meaning 'omen'.[102] By borrowing from the vocabulary of magic, the Anglo-Saxon church accidentally or deliberately assimilated exorcism to the most powerful rites of pre-Christian English religion.

Once the water was mixed with exorcized salt, the exorcism was completed by the reading of the Passion. The water could now be placed in a font or a large vessel from which the faithful could take it back to their homes; alternatively it could be used as part of the exorcism of a demoniac. At this point the Pontifical, abruptly assuming the presence of a demoniac, instructs 'make this adjuration over him' (*hanc facias super eum adiurationem*), followed by the three 'great adjurations' (*SG* 2405), here divorced from their liturgical context.[103] The prayer that follows is not taken from the Gelasian Sacramentary[104]:

> Almighty and merciful God, the Father of our Lord Jesus Christ, we suppliants beseech you, command the devil, who now restrains this servant N., that he should draw back from this man, and free him who believes in the true liberator, our Lord Jesus Christ; so that having been purged of every failing of iniquity by your majesty, he may consequently devotedly serve the grace of the Holy Spirit, who with the Father and the Son and the Holy Spirit lives and reigns to the ages of ages.

---

[102] Chardonnens, L. S., *Anglo-Saxon Prognostics, 900–1100: Study and Texts* (Leiden: Brill, 2007), p. 110. Gustav Hübener, in 'Beowulf and Germanic Exorcism', *Review of English Studies* 11 (1935), pp. 163–81, at pp. 176–7 argued that Beowulf's defeat of Grendel was representative of a distinctive Germanic tradition of 'heroic exorcism', involving a confrontation between the exorcist and a ghost or spirit, usually dwelling in a cave, that still existed around Lake Lucerne in Switzerland in the eighteenth century. Hübener speculated (p. 180) that pagan Germanic exorcists drank blood, the food of demons, in order to gain clairvoyance and the strength to fight the demons. If true, this might explain the semantic link between exorcism and divination in the Old English word *halsung*.

[103] *Pontificale Lanaletense*, pp. 112–13. The opening prayer from the Gellone Sacramentary, *SG* 2400 (*Omnipotens sempiterne deus a cuius facie celi distillant*) does appear in the Lanalet rite, but it is moved to the very end (p. 115).

[104] *Pontificale Lanaletense*, p. 114: *Omnipotens et misericors deus pater domini nostri ihesu christi te supplices deprecamur Impera diabolo qui hunc famulum N detinet ab hoc recedat et libera eum qui credit in uerum liberatorem dominum nostrum ihesum christum ut expurgatus ab omni labe iniquitatis maiestati tue pura mente deseruiat consecutus gratiam spiritus sancti qui cum patre et filio et spiritu sancto uiuit et regnat in secula seculorum.*

A liturgical structure similar to that of the Lanalet Pontifical can be found in the Samson Pontifical, produced at Winchester in the second half of the eleventh century. In both pontificals, *SG* 2405 follows immediately after the blessing of holy water. Furthermore, both the Lanalet and Samson Pontificals borrow *SG* 2412 (*Non ego tibi impero neque peccata mea*), which includes a detailed enumeration of body parts that the devil is forbidden from harming.[105] The merging of the Gelasian Sacramentary's exorcism of an energumen with the blessing of holy water suggests that it was primarily the virtue of the holy water itself, rather than the words of the exorcist, that was thought to be effective in expelling the demon.

The most elaborate exorcism of all in the Lanalet Pontifical was reserved for the judicial 'ordeal by cold water'. The right to host ordeals was a fiercely guarded privilege of major churches and a mark of their status, as well as an opportunity for the church to maintain a certain amount of control over the administration of justice.[106] The parties in dispute were expected to fast for three days and then come to the church, where they heard mass. After mass the priest pronounced the customary exorcism of holy water, with the addition of various adjurations addressed to the water itself[107]:

> I adjure you, creature of water, that you should become exorcized water, so that he who is made empty of the burden of goodness should not be submerged in you at all, that you should not permit him to be dragged to the depths, but that you should repel and reject him, nor suffer to receive his body.

The participants then drank the holy water and were led to a body of water, where they were lowered in by ropes one at a time; they were deemed guilty if they floated.

The structure and liturgical emphasis of Anglo-Saxon rites of exorcism suggest that the exorcism preceding the cold water ordeal was a quasi-

---

[105] *Pontificale Lanaletense*, pp. 114–15; Cambridge, Corpus Christi College, Parker Library MS 146, fols 315–18. *SG* 2405 is followed by a variant of *SG* 2400 (fol. 317r), a variant of *SG* 2412 (fol. 317v) and two more prayers, the last based on *SG* 2400 (fol. 318r).

[106] Blair, J., *The Church in Anglo-Saxon Society* (Oxford: Oxford University Press, 2005), p. 448.

[107] *Pontificale Lanaletense*, pp. 120–2: *Adiuro te creatura aque ... ut fias aqua exorcizata ... ut nullatenus eum in te submergi. aut in profundum trahi permittas sed a te repellas atque reicias nec patiaris recipere corpus quod ab honere bonitatis inane est factum.*

magical means of coercing nature to reveal the divine will, while it was the making of holy water that really counted rather than the pronouncement of exorcistic formulas over a possessed person. Exorcism was adapted to fit the priorities of Anglo-Saxon society, in which the church's endorsement of judicial ordeals mattered more than exorcism of demoniacs. However, Raiswell and Dendle were mistaken in thinking that there is no reference to exorcism in the pastoral writings of the tenth and eleventh centuries.[108] In his pastoral letter to Wulfsige III, then Abbot of Westminster (c. 995), Ælfric of Eynsham described each of the orders of the clergy as part of a defence of clerical celibacy. The exorcist was 'he who adjures with an oath in the Saviour's name the accursed spirits, who wish to torment men, that they should forsake men'.[109] This suggests that Ælfric believed an exorcist was empowered to exorcize energumens, rather than being an order bestowed on a cleric as a symbol of his power to exorcize catechumens. However, in a later letter to Wulfstan, Bishop of Worcester, Ælfric described an exorcist as an 'adjuror, who reads over the insane and infirm'.[110] There was no mention of demons or possession. In the same letter, Ælfric denied that it was possible for the devil to harm anyone without their consent: 'It cannot harm us, if anything comes upon us, sleeping or waking, against our will from the devil through his wiles'.[111] Whilst this view does not necessarily exclude the possibility of possession, it implies that only sinful people who opened themselves up to the devil were in danger of being possessed.

Exorcism was mentioned in the Ecclesiastical Ordinance of the Laws of King Cnut, promulgated by the new Danish king of England at Christmas 1020. Here it was declared that 'Great is the exorcism and glorious the consecration, which drives away and puts to flight devils, as often as one baptizes, or consecrates the host; and holy angels hover around there and protect those acts, and through God's power help the priests, as often as

---

[108] Raiswell and Dendle (2008), p. 743.

[109] *Councils and Synods with other Documents relating to the English Church: I A.D. 871–1204*, ed. D. Whitelock, M. Brett and C. N. L. Brooke (Oxford: Clarendon, 1981), vol. 1, pp. 202–3: 'Exorcista is on englisc se þe mid aðe halsað þa awyrgedan gastas, þe willað menn dreccan, þurh þæs Hælendes naman, þæt hy þa menn forlæton'.

[110] *Councils and Synods* I, vol. 1, p. 282: 'Exorcista is halsiend, se þe ræt ofer þa witseocan men ofer þa untruman'.

[111] Ibid. vol. 1, p. 281: 'þæt us ne mæg derigan, gif us hwæt unþances of þam deofle becymð þurh his searocræftas, slapende oþþe wæccende'.

they serve Christ rightly'.[112] This statement contains some confusion with regard to the liturgy, since no Latin liturgy of the mass has ever contained an exorcism. However, the blessing of holy water might take place before mass, and if this was established practice then the misconception could arise that it was a rite intended to drive the devil away from the church so that mass could be celebrated. The Ecclesiastical Ordinance demonstrates that Anglo-Saxon clergy in the early eleventh century still understood exorcism as the driving away of evil spirits; the use of the term 'exorcism' for the blessing of bread and cheese in the later pontificals suggests that, by the end of the century, the distinction between exorcism and blessing was blurred.[113] On the other hand, exorcism was exclusively understood as part of other rites (baptism and the mass) and there was no mention of exorcism of demoniacs.

From its foundation in 1123, St Bartholomew's Hospital in Smithfield regularly treated those who were molested by demons. Basil Clarke observed that, while mental disturbance in those treated at St Bartholomew's was often attributed to elves and demons, this was rarely presented as a punishment for sin.[114] Furthermore, although prayers were offered for patients by the Augustinian Canons, there is no evidence that exorcism was part of the treatment for the insane.[115] Instead, the treatment usually involved a form of 'incubation' in which patients were visited and cured by St Bartholomew himself in therapeutic dreams. The use of the demonically neutral term *witseocan* (literally 'wit-forsaken') by Ælfric to describe the insane supports Clarke's argument that, whilst mental illness was often construed in demonic terms, there was a conceptual distinction between the possessed and the insane. In the twelfth century insanity was often portrayed as a consequence of contact with demons who took the form of beautiful men or women who seduced the victim.[116] This was how the seer Meilyr of Caerleon came to be troubled by demons who appeared to him as huntsmen, since they were hunting human souls. The demons gave Meilyr secret knowledge of people's sins and allowed him to point

---

[112] Ibid. vol. 1, p. 473: 'Mycel is seo halsung mære is seo halgung, þe deofla afyrsað on fleame gebringeð, swa oft swa man fullað oððа husel halgað; halige englas þær abutan hwearfiað þa dæda beweardiað þurh Godes mihta þam sacerdon fylstað, swa oft swa hig Criste ðeniað mid rihte'.
[113] *Pontificale Lanaletense*, pp. 123–5; BL MS Add. 57337 fol. 80v (Anderson Pontifical); Parker Library MS 146, fols 312–13 (Samson Pontifical).
[114] Clarke (1975), p. 144.
[115] Ibid. p. 149.
[116] Ibid. pp. 146–7.

out false statements in books, even though he was illiterate. Meilyr was a victim of the demons rather than their master, and when he wanted relief from them John's Gospel was placed on his lap and they flew away. When Geoffrey of Monmouth's fantastical *History of the Kings of Britain* took its place, the demons returned in even greater numbers.[117]

Sluhovsky has argued that it was not until the fifteenth century that possessed people were regarded as points of access to the beyond; in the Middle Ages possession was 'a relatively unimportant occurrence' and demoniacs were not treated as mediums.[118] In the case of Meilyr this generalization does not hold true; although the placing of the Gospel on Meilyr's lap was a kind of exorcism, there is no other sign that anyone made any attempt to deliver Meilyr from the demons. The large number of accurate prophecies attributed to him would suggest that Meilyr was deliberately denied exorcism so that individuals could benefit from his prophecies.[119] Meilyr's story may well belong to a Welsh folk tradition of healers and seers who acquired their powers through liaisons with spirits in the form of human beings, but the fact that an educated churchman (Gerald of Wales) gave an account of him indicates that medieval interpretations of possession were not always as simplistic as Sluhovsky supposed.

The decline of exorcism in England is exemplified by the poor understanding of baptismal theology amongst even the most senior clergy. At the Council of Lambeth in October 1281, Archbishop John Pecham forbade the rebaptism of children who had already been baptized by a layperson when they were in danger of death (instead he recommended conditional baptism). However, he instructed that the exorcisms and catechism should be read over infants even if it was certain that they were previously baptized, 'on account of reverence for the statutes of the church'.[120] The reading of the exorcisms after baptism was entirely at odds with Alcuin's view, five hundred years earlier, that the pre-baptismal exorcisms put the devil to flight and made room for Christ; belated exorcism made no theological or liturgical sense. However, the reason given by Archbishop Pecham for

---

[117] Gerald of Wales (trans. L. Thorpe), *The Journey through Wales and the Description of Wales* (Harmondsworth: Penguin, 1978), pp. 116–20.
[118] Sluhovsky (2007), p. 6.
[119] Ross, A., *Folklore of Wales* (Stroud: Tempus, 2001), pp. 113–17.
[120] *Councils and Synods with other Documents relating to the English Church: II A.D. 1205–1313*, ed. F. M. Powicke and C. R. Cheney (Oxford: Clarendon, 1964), vol. 2, pp. 896–7: ... *sed super* sic *baptizatos dicantur exorcismi et catecismi, propter reverentiam ecclesiae statuentis.*

the reading of the exorcisms was neither theological nor liturgical; laypeople who baptized did so without the traditional preparatory rites of the church, and out of respect for the church's authority the whole rite had to be pronounced even though the infant was validly baptized. In other words, the reading of the exorcisms was purely political.

If formal exorcism of demoniacs was a practice of diminished significance in medieval England and baptismal exorcism had dwindled to little more than a required formula, other forms of exorcism thrived. Demoniacs continued to resort to the shrines of the saints, where cures were usually effected by incubation and dream visions,[121] and the fifteenth-century canonist William Lyndwood (1417–c. 1429) declared that it was permissible for a demoniac to carry stones and herbs about his person, provided he did not seek the help of magical incantations, making no mention of official exorcisms.[122] One possible reason for the relative insignificance of exorcism in medieval England was that the population at large was less concerned about demons possessing living bodies than the prospect of them possessing dead bodies. Medieval English folklore is replete with tales of revenants. William of Newburgh told the story of a friar who waited in a churchyard at Melrose in the Scottish borders, expecting a corpse to rise from the grave. When it did he decapitated it, an act that Sara Butler saw as 'a form of exorcism'.[123] Those who encountered ghosts protected themselves by means of relics and the sign of the cross and addressed spirits with the word *coniuro*, requiring them to answer questions much as exorcists did,[124] and Caciola has argued that references to the soul as the clothing of the body encouraged a parallelism between the exorcism of demons from the bodies of the possessed and exorcism of demons animating the bodies of the dead.[125]

---

[121] Hughes, J., *Pastors and Visionaries: Religion and Secular Life in Late Medieval Yorkshire* (Woodbridge: Boydell, 1988), pp. 325, 341.

[122] Kelly, H. A., 'Canon Law and Chaucer on Licit and Illicit Magic', in Karras, R. M., Kaye, J. and Matter, E. A. (eds), *Law and the Illicit in Medieval Europe* (Philadelphia, PA: University of Pennsylvania Press, 2008), pp. 210–21, at pp. 212–13.

[123] Butler, S. M., 'Cultures of Suicide? Suicide Verdicts and the "Community" in Thirteenth- and Fourteenth-Century England', *Historian* 69 (2007), pp. 427–49, at p. 436.

[124] Simpson, J., 'Repentant Soul or Walking Corpse: Debatable Apparitions in Medieval England', *Folklore* 114 (2003), pp. 389–402, at p. 396. See also Watkins, C. S., 'Sin, Penance and Purgatory in the Anglo-Norman Realm: The Evidence of Visions and Ghost Stories', *Past and Present* 175 (2002), pp. 3–33, at p. 23.

[125] Caciola, N., 'Wraiths, Revenants and Ritual in Medieval Culture', *Past and Present* 152 (1996), pp. 3–45, at p. 12. On revenants and spirits of the dead possessing human bodies see Sluhovsky (2007), pp. 17–21.

The Anglo-Saxon pontificals shifted the emphasis of exorcism from possessed persons to exorcisms of things. This in turn led to exorcisms of specific body parts. John Blair has described these exorcisms as 'encouraged magic', a substitute for suppressed pagan practices that existed at the margins of the church,[126] while for Jonathan Hughes they represented 'the uncertain powers and remedies of the rural pagan world'.[127] However, Bridget Nichols has argued that the inventiveness, sophistication and biblical allusions found in medieval blessings and exorcisms lift them out of the realm of mere 'popular religion'.[128] Eamon Duffy likewise maintained that the exorcistic and apotropaic practices of pre-Reformation England were deeply rooted in authentic Christian liturgical practices rather than 'pagan' magic.[129] Exorcisms were liturgical and were performed in ecclesiastical contexts: to label them as pagan, just because they do not conform to the norms of contemporary Christianity, seems circular.

In a leaf from a thirteenth-century English pontifical an exorcism of salt and water, intended for use on humans and animals, is followed by an exorcism of aching pain (probably for the teeth) with strong similarities to an Anglo-Saxon charm against toothache from the *Lacnunga Manuscript*.[130] This, the only surviving exorcistic text from thirteenth-century England, is testimony both to the longevity of Anglo-Saxon charms and the extent of the ecclesiastical approval they received. The thirteenth-century version, unlike the charm in the *Lacnunga*, is elaborated to include all parts of the body; the inspiration for this may have been from a pontifical containing a text similar to the Gellone Sacramentary's thorough exorcism, body part by body part[131]:

---

[126] Blair (2005), p. 167.
[127] Hughes (1988), p. 326.
[128] Nichols and MacGregor (2003), p. 2.
[129] Duffy (1992), pp. 281–3.
[130] BL MS Harley 585 fol. 183; see Cockayne, T. O., *Leechdoms, Wortcunning and Starcraft of Early England* (London: Longman, Roberts and Green, 1866), vol. 2, p. 64. On Anglo-Saxon charms and exorcisms see Clarke (1975), pp. 46–9; Skemer, D. C., *Binding Words: Textual Amulets in the Middle Ages* (University Park, PA: Pennsylvania State University Press, 2006), pp. 77–9.
[131] BL MS Add. 34652, fol. 14r: *Adjuro te gutta migranea per dominum et dominum nostrum iesum christum per patrem et filium et spiritum sanctum et non habeas potestatem in capite isto stare. ne in dentibusque morari. ne in manibus. ne in pedibus. ne in ullo loco dominari. Sic libera famulum tuum dic agyos. agyos. agyos.* Compare this with *SG 2412: Recedo ergo a capite, a capillis, a lingua, a sublingua, a brachyum, a naribus, a pectore, ab oculis, ab aenis, ab intistino maiore et minore.*

I adjure you aching spot by the Lord and Our Lord Jesus Christ, by the Father and the Son and the Holy Spirit, that you shall not have the power to stay in this head. Nor to remain in the teeth. Nor in the hands. Nor in the feet. Nor to dominate in any part. Thus free your servant, say *Agyos, Agyos, Agyos.*

On the reverse side of the leaf is a canticle adapted from Apocalypse 8 beginning '...before the altar of the temple, having a censer' ([*ante*] *aram templi habens turribulum*), with the syllables separated and spaces between the lines for musical notation. This is followed by an adapted reading from Apocalypse 7 beginning 'I, John, saw in the middle a throne ...' (*Ego Johannes vidit* [sic. for *vidi*] *in medio thronum*).[132] The juxtaposition of this fragment of sung liturgy with the exorcism can be explained in at least two ways. On the one hand, it is possible that the musical notation has nothing to do with the exorcism and the scribe was just re-using some vellum. On the other hand, the apocalyptic overtones of the verse chosen could suggest that it was part of the exorcism, which was to be conducted in the traditional liturgical context of a church rather than as an extension of the priest's pastoral work into the realm of 'popular religion'.

With the exception of the liturgical exorcisms of holy water and salt in missals and pontificals, 'medical' exorcisms are the most common form of exorcism in early English texts. The *Liber de diversis medicinis*, compiled in the mid-fifteenth century but probably containing older vernacular material, included the formula *adiuro te gutta migranea*, accompanied by appeals to Ss Appollonia and Laurence, in a treatment for toothache.[133] Vernacular 'medical' exorcisms existed too, in Norman French translations of lapidaries, treatises on the properties of minerals and stones.[134]

In the late thirteenth century an internal challenge to the English church emerged in the form of the Lollards, individuals inspired by the writings of John Wyclif (c. 1320–84) to reject the authority and sacraments of the Catholic church. When the Lollards rejected exorcism in the fifth of their 'Twelve Conclusions', nailed to the doors of Westminster

---

[132] BL MS Add. 34652, fol. 14v.
[133] Ogden, M. S. (ed.), *The 'Liber de Diversis Medicinis' in the Thornton Manuscript (MS. Lincoln Cathedral A.5.2)* (London: Early English Text Society, 1938), p. 18.
[134] Vising, J., *Anglo-Norman Language and Literature* (Oxford: Oxford University Press, 1923), pp. 50, 68; Dean, R. J., *Anglo-Norman Literature: A Guide to Texts and Manuscripts* (London: Anglo-Norman Texts Society, 1999), 357 (p. 197). On the use of precious stones in exorcisms see Sluhovsky (2007), p. 68.

Abbey and St Paul's Cathedral in 1395, they made no mention of exorcism of demoniacs but anticipated the arguments of later reformers against exorcisms of objects.[135] The Lollards appealed to experience and observed that no change was noticeable in blessed or exorcized things, showing that exorcism was 'necromancy' and a falsehood spread by the devil. They singled out holy water, noting that experience contradicted the claims made in its favour by the clergy.[136] However, whilst Lollardy proved a persistent feature of late medieval English religion, the Lollards were a tiny minority of the population. Duffy has argued that their continued existence was overshadowed by the outpouring of Catholic catechetical and devotional literature in the late fifteenth and early sixteenth centuries,[137] and it was Henry VIII and his ministers, not the Lollards, who led the English Reformation. The late Middle Ages in England saw a revival of the cult of the saints, including two native pseudo-saints who were associated with exorcism: John Schorne and King Henry VI. In this respect England was strikingly conservative, retaining the early medieval approach to exorcism through the saints rather than clerical involvement, although the mass of St Raphael in the Sarum missal was sometimes used as a means of driving demons out of a person.[138]

Master John Schorne was rector of North Marston in Buckinghamshire 1290–1314. Immediately after his death he was venerated for his sanctity and, although he was never officially canonized, by the fifteenth century his cult had spread throughout England. Schorne was supposed to have imprisoned the devil in a boot, and representations of the 'saint' invariably

---

[135] Wyclif condemned the multiplication of orders of the clergy, including the order of exorcist, in his short treatise *De Gradibus Cleri Ecclesiae* (1382) (Wyclif, J. (ed. J. Loserth) *Johannis Wyclif Opera Minora* (London: Wyclif Society, 1913), pp. 140–4).

[136] Cronin, H. S., 'The Twelve Conclusions of the Lollards', *English Historical Review* 22 (1907), pp. 292–304, at p. 298: 'Exorcismis and halwinge, made in þe chirche, of wyn, bred, and wax, water, salt, and oyle and encens, þe ston of þe auter, upon uestiment, mitre, crose, and pilgrimes stauis be the uerray practys of nigromancie rathere þanne þe holi theologie. Þis conclusion is prouid þus. For be suche exorcismis creaturis been charged to ben of heygere uertu þan here owne kynde, and we sen no þing of chaunge in no sich creature þat is so charmid but be fals beleue, þe whiche is þe principal of þe deuelis craft. Þe correlary of þis, þat if þe bok þat charmith haliwater spred in holy chirche were al trewe us thinkis uerrily þat holy water usid in holi chirche schulde ben þe beste medicine to alle manere of sykenesse. Cuius contrarium experimur'.

[137] Duffy (1992), pp. 2–3.

[138] Sangha, L., *Angels and Belief in England, 1480–1700* (London: Pickering and Chatto, 2012), p. 26.

depict him holding a boot in his left hand, from the top of which pokes the face of the devil, while the 'saint's' gestures with his right hand suggest an adjuration or exorcism. On the rood screen of St Helen's church, Gateley, in Norfolk, John Schorne is depicted in a Doctor of Divinity's robes, and the figure of Satan is tiny. On the rood screen of St Gregory's, Sudbury, in Suffolk, the devil is scowling comically, and a seventeenth-century visitor who saw another depiction at Cawston, Norfolk, described the devil as a 'moppet'. At North Marston itself, pilgrims were supposedly treated to the spectacle of the devil moving up and down in Master Schorne's boot, which in turn may have been the origin of the children's toy, the jack-in-the-box.[139]

Curiously, in spite of the fact that he was medieval England's most famous exorcist, there is little evidence that Master John Schorne's cult was ever associated with exorcism.[140] Rather, his image was supposed to be a good cure for the ague. The devil in John Schorne's boot, like the devil in some medieval English mystery plays, was a comic figure rather than an object of fear.[141] However, Schorne's imprisonment of the devil had a lasting influence on English folklore, which recounted the exploits of parsons who imprisoned the devil in bottles, snuff boxes and other receptacles centuries after the Reformation.[142]

Instead of John Schorne's shrine at North Marston, it was the shrine of King Henry VI (1421–71), who was twice deposed by Edward IV and finally put to death in the Tower of London, that was associated with deliverance of demoniacs.[143] Henry, like St Bartholomew, was an 'exorcist saint' whose very presence banished demons, rather than his shrine being a centre of liturgical exorcism. Indeed, there is no evidence that the

---

[139] On the legend and cult of Master John Schorne see Kelke (1869), pp. 60–74; Simpson (1870), pp. 354–69; Clarke (1975), pp. 214–15.

[140] On 30 July 1537 two Englishmen and a Dutchman met with an English priest living in the Low Countries named Doctor Clene, who was otherwise known as 'Sir John Skarme', 'because he can cumber the devil as is said' (*Letters and Papers, Foreign and Domestic, of the Reign of Henry VIII*, ed. J. Brewer, J. Gairdner and R. Brodie (London: HMSO, 1892), vol. 13:1, p. 1383).

[141] On the development of the devil as a comic character see Russell (1984), pp. 259–61.

[142] For English folklore concerning exorcisms see Leather, E. M., *The Folk-lore of Herefordshire* (Hereford: Jakeman and Carver, 1912), pp. 29–31; Hole, C., *English Folklore* (London: Batsford, 1940), pp. 162–4; Brown, T., 'Examples of Post-Reformation Folklore in Devon', *Folklore* 72 (1961), pp. 388–99. The example of John Schorne's boot demonstrates that these legends do not construe exorcism 'in Protestant ... terms' (Simpson (2003), p. 398).

[143] Clarke (1975), pp. 163–5.

popularity of exorcism manuals in Continental Europe had any effect in England at all. Nevertheless, some theological understanding of exorcism circulated in pre-Reformation England. Andrew Chertsey (fl. 1502–27) translated *The Ordynarye of Crystyanyte or of Cristen Men* into English from a French devotional treatise, and it was printed twice by Wynkyn de Worde in 1502 and 1506. The *Ordynarye* consisted of an exposition of each of the sacraments, along with Latin texts and English translations of the liturgy, including an explanation of the purposes of pre-baptismal exorcism. The theology of the *Ordynarye* was thoroughly Augustinian: the purpose of exorcism was to free the infant from 'the puyssaunce of the devyll'. However, the *Ordynarye* echoed the objections of the Lollards by assimilating exorcism to the blessing of inanimate objects:

> Whan Adam & Eve unto whome god had gyven dominacyon of all the worlde disobeyed unto god the devyll toke power upon theym & in lyke wyse upon all theyr dominacyon as were the ayre the water & these other creatures the whiche were made & create for man ... And for so moche all these thyngis the whiche be spoken & consecrate unto god & unto his dyvyne servyce as chirches chircheyardes awters corporaces chalyces towelles vestymentes apperteynynge unto the holy mysterye of the awter be exorcyses by the benediccion & by the holy oryson of preestes bysshops. That is to saye th[a]t the puyssaunce of the enmye infernall is coniured & put out of these sayd thynges.

As Nichols has observed, a potential danger to faith lurked in the idea that exorcism was necessitated by the radical corruption of nature by the Fall, since this raised questions about the completeness of Christ's victory over evil.[144] Ironically, the Reformers opposed exorcism, yet the Calvinist emphasis on the total depravity of nature and human beings provided a theological rationale for universal exorcism. In England, where liturgical exorcism of the possessed had never been significant, the Reformers attacked exorcism of objects instead.[145] Furthermore, the early Reformers'

---

[144] Nichols and MacGregor (2003), p. 10.

[145] In 1554 the exiled Protestant Nicholas Nicastor published English translations of the exorcism of water and salt, the blessing of bread and candles, the blessing of ashes, palms, the Easter fire, the Paschal candle, Paschal lamb, wedding ring and blessings for pilgrims in his *Doctrine of the Masse Booke* (Wittenberg, 1554), but made no mention of exorcizing the possessed.

emphasis on ghosts as the subjects of fake exorcisms by Catholic clergy may well have derived from the English tradition of exorcizing revenants.[146]

One late pre-Reformation instance of possession well demonstrates the insignificance of liturgical exorcism in England. In April 1516 a twelve-year-old girl from Gosfield in Essex, Jane Wentworth, visited the shrine of Our Lady of Grace in Ipswich to give thanks for her deliverance from possession by a vision of the Virgin Mary on Lady Day (25 March). Whilst at the shrine, Jane was possessed again and delivered visionary sermons calling on others, including members of her own family, to be reconciled to God. The proceedings were witnessed by local notables including Lord Curzon and John Reeve, the Abbot of Bury St Edmunds and Suffolk's leading churchman. Jane harangued the clergy, declaring 'ye shall see what good ye all do to me with your arguments for I shall be by and by in the same case I was that day I was holpen by Our Blessed Lady'.[147] In other words, exhortations and exorcisms (and there is no evidence that liturgical exorcisms were deployed on Jane) were of no effect in comparison with the *virtus* of Our Lady of Grace. The case of Jane Wentworth demonstrates that, even at the eve of the Reformation, traditional shrine-exorcisms still trumped liturgical exorcism in England.

Liturgical exorcism largely failed to make an impact in medieval England, where the crisis of exorcism that affected the whole of Catholic Europe between the eleventh and thirteenth centuries was particularly acute. From the very beginning, the Anglo-Saxons adapted liturgical exorcism to the needs of a post-pagan Germanic culture. Exorcism of demoniacs receded in importance and in some liturgical books became a mere adjunct to the far more important exorcism of holy water. At the same time, the *virtus* of the saints trumped liturgical exorcism in many stories. The rising fear of magic and sorcery in fourteenth-century Europe had comparatively little effect in England, and the idea of demonic possession never seems to have taken hold (and, in any case, a judicial preoccupation with witchcraft in Europe led to further denigration of the significance of exorcism). The word 'exorcism' in late medieval England came to refer primarily to a component of the rite of baptism and the blessing of objects.

---

[146] On the English Reformers' preoccupation with fake ghosts see Davies, O., *The Haunted: A Social History of Ghosts* (Basingstoke: Palgrave MacMillan, 2007), p. 166.

[147] Rex, R., 'Wentworth, Jane [Anne; *called* the Maid of Ipswich] (*c*. 1503–1572?)' in *The Oxford Dictionary of National Biography* (Oxford: Oxford University Press, 2004), vol. 58, pp. 127–8.

As late as the fifteenth and sixteenth centuries, people who were molested by the devil continued to be treated at shrines of the saints.[148] The example of England, extreme as it was when compared to the religious culture of its European neighbours, demonstrates that liturgical exorcism of demoniacs was a fairly marginal activity for much of the Middle Ages.

---

[148] On exorcism at shrines in the late Middle Ages see Sluhovsky (2007), pp. 49–59.

CHAPTER 4

Exorcism in Counter-Reformation Europe

In the winter of 1604, in the town of Laurac in the south of France, a twenty-one-year-old man was being exorcized to free him from an evil spirit with which he had made a pact in return for wealth.[1] The exorcist, Béringer, assisted by the prayers of a crowd of laypeople in the room, finally achieved a result after many days[2]:

> At last, on the fourth Tuesday of January between 10 and 11 o'clock in the evening in the presence of the said Seigneur Béringer and thirty or forty persons, the evil spirit went out of the body of this man in the form of a flame of fire like a band made of gunpowder from a cannon, with a great stench and of such force that it gave a great blow to the two assistants, one of them on the face and the other on the ear, from which he remains deaf

---

[1] On the acquisition of wealth by magical means see Thomas (1971), pp. 279–82; Davies, O., *Popular Magic*, 2nd edn (London: Hambledon Continuum, 2007), pp. 93–6; Davies, O., *Grimoires: A History of Magic Books* (Oxford: Oxford University Press, 2009), p. 39.

[2] BL MS Cotton Caligula E XI, fols 237–8, Guillaume de Nautonier to unknown recipient, 14 January 1605: 'Finalement, le mardj 4ni du Fin[a]l mois Janvier entre 10. et 11. heures du soir en pr[es]ence d[u] [d]it S[eigneu]r Beringer & 30. ou 40. Persones, Le malni esprit sort du corps de cet home en forme d'une flamme de feu come une fasce faite a poudre a canon d'une grande puanteur et de telle poideur qu'elle dona a deux des assistans Un grand coup, a L'un sur le visage a L'au[tr]e sur L'oreille dont il demeura sourd … L'Esprit sorty voltigeoit en L'air et fascoit effort de rentrer au cors d[u] [d]it home, Et au mesme instant Les bois mis de La d[it] maiso[n] ouïllent un grand bruit du q[ue]l aucunes des d[ite]s maisons tremblerent estra[n]g[e]m[en]t'.

© The Editor(s) (if applicable) and The Author(s) 2016
F. Young, *A History of Exorcism in Catholic Christianity*,
DOI 10.1007/978-3-319-29112-3_4

> ... the departed spirit flitted about in the air and made an effort to return to the body of the said man, and at the same moment they heard the timber sent from the said house, a great noise from which several of the said houses strangely shuddered.

This story is typical of hundreds of exorcism narratives from the sixteenth and seventeenth centuries. The man became possessed through a pact with an evil spirit, the exorcism was dramatic and public, and the emphatically physical nature of the spirit was not without risks to the exorcists and onlookers. However, this is not a Catholic exorcism narrative; its author, Guillaume de Nautonier (1560–1620), was a Huguenot Protestant and a man of science. The Lauragais region was divided between Catholics and Protestants, and one of the issues they disputed most hotly was the efficacy and necessity of exorcism.[3] The martial imagery of this exorcism, during which the demon came out of the man's body like the flash of a cannon, is an apt illustration of the explosive propaganda potential of exorcism, which was genuinely a weapon in the war between Catholic and Protestant models of authority.

The Counter-Reformation was a global religious and cultural movement that can be defined as the totality of the Catholic response to Protestantism and the subsequent Catholic reform movement. Consequently, although the Council of Trent (1545–63) was central to the Counter-Reformation, the Counter-Reformation began before Trent and continued after the Council. The Counter-Reformation was a protracted process because the Catholic church was a collection of separate institutions with a common loyalty rather than a single institution in any real sense, and it would be a mistake to reify the Counter-Reformation as a united movement against Protestantism. Competing religious orders with competing models of Catholic reform contended with one another to define the post-Tridentine church.

In the case of exorcism the struggle was particularly acute. Arguments raged over the acceptability of lay exorcism,[4] but even after these were resolved in favour of the clergy's sole right to administer the sacramental, differences of emphasis remained. The Franciscans defended the frequent deployment of elaborate exorcisms as a quasi-magical aid to popular faith. The Jesuits likewise promoted exorcism as an evangelistic tool, but favoured a 'charismatic' based on relics rather than liturgy. At least some Dominicans approached exorcism with suspicion, as a door through which

---

[3] On Huguenot attitudes to exorcism see Ferber (2004), pp. 32–3.
[4] Sluhovsky (2007), pp. 69–78.

enthusiastic and heretical spiritualities could enter the church, and diocesan clergy were wary of the enthusiasm whipped up by the religious orders. In 1614 the humanist scholar Cardinal Giulio Antonio Santori cut through the controversy, reviving the liturgy of the Gelasian Sacramentary in the *Rituale Romanum*, accompanied by stringent criteria of discernment. In an age when spiritual authority was everything, exorcism was the one rite through which Catholics could tangibly demonstrate the truth of the Catholic faith and put heretics to shame, yet in reality there were few issues on which Catholics were more divided, and the codification of an official rite in 1614 did not put an end to dissension.

In exorcisms, Catholics sought certainty from the mouths of demons concerning the foundations of their faith, at a time of growing fear of witchcraft and magic, when eschatological obsessions were fostered by the violence of religious conflict.[5] Exorcisms became ever more dramatic and demonic manifestations ever more extreme; the conditions of the sixteenth century allowed for a 'limitless expansion' of exorcism,[6] culminating in witchcraft allegations and a series of mass possessions in the mid-seventeenth century that captured the attention of the entire French nation and beyond. The evidential base for exorcism in the sixteenth and seventeenth centuries is vast, and the scholarly literature correspondingly so. However, with the exception of two chapters by Sluhovsky and one by Guido dall'Olio,[7] little attention has been paid to the liturgical, canonical and theological development of exorcism within the Counter-Reformation church. The majority of studies concentrate on possession and witchcraft which, while intimately related to exorcism, have a distinct history. The purpose of this chapter is to set exorcism in the early modern period in its historical context as just one chapter in a much longer process of development.

The Challenge to Exorcism

Euan Cameron has argued that pre-Tridentine exorcism was 'a flexible and varied business'.[8] No standard, accepted rite of exorcism existed, although some were more popular than others, and exorcistic formulae were often used in magic. Exorcism was as likely to be applied to

---
[5] On exorcism and apocalypticism see Clark (1997), p. 409.
[6] Ferber (2004), p. 4.
[7] Dall'Olio, G., 'The Devil of Inquisitors, Demoniacs and Exorcists in Counter-Reformation Italy', in Dendle, P. and Raiswell, R. (eds), *The Devil in Society in Pre-Modern Europe* (Toronto: Centre for Reformation and Renaissance Studies, 2012), pp. 511–36.
[8] Cameron (2010), pp. 59–60.

animals and inanimate objects as it was to human beings.[9] If there was one constant that united the spiritual concerns of the late fifteenth century and the early 1500s with those of the Counter-Reformation it was witchcraft, whose significance grew rather than diminished as the threat of Protestantism emerged.[10] Midelfort has described the association between possession and witchcraft as a 'dangerous cultural invention' of the sixteenth and seventeenth centuries that had far-reaching implications.[11] Catholic authors stressed the apostasy inherent in witchcraft, which was conceptualized as formal worship of the devil and renunciation of Christianity, often accompanied by such accoutrements as the witches' Sabbath, ritual cannibalism and sexual deviance.[12] Whilst discussion of witchcraft was more muted in Spain, Portugal and the Kingdom of Naples, the Spanish and Portuguese Inquisitions remained concerned about the proliferation of sorcery.[13]

In 1500, the Cologne printer Johann Besichen produced a new edition of *Coniuratio malignorum spirituum*, the most successful exorcism text of the early years of printing (it had already been through three editions by 1500). The *Coniuratio* was short, at only fourteen pages, and its popularity may have lain in its claim to be the liturgy used on demoniacs in St Peter's Basilica itself. The *Coniuratio* consisted of twenty-six separate stages, only three of which were derived from the ancient exorcism liturgies. The prayer *Exorcizo te im[m]unde spiritus*, lifted from the baptismal liturgy, was followed by *Deus angelorum, Deus archangelorum* (*SG* 2403), and the prayer *Deus celi, deus angelorum*, derived from the Paris Supplement and later included in the *Rituale Romanum* of 1614 (*RR* 903). Crucially, however, the three 'great adjurations' (*SG* 2405) did not feature in the rite, and instead the *Coniuratio* culminated, as its title suggests, with six 'conjurations'. The devil

---

[9] Ibid. pp. 38–9.

[10] On Counter-Reformation responses to witchcraft see Clark (1997), p. 527; Clark, S., 'Protestant Witchcraft, Catholic Witchcraft' in Oldridge, D. (ed.), *The Witchcraft Reader* (London: Routledge, 2002), pp. 165–77.

[11] Midelfort (2005a), p. 9.

[12] Cameron (2010), pp. 193–5.

[13] On the Spanish Inquisition's attitude to witchcraft see Weber (2005), p. 188; Henningsen, G., *The Witches' Advocate: Basque Witchcraft and the Spanish Inquisition (1609–1614)* (Reno, NV: University of Nevada Press, 1980); Henningsen, G., '"The Ladies from Outside": An Archaic Pattern of the Witches' Sabbath' in Ankarloo, B. and Henningsen, G. (eds.), *Early Modern European Witchcraft: Centres and Peripheries* (Oxford: Oxford University Press, 1990), pp. 191–215, at p. 194.

was conjured to depart by the Trinity, by the Passion, by the keys of St Peter, by the lance that pierced Christ's side, by the death and entombment of Christ, by the Resurrection, and by the Ascension.

The reference to St Peter's keys further strengthened the association between the *Coniuratio* and Rome at a time before the Papacy exercised a significant degree of central control on the liturgy. The *Coniuratio* was printed twice more, by Marcellus Silber in 1501 and in 1510. Although it was derived in part from ancient liturgical sources, the direct borrowing of exorcisms from the baptismal liturgy and the absence of the great adjurations (the central and unvarying component of the oldest liturgies of exorcism) demonstrated that the compilers of the *Coniuratio* had little knowledge of the liturgical history of exorcism. The *Coniuratio* drew upon the mysteries of the faith for power over demons, and this set the pattern for the elaborate conjurations of later exorcists such as Girolamo Menghi. However, it is clear that the *Coniuratio* could easily be used for magic, and Owen Davies has aptly described exorcism manuals as 'the most influential occult products of the print age', classing them with grimoires as well as liturgical texts.[14]

The critique of Catholic exorcism that came to be associated with the Protestant Reformers emerged from a Catholic source. In Erasmus's colloquy *Exorcism or, The Spectre* (1524), the principal speaker, Anselm, describes how a man named Polus tricked a self-important priest called Faunus into performing an exorcism. He managed to convince Polus that a churchyard was haunted by a soul suffering torment in purgatory, faking strange lights in the churchyard by fixing candles to the backs of crabs and making wailing sounds. Faunus performed the exorcism and the manifestations stopped, and the priest subsequently received a letter, purportedly from the suffering soul, claiming that he had been released from purgatory.[15] Erasmus's comic tale was intended to ridicule popular superstitions of the day; the idea that souls from purgatory returned, demanding prayers and masses, and the alleged 'miraculous letters' that circulated, purporting to have been written by saints. None of these phenomena were accepted without reservation by serious late medieval theologians, and it is very

---

[14] Davies (2009), p. 59.
[15] Erasmus, D., *The Colloquies of Erasmus* (trans. C. R. Thompson) (Chicago, IL: University of Chicago Press, 1965), pp. 231–327. On Erasmus's colloquy see Cox, J. D., *Seeming Knowledge: Shakespeare and Skeptical Faith* (Waco, TX: Baylor University Press, 2007), pp. 3–4.

unlikely that Erasmus intended that his satirical observations on superstitious folly should become acerbic anti-Catholic propaganda.

Other Catholic authors hostile to exorcism in the early sixteenth century included Pedro Ciruelo, Martín de Castañega and the authors of the *Malleus maleficarum*, Sprenger and Kramer.[16] These authors showed a concern for apostolic authenticity by drawing on evidence such as the decrees of the Council of Carthage in 398. However, the extent of Catholic opposition to exorcism should not be exaggerated. In many cases, objections were raised to exorcism of animals and objects rather than people. Critical authors simply created 'a mood or climate which privileged the need for discernment' rather than threatening the continued existence of exorcism.[17] Indeed, there was nothing intrinsically at odds with the conditions laid down by these reforming authors in the famous exorcisms of the sixteenth century, since they were primarily concerned to ensure that exorcisms were performed by the right people.

Nevertheless, Erasmus's critique of exorcism went on to form the basis of a Protestant attack on the practice driven by resistance to the idea of sacramentals, rites whose effectiveness was guaranteed not directly by God but indirectly by the church. As such, Protestant hostility to exorcism had its roots in Luther's original objection to the doctrine of indulgences and the idea of the church's 'treasury of merit'; any claim by the church to be able to distribute grace was presumptuous blasphemy. The classic biblical critique of exorcism came from the Swiss reformed theologian Benedikt Marti (known as Aretius, 1522–74), who argued that the Greek word *exorcizō* originally meant nothing but 'to bind by oath', and that the word *ekballō* ('to cast out') was the one used in the Gospels to describe Jesus' exorcisms. Liturgical exorcism was nothing more than magic, a practice with no biblical foundation, and the difference between a magician seeking favours from spirits and an exorcist commanding them was slight.[18] However, Protestant authors did not question the underlying demonological assumptions of medieval Catholicism. Demonic possession was real, but the church's claim to be able to cast out devils was fraudulent. The Protestant critique was therefore based less on a fundamental theological disagreement than on different ideas about authority.

---

[16] On Catholic criticism see Ferber (2004), pp. 17–22.
[17] Ibid. p. 21.
[18] On the Protestant critique see Cameron (2010), pp. 205–8.

The Catholic Response

The Counter-Reformation saw the consolidation and clarification of Catholic practices rather than unqualified acceptance of the humanist arguments for reform that initially inspired the Protestant attack.[19] Lyndal Roper and David Lederer identified the exorcisms performed by the Jesuit Peter Canisius (1521–97) during his time as a preacher in Augsburg as the first in a series of 'staged' exorcisms designed to promote the Catholic faith. Between 1560 and 1580 Augsburg experienced 'the years of exorcism mania'.[20] However, the best publicized of the early 'theatrical' Counter-Reformation exorcisms was the protracted ordeal of sixteen-year-old Nicole Aubry in Laon Cathedral in northern France between November 1565 and February 1566. The 'Miracle of Laon' occurred at a time when France was politically divided between Catholics and Huguenot Protestants. The Edict of Amboise (1563), signed by Catherine de Medici as regent for her son, Charles IX, ended the first confessional war in France with the provision of limited toleration for the Huguenots, yet the competing factions remained armed and tensions ran high.

Nicole was possessed after her family were unable to fulfil a pilgrimage to Santiago de Compostela requested by the ghost of her grandfather. Her possession was diagnosed by a lay teacher in her home town of Vervins, where a Dominican friar, Pierre de la Motte, began the exorcisms. Nicole claimed to be possessed by her grandfather's ghost, but De la Motte rejected this interpretation. He found that Nicole's seizures were alleviated only by consecrated hosts, and during her periods of possession she

---

[19] On the Tridentine revision of baptismal rites of exorcism see Kelly (1985), pp. 261–2.

[20] Roper, L., *Oedipus and the Devil: Witchcraft, Sexuality and Religion in Early Modern Europe* (London: Routledge, 1994), p. 185; Lederer, D., 'Exorzieren ohne Lizenz...' in De Waardt et al. (2005), pp. 213–31, at pp. 214–18. On exorcism as Counter-Reformation propaganda see Venard, M., 'Le Démon controversiste' in Péronnet, M. (ed.), *La Controverse Religieuse (XVIe–XIXe siècles): Actes du Ier Colloque Jean Boisset* (Montpellier: Université Paul Valery, 1980), vol. 2, pp. 45–60; Walker, D. P., 'Demonic Possession used as Propaganda in the Later Sixteenth Century' in Garfagnini, G. (ed.), *Scienze, credenze occulte, livelli di cultura* (Florence: Olschki, 1982), pp. 237–48; Weber (1983), pp. 79–101; Pearl, J. L., 'Demons and Politics in France, 1560–1630', *Historical Reflections* 12 (1985), pp. 241–51; Pearl, J. L., '"A School for Rebel Soul": Politics and Demonic Possession in France', *Historical Reflections* 16 (1989), pp. 286–306; Hanlon, G. and Snow, G., 'Exorcisme et Cosmologie Tridentine: trois cas agenais en 1619', *Revue de la Bibliothèque Nationale* 28 (1988), pp. 12–27; Soergel, P. M., *Wondrous in His Saints: Counter-Reformation Propaganda in Bavaria* (Berkeley, CA: University of California Press, 1993), pp. 99–158.

was able to answer questions posed in Latin, French, German and Flemish and reveal the secret sins of bystanders. Soon the church at Vervins was too small for the spectators the exorcism attracted, and the performance was moved to Laon. Nicole was brought to the cathedral in procession and exorcized twice a day on a dais erected for the purpose; the more hosts she was fed, the more her symptoms were alleviated. In the meantime she identified the demon possessing her as Beelzebub (a leader of the Huguenots), proclaimed the real presence of Christ in the Eucharist, and eventually declared that she was free from the spirits, who had returned to Calvinist Geneva.[21]

The exorcism of Nicole Aubry led to confrontation between Protestants in Laon, who wanted the processions stopped, and local Catholics. Nicole was rewarded by King Charles IX, who visited Laon during a tour of France intended to restore order, for her services to the Catholic faith. However, the events were not uncontroversial amongst Catholics; the local bishop attempted to make the exorcisms more private and the use of consecrated hosts in large numbers for exorcistic purposes was not only unprecedented but also undermined the Council of Trent's insistence that every host contained the entire person of Christ, 'body, blood, soul and divinity'. As D. P. Walker noted, 'these pious Catholics ... came near to using the host as a medicine'.[22] Both Ferber and Sluhovsky have argued that Nicole set the pattern for subsequent sixteenth-century French possessions, which tended to involve laywomen and did not involve any accusations of witchcraft,[23] such as the widely publicized possession of Marthe Brossier at Romorantin and Paris in 1598–99.[24] As the threat from Protestantism receded (or at least became less immediate), exorcisms began to expose witches and sorcerers rather than heretics.

---

[21] Sluhovsky (1996), pp. 1039–42. On the Laon case see also Walker (1981); Crouzet, D., 'A Woman and the Devil: Possession and Exorcism in Sixteenth-Century France' in Wolfe, M. (ed.), *Changing Identities in Early Modern France* (Durham, NC: Duke University Press, 1996), pp. 191–215; Ferber (2004), pp. 23–39; on contemporary reactions see Backus, I., *Le Miracle de Laon: le deraisonnable, le raisonnable, l'apocalyptique et le politique dans les recits du Miracle de Laon, 1566–1578* (Paris: J. Vrin, 1994).

[22] Walker (1981), p. 24.

[23] Ferber (2004), p. 6; Sluhovsky (1996), p. 1043.

[24] On the Brossier case see Walker, A. M. and Dickerman, E. H., '"A Woman under the Influence": a case of alleged possession in sixteenth-century France', *Sixteenth Century Journal* 22 (1991), pp. 535–54; Ferber (2004), pp. 40–59.

GIROLAMO MENGHI AND MAGICAL EXORCISM

Counter-Reformation Catholicism responded to demoniacs at two extremes, and between these lay a continuum of treatment and diagnosis. At one extreme was the sympathetic approach, whose most dramatic instances were the exorcisms at Laon and Loudun, when demoniacs were elevated almost to the level of living saints. At the other extreme, the possessed were judged to have made a pact with Satan, meaning that demoniacs were tainted by witchcraft and diabolism; the Jesuit Peter Thyraeus suggested that it was sometimes difficult to distinguish between a demoniac and a witch.[25] Between these two approaches, possession might or might not be seen as the consequence of sin, but the demoniac was usually construed as a victim of the devil in some sense, either directly or indirectly by means of witchcraft. Richard Raiswell and Peter Dendle's four-fold classification of roles assigned to the devil in medieval and early modern Christianity is helpful here: the devil could be God's agent, God's rival, God's frustrated opponent or God's dupe.[26] In early modern exorcism the devil usually passed from the roles of rival to frustrated opponent, but he was also just as likely to be seen as acting as an agent of God to reveal heresy, witchcraft and other sins.

The most famous Catholic exorcist of all was the Italian Observant Franciscan friar Girolamo Menghi (1529–1609), who tested the boundaries between exorcism and magic as never before. Menghi was born at Viadana and entered the Franciscans in 1550, serving as provincial of the order at Bologna between 1598 and 1602.[27] Based mainly in Bologna, Menghi performed exorcisms in northern Italy for forty years and was the author of three Latin works on exorcism, *Flagellum daemonum* ('The Scourge of Demons', 1577), *Fustis daemonum* ('The Club of Demons', 1584) and *Eversio daemonum* ('The Overthrow of Demons', 1588). However, Menghi's earliest work was the 1572 vernacular *Compendio dell'arte essorcistica* ('Compendium of the Exorcist's Art'), the first complete manual of exorcism to appear in print. Menghi's theology was nakedly apocalyptic. He was convinced that the history of the world had entered its last phase; the final victory of God was approaching, and in response the raging devil

---

[25] Thyraeus, P., *De demoniacis liber unus* (Cologne 1594), pp. 36–8.
[26] Raiswell and Dendle (2012), pp. 537–51.
[27] Romeo (1990), p. 115.

was letting his power loose in the world.[28] Menghi placed a strong emphasis on the corporeality of spirits in the *Compendio*, defending the existence of incubi and succubi and claiming that demons could assume the appearance of any body they chose, including those of animals. Menghi quoted Augustine's *On the Literal Meaning of Genesis*, in which he described the aerial bodies of spirits.[29] Menghi took the medieval Franciscan tradition concerning demonic corporality to its ultimate conclusion, free this time from any obvious debt to Aristotelian philosophy.

Menghi's works were produced in pocket versions, 'ideal for itinerant lay and ordained exorcists',[30] but the ready availability of his manuals also allowed for their creative use by clergy and laity alike. The absence of a single accepted rite of exorcism for the whole church, and the ignorance of many of the laity, was certainly a factor that enabled the sexual abuse of demoniacs in Modena in the 1580s.[31] Giovanni Romeo has demonstrated that exorcists were prosecuted for conducting 'Menghian' exorcisms using suffumigations of roots and herbs as early as 1590,[32] and soon the exorcisms were being used as grimoires for finding treasure and curing impotency.[33] In 1643 a monk named Zorzi used the *Flagellum daemonum* to conjure up demons and create talismans for gambling.[34] This was no accident, since exorcists deployed methods strikingly similar to those of

---

[28] On Menghi's apocalypticism see Clark, S., *Thinking with Demons* (Oxford: Clarendon 1997), p. 409. On Menghi's life and influence see M. R. O'Neill, 'Discerning Superstition: Popular Errors and Orthodox Response in Late Sixteenth-Century Italy', unpublished PhD thesis, Stanford University, 1981; Romeo (1990), pp. 114–44; Sluhovsky (2007), pp. 78–87; Probst, M., *Besessenheit, Zauberei und ihre Heilmittel: Dokumentation und Untersuchungen von Exorcismushandbüchern des Girolamo Menghi (1523–1609) und des Maximilian von Eynatten (1574/75–1631)* (Münster: Aschendorff, 2008).

[29] Menghi, G., *Compendio dell'arte essorcistica* (Venice, 1605), p. 24. See Augustine, *De Genesi ad litteram* (PL 34.284). On Menghi's demonology see Maggi (2001), pp. 104–36; Maggi, A., *In the Company of Demons: Unnatural Beings, Love, and Identity in the Italian Renaissance* (Chicago, IL: University of Chicago Press, 2006), pp. 1–5.

[30] Sluhovsky (2007), p. 45.

[31] On sexual and physical abuse by early modern exorcists see ibid. pp. 45–9; 68–9.

[32] Romeo (1990), pp. 145–68.

[33] Thorndike, L., *A History of Magic and Experimental Science* (New York: Columbia University Press, 1923–58), vol. 6, pp. 556–9; Sluhovsky (2007), p. 78; Gentilcore (1992), pp. 107–11.

[34] Barbierato, F., 'Magical Literature and the Venice Inquisition from the Sixteenth to the Eighteenth Centuries' in Gilly, C. and Van Heertum C. (eds), *Magia, Alchimia, Scienza dal'400 al'700; l'influsso di Ermete Trismegisto* (Florence: Centro Di, 2002), pp. 159–75, at p. 160.

magicians. Pietro Antonio Stampa's *Fuga Satanae* ('Flight of Satan') advised that an individual under the oppression of witchcraft might speak the name of the offending demon, in which case the name should be written on a piece of paper and burned. Stampa then instructed[35]:

> Prepare two images, the one beneath the image of a demon with its name; the other the ill-wishing person whom the demon has used in this witchcraft. In putting this together, add some name to it such as 'diviner', 'sorcerer', 'magician', 'witch' or something similar.

The constraint of spirits by ritual burning of their names or images was as old as the Greek Magical Papyri and featured in magical texts like the *Key of Solomon*.[36] Counter-magic was still magic, and little other than holy orders distinguished exorcists from lay 'magicians' such as Johann Weiss, the son of a Bavarian priest who believed that he could free people from being possessed by spirits from purgatory in 1579.[37]

Exorcism, Witchcraft and Haunted Houses: Stampa's Fuga Satanae (1597)

In 1608 the Cologne printer Lazarus Zetzner collected the major works of the Franciscan exorcists in a single volume, *Thesaurus exorcismorum* ('Treasury of Exorcisms'),[38] which included the *Practica exorcistarum* ('Practices of the Exorcists', 1585) and *Dispersio daemonum* ('Dispersal of Demons', 1587) of Valerio Polidori of Padua,[39] Menghi's

---

[35] Stampa, P. A., *Fuga Satanae* in *Thesaurus Exorcismorum* (Cologne 1608), pp. 1245–6: *Praepara duas imagines, alteram sub effigie daemonis cum nomine: alteram, quae personam maleficam, quam daemon usus est, in illo maleficio. Componendo, cui adde nomen aliquod, ut v. g. Pytho, maleficus, magus; strigha, vel aliquod simile.*

[36] Butler, E. M., *Ritual Magic* (Cambridge: Cambridge University Press, 1949), p. 58.

[37] Lederer, D., *Madness, Religion and the State in Early Modern Europe: A Bavarian Beacon* (Cambridge: Cambridge University Press, 2006), pp. 216–18. In his analysis of early modern Bavarian exorcisms, Lederer has demonstrated that the authorities in southern Germany were determined to control exorcism, occasionally prosecuting unlicensed exorcists and sending demoniacs to designated shrines such as the shrine of St Anastasia at Benediktbeuern. Furthermore, in one case the secular authorities undermined the clergy by licensing a female lay exorcist, Rosina Huber, who worked for prominent families in Bavaria throughout the 1650s (see Lederer (2005), pp. 213–31).

[38] For detailed studies of the *Thesaurus* see Maggi (2001) and Kallendorff (2005).

[39] *Thesaurus exorcismarum* (Cologne 1608), pp. 1–196, 197–284.

Flagellum and *Fustis*,[40] Zaccaria Visconti's *Complementum artis exorcisticae* ('Complement to the Exorcist's Art', 1589)[41] and Stampa's *Fuga Satanae* ('Flight of Satan', 1597).[42] These exorcistic works shared many similarities, and all were preoccupied with witchcraft. The latest of them, Stampa's *Fuga*, which was the product of twenty years of intensive writing on exorcism by professional demonologists, will be examined here as just one example of the genre. Stampa's approach to exorcism was superficially liturgical but not truly grounded in liturgical tradition. In its merging of exorcism, counter-witchcraft and apotropaic practices, Stampa's approach comes closer to contemporary 'deliverance ministry' (discussed in Chap. 8) than the liturgical exorcisms of the *Rituale Romanum*.

Stampa's initial liturgy consisted of twelve stages, combining theological instruction with deprecatory and imperative exorcisms. These included an 'Exposition of the deceits of the devil' (*Exponuntur insidiae diaboli*),[43] 'Preparation of the exorcist' (*Praeparatio exorcistae*),[44] 'Imprecation against the demons and their co-workers' (*Imprecatio in Daemones, & cooperantes*)[45] and a list of 'Commands to be made to devils' (*Praeceptum Diabolis faciendum*).[46] At no point in Stampa's liturgy did the exorcist use any of the ancient rites of exorcism. Stampa advised that the exorcist should omit the first ten stages if the demoniac was 'potentially' (*potestative*) possessed, a state akin to obsession, or possessed 'by witchcraft alone' (*per sola maleficia*), rather than 'actually' (*praesentialiter*) possessed.[47] The next seven sections of the exorcisms were devoted entirely to dealing with witchcraft, and included 'Breaking witchcrafts' (*Solutio Maleficiorum*),[48] a 'Method of burning instruments of witchcraft' (*Modus comburendi*

---

[40] Ibid. pp. 285–526, 527–756.
[41] Ibid. pp. 757–1192.
[42] Ibid. pp. 1193–1272.
[43] Ibid. pp. 1202–4.
[44] Ibid. pp. 1218–21.
[45] Ibid. pp. 1221–5.
[46] Ibid. pp. 1226–9 (this section included the *Praecipio tibi*).
[47] Ibid. p. 1225.
[48] Ibid. pp. 1230–2: *Deus qui Beato Petro Apostoli tuo collatis clavib[us] regni coelestis, animas ligandi, atq[ue] solvendi Pontificium tradidisti concede: Ut intercessionis ejus auxilio a peccatorum nexibus, & diabolicis vinculis hic famulus tuus N. liberetur. Per eum qui est morti mors, et inferno morsus, & qui cum Patre, & Spiritu sancto venturus est judicare saeculum per ignem.*

instrumenta Maleficialia),[49] 'Suffumigation of a person oppressed by the devil' (*Suffumigatio ... personae a Diabolo oppressae*),[50] and a rite for 'Burning of the written names and images of demons' (*Dominis* [sic. for *Nominis*] *scripti, et imaginis daemonis combustio*).[51]

Stampa included a section on 'the use of the stole, concerning the means of binding the stole to the neck of the sufferer' (*Usus stolae de modo ligandi Stolam ad collum patientis*),[52] which involved creating an invisible spiritual bond by tying knots in the stole, a clear example of counter-witchcraft. Furthermore, he added an 'exorcism of any object', a blessing of candles and a 'blessing of a house from Satan' (*Satanae benedictio domus*) that included some exorcistic and apotropaic elements.[53] The priest pronounced the usual exorcisms of water and salt, and sprinkled the house with holy water, then a series of deprecatory exorcisms implored God to protect the house's inhabitants from 'all hidden traps of the enemy' (*omnes insidiae latentis inimici*), but this was understood in very general terms. For instance, the priest prayed against 'the spirit of pestilence' (*spiritus pestilens*) and 'the corrupting atmosphere' (*aura corrumpens*).[54] The exorcism was thus an ecclesiastical disinfectant against natural hazards that might or might not be the direct work of the devil, rather than an exorcism proper. The rite concluded with the placing of an apotropaic amulet in the house, a wax cross inscribed with the words *Vicit leo de tribu Juda radix David. Fugite partes adversae.*

Preoccupation with witchcraft was not a new element in exorcism, but the idea of exorcizing a domestic space was distinctive to the sixteenth century. Timothy Chesters has argued that the trope of the haunted house was an invention of the Swiss Protestant theologian Ludwig Lavater (1527–86), who presented the house haunted by noisy spirits as the theatre of an ideological battle in which Protestants attempted to

---

[49] Ibid. pp. 1238–44: This, the most elaborate part of the whole exorcism, required the priest to prepare sulphur and pitch, which were set alongside the instruments of witchcraft. After a series of readings, prayers and addresses to the demons, the priest blessed a fire with holy water and then threw the sulphur and pitch into the fire, each action being accompanied by a distinct prayer. Finally the priest threw the instruments of witchcraft themselves into the fire.
[50] Ibid. pp. 1244–5 (for the sick).
[51] Ibid. pp. 1245–6.
[52] Ibid. pp. 1268–72.
[53] Ibid. pp. 1253–64.
[54] Ibid. p. 1257.

seize spiritual control of domestic space.⁵⁵ It was in response to Lavater that the Jesuit Peter Thyraeus first addressed the problem of haunted houses from a Catholic perspective. Thyraeus provided a rite for the exorcism of buildings in his *Locis infestis* (1604), including invocations of God, the Virgin Mary and all the saints, the recitation of the gradual psalms, the reading of a portion of St John's Gospel, and the use of incense.⁵⁶ Exorcisms of houses even made it into more official liturgies: one Spanish edition of the *Rituale Romanum* (1631) included a rite entitled *Exorcismus domus a daemonio vexatae* ('Exorcism of a house troubled by a demon').⁵⁷ Regular exorcism of buildings is one legacy of the Counter-Reformation that is still very much alive.

Dominicans and Jesuits

In contrast to Franciscans like Menghi, the Spanish Dominicans, who effectively ran the Spanish Inquisition and dominated the church in Spain and its territories, were deeply suspicious of the new vogue for exorcism. In Italy outside the Kingdom of Naples, where the Sacred Congregation of the Holy Office carried out the duties of the Inquisition, the persistent attention paid to abusive and disobedient exorcists meant that inquisitors and exorcists were almost always at odds. Pope Sixtus V's bull *Coeli et terrae* (5 January 1586) urged the suppression of witchcraft and drew attention to demoniacs as potential witches: 'Even in the bodies of obsessed, distracted and mad women the demons search out future or hidden things, so that vain and lying replies might be returned by those whom the Lord in the Gospel commanded to be silent'.⁵⁸ The implication

---

⁵⁵ For Lavater's condemnation of Catholic teachings on apparitions of the dead see Lavater, L., *De spectris, lemuribus et magnis insolitis fragoribus* (Leiden, 1659 [1570]), pp. 111–23. On Lavater see Chesters, T., *Ghost Stories in Late Renaissance France* (Oxford: Oxford University Press, 2011), pp. 77–83.

⁵⁶ Thyraeus, P., *Benedictio domus novae aut daemonibus infestae* in *Daemoniaci cum locis infestis et terriculamentis nocturnis* (Cologne 1604), pp. 242–54.

⁵⁷ For a translation of this rite see, 'Appendix: The Exorcism of Haunted Houses' in Thurston, H. (ed. J. H. Crehan), *Ghosts and Poltergeists* (London: Burns and Oates, 1953), pp. 204–8.

⁵⁸ *Bullarum diplomatum et privilegiorum sanctorum Romanorum Pontificium Taurinensis editio* (Turin: A. Vecco, 1863), vol. 6, pp. 648–9: *Etiam in corporibus obsessis vel lymphaticis et fanaticis mulieribus daemones de futuris vel occultis rebus aut factis exquirunt, ut merito ab eis, quos Dominus in Evangelio tacere imperavit, vanas mendacesque referent responsiones.*

for exorcists was clear: by giving a voice to demoniacs through elaborate conjurations, they were potential enablers of witchcraft.

Between 1575 and 1579 the Dominican Alonso de la Fuente attempted to persuade King Phillip II and the Inquisition that he had discovered a sect in Extremadura and western Andalusia known as the *alumbrados*, who made pacts with the devil under the cover of enthusiastic spirituality.[59] According to Fray Alonso the *alumbrados* were then 'exorcized' by Jesuits who were really Satan-worshippers. The Inquisition eventually investigated *alumbradismo*, but on account of allegations of improper sexual conduct between priests and devout laywomen rather than because they suspected Satanic activity. Witchcraft was never mentioned in the official indictments of the *alumbrados*,[60] and although a woman who demonstrated super-human agility by climbing into a pulpit was whipped for her defiance of the Inquisition, she was neither exorcized nor accused of witchcraft.[61] Fray Alonso continued his campaign, driven partly by paranoia and partly by hostility to the Jesuits, but the Jesuits had powerful supporters and Alonso was silenced, at least briefly.[62]

Fray Alonso's accusations may be seen as just one skirmish in an ongoing struggle for spiritual supremacy in Spanish territories between the Dominicans and Jesuits, which expressed itself in demonological disagreements. Acceptance of the total reality of witchcraft remained controversial in many parts of Catholic Europe. Whilst Toby Green has interpreted the Spanish Inquisition's apparent reluctance to go after witches as a historical accident—there were other scapegoats readily available in the Iberian peninsula—for Julio Caro Baroja, the diversity of opinions amongst theologians is evidence of rivalry between the Jesuits and Dominicans.[63] Where the Dominicans were determined to uphold a demonological 'realism' concerning physical manifestations of the devil derived from the *Malleus*,

---

[59] On Fray Alonso see Weber, A., 'Demonizing Ecstasy: Alonso de la Fuente and the Alumbrados of Extremadura' in Boenig, R. (ed.), *The Mystical Gesture: Essays on Medieval and Early Modern Spiritual Culture in Honor of Mary E. Giles* (Aldershot: Ashgate, 2000), pp. 141–58; Weber, A., 'The Inquisitor, the Flesh, and the Devil: Alumbradismo and Demon Possession' in De Waardt et al. (2005), pp. 177–89.

[60] Weber (2005), p. 182.

[61] Ibid. p. 180.

[62] Ibid. p. 185.

[63] Green, T., *Inquisition: The Reign of Fear*, 2nd edn (London: Pan MacMillan, 2008), pp. 9–10; Baroja, J. C., 'Witchcraft and Catholic Theology' in Ankarloo, B. and Henningsen, G. (eds), *Early Modern European Witchcraft: Centres and Peripheries* (Oxford: Oxford University Press, 1990), pp. 19–43, at pp. 40–2.

Jesuits tended to take a more sceptical approach. For instance, in the 1660s the Bavarian Jesuit Bernhard Frey strictly applied the diagnostic criteria of the *Rituale Romanum* and spoke against witchcraft, arguing that the defence of insanity should be accepted by the courts and that 'demoniacs' should be remanded to hospitals for the insane.[64]

The development of late Scholastic philosophy was also a determining factor in attitudes to demonology. Francisco Suárez (1548–1617), the leading Jesuit philosopher of the Counter-Reformation, explored the problems of demonic locality and activity in his treatise *De malis angelis* ('On the Evil Angels'). Whilst Suárez considered that the entry of the Gerasene demoniac's demons into the pigs demonstrated 'that some demons were turned out into the air' (*Quod aliqui daemones in hoc aere versentur*) and therefore occupied physical space in the natural world,[65] he was reluctant to accept without reservation the idea that demons could range through the world unchecked. In answer to the question 'Whether the liberty of demons to wander should endure even under the law of grace?' (*an ... daemonum vagandi libertas duret etiam in lege gratia*), Suárez concluded[66]:

> It is very certain that even now a multitude of demons has been turned out into the air; for the demons trouble men, even the faithful, and therefore the obsessed are exorcized by the Church. It must be said that a demon cannot be said to be bound as to being held personally in a certain place, but insofar as it has the use of the power to tempt men ... not because they are not permitted to tempt or trouble men everywhere, for the opposite is true (as I have said), but because they are not permitted to tempt as much as they desire and are able, nor as much as they were accustomed before the coming of Christ. And they are greatly bound in this way with respect to Christians and the members of Christ's Church, especially the predestined, as Augustine holds.

---

[64] Lederer (2005), pp. 224–7.
[65] Suárez, F., *De malis angelis* 16.29, in *Opera omnia* (Paris: Vivès, 1856), vol. 2, p. 1066.
[66] Ibid. 18.7 (pp. 1066–7): *Certissimum est, etiam nunc daemonum multitudinem in hoc aere versari; nam ... nunc etiam daemones vexant homines, etiam fideles, et ideo ab Ecclesia obsessi exorcizantur. Dicendum est, daemonem non dici ligari quoad detentionem personae in certo loco, sed quoad usum potestatis tentandi homines ... non quod omnino non sinantur homines tentare, aut vexare, contrarium enim constat (ut dixi), sed quia non permittuntur tentare quantum possunt et cupiunt, nec quantum ante Adventum Christi solebant. Maximeque ligati sunt hoc modo respectu Christianorum et membrorum Ecclesiae Christi, et praesertim praedestinatorum, ut vult Augustinus.*

Indeed, Suárez went even further in restricting the activity of demons: 'The power of demons would seem to have been bound, not only with respect to the predestined after the coming of Christ, but even before, on account of the foreseen merits of Christ; for it was never permitted to a demon to tempt the elect'. Furthermore, contemporary non-believers also enjoyed the benefit of Christ's 'foreseen merits' as protection against demons.[67] Most significantly of all, Suárez made clear that Satan himself was literally bound in the abyss of hell and would not be released until the coming of Antichrist.[68] Therefore, although the demons who escaped into the air at the time of their fall had the power to possess human beings, no-one could be possessed by the devil himself. Suárez never addressed the subject of exorcism explicitly, and he may not have realized the consequences of his claim that diabolic, as opposed to demonic possession, was impossible. An obvious question that arises from Suárez's view concerns the ancient formulae of exorcism: if Satan is incapable of possessing a human being, why is it Satan who is directly addressed by the exorcist?

Other Jesuits were more explicitly critical of contemporary approaches to exorcism. The Spanish Jesuit Martín Del Rio (or Delrio), an influential writer on magic, witchcraft and exorcism, condemned Menghi's suffumigations on the grounds that no physical thing could have power over an immaterial substance.[69] Lynn Martin has argued that French Jesuits were especially reluctant to make use of 'the official magic of the Catholic church',[70] and Thyraeus rejected twelve of the accepted signs of possession as unreliable.[71] Nevertheless, there was a diversity of views amongst Jesuits and few adopted as stringently sceptical an approach to exorcism as Frey. Instead, they avoided the epistemological questions thrown up by the rite of exorcism by using other sacramentals such as holy water blessed in the name of St Ignatius, Agnus Deis, relics of Jesuit saints such as St Francis

---

[67] Suárez, *De malis angelis* 18.8: *non solum videtur ligata potestas daemonum respectu praedestinatorum post Christi adventum, sed etiam antea, propter Christi merita praevisa; nunquam enim permissus est daemon ita electos tentare.*

[68] Suárez, *De malis angelis* 18.9–10.

[69] Del Rio (2000 [1595]), pp. 115–16. On Del Rio see now Machielsen, J., *Martin Delrio: Demonology and Scholarship in the Counter-Reformation* (Oxford: British Academy, 2015).

[70] Martin, A. L., *The Jesuit Mind: The Mentality of an Elite in Early Modern France* (Ithaca, NY: Cornell University Press, 1988), pp. 136–40.

[71] Kelly (1968), p. 87. On Thyraeus see Lederer (2005), p. 221.

Xavier and consecrated oils and medals.[72] These, if successful, proved that an individual had been under demonic influence, whilst simultaneously promoting Jesuit saints and the Jesuits' generous view of the efficacy of means of grace.

THE LITURGICAL REFORM OF 1614

The *Rituale Romanum* of the Council of Trent, which contained the liturgy of the sacraments of baptism, confession, extreme unction and matrimony as well as the approved blessings and exorcisms of the church, was the last of the Tridentine liturgical books to be published. Its immediate predecessors were Alberto Castellani's *Liber sacerdotalis* (1523), Francesco Samarini's *Sacerdotale* (1579) and Cardinal Santori's *Rituale* (1584). Santori, who was asked by Pope Gregory XIII to begin drafting a new *Rituale Romanum* for the Council in 1584, completed a rite of exorcism based not on the work of contemporary Italian exorcists such as Menghi, but on the most ancient available sacramentaries. For his instructions on the diagnosis of possession Santori relied on Castellani.[73] The historical significance of Santori's decision to ignore the contemporary vogue for exorcism by grounding his liturgy in the language of *Ordo Romanus XI* and the Gelasian Sacramentary cannot be overemphasized. By doing so he eventually transformed official Catholic attitudes to exorcism, turning it from a common event into an exceptional procedure strictly governed by canon.

The 1614 rite was simultaneously liturgical and unusually flexible and open-ended, since the length of time taken by an exorcism could vary. Indeed, the rite was a balance between two extremes: the complete 'sacramentalization' of exorcism as an infallibly effective set of words, and

---

[72] See, for example, the exorcism of Anna de la Haye performed by Jesuits in Bavaria in 1664 (Johnson, T., 'Besessenheit, Heiligkeit und Jesuitspiritualität' in De Waardt et al. (2005), pp. 234–47). On the Jesuit approach to exorcism see also De Waardt (2009), pp. 344–59; Young (2013), pp. 203–9.

[73] Santori, G. A., *Rituale sacramentorum Romanum Gregorii XIII Pont. Max. iussu editum* (Rome, 1584), pp. 672–712. On the development of the *Rituale* of 1614 see Sodi, M. and Flores Arcas, J. J., 'Introduzione' in *Rituale Romanum Editio Princeps (1614)*, Monumenta Liturgica Concilii Tridentini 5 (Vatican City: Libreria Editrice Vaticana, 2004), pp. xxxvi–xlii; Haag, H., *Teufelsglaube* (Tübingen: Katzmann, 1974), pp. 391–439; Dondelinger-Mandy, P., 'Le rituel des exorcismes dans le *Rituale Romanum* de 1614', *Le Maison-Dieu* 183/184 (1990), pp. 99–121; Sluhovsky (2007), pp. 87–8.

a charismatic process whose shape was to be determined entirely by the exorcist. The instructions prefaced to the rite acknowledged the usefulness of both authority and experience when they suggested that the 'priest, or other legitimate minister of the Church ... should study to acquire knowledge from approved authors and from practice'.[74] Sluhovsky has argued that the rite of 1614 led to a 'quasi-sacramental approach',[75] while Ferber has drawn attention to a paradox inherent in the sacramentalization of exorcism. The order of exorcist was one of the lowest of the clergy, and exorcism did not require a priest in Canon Law, yet sixteenth-century exorcisms became a proving ground for priestly authority, not least because the consecrated host was often involved. However, unlike the mass, a successful exorcism reflected the holiness of the exorcist, meaning that exorcism became nothing less than a 'super-sacrament', something suitable only for the most heroic priests to attempt. Exorcism thus served to distinguish the 'best' priests from those less worthy, and in the case of Louis Gaufridy, it even allowed a priest to be designated a magician by his confreres.[76]

If the consolidation of the rite in 1614 did indeed create a 'super-sacrament', this does not seem to have been the intention of its authors. The rite retained a careful balance between scepticism and credulity: 'Let [the exorcist] not easily believe that someone is obsessed by the devil; but let him have those known signs, by which a person obsessed shall be distinguished from those who labour under an atrabilious or some other sickness'.[77] These signs were speaking an unknown language 'in many words' (*pluribus verbis*) or understanding one, the ability to make known distant and unknown things, and a person's manifestation of strength 'beyond his age or natural condition' (*supra aetatis, seu conditionis naturam*). The strict application of these criteria in the eighteenth century, when church authorities veered towards scepticism, made exorcism almost impossible.

On the other hand, the exorcist was warned that demons sometimes hid themselves, or pretended to leave the demoniac; they might even mimic the symptoms of natural illness. Clearly, such warnings would have the effect of encouraging the exorcist to persist even when a person did not show obvious signs of possession. The rite of 1614 did not assume that all

---

[74] RR 861–2: *Sacerdos, seu quis alius legitimus Ecclesiae minister ... ex probatis auctoribus, & ex usu nosse studeat.*
[75] Sluhovsky (2007), pp. 88–9.
[76] Ferber (2004), pp. 63–9.
[77] RR 863: *In primis, ne facile credat, aliquem a daemone obsessum esse; sed nota habeat ea signa, quibus obsessus disgnoscitur ab iis, qui vel atra bile, vel morbo alio laborant.*

possessions were the result of witchcraft, but it did endorse the prevailing view that a witch could bring about possession by means of instruments of witchcraft.[78] Here lay one of the rite's 'loopholes'[79]; it instructed that instruments of witchcraft should be destroyed, but did not provide a liturgical context in which this could take place:

> And he should command the demon to say whether it is held in that body on account of any work of magic, or by an image or instrument of witchcraft, which if the obsessed person received by his mouth, he should vomit; or if there should be anything outside the body, it should reveal it, and having been found it should be burnt.

Nevertheless, the rite also restricted the curiosity of the exorcist to asking for the demon's name and the time of its departure, and insisted that the demoniac should be involved in the process as well, through fasting, confession and communion.[80] The instructions stipulating that, under normal circumstances, the exorcism should take place in a church and that there should be witnesses present at exorcisms of women were genuinely intended to prevent abuse.[81] However, since the majority of demoniacs were women, this also gave a licence for exorcisms to become events with lay spectators. The recommendation that the exorcism should take place after mass linked exorcism to the supreme liturgical act of Counter-Reformation Catholicism,[82] although it is unclear how often this stipulation was followed.

The rite began with responses and deprecatory prayers before the first imperative exorcism, the *Praecipio tibi* (RR 887), followed by a selection of New Testament readings: Jesus' commission to the disciples in Mark 16 ('In my name they will cast out demons'), the return of the seventy-two disciples in Luke 10, and Jesus' response to the accusation that he cast out devils by Beelzebub in Luke 11 (*RR* 889–91). Further deprecatory prayers followed before the second imperative exorcism, *Exorcizo te, immundissime spiritus* (*RR* 896–97), and the ancient deprecatory

---

[78] *RR* 879: *Iubeatque daemonem dicere, an detineatur in illo corpore ob aliquam operam magicam, aut malefica signa, vel instrumenta, quae si obsessus ore sumpserit, evomat; vel si alibi extra corpus fuerint, ea revelet, & inventa comburantur.*
[79] Ferber (2004), p. 12.
[80] *RR* 873, 871.
[81] *RR* 870, 878.
[82] *RR* 881.

exorcism *Deus conditor* (*RR* 898–99), which included the signing of the demoniac's breast with the cross. The three-fold great adjurations followed, punctuated by the ancient prayer *Deus caeli* (*RR* 900–904). The final adjuration constituted the climax of the rite; all that followed was optional material that might be 'said devoutly over the obsessed' (*super obsessum devote dicere*). This included the Magnificat, the Apostles' Creed, the Athanasian Creed, and Psalms 90, 67, 69, 53, 117, 34, 30, 21, 3, 10 and 12.

The 1614 rite remained the Catholic church's official liturgy until January 1999, making it the longest-lived of all Tridentine liturgies; vernacular versions were never authorized. The rite was simple and flexible, embodying the Renaissance humanist antiquarian concern for ancient texts and Trent's spirit of reform and sympathy for the simplification of rites. Erik Midelfort has argued that the *Rituale* advanced a markedly sceptical view of possession for its time; in contrast to Menghi, who acknowledged that some cases of possession might be natural illness, the *Rituale* insisted that 'every phenomenon was to be considered natural unless it was obviously supernatural', making possession a kind of 'negative miracle' that was extremely difficult to prove.[83] Midelfort rightly acknowledged that the doctrine of the *Rituale* was not fully accepted by most clergy until the eighteenth century, but the epistemological implications of the *Rituale*'s prescriptions did begin to be felt in the seventeenth century.

Kelly expressed the view that 'Overall the instructions [in the 1614] rite achieved their desired effect of decreasing the irresponsible and incendiary use of exorcism'.[84] If this was true over the four centuries in which the *Rituale* remained in use, it was certainly not true of the rite's immediate impact. In the first four decades of the seventeenth century the 'exorcism industry' showed little sign of slowing down, and it was up to individual bishops whether priests in their diocese made use of the *Rituale* or some other text. In the case of the regular clergy, it was difficult for the bishop to influence their activities anyway. As late as 1639 the Theatine Canon Hilario Nicuesa published his *Exorcismarium*, a series of elaborate liturgical exorcisms to be used on appropriate feast days throughout the year, emphasizing the everyday nature of exorcism.[85]

---

[83] Midelfort, H. C. E., 'Natur und Besessenheit: Natürliche Erklärungen für Besessenheit von der Melancholie bis Magnetismus' in De Waardt et al. (2005), pp. 73–87, at pp. 84–7.
[84] Kelly (2006), p. 306.
[85] Nicuesa (1639), pp. 1–15.

Sluhovsky has argued that, in spite of the pressure towards centralization and a uniform Roman liturgy in the aftermath of Trent, the church did not make as much effort as it might have done to enforce the *Rituale Romanum* because exorcism was both 'messy' and unimportant in comparison with other rites. Exorcism tainted priests, who were never quite free from the stigma of wandering friars, conjurers and lay folk-healers.[86] Exorcism was an 'intricate' business which easily slipped over into magic, or even physical and sexual abuse. However, the longevity of the 1614 rite and its extraordinary adaptability to the conditions of four succeeding centuries is testament to the skill of Santori and the other redactors. Whilst the Curia left the implementation of the new rite to individual bishops, the existence of an official rite firmly grounded in ancient liturgical tradition challenged the continued survival of unapproved quasi-magical practices and furnished bishops with an alternative with which to confront troublesome clergy.

Convent Possessions

A distinctive feature of the development of exorcism in the seventeenth century was the centrality of nuns to cases of possession, which were invariably linked with witchcraft and magic and often involved large numbers of demoniacs.[87] The earliest example of a case of this kind occurred at Aix-en-Provence in 1609, when a young Ursuline nun, Madeleine Demandolx de la Palud, blamed her possession on bewitchment by her confessor, Louis Gaufridy. Gaufridy convinced the ecclesiastical authorities of his innocence but the Dominican inquisitor Sébastien Michaelis invoked the secular authorities, in this case the Parlement of Aix, which eventually convicted Gaufridy of witchcraft and heresy, for which he was burnt at the stake. Michaelis's account of the Gaufridy trial became an influential demonological text in its own right.[88] Michaelis's preoccupation with witchcraft

---

[86] Sluhovsky (2007), pp. 91–3.

[87] On 'convent possession' see Hallett, N. (ed.), *Witchcraft, Exorcism and the Politics of Possession in a Seventeenth-Century Convent: 'How Sister Ursula was once bewitched and Sister Margaret twice'* (Aldershot: Ashgate, 2007), pp. 17–18; Sluhovsky (2007), pp. 233–64.

[88] Michaelis, S., (trans. W. B.), *The Admirable History of the Possession and Conversion of a Penitent Woman* (London, 1613), pp. 1–116. On the Gaufridy case see Marshman, M., 'Exorcism as Empowerment: A New Idiom', *Journal of Religious History* 23 (1999), pp. 265–81; Ferber (2004), pp. 70–88; Po-chia Hsia, R., *The World of Catholic Renewal, 1540–1770* (Cambridge: Cambridge University Press, 2005), pp. 155–8.

EXORCISM IN COUNTER-REFORMATION EUROPE 121

was a throwback to Sprenger and Kramer, the Dominican inquisitors of the late Middle Ages, and sat uneasily with the relative indifference shown to witchcraft and possession by the Iberian Dominicans.

Events at Aix were just the beginning. The mass possession of Ursuline nuns at Loudun in the French diocese of Poitiers between 1632 and 1638 remains the most famous case of demonic possession in Catholic history, and has become a cultural archetype through its endless reinterpretation. It was to Loudun that nineteenth-century French physicians turned to argue that possession was nothing more than mental illness (a development to be examined in Chap. 7). In the twentieth century Aldous Huxley's successful book *The Devils of Loudun* (1952) portrayed the possessions in Freudian terms as the consequence of sexual repression and inspired John Whiting's play *The Devils* (1960), which was adapted into an opera by Krzysztof Penderecki and two films, Jerzy Kawalowericz's 1961 *Matka Joanna od Aniołów* ('Mother Joanna of the Angels') and Ken Russell's notorious film *The Devils* (1971). William Friedkin even borrowed an incident from the life of Jean-Joseph Surin, the Jesuit exorcist at Loudun, for the concluding scene of *The Exorcist* (1973).

Loudun's influence extends beyond popular culture. In a curious reversal of its role in the nineteenth century as confirmation of mass hysteria, Thomas Killigrew's letter describing the nuns of Loudun was produced in an Australian court in 1993 as evidence of the reality of demonic possession.[89] Loudun represented the Baroque culmination of Counter-Reformation Europe's obsession with exorcism and possession, yet it also marked the beginning of the end for exorcism's golden age. The possessions lasted for so long and were so extensively publicized that they came under significant scrutiny, generating scepticism as well as confirming faith.

Michel de Certeau has connected the trauma of the plague which ravaged Loudun with the 'apparitions' that the nuns of the Ursuline Convent began to see on the night of 21 and 22 September 1632.[90] At first they were the ghosts of the dead, but on 7 October an apparition of a living priest, Urbain Grandier, triggered the first convulsions amongst the nuns. On 12 October Pierre Barré, a priest from Chinon regarded as an authority

---

[89] Ferber, S. and Howe, A., 'The Man who Mistook his Wife for a Devil: Exorcism, Expertise and Secularisation in a Late Twentieth-Century Australian Criminal Court' in De Waardt et al. (2005), pp. 281–92.

[90] De Certeau (1980), pp. 21, 24.

on exorcism, arrived to take charge, assisted by seven local Carmelite friars, Jean Mignon, the almoner of the convent, three Franciscans (one Observant and two Capuchins) and several other local priests.[91] By 5 October, Barré's questioning of the demoniacs had established that the possessions were the result of sorcery, and by 11 October Urbain Grandier had been denounced as the culprit.[92] The following day he was apprehended by the civil authorities, and on 24 November the Bishop of Poitiers, Henri de Chasteignier de la Rocheposay, gave his official permission for the exorcisms that were already well underway.[93]

A month later, however, new instructions arrived from the Archbishop of Bordeaux, Henri d'Escoubleau de Sourdis, who ordered that the demoniacs should be isolated and examined by Catholic doctors, watched for several days and purged; only then should subsequent supernatural phenomena be taken to confirm the diagnosis of possession.[94] The Archbishop insisted, in effect, on the rigorous application of the diagnostic criteria of the *Rituale Romanum*. De Certeau argued that the questioning of the demoniacs produced a distinctive demonic discourse in which the demons identified themselves by name and engaged in verbal jousting with the exorcist priests.[95] The *Rituale* called for knowledge of languages unknown to the demoniac, and while the demons seemed able to respond in Latin, Barré made several attempts to make the demons speak Irish (*lingua Scotica*) and Hebrew but was accused of excessive curiosity by the demons (a fault specifically condemned in the *Rituale*).[96] Soon the demons began to disobey the exorcists and assume a prophetic role, denouncing Protestants and proclaiming the truth of the Catholic faith.[97]

Loudun was a city divided; the Edict of Nantes (1598) made Loudun a 'place of safety' for the Huguenots, and they remained there in large numbers in 1632. However, throughout the first three decades of the seventeenth century Catholic clergy and religious deliberately colonized Loudun in an effort to put Catholics in the majority.[98] One of the exorcists, the Capuchin friar Tranquille, declared that the sign of the cross was

---

[91] Ibid. p. 25.
[92] Ibid. pp. 29–31.
[93] Ibid. pp. 57–8.
[94] Ibid. pp. 58–9.
[95] Ibid. pp. 60–3.
[96] Ibid. pp. 65–7.
[97] Ibid. pp. 67–8.
[98] Ibid. pp. 39–42.

insufficient to crush the head of the dragon, and only a blow from the sceptre could drive the demons away.[99] The implication was that the possessions were a punishment from God for the French monarchy's toleration of Protestantism. De Certeau argued that the exorcists at Loudun quickly lost control of the discourse of possession, which fell into the hands of the demoniacs and the citizens of Loudun. The loss of control was marked by the progressive movement of the exorcisms to ever more public places: first the room of the Prioress, Jeanne des Anges, then the Ursuline chapel, then the parish churches and finally the city's public spaces.[100]

In the early part of 1633 Grandier's trial began and the Ursuline nuns were isolated in different houses around the city.[101] Barré and Mignon were replaced as exorcists by four Capuchins.[102] The new team was the choice of the Bishop of Poitiers rather than the Archbishop of Bordeaux, and the choice of Capuchins represented a return to traditional modes of exorcism. In the spring of 1633 the exorcisms spilled onto the streets of Loudun, and it was here that they were witnessed by a number of foreign visitors including Thomas Killigrew.[103] The Capuchins elicited elaborate lists of demons from the nuns, following the pattern set by Menghi.[104] Frankfurter has argued that past and contemporary exorcistic cults tend to value 'demonic lists and hierarchies', 'in order to gain a sense of control over possession performances that could be quite disruptive', but also because 'exhaustive demonologies also provide those in the process of embracing the role of demon-possessed with a cast of characters and a script for behavior'.[105]

The Loudun exorcisms continued into the summer of 1633, and on 23 June the Capuchin Lactance suggested that they might be more successful

---

[99] *Véritable Relation des justes Procédures observées au fait de la Possession des Ursulines à Loudun et au procès de Grandier* (Paris, 1634), pp. 310–32. On the political state of Loudun see De Certeau (1980), pp. 99–114.

[100] De Certeau (1980), pp. 76–7.

[101] On Grandier's trial see ibid. pp. 81–96, 117–26.

[102] Ibid. p. 130.

[103] For the text of Killigrew's letter see Lough, J. and Crane, D. E. L., 'Thomas Killigrew and the Possessed Nuns of Loudun: the text of a letter of 1635', *Durham University Journal* 78 (1986), pp. 259–68.

[104] De Certeau (1980), pp. 135–40.

[105] Frankfurter (2008), pp. 27–8. The creation of a complete list of possessing demons formed part of the exorcism of two English Carmelite nuns, Elizabeth and Margaret Mostyn, at Lierre in 1651 (Hallett (2007), pp. 92–106). On the Lierre exorcisms see also Young (2013), pp. 209–17.

if Grandier himself performed the exorcisms. Grandier was duly produced and the demoniacs revealed more details of his initiation as a magician and went into convulsions.[106] Grandier was convicted of sorcery on 18 August and publicly executed by burning on the same day.[107] The possessions and the execution of Grandier produced an outpouring of literature in the form of books, pamphlets and ballads, peaking in 1634 after the execution and tailing off by the end of the 1630s.[108] Yet the possessions did not end with Grandier's death, and it was not long before the Jesuit Jean-Joseph Surin (1600–65) was called in as a new exorcist. Surin identified the possession of the mother superior, Jeanne des Anges, as the centre of the problem and concentrated his attention on her. The exorcism became a personal spiritual battle for Surin in which he experienced strong temptations and sought to replace the love-magic of Grandier with the love of Christ. Eventually, Surin felt such an overflow of Christ-like love for Jeanne that he wanted to share in all her sufferings, including her possession.[109] His desire was granted, and he suffered possession for the next twenty years.[110]

Surin's 'expiatory possession' was perhaps the most unusual feature of the Loudun case, and Surin was a most unusual exorcist. However, his exorcism of Jeanne des Anges belongs as much to the history of Jesuit spirituality as it does to the history of exorcism. Surin's possession was a suffering endured for Christ that enhanced his spiritual life, and his Jesuit spirituality was focused on the love of Christ and its devotional embodiment, the Sacred Heart. The Oratorian priest Jean Eudes (1601–80), who can be considered the founder of devotion to the Sacred Heart, patronized a controversial female visionary, Marie des Vallées, who was accused of being both a demoniac and a witch,[111] and by becoming possessed himself Surin was simply taking the role of confessor to a demoniac mystic one stage further.

---

[106] De Certeau (1980), pp. 158–9.
[107] On the trial and execution of Grandier see ibid. pp. 225–62.
[108] Ibid. pp. 265–75.
[109] Surin, J.-J. (ed. M. de Certeau), *Triomphe de l'Amour Divine sur les Puissances de l'Enfer* (Grenoble: J. Millon, 1990), p. 27.
[110] On Surin see De Certeau, M., *Les aventures de Jean-Joseph Surin* (Grenoble, 1990); Marin, J. M., 'A Jesuit Mystic's Feminine Melancholia: Jean-Joseph Surin SJ (1600–1665)', *Journal of Men, Masculinities and Spirituality* 1 (2007), pp. 65–76.
[111] On Marie des Vallées see Ferber (2004), pp. 127–35; Lecouturier, Y., *Sorciers, Sorcières et Possédés en Normandie: procès en sorcellerie du Moyen Âge au XVIIIe siècle* (Rennes: Editions Ouest-France, 2012), pp. 107–13.

STIRRINGS OF SCEPTICISM

Scepticism amongst Catholics concerning the reality of possession and the effectiveness (or appropriateness) of exorcism was not new to the 1630s and 1640s, at least in France.[112] As early as 1583 the Synod of Rheims, under the influence of moderate Catholics in opposition to the Catholic League, cautioned against the use of exorcism, noting that many people had more need of a physician than an exorcist,[113] and in probative exorcisms organized by Henri IV in the Marthe Brossier case, holy water was secretly administered to the supposed demoniac as an early form of 'placebo control'.[114] Focusing on the example of the sixteenth-century Dutch physician Jason van de Velde, Nadine Metzger has shown that the medical treatment of demonic possession was an established method: exorcism was not the only solution.[115] For Sluhovsky, the shift in emphasis from the therapeutic to the probative exorcism was a fundamental characteristic of early modern (as opposed to medieval) exorcism.[116] On this reading, early modern exorcism contained within itself the reason for its own decline: its purpose was to prove possession, yet it was precisely because possession was so hard to prove that the church eventually turned against exorcists in the eighteenth century.

An early indication of doubt concerning the Loudun possessions occurred in a letter of 2 August 1634 from a Loudun magistrate to Mademoiselle de la Motte Le Voyer in Paris. The magistrate described several supposed revelations from the demons, and noted that the demons were able to know the thoughts of the exorcists, 'although St Thomas and the greatest theologians hold that the devil cannot know our interior thoughts'.[117] The Aristotelian inheritance of Scholastic philosophy

---

[112] On sceptical responses to exorcism in the early seventeenth century see Pearl, J. L., 'French Catholic Demonologists and their Enemies in the Late Sixteenth and Early Seventeenth Centuries', *Church History* 52 (1983), pp. 457–67, at pp. 460–6.

[113] On the Synod of Rheims and its political implications see Pearl (1999), p. 50.

[114] Kaptchuk, T. J., Kerr, C. E. and Zanger, A., 'The Art of Medicine: Placebo Controls, Exorcisms, and the Devil', *The Lancet* 374 (October 2004), pp. 1234–5.

[115] Metzger, N., 'Incubus as an Illness: Taming the Demonic by Medical Means in Late Antiquity and Beyond' in Raiswell, R. and Dendle, P. (eds.), *The Devil in Society in Pre-Modern Europe* (Toronto: Centre for Reformation and Renaissance Studies, 2012), pp. 483–510.

[116] Sluhovsky (2007), p. 93.

[117] Quoted in De Certeau (1980), p. 214: 'Cependant saint Thomas et les plus grands théologiens tiennent que le diable ne peut connaître ce que nous pensons intérieurement'.

had always sat rather uneasily with traditional Christian beliefs about the activities of disembodied spirits on earth, and whilst Suárez's rejection of the idea of diabolic possession may not have filtered down to ordinary Catholics or even ordinary Jesuits, the philosophical idiom of late Scholasticism contained more than enough potential to cause trouble for advocates of exorcism.

A manuscript treatise on exorcism composed by a Jesuit at a college in the Loire valley, probably in the 1640s, reveals the epistemological anxieties about exorcism that beset the French church, and the Jesuits in particular, in the aftermath of the Loudun case. The author of *De sacris exorcismis*, 'G. T.', noted that several of his colleagues remembered the Loudun exorcisms.[118] The treatise took the form of a Scholastic quodlibetal disputation, with questions followed by doubts then answered by the author. G. T.'s approach challenges Sluhovsky's argument that exorcism became ever more 'sacramentalized', since the Jesuit strongly affirmed both the conditional effectiveness of exorcisms and even the possibility of lay involvement.

The first question considered, 'In what manner are demons expelled by the church by exorcisms?' (*Qualiter Exorcismis Ecllesia pellantur Daemones*), addressed a doubt concerning the efficacy of exorcism. Given that Christ gave an infallible promise, 'In my name they will cast out demons', exorcisms should always be effective if the exorcist has faith. This promise was made not only to those ordained as exorcists but to the church as a whole. However, founding ecclesiastical exorcisms on this promise of Christ was problematic, because Christ did not institute an order of exorcists: 'This power and this faith is not uniquely joined to the orders of the clergy, since thanks to given grace, it is accustomed to have been given by God even to women, [therefore] the ordinary power of our exorcists ought not to be founded proximately on this promise of Christ'.[119]

G. T. solved this problem by appealing to the distinction between sacraments and sacramentals. Sacraments, which were directly instituted by Christ himself, applied the merits of Christ to the recipients, whereas sacramentals, instituted by the church, applied the merits of the church.

---

[118] BL MS Add. 8289 fols 340r–352r.

[119] Ibid. fol. 340r: *hac potestas et hac fides non est Uni Clericorum ordinis alligata cum sit gratia gratis data solita etiam á Deo datj foeminis, non debet ordinaria potestas nostrorum Exorcistarum fundarj proximie in hac Christi promissione.*

Sacramentals were 'founded in the common treasury of merit' (*fundatum ... in communis thesauro meritorum*); in other words, Christ gave a treasury of merits to the church, and the church can apply these merits within the limits set by God, including for the purposes of exorcism.[120] However, if God should choose to make an exorcism ineffective, we cannot enquire into God's reasons or seek to restrict the freedom of divine will.[121] G. T. argued that exorcism was *ex opere operantis*, dependent on the intentions and holiness of the exorcizing priest, rather than *ex opere operato* like the mystery of transubstantiation, which even the words of the unworthiest priest could validly effect.[122] This in turn gave rise to a new doubt. If the effectiveness of exorcism depended on God's arbitrary will, then how could the use of imperative language by the exorcist, which seemed to presuppose certainty about the exorcist's power, be justified? For G. T., imperative exorcism was justified on the grounds that the church always commanded in the name of Christ; the exorcist did not command by virtue of his own authority.[123]

G. T. passed on to epistemological anxieties with the question 'Whether a demon, legitimately adjured and questioned, always gives responses of infallible truth?' (*Utrum Daemon legitime adiuratus et interrogatus det semper responsa infallibilis veritatis*). He noted that the *Rituale Romanum* gave the impression that exorcism compelled spirits to speak the truth. A demon would always lie when it spoke on its own behalf, but 'having been forced by the power of the exorcisms, it does not speak from itself or of its own accord but by the virtue of the divine name invoked by the church'.[124] Unusually, rather than advancing a theological case against this opinion, G. T. took issue with it on the grounds of personal experience, not his own but that of his fellow Jesuits, who personally witnessed the events at Loudun: 'I have taken [the story] concerning these events from many witnesses by sight and hearing with me in the college'.[125] G. T. also

---

[120] Ibid. fol. 342r. Franz (1909), vol. 1, p. 15 held a similar view in the twentieth century: 'Sacramentals are in their elements of Christ, but in their concrete identity they are founded by the Church'.
[121] BL MS Add. 8289, fol. 340v.
[122] On exorcism as *ex opere operantis* see Sluhovsky (2007), p. 69.
[123] BL MS Add. 8289, fols. 341r–v.
[124] Ibid. fol. 342v: *At coactus vi Exorcismorum non á seipso et sponte suá sed Virtute divinj nominis per Ecclesiam invocatj Loquitur.*
[125] Ibid. fols 342v–343r: *á pluribus oculatis et auritis testibus mecum in collegio de eventibus arrepi.*

cited the case of 'the energumens of Nantes', which took place on 30 January (since no date was given, this case may have occurred in the same year in which G. T. was writing).[126] G. T.'s willingness to accept personal testimony concerning the mendacity of demons represented an appeal to experience at odds with traditional Scholastic orthodoxy and betrayed his anxiety that a credulous exorcist might be misled by unscrupulous 'demoniacs'.

Having considered the question of whether demons could act as oracles of the future (which he predictably condemned as a superstitious error),[127] G. T. moved to the question 'Whether it is permitted, or not permitted, to believe the demons' responses of this kind?' (*Quatenus Licet, Vel non Licet, credere huiusmodj Daemonum responsis*). He considered two possible answers; on the one hand, by believing the replies given by demons during exorcisms, we might give honour and worship to the devil; on the other hand, to believe the demons was only to believe that the power of God compelled them to answer. G. T. proposed four guidelines for dealing with the demons' answers[128]:

1. The exorcist should never trust in the authority of demons, properly speaking, but only in God who compelled them to speak;
2. The exorcist should never take the word of demons as the sole indicator of truth;
3. If a demon should accuse someone of magic or witchcraft, this did not constitute sufficient grounds for suspicion;
4. Notes taken during an exorcism should never be used to incriminate anyone.

It is highly likely that the last two suggestions were influenced by the incrimination of Urbain Grandier by the demoniac nuns. The continuation of the possessions after Grandier's death, which might have been expected to break the original magic pact, cast some doubt on his alleged involvement in the proceedings. During the course of the seventeenth century, restrictions on using 'evidence' of crime obtained from interrogating demoniacs in several countries became increasingly stringent, and

---

[126] G. T. referred to an account of the Nantes demoniacs by Jean Guéret; I have been able to identify no published works by this author.
[127] Ibid. fols 344r–345r.
[128] Ibid. fol. 346v.

by the eighteenth century a Spanish treatise on exorcism, discussed in Chap. 6, deemed it a mortal sin to do so.

To the question 'What sort of sin is it to consult a demon concerning secret things or to learn these from it?' (*Quod qualeve peccatum est consulere Daemonem de rebus occultis vel has ib illo discere*), G. T. responded that the exorcist should force the devil to confess rather than testify, although the only apparent difference between confession and testimony was that the former was given under duress while the other was not.[129] Exorcism thus corresponded to judicial torture, recalling the language of torment favoured by the Church Fathers. The final question of the treatise considered the question 'Whether it is permitted for an exorcist to force a demon to confirm its answer by oath?' (*Liceatne Exorcistis cogere Daemonem ad confirmandu[m] Juramento suum responsum*).[130] The author noted that, although the *Rituale Romanum* made no provision for the swearing of oaths by demons, the Ambrosian Rite did allow this. The differences between the Roman and Ambrosian rites was an important one in the post-Tridentine context, since the Council suppressed all local rites in favour of the Roman rite unless, like the ancient Ambrosian rite of Milan, they were of proven antiquity. The Ambrosian rite could therefore be taken as a source of sound doctrine. However, G. T. showed once again that he erred on the side of caution by insisting that the oaths of demons could not be trusted, and no exorcist should be permitted to engage in this practice. The author's awareness of the controversial nature of this position is suggested by his choice of words: 'I dare at last to fix on this [opinion]' (*Illud ad extremum audeo hic defigere*), but his reference to demonic blasphemies suggests that, once again, he was drawing upon his colleagues' personal experience of Loudun to reach his conclusions.

Loudun was the crisis in European exorcism that, over time, served to divide Catholic opinion. It was by no means the last mass exorcism in France, as events at Louviers in Normandy were to prove between 1642 and 1647,[131] but the sceptical voices that rejected the possessions at Louviers, led by the royal physician Pierre Yvelin, were confident and

---

[129] Ibid. fols 348r–v.
[130] Ibid. fols 350r–352r.
[131] On the Louviers possessions see Ferber (2004), pp. 89–112; Lecouturier (2012), pp. 73–106.

vociferous.[132] Loudun divided French Catholics into believers, outright sceptics and a majority amongst the senior clergy for whom the excesses of the nuns were both implausible and distasteful. The manifestations of the devil at Loudun were so excessive and destructive that to reject them was not to reject Catholic truth, but rather an inflated view of the power of magic and witchcraft and an 'enthusiastic' spirituality inimical to good order within church and state. By the second half of the seventeenth century, contempt was an acceptable Catholic response to exorcists.

---

[132] On the controversy following the Louviers possessions see Lecouturier (2012), pp. 90–105.

CHAPTER 5

Catholic Exorcism Beyond Catholic Europe

Exorcism fulfilled two distinct functions in the global Counter-Reformation. For clergy in the New World, struggling to impose Christianity and colonial government (often scarcely distinguished from one another) on alien cultures, exorcism of sacred sites as places of Satanic worship and the designation of religious leaders as witches served a useful function, demonizing the traditional religions of indigenous peoples. In Protestant Europe and China, by contrast, exorcism was a tool of mission rather than cultural subjugation, demonstrating the superior authority and spiritual power of Catholic missionaries over Christians of other confessions or, in the case of China, Daoist priests and Buddhist bonzes. However, missionary environments were often far removed from church authorities, and the inevitable fusion of cultures that occurred in such environments also allowed exorcism in these jurisdictional borderlands to preserve troubling overtones of 'enthusiasm' that had largely disappeared from official practice in Catholic Europe into the eighteenth century and beyond.

The European Reformation sundered Christendom in the same century as two of the great Catholic powers, Spain and Portugal, were beginning their conquest of the New World. From the very beginning, the Catholic Counter-Reformation was an outward-looking missionary movement whose priorities included not only the re-conversion of European Protestants but also the triumph of Catholic Christianity in every corner of the globe. Spanish and Portuguese mastery of the oceans propelled the religious orders to the furthest ends of the earth, where they encountered baffling cultures and religions that challenged the European imagination as never before. At the forefront of Counter-Reformation missionary activity was the Society of Jesus, founded and organized with military discipline by Ignatius Loyola in 1534. The Jesuits' first great international missionary, Francis Xavier, travelled as far as Japan before his death off the coast of China in 1552. Xavier's ambition to evangelize China was achieved by Matteo Ricci in 1582. The mendicant orders, although older than the Jesuits, were almost as successful in adapting to the new conditions. In 1510 the Dominicans established a mission on the island of Hispaniola, the first Spanish territory of the New World, challenging the conquerors' enslavement of the natives.

The friars followed the Conquistadors into the interior of Central America, and the Observant Franciscans arrived in Mexico in 1524, retaining a dominant position in the Mexican church into the eighteenth century and beyond. In the New World, as in the Old, the differing attitudes of the religious orders towards exorcism had a profound effect on their approach to indigenous religions. Exorcism could be deployed to demonize indigenous religion, but it was also the Catholic practice most amenable to incorporation in a syncretistic marriage with indigenous belief. The isolation of Christian communities in the Americas produced eccentric forms of exorcism, yet geographical isolation was not the only factor that contributed to the individuality of exorcistic practices beyond Catholic Europe. Catholics living under Protestant regimes in England and the Low Countries were at times almost as isolated from the Catholic world as their coreligionists in China and the New World, and the purposes to which exorcism was put in these countries mirrored missionary activity much further afield. Given the centrality of mission to the Counter-Reformation, exorcism in territories beyond the heartlands of Catholic Europe should not be seen as marginal to the story of Catholic exorcism.

Exorcism as Mission

The continued existence of Catholics in Protestant territories such as England, Scotland and the Netherlands created an opportunity for better-trained Catholic clergy to return and evangelize populations with little understanding of, or sympathy for, the new religion. Since the Protestant Reformers advocated the reality of demonic attacks, yet offered no convincing remedies for them, exorcism was a unique selling-point of Catholicism that became an indispensable weapon in the arsenal of the

Counter-Reformation. In both England and the Protestant Netherlands, Catholics pointed out the new faith's failure to produce miracles. A lingering belief in the power of Catholic priests combined with a desire for protection against witchcraft created an ideal environment for Catholic exorcists.[1] Exorcism made converts, and in the sixteenth and seventeenth centuries it was a grave threat to Protestant Europe. The deployment of exorcism by Jesuits and Dominicans in China was strikingly similar to the methods of their confreres at the other end of the world. In China, as in Protestant Europe, exorcists faced a highly literate and learned elite sceptical of their efforts, combined with considerable demand from the rural population. However, while Catholic missionaries in China contended with significant challenges of cultural translation, European evangelists belonged to the same culture as their congregations and shared their preconceptions. Nevertheless, when it came to exorcism, the similarities between China and Europe are more striking than the differences.

The evidence presented in Chap. 3 demonstrates that liturgical exorcism never took hold in England before the Reformation, and therefore the idea of exorcisms performed by the exercise of priestly power rather than through the *virtus* of a saint were a novelty in post-Reformation England, even for the most steadfast of Catholics. Christopher Haigh was right to claim that 'the priest was a powerful magical figure in the popular imagination' in rural England, but exorcism should not be classed as part of the 'conservative cultural framework' of ordinary parishioners.[2] The definitive separation of Catholics from the rest of the population did not take place in England until 1559, when Queen Elizabeth I's Act of Uniformity made it illegal to refuse to attend the parish church (recusancy), where all services were performed according to the English prayer book. Catholics were forced to choose between deliberate defiance of the law, exile and a range of compromises. Church attendance for the sake of evading fines and imprisonment was strenuously condemned by the leaders of the English Catholic community in exile, and in 1570 the first priests trained in a seminary modelled on the decrees of Trent returned to England; they were soon followed by the first English Jesuits and representatives of other religious orders. These priests incurred the death penalty for treason

---

[1] Thomas (1991), pp. 586–7.
[2] Haigh, C., 'The Continuity of Catholicism in the English Reformation' in Haigh (ed.), *The English Reformation Revised* (Cambridge: Cambridge University Press, 1987), pp. 176–208, at pp. 206–7.

just by setting foot in England, and for this reason the evidence for their activities presents the historian with particular challenges. Although it was in their interest to report their successes, including exorcisms, it was often impossible for Catholic missionaries to offer any details of the exorcisms they performed.

Whilst it is possible that some priests made use of Cardinal Santori's sacramentary (1584) and the *Rituale Romanum* after 1614, the liturgical manuals produced for the English mission in the seventeenth century perpetuated the ceremonies of the medieval Sarum Rite and did not include a rite of exorcism. The first of these manuals was published by Laurence Kellam at Douai and was printed in 1604 and again in 1610.[3] It contained rites for baptism, matrimony, confession, extreme unction and burial. The annotations to the rite of baptism advised that even if a child had been baptized by a layperson in the absence of a priest (which was not an uncommon occurrence if a child's life was thought to be in danger), the exorcisms should be said subsequently by a priest. Unlike Archbishop Pecham in the thirteenth century, Kellam offered a theological justification of this practice derived from his interpretation of Augustine[4]:

> If the infant was previously baptized, those things which are said in the prayers, adjurations or exorcisms written below concerning the grace or gift of baptism, to the fuller effect or gift, to be perceived for the rest of its life, ought to be given by the baptizer. Just as even the flight, ejection or destruction of Satan here frequently commemorated ought to be recalled little by little, to a perfect ejection and a more complete purgation.

Kellam's annotations suggest that the baptismal exorcisms were understood as a form of apotropaic protection as well as a symbolic 'commemoration' of Christ's victory over Satan, although he stopped short of any clear statement that Satan was actually expelled by baptismal exorcisms.

---

[3] For a list of post-Reformation English Rituals, see Allison, A. F. and Rogers, D. M., *A Catalogue of Catholic Books in English printed abroad or secretly in England 1558–1640* (Bognor Regis: Arundel Press, 1956), nos 717–24.

[4] Kellam, L. (ed.), *Sacra Institutio baptizandi ... iuxta usum insignis ecclesiae Sarisburiensis* (Douai, 1604), p. 169; Kellam, L. (ed.), *Manuale Sacerdotum ... iuxta usum insignis ecclesiae Sarisburiensis* (Douai, 1610), p. 274: *Si infans antea fuerit baptizatus quae in orationibus, adiurationibus, seu exorcismis infra praescriptis, de dono seu gratia Baptismi dicuntur, ad uberiorem gratiae aut doni effectum, tota vita reliqua percipiendum, a baptizante referantur. Quomodo etiam frequens ibi memorata Satanae eiectio, fuga, aut exitus referenda sunt ad perfectionem eius paulatim eiectionem, ac pleniorem purgationem.*

The testimony of printed exorcisms alone does little to reveal the history of exorcism in post-Reformation England, the evidence for which is to be found in accounts of exorcisms by both Catholics and Protestants. The study of Catholic exorcism in early modern England is fraught with difficulty, owing to the hostile or vague nature of many sources, yet the evidence strongly suggests that exorcism was a key component of Catholic missionary work in the country,[5] even if it did not always take the form of liturgical exorcism of demoniacs by a priest.

Uniquely amongst European nations, Ireland was a Catholic country under a Protestant government. Officially, Catholic worship was outlawed in Ireland for much of the early modern period, but in practice it was difficult for the Protestant 'ascendancy' to enforce measures against the Catholic clergy, and exorcism was crucial to the prestige of priests who publicly exorcized both people and animals using relics and other sacramentals. The Discalced Carmelite Steven Browne specialized in exorcizing by means of the eucharist or taking on cases that Protestants were unable to solve.[6] In the first half of the seventeenth century, failure to enforce Protestantism in large parts of Ireland led to the re-establishment of monastic life. The reacquisition of relics and buildings by Catholic clergy was a crucial component in the church's campaign to reclaim control of Ireland's sacred space, and exorcism played its part in this.[7]

In 1603 the Cistercian Abbey of Holy Cross in County Tipperary, famous for its relic of the true cross, was re-established under Abbot Richard Foulow.[8] In 1609 a woman from Callan, County Kilkenny, came to the Abbey seeking deliverance from magic spells. Foulow put a belt that had touched the relic of the cross around her waist and she vomited strange items such as cloth, wool and wood for a month.[9] Exorcisms of this kind had the potential to re-establish the restored monasteries at the centre of

---

[5] On Catholic exorcism as mission see Young, F., 'Catholic Exorcism in Early Modern England: Polemic, Propaganda and Folklore', *Recusant History* 29 (2009), pp. 487–507; Young (2013), pp. 189–229. For an alternative view of exorcism as a healing ministry see Walsham, A., 'Miracles and the Counter-Reformation Mission to England', *The Historical Journal* 46 (2003), pp. 779–815.

[6] Gillespie, R., *Devoted People: Belief and Religion in Early Modern Ireland* (Manchester: Manchester University Press, 1997), pp. 67–8.

[7] Ibid. pp. 160–1.

[8] Colmcille, Fr, 'Three Unpublished Cistercian Documents', *Journal of the County Louth Archaeological Society* 13 (1955), pp. 252–78, at p. 267.

[9] Kiely, D. M. and McKenna, C., *The Dark Sacrament: Exorcism in Modern Ireland* (Dublin: Gill and MacMillan, 2006), pp. 44–5.

their communities, as well as boosting the prestige of relics they claimed to possess and challenging Protestant claims to authority. Exorcism was also a force for the conversion of Protestants in Ireland. In April 1665 a Protestant landlord, Edmond Nangle of Cloandaragh Castle in County Longford experienced a dramatic waking vision of hell, declaring that he was surrounded by devils and speaking to them. Nangle's cousin, Garret Nangle, tied Nangle to a chair and summoned the Protestant Dean of Ardagh, John Carre. Nangle later related that he mistook Carre for the devil[10]:

> I begin to cry out against all that were about me in generall, judging them as well as Mr. Carre to be all Devils, which occasioned my couzen Garret Nangle and the rest (as well they might) to judge that I was now possessed with Devils that made me talk so, and making the tyes now again much faster on my hands, legs, and body, my couzen Nangle now and then gave me some whips on the face and breast when I begun to talk of Devils, or offer to break loose, requiring me to hold my tongue, which in truth made me now to judge that he and the rest of my friends did intend to murder me.

Garret Nangle's attempts to 'exorcize' his cousin by means of physical violence resembled Menghi's techniques, and Nangle managed to dislocate both his shoulders trying to free himself from the chair into which he was tied. In the end, however, in spite of the fact that a Catholic priest was summoned, Nangle exorcized himself. When he began to pray, 'severall bright lightenings from the Heavens ... chaced away all the diabolicall spirits that were about me, which lay numberless in my bed cloaths that were over me, and within the cushions that people laid under my head and shoulders'. Nangle then had a vision of the Virgin Mary, who completed the exorcism in a rather unexpected manner: 'through her Intercession there descends from Heaven a great number of blessed bees, which entred my belly and all my bowels, driving out as well the vermin that were in me'.

As a consequence of his visionary experience and deliverance from evil spirits by means of invisible bees sent by the Virgin Mary, Nangle converted to Catholicism. Fifteen months later, in July 1666, Edmond Nangle led two hundred men in an armed raid on Lord Aungier and his troop of horse in the town of Longford. Nangle was killed but the rest

---

[10] Nangle, E., *From Cloandaragh the First of April in the Year of our Lord God 1665* (n.p., 1665), pp. 10–11.

of the Irish attackers escaped, causing the government considerable concern.[11] Nangle, it seems, was emboldened by his experience of exorcism to embrace Catholicism and turn against the ruling class of which he himself was a member. His story is evidence that Catholic emphasis on the devil and exorcism in Ireland not only sustained the faith but empowered rebellion against authority.

The situation of Catholics in the United Provinces of the Netherlands (the Dutch Republic) paralleled that of Catholics in England and Ireland; from its independence from Spain in 1581 the Republic was officially Protestant and Catholic worship was outlawed. However, unlike England, where strong central government drove the Reformation, the Republic was a collection of provinces that enjoyed a degree of autonomy and contained significant pockets of Catholic population. Furthermore, the Republic permitted freedom of conscience and made no attempt to enforce compulsory attendance of Protestant services. In practice, if not in theory, the Dutch Republic was a more or less open religious marketplace in which Catholic clergy competed with a variety of Protestant denominations for the souls of the inhabitants.[12] Furthermore, the Republic was bordered by Catholic states and its territory fluctuated throughout the late sixteenth and seventeenth centuries, bringing more Catholics under the authority of the States General.

There is some evidence that exorcism was used by Catholics as a weapon against the Protestant authorities in the Netherlands. In 1629 the Republic acquired the city of 's-Hertogenbosch and its surrounding country, known as the Meierij, in the northeastern corner of the Duchy of Brabant, from the Spanish Netherlands. The Meierij, an area that had undergone the Counter-Reformation, was subjected to Reformation of its government (the purging of Catholics from positions of authority). Furthermore, Protestant magistrates began to claim all church property for the state. Catholics found ways to avoid this, hiding church property in private houses and setting up chapels just over the border in domains not under the jurisdiction of the Dutch States General. In 1650 a dramatic confrontation occurred at one such chapel between a Protestant bailiff, Cornelis Prouninck van Deventer, and a Catholic priest named

---

[11] O'Hara, T., 'A Vision of Hell in Early Modern Ireland', *Archivium Hibernicum* 51 (1997), pp. 87–99, at p. 87. On Nangle see also Gillespie (1997), p. 32.

[12] De Waardt, H., 'Jesuits, Propaganda and Faith Healing in the Dutch Republic', *History* 94 (2009), pp. 344–59, at pp. 345–6.

Joannes Houbraken who was in the act of exorcizing a group of demoniacs. Houbraken, enraged by the intrusion of the Protestant, declared that he would be torn to pieces by the demoniacs, although this did not happen.[13] Houbraken was a controversial figure even within the Catholic community, 'extorting' money from his congregation and denouncing the authorities in apocalyptic terms. For Marc Wingens, the powerlessness of the demoniacs to harm the Protestant bailiff reflected the political reality of Catholics in the Protestant Republic; they could make a political protest but do little else.[14]

Exorcism was originally a powerful instrument for the conversion of Dutch Protestants, but it was not long before it came to play a role in dividing Dutch Catholics. Jesuits operating in the Republic refused to recognize the Vicar Apostolic of Utrecht Sasbout Vosmeer's (1548–1614) claim to be the successor of the Bishops of Utrecht, and operated mission stations along the same lines as those in England and the Americas, which brought them into conflict with the parochial structures that Vosmeer had struggled to establish. This dispute eventually escalated to a full-blown schism in 1723, when the Old Catholic Church of Utrecht, led by the Vicar Apostolic, broke with Rome altogether. However, this jurisdictional dispute had theological overtones; the secular clergy under the authority of the Vicar Apostolic were increasingly influenced by austere Augustinian theology that emphasized the difficulty of obtaining grace from God. Whilst the label 'Jansenist' was often applied indiscriminately to anyone sceptical of the claims of Papal authority and hostile to the Jesuits, Jansenists tended towards scepticism concerning demonic possession. One of Vosmeer's successors as Vicar Apostolic, Johannes van Neercassel (d. 1663), even suggested that most demoniacs were fraudulent.[15]

Catholic exorcists in Qing dynasty China made use of exorcism in ways strikingly similar to their colleagues in England and the Netherlands. The Jesuit Matteo Ricci arrived in China in 1582 and was followed by Dominicans, although the two religious orders differed on the question of whether missionaries should adopt local dress and endorse Chinese customs such as offerings to the Emperor. Chinese religion defied the traditional European categorization as idolatry, and the self-conscious

---

[13] Wingens (2005), pp. 249–52.

[14] Ibid. p. 261. On exorcism in the Dutch Republic see also Kaplan, B. J., 'Possessed by the Devil: a very public dispute in Utrecht', *Renaissance Quarterly* 49 (1996), pp. 738–59.

[15] De Waardt (2009), p. 349.

sophistication of Chinese civilization proved a unique challenge to the missionaries. Eventually, in 1715, Pope Clement XI ruled against the Jesuits' compromise with local traditions. Deprived of their ability to conduct services in Chinese, exorcism remained one of the few practices that the clergy could use to market Christianity in eighteenth-century China.[16]

In Chinese culture, exorcisms were regularly performed as part of Buddhist and Daoist funerary rituals and supported by the state. Minor exorcisms, known as *xiaofa*, were also performed by itinerant Daoist priests and Buddhist monastics. Catholic missionaries in China, unwilling to expose themselves to the publicity generated by a large-scale, operatic exorcism of the kind performed at temples, restricted themselves to *xiaofa*. In Fujian, the Jesuits did not get involved in exorcisms, leaving this to the Dominicans.[17] In the 1650s the native Chinese priest Gregorio Luo Wenzao performed exorcisms of both people and places in direct competition with the Buddhist bonzes.[18] However, priests were few and far between, and it was unrealistic for the clergy to do anything more than initiate exorcisms that were actually performed by laypeople. As early as Ricci's mission in the 1580s, missionaries in China delegated the power of using minor exorcisms to lay catechists and members of confraternities, and this was standard practice by the eighteenth century.[19] The development was not unique to China; during the period of Dutch rule in Sri Lanka (1656–1798) there was a shortage of Catholic priests and the tradition of lay exorcism that developed continued into the nineteenth century, in spite of attempts by the church to suppress it.[20]

A Ming Fujian collection of Christian stories compiled in the 1630s or 1640s related how a man who resorted to a medium, unable to rid his house of a presence, went to his Christian neighbour who put him in touch with the Jesuit Bento de Matos (1600–52). De Matos said mass

---

[16] On the role of exorcism in the Chinese rites controversy see Mungello, D. E., *The Chinese Rites Controversy: its History and Meaning* (Nettetal: Steyler Verlag, 1994), pp. 117, 122–3.

[17] Menegon (2010), pp. 222–3. On exorcism in eighteenth-century China see also Zhang Qiong, 'About God, Demons and Miracles: The Jesuit Discourse on the Supernatural in Late Ming China', *Early Science and Medicine* 4 (1999), pp. 1–36, at pp. 6–16.

[18] Menegon (2010), p. 224.

[19] Tacchi Venturi, P., *Opere Storichi del Padre Matteo Ricci S. J.* (Macerata: Giorgetti, 1911–13), vol. 2, pp. 315, 319–20.

[20] Stirrat, R. L., *Power and Religiosity in a Post-Colonial Setting: Sinhala Catholics in Contemporary Sri Lanka* (Cambridge: Cambridge University Press, 1992), pp. 79–80.

in the house and brought holy images, holy water and candles, as well as having local Christians pray in the house. Yet the priest, unwilling to create a dependency on his power given the scarcity of clergy, did not join the people.[21] On other occasions, however, lay exorcisms were not enough. In 1676 the soldier husband of a possessed woman in Fuan took her to the shrine of the Chinese god of war, Guandi, while a local Muslim official attempted to exorcize her by marching his troops to the soldier's house and threatening the demon. The demon attacked him in the house and he fled in terror; subsequently mandarins sent written instructions to the demon to depart. The Dominican Francisco Varo reported that the demon laughed at the instructions and identified itself as a sort of 'goblin' (*duende*). A Christian neighbour then proposed that a priest might be successful, but since Varo was away the local Christians started anyway, bringing a crucifix and holy water to the house. The local communities fasted for eight days and recited litanies, but without results. Varo finally put the spirit to flight by vowing to celebrate fifteen masses in honour of St Dominic.[22]

A notable feature of exorcism accounts from China was the prevalent belief in spirits' tendency to haunt places as well as people, an aspect of Chinese belief that Thyraeus's emphasis on dealing with haunted houses equipped the priests to solve. Furthermore, in a culture where spiritual power was associated with ancestors as well as deities, spirits were often identified as the ghosts of the dead. In 1657 Victorio Riccio exorcized a house haunted by the ghost of a woman who had committed suicide after arguing with her Christian husband; the priest entered the house wearing his stole and blessed it with holy water, driving away the spirit.[23] The Dominicans adopted a more aggressive approach than the Jesuits and labelled local mediums as *hechiceros*, thus adopting the same vocabulary used against cunning-folk in Spain and local spiritual figures in the New World.[24] González de San Pedro, reluctantly acknowledging that Daoist exorcisms sometimes worked, argued that this was because the spirits were weak and had already decided to leave the body of the possessed. Only Catholic exorcists could hope to expel more powerful spirits. The success of Jesuit and Dominican exorcisms did not impress the authorities; the

---

[21] Menegon (2010), p. 222.
[22] Ibid. p. 225.
[23] Ibid. p. 224.
[24] Ibid. pp. 223–4.

Qing code condemned sorcery, and the Daoist, Buddhist and Confucian intelligentsia suspected that the friars and Jesuits were involved in magic.[25]

Eugenio Menegon's analysis of Catholic exorcisms in Fuan during the period 1697–98 has led him to the view that exorcism was strongly linked with baptism, and spirits were usually driven away when those involved accepted baptism. Amulets, blessings and confession were usually effective for those who were already baptized. In 1729 a priest successfully rid a house in Luojiaxiang of a demon by entrusting the family with an Agnus Dei and instructing them to shout an exorcistic formula. Three days later, at night, the demon announced through a young girl that he was leaving the village. The priest returned, blessed the affected houses, adjured the demon and celebrated mass. Exorcism was also linked with recovery from illness and the Dominicans especially engaged in ritual healing.[26] The evidence suggests that exorcism was one aspect of Christianity that ordinary Chinese people had little difficulty understanding. Just as in seventeenth- and eighteenth-century Sri Lanka, where Catholic missionaries from Brahmin backgrounds trained in Goa were quite at ease working with Tamil and Sinhalese demonological traditions, so in China exorcism was a point of contact between European and local beliefs.[27] Even after Clement XI's decree *Ex illa die* curtailed accommodation of Chinese culture, exorcism empowered Catholic missionaries in a context where they would otherwise have had little political influence.

Exorcism and Conquest

Michel De Certeau laid the groundwork for the classic interpretation of exorcism in the New World when he argued that the Spanish conquistadors were the analogues of European exorcists, driving out the devil by imposing colonial authority on the alien world of the Americas.[28] Whilst De Certeau's argument is supported by the close collaboration of religious and civil authorities in the ritualized destruction of indigenous sacred sites, it creates the misleading impression that liturgical exorcism on the

---

[25] Ibid. pp. 227–8.
[26] Ibid. p. 226.
[27] Županov, I. G., 'Goan Brahmins in the Land of Promise: Missionaries, Spies and Gentiles in Seventeenth- and Eighteenth-Century Sri Lanka' in Flores, J. (ed.), *Re-exploring the Links: history and constructed histories between Portugal and Sri Lanka* (Wiesbaden: Harrassowitz Verlag, 2007), pp. 171–210, at pp. 197–8.
[28] De Certeau, M., *L'Ecriture de l'Histoire* (Paris: Gallimard, 1975), pp. 243–4.

European model did not exist in the New World—or, if it did exist, that it was just a European practice transplanted into a colonial context. In fact, exorcists not only existed but flourished in the territories of Spain and Portugal, adapting their practices to suit local beliefs and circumstances. Furthermore, Stuart Clark has drawn attention to the extent to which exorcism as a response to 'idolatry' in the Americas drew on precedents from Christian antiquity.[29]

Early encounters with paganism in the age of discovery were marked by curiosity rather than hostility. In 1341, when Portuguese sailors arrived in the Canary Islands, they discovered an idol inside a small shrine and brought it back to Lisbon.[30] The Guanches of Gran Canaria were encouraged to venerate the Virgin Mary in the places where they had previously worshipped their gods, echoing an earlier practice recommended by Gregory the Great to missionaries in sixth-century England.[31] Fernando Cervantes has argued that, as a consequence of the Christian conquest of Muslim Spain and diplomatic contacts with the Mongols, a strand of 'favourable perception of non-Christians' developed in the late Middle Ages.[32] However, the discovery of the Americas and the gradual realization that this new land was not part of Asia but a 'New World' was accompanied by apocalyptic expectations that rendered it qualitatively different from previous Catholic encounters with pagan religion. The early friars regarded the discovery of the peoples of the Americas as a sign of the end of the world, permitting them to fulfil the Gospel's imperative to preach the good news to all people.[33] Furthermore, the discovery that God had permitted so many people to live without knowledge of the Gospel for centuries before the arrival of Europeans was a disquieting one.

Cervantes has argued that, given the dubious legality of the grant of the Indies to Spain by Pope Alexander VI in 1493, the primary pillar of Spain's claim to the New World was the duty of evangelizing the natives, providentially granted to Spain by God and reinforced by the burgeoning Counter-

---

[29] Clark, S., 'Magic and Witchcraft' in Molho, A., Curto, D. R. and Koniordos, N. (eds), *Finding Europe: Discourses on Margins, Communities, Images ca. 13th–ca. 18th centuries* (Oxford: Berghahn Books, 2007), pp 115–30, at pp. 118–19.

[30] Bontier, P. and Le Verrier, J., *The Canarian* (London: Hakluyt Society, 1872), p. vi.

[31] Bede, *Historia Ecclesiastica* 1.30 (*PL* 95.70C–71B).

[32] Cervantes (1994), p. 12.

[33] Weber, D. J., 'Conquistadores of the Spirit' in Katz, S. N., Murrin, J. M. and Greenberg, D., (eds), *Colonial America: Essays in Politics and Social Development* (New York: McGraw Hill, 2001), pp. 127–56, at p. 129.

Reformation. The greater the extent to which the natives could be shown to be under the dominion of Satan, the more pressing that duty was.[34] The Spanish encounter with native religions in the Americas produced heated theological debate concerning the nature of the devil's involvement. The priest and former slave owner Bartolomé de las Casas (c. 1484–1566) argued that the Indians were essentially good and advocated conversion through finding the similarities between their religious outlook and Christianity. The Conquistador Hernán Cortés, who captured the Aztec capital of Tenochtitlan, recognized that the civilizations he encountered were just as sophisticated as his own. He destroyed idols but left shrines intact, leaving the indigenous religious officials in charge of crosses and images of the Virgin Mary.[35] The cathedral church of Mexico City was eventually built on the site of one of Tenochtitlan's greatest temples.

The Spanish conquest of the Inca Empire began in 1531, led by Francisco Pizarro accompanied by the Dominican friar Vincente de Valverde. Valverde adopted a policy of destruction of religious sites, and destroyed images at the oracle-temple of Guaribilca at Xauxa in 1533.[36] The 'destructive exorcisms' pioneered by friars in the New World to designate sacred space and Christianize the sacred spaces of indigenous peoples were unprecedented in the history of exorcism in Europe. Exorcisms of place in the Americas were a meeting point between choreographed iconoclasm, sometimes involving the civil authorities as well, and spiritual cleansing performed by the clergy. Whether these rites were 'exorcisms' in the true sense is perhaps less important than the fact that the authors who recorded them regarded them as such. Unlike European exorcisms of haunted localities, they were not provoked by spectral appearances but by the fact that 'Satanic' worship had been practised on a given site.

A remnant of the Inca Empire survived in the remote Andean province of Vilcabamba and, until the Spanish conquest of this Inca state in 1572, the only Europeans in the area were two Augustinian friars, Marcos García and Diego Ortiz. Although the Incan authorities prevented them from evangelizing Vilcabamba itself, the friars established flourishing Christian communities. Ortiz embarked on an ambitious plan of iconoclasm of indigenous religious sites that involved 'exorcism by fire'. He equipped

---

[34] Cervantes (1994), pp. 8–9.
[35] Ibid. p. 11.
[36] MacCormack, S., *Religion in the Andes: Vision and Imagination in Early Colonial Peru* (Princeton, NJ: Princeton University Press, 1998), pp. 84–5.

acolytes with firewood and marched with a group of Christian converts to the great shrine of Chuquipalta, containing the sacred white rock of Yurak-Rumi. Ortiz set light to the surrounding thatched temples and 'exorcized' the rock.[37] Baltasar de Ocampo gave some indication of the methods adopted by Ortiz, recording that he 'destroyed many sanctuaries from which devils were seen to come out, unable to resist the prayers, exhortations and exorcisms offered up by the said Father, and fumigations with which he tormented and afflicted them'.[38] Ortiz's practice pre-dated Girolamo Menghi's recommendation to use noxious suffumigations to expel demons in his *Flagellum daemonum* (1577).

The isolated site of Yurak-Rumi was an easy target compared with the temples of Vilcabamba, but its destruction provoked considerable anger from Inca leaders. Ortiz successfully converted the Inca Titu Cusi to Christianity but was put to death by his brother, Tupac Amaru. In the 1630s another Augustinian, Antonio de la Calancha, argued that the Spanish were the agents of God's justice for the death of Ortiz when they destroyed Vilcabamba a year later.[39] In the 'Valladolid Controversy' concerning Spain's justification for the conquest of the New World, the humanist Juan Ginés de Sepúlveda argued that all native religion was honouring the devil, and in Peru José de Acosta defended the idea that native religion was the devil's creation. The Jesuit José Pablo de Arriaga drew up a programme for the extirpation of indigenous beliefs in the Andes by assimilating them to European preconceptions about *maleficium*.

The Inquisition in Peru applied the term *hechicería maléfica* indiscriminately to native healers, practitioners of pre-Conquest religion and those genuinely intending to curse and harm.[40] In the seventeenth century, the Inquisition repeatedly pressured Juana Icha, an Incan woman accused of worshipping the mountain deity Apo Parato, to admit to having sex with

---

[37] Hemming, J., *The Conquest of the Incas*, 2nd edn (London: Pan MacMillan, 1993), pp. 311–14.

[38] De Ocampo, B., 'Account of the Province of Vilcapampa and a Narrative of the Execution of the Inca Tupac Amaru' in Markham, C. (ed.), *History of the Incas and the Execution of the Inca Tupac Amaru* (Cambridge: Hakluyt Society, 1907), p. 233.

[39] MacCormack, S., *On the Wings of Time: Rome, the Incas, Spain, and Peru* (Princeton, NJ: Princeton University Press, 2007), pp. 60–1. On Calancha's views of demonic possession see MacCormack (1998), p. 378.

[40] Ebright, M. and Hendricks, R., *The Witches of Abiquiu: the Governor, the Priest, the Genizaro Indians, and the Devil* (Albuquerque, NM: University of New Mexico Press, 2006), pp. 163–4.

him, since this conformed to European expectations concerning demonic pacts. Furthermore, they insisted that she should confess to performing witchcraft using 'instruments', after the European pattern. However, Juana's descriptions of Apo Parato portrayed a hungry, enfeebled deity unable to grant her wishes and afraid of the Spaniards, a situation which Irene Silverblatt interpreted as a consequence of the Incans' failure to 'feed' their gods by regular worship.[41]

It would be overly simplistic to regard colonial South America as a collection of pagan societies on whom Catholic Christianity was imposed by coercion and violence, and in which any manifestation of paganism was labelled as witchcraft. Indeed, Silverblatt has argued that the Incans demonized their own gods, the *huacas*, partly because they had failed to protect them against the invaders and partly because the Incans, unable to honour the gods appropriately in the new political environment, became increasingly afraid of the vengeance they might exact.[42] Nevertheless, exorcism in the Americas frequently took on violent and oppressive overtones. In seventeenth-century Florida, priests whipped and beat newly converted native people suspected of idolatry and exorcized the churches 'to conjure and banish the devil'.[43] The devil was regularly made to confess the deceitfulness of native religion. Las Casas reported that a young Dominican, Pedro de Cordoba, exorcized a demon from a young woman in Paria. When the demon claimed that it took the souls of those who worshipped it to 'pleasant and delightful places', Cordoba forced the demon to admit that it really took their souls to hell.[44] In the early seventeenth century the Augustinian friar Ramos Gavilán proudly recorded that he forced a possessed woman to confess the deceits introduced by the devil among the native people.[45]

Clergy in the New World continued to respond to the evidence of non-Christian religion with exorcism. In 1634 Franciscan friars exorcized a boulder that used to be held in fear by people and animals, bearing 'the marks of the claws of a witch', just by saying mass over it.[46] It is

---

[41] Silverblatt, I. M., *Moon, Sun and Witches: Gender Ideologies and Class in Inca and Colonial Peru* (Princeton, NJ: Princeton University Press, 1987), pp. 184–6.

[42] Ibid. p. 194.

[43] Weber (2001), pp. 140–1.

[44] Las Casas, B. (ed. E. O'Gorman), *Apologética Historia* (Mexico City: Universidad Nacional Autónoma de México, 1967), pp. 550–1.

[45] Gavilán, R., *Historia del celebre santuario de Nuestra Señora de Copacabana* (Lima, 1621), p. 52.

[46] Simmons (1974), p. 129.

likely that the marks of claws were pre-Columbian rock art, which also provoked a witchcraft scare between 1756 and 1766 at the remote mission of Abiquiu, New Mexico, in the territory of the Genízaro Indians. This led the Franciscan friars there to exorcize sites supposedly connected with Satanic worship as well as possessed women and girls. However, the Mexican Inquisition's lack of interest in possession and exorcism frustrated the friars' attempts to have the 'witches' punished. In their analysis of the events at Abiquiu, Malcolm Ebright and Rick Hendricks designated the exorcisms of the possessed as the third phase in a process that began with complaints from one of the friars, Juan José Toledo, that he was being bewitched by Genízaros from Abiquiu. An indigenous informer then led the governor and other civil officials to sites of supposed idolatry. These sites were 'exorcized' by the combined efforts of the friars and the civil authorities, who ensured that native rock-art was erased and crosses inscribed in its place.[47] In June 1763 Toledo approached an inscribed stone wearing a surplice and stole and carrying a crucifix and holy water; he threw the stone down and it broke into pieces. The priest then exorcized the four elements and addressed Satan directly, a rite clearly taken from Menghi's *Flagellum*.[48] The possessions began the same month, when a woman named María Trujillo fainted in church at the exorcism of salt and water before mass; her symptoms steadily worsened until Toledo agreed to exorcize her in December 1763.[49]

However, more possessions followed, accompanied by unruly behaviour at mass and disrespect for Toledo's authority. In February 1764 the Governor of New Mexico, Vélez Capuchín, ordered the convening of a *junta* to discuss the possessions, without Toledo. The *junta* consisted of the Vicar General of New Mexico, Santiago Roybal, and six friars. They dealt with the exorcisms by condemning the friars, and Toledo in particular, as irresponsible; they agreed that the demoniacs were genuinely possessed but accused them of sorcery, and ordered the punishment of the demoniacs and the destruction of idolatrous sites.[50] In other words, civil punishment rather than exorcism was the best way to deal with the demoniacs of Abiquiu.

---

[47] Ebright and Hendricks (2006), p. 167.
[48] Ibid. p. 190. For the exorcism of the elements see Menghi, G., *Flagellum daemonum, seu exorcismi terribiles, potentissimi et efficaces* (Bologna, 1578), pp. 141–7.
[49] Ebright and Hendricks (2006), p. 181.
[50] Ibid. pp. 196–8.

Exorcism at the Margins

The immense size of Spanish and Portuguese territories in the New World and the vast distances between major settlements meant that, in spite of the church's best efforts, the Americas remained a frontier territory in which ecclesiastical discipline was difficult to enforce. Instead of the parish system that prevailed in Europe, the friars and Jesuits established missions in which indigenous people were permitted to live once they converted to Christianity. By the eighteenth century the challenge to the church from native religion had receded in all but remote areas like Abiquiu, yet Latin American Catholicism acquired distinctive features through its engagement with indigenous beliefs and preoccupations, such as the use of exorcism against storms.[51] As Cervantes has observed, Catholicism did not sit 'like a layer of oil' on top of indigenous beliefs, but engaged in a process of exchange and mutual influence.[52] The dominance of the Franciscans in many parts of Central and South America, combined with the conservative instincts of Spanish missionary clergy, ensured that the works and techniques of Menghi and other European exorcists of the 'golden age' remained in use in the New World long after they had fallen out of favour in Europe.

Watching over the activities of missionaries was the Inquisition, officially established in Mexico City in 1571. The Inquisition had no authority at first over the indigenous people, who were considered too new to the faith.[53] Furthermore, the Inquisition's purpose was disciplinary rather than evangelistic; to regulate the mission rather than to advance it by coercion. Indeed, one of the Inquisition's most important roles was to keep in check the spirituality and conversion methods of evangelizing clergy, and the Mexican Inquisition inherited its Spanish counterpart's coolness towards possession and exorcism. In 1613 the Mexican Inquisition concluded that the priest Alonso Hidalgo was mad after he wrote a letter claiming to be possessed by Beelzebub, who tempted him to suicidal thoughts and told him he would be damned eternally. Cervantes has argued that Hidalgo's belief that he was possessed gave him hope that his despair was external to himself, yet the Inquisition was not prepared to accept the possession hypothesis.[54]

---

[51] MacCormack (1998), p. 42.
[52] Cervantes (1994), p. 58.
[53] On the Mexican Inquisition see Behar, R., 'Sex and Sin, Witchcraft and the Devil in Late-Colonial Mexico', *American Ethnologist* 14 (1987), pp. 34–54, especially pp. 34–5.
[54] Cervantes (1994), pp. 98–102.

Although there were early cases in which the Inquisition showed an 'obsessive interest' in diabolism (especially witchcraft), by the end of the seventeenth century it was beginning to adopt a more dismissive attitude.[55] However, in 1691 exorcism came to the attention of the Inquisition once again in the town of Querétaro, northwest of Mexico City. A number of local women, influenced by the preaching of friars at the Franciscan College of Santa Cruz de Querétaro, had taken to wearing Franciscan habits. On 10 August 1691 one of the women anxiously called on Fray Pablo Sarmiento to inform him that her daughter seemed to have gone mad. Fray Pablo found that the daughter, Francisca Mejía, was dumb and her mouth so tightly sealed shut that it could be opened only by applying relics. After several exorcisms the demoniac began to speak, revealing that a confederacy of witches led by 'the mice-sucker' (*La Chuparratones*) had bewitched her and other women in the town. Fray Pablo exorcized Francisca by means of 'holy potions' taken from Menghi's *Flagellum*, as a result of which she vomited up a range of objects including avocado stones, a toad and a snake. Again, Fray Pablo followed Menghi's prescriptions and burnt these *maleficalia*.[56]

The possession spread to another woman, Juana de los Reyes, who expelled hundreds of objects from her body and a corresponding number of devils, who refused to obey on the grounds that they were forced to serve the wishes of *La Chuparratones* and the other witches.[57] The possessions spread until, in December 1691, a commissary of the Inquisition in Querétaro observed that a new demoniac came out of the Franciscan College every evening.[58] Another commissary of the Inquisition, José de Frias, referred contemptuously to the 'conjuring tricks' of the friars; the municipal magistrates adopted a similarly sceptical stance.[59] The Carmelites, Augustinians, Jesuits and Dominicans rejected the authenticity of the Querétaro possessions, revealing the tensions created by Franciscan dominance of missions in Mexico. The Carmelite Manuel de Jesús María was especially critical, arguing that the Franciscans were preaching an intense spirituality unsuitable for the Mexican women and encouraging an inappropriate familiarity between confessors and penitents.

[55] Ibid. p. 125.
[56] Ibid. p. 116.
[57] Ibid. pp. 117–18.
[58] Ibid. p. 115.
[59] Ibid. p. 119.

Fray Manuel's words did not seem unfounded; in January 1692 Juana de los Reyes gave birth to a child, giving rise to suspicion that one of the Franciscan friars was the father. In spite of Fray Pablo's insistence that the child was conceived by an incubus, the protestations of Fray Manuel and the Dominican Provincial carried more weight with the Inquisition. Fray Manuel noted that the exorcisms of the women involved frequent touching all over the body. Although exorcism was not, in itself, of any particular interest to the Inquisition, at the very faintest whiff of clerical misconduct the Inquisition was roused to action. Finally, on 18 January 1692, the Inquisition accused Francisca Mejía, Juana de los Reyes and the other demoniacs of feigning possession as an excuse to blaspheme. Any further exorcisms, or even the mention of the possessions, was forbidden, and Fray Pablo was severely reprimanded for causing division.[60]

Toby Green has interpreted the events at Querétaro as a product of neuroses produced by the 'extreme religious orthodoxy' encouraged by the Inquisition: 'from repression came fantasy and a sexual cycle of exorcism'.[61] On this reading, the Inquisition was both the cause and the remedy of the Querétaro possessions. Aside from the difficulties inherent in reading Freudian psychological terminology back onto the past, the criticism that the Franciscans attracted from their no-less-devout confreres in other religious orders suggests that it was the particular spiritual preoccupations of the Franciscans, rather than the atmosphere of religiosity encouraged by the Mexican Inquisition, that were to blame for the behaviour of the women of Querétaro. Nevertheless, the Inquisition remained relatively uninterested in possession cases, as their attitude to events at Abiquiu in the 1760s demonstrates. Even the involvement of senior clergy did not arouse the interest of the Sacred Tribunal. A woman named Josefa de Saldaña manifested the symptoms of possession in 1748 after she was bewitched by her lover, Juan de Cadena. The Vicar General of the Archbishop of Mexico, Francisco Javier Gómez de Cervantes, endorsed the case in the hope that Juan de Cadena would be accused of witchcraft. Events escalated when Josefa's protector, Nicolás Fernando de Tapia, began to study exorcism manuals and urged the clerical exorcists to carry on a dialogue with the demon in Latin. In spite of the involvement of senior clergy in the form of Gómez de Cervantes, the Inquisition's only

---

[60] Ibid. pp. 120–4. On the Querétaro case see also Ebright and Hendricks (2006), pp. 171–2.

[61] Green (2008), pp. 301–5.

action was to prohibit the exorcisms on pain of excommunication, on the grounds that the participants showed excessive credulity.[62]

The Inquisition reserved its severest interventions for accusations of sexual misconduct against exorcists. In 1572 a young woman from Mexico City named María Pizarro claimed to be having visions of angels with whom she regularly conversed. She was exorcized by a Jesuit, Luís Lopez, and two Dominicans.[63] Lopez insisted that he should sleep in the same room as María, and both he and one of the Dominicans, Jerónimo Ruiz de Portillo, had sex with her as part of their 'exorcisms'. The Inquisition interpreted all of this as evidence of a genuine demonic pact. In 1740 the Portuguese Inquisition intervened against a Carmelite friar from the province of Bahia in Brazil, Luís de Nazaré, who practised a form of medical exorcism that was magic at best and sexual abuse at worst. On one occasion he ordered a pig to be slaughtered and a salve to be made from the quarters and side, while the pig's cooked entrails should be buried at night at the crossroads. De Nazaré exploited his reputation amongst illiterate black *crioula* slaves, claiming that his book of exorcism required him to strip them naked and have sex with them. For a long time the women seem to have accepted the 'magical logic' of De Nazaré's bizarre behaviour, until he was eventually denounced to the Inquisition. Tried in Lisbon in 1740, De Nazaré admitted his crimes but blamed the condition of the colony, where lust 'enjoyed great strength and dominion'. The Inquisition sent him to a remote monastery for five years but did not take away his priestly status.[64]

Luís de Nazaré was a respected exorcist who had a good reputation in Salvador, where he had been authorized to exorcize by the Carmelite order. De Nazaré made use of Candido Brugnoli's *Mestre da vida* ('Master of Life') and *Opus de maleficiis* ('Work concerning Witchcrafts'), both of which had been banned Rome by 1740.[65] De Nazaré claimed that he did not know this, and indeed a priest from a remote corner of the Portuguese empire would not necessarily have been aware which books were on the Index.[66] The evidence suggests that De Nazaré was an ordinary exorcist, tempted to sexual misconduct, who exploited his

[62] Cervantes (1994), pp. 138–41.
[63] Green (2008), p. 304.
[64] De Mello e Souza (2003), pp. 109–11.
[65] Davies (2009), p. 60.
[66] De Mello e Souza (2003), pp. 166–7.

position and authority. Yet this does not necessarily mean that he did not also believe in the magical logic of his unorthodox practices, and Laura de Mello e Souza has suggested that De Nazaré really thought semen had curative properties.[67]

Whether De Nazaré was a manipulative sexual predator or an innovative exorcist (or both), his story is a reminder that in many parts of the New World the church engaged not only with the beliefs of indigenous peoples but also with the black slave community. In 1715 another Carmelite friar exorcized an entire family in Pernambuco who had been bewitched, causing them to vomit strange objects from every orifice, yet after the liturgical exorcisms were concluded the trouble continued, and exorcism was continued by a black *curandeiro* (healer) with 'purgatives of herbs and roots'.[68] Portuguese families in colonial Brazil were prepared to accept that supernatural knowledge was available to their black slaves, who developed their own syncretic forms of Catholicism that still exist in contemporary Brazil in the forms of Macumba and Umbanda.[69]

Ethnic diversity and religious syncretism were not the only causes of eccentric approaches to exorcism in the Americas. The vast size of colonial territories and the remoteness of settlements, especially in North America, created their own problems. From the foundation of Quebec City in 1608 until defeat by Britain in the French and Indian War in 1763, France and the Jesuits dominated vast tracts of uncharted territory in the continent's interior. Settlers imported French rural ritual traditions to New France which were given new urgency by the harshness of the land, especially in Quebec. The edition of the *Rituale Romanum* for use in Quebec, published in 1703, included exorcisms against storms and exorcisms 'against witchcraft and mortality' alongside blessings for crops and animals as well as an exorcism for houses and the usual rite for demoniacs.[70] When the Quebecois *Rituale* was reprinted in 1836 it contained only one exorcism and a warning against superstitious practices, but special permission continued to be sought for the excluded processions and benedictions.[71]

---

[67] Ibid. p. 110.
[68] Ibid. pp. 122–3.
[69] On religious syncretism in the black community in Brazil see De Mello e Souza (2003), pp. 50–1.
[70] Hubert, O., *Sur la Terre comme au Ciel: La Gestion des Rites par l'Eglise Catholique du Québec (fin XVIIe–mi-XIXe siècle)* (Quebec City: Les Presses de L'Université Laval, 2000), pp. 46–7.
[71] Ibid. pp. 49–50.

Between 1755 and 1763 French settlers in Newfoundland, known as Acadians, were deported to the thirteen British colonies of North America or back to Europe, while the indigenous tribes who had supported France were punished. French-speaking communities gradually returned to British North America after this dramatic disruption, known as the *Grand Dérangement*, bringing with them half-remembered folk traditions from *le temps de l'Acadie* ('the time of Acadia'). One reconstituted community was Bas-de-Tousquet, a fishing community at the southwest tip of Nova Scotia, which from 1799 was in the parish of St Anne, a large area of several villages served by the secular priest Jean Mandé Sigogne. Sigogne was an exile of a different kind, having fled from the Revolution in France in 1792 to England; a French community in Nova Scotia under the flag of the British Empire was a logical home for such a priest. However, the Acadians were used to life in scattered and remote communities far from any priest, and when in September 1810 a young girl named Rosalie Cotrau began to show symptoms of possession they drew on earlier traditions to deal with it.[72] Rosalie's father later described what happened[73]:

> First we prayed so that God would bless our enterprise, having made a company of my neighbours come for this purpose; after that we took a pot of new earth with a hundred eels and two hundred pins and a completely new knife with the heart of a black cock and the person's urine. We boiled this together, but it could not succeed to the end on account of lack of urine.

Rosalie's father understood that he and his neighbours had committed the sin of engaging with magic (*sort*), probably because Sigogne had already told him so, and he asked pardon for himself and the rest of the community. However, it was because the exorcism failed that Cotrau wrote to Sigogne, seeking his assistance. Sigogne responded by warning the community against accusing another woman in the village, Germain Corporon, of causing the possession, but within a month the possession had spread

---

[72] Boglioni, P. and Boudreau, G., '"Du tems de la cadi": possessions diaboliques et exorcismes populaires en Acadie au début du XIXe siècle', *Revue d'Histoire de l'Amerique Française* 60 (2007) pp. 487–515, at pp. 487–9.

[73] Ibid. p. 491: 'Nous ont prémierement fait la priere afin que Dieu benissie notre entreprise, aÿant fait venire pour cela une compagnie de mes voisins après cela nous on prie un pot de terre neuf avec cent Eguilles et deux cent Epeingles et un ganif tous neuf avec le coeur d'une Poul noire et de l'urine de la personne nous ont bouilli cela ensemble, mais cela n'a put réussir jusqu'aux bout par faute d'urine'.

beyond Rosalie Cotrau to another girl, Anne Doucet. This precipitated a visit by Sigogne, who celebrated Sunday mass. On the same day the community performed another makeshift exorcism, this time on Anne, which was later reported to the priest[74]:

> Anne Doucet was cured on the Sunday that you were here; we took her in two canoes, fearful of capsizing; we carried her into the middle of the river and plunged her in it four times without telling her what they wished to do to her, after which she said that she was cured.

The prayers that Sigogne had said on Sunday (perhaps the exorcisms of salt and water preceding the mass) compelled the spirit to reveal itself as Joseph Frédéric Mius, a dead relation of Germain Corporon.[75] However, there is no evidence that Sigogne himself performed an exorcism on Rosalie or Anne as an alternative to the makeshift exorcisms performed by the Acadians. Instead, he discouraged any insinuations of witchcraft and this may have been the reason why he did not want to endorse the idea of possession. However, this did not stop the Acadians interpreting the success of their exorcism as a consequence of the priest's visit. In this way, the reluctance of the French priest to engage with the beliefs of a people far removed from the culture of France merely served to confirm them in their 'superstitious' practices.

Conclusion

Exorcisms in contexts beyond Catholic Europe, whether as part of Catholic missions in the Protestant-dominated British Isles and Dutch Netherlands or in the New World and Asia, were considerably harder for the church to control and regulate than exorcisms in the Counter-Reformation heartlands of Italy, Iberia and southern Germany. There was also considerably less incentive for the imposition of a more sceptical and cautious approach to exorcism in these areas, since the practice often appealed to indigenous peoples with a vivid awareness of interaction with the spirit world and acted as a stimulus to conversion. To a certain extent, the recogni-

---

[74] Ibid. p. 493: 'Anne Doucet fut guérie le Dimanche que vous étiez ici on la prit dans deux canoux crainte de chavirer on la porta aux milieu de la rivière et on la plonga par quatre fois sans lui dire ce qu'on vouloient faire d'elle après quoi elles dit qu'elle étoit guéri'.

[75] The original rite used to exorcize Rosalie seems to have had its roots in attempts to contact the dead through magic (Boglioni and Boudreau (2007), p. 507).

tion that exorcism needs to be treated differently in rural tribal societies compared with the developed world remains a feature of the Catholic church's approach to exorcism. The revision of the rite in 1999 left it up to individual bishops' conferences which version of the rite they preferred exorcists in their country to use, and it is likely that the continued provision of imperative exorcisms was aimed at Africa, Asia and South America. Chapter 7 explores the asymmetry in the nineteenth century between a Catholic Europe in which exorcism was increasingly side-lined and a colonial context in which the church remained more willing to deploy it as an evangelistic tool.

CHAPTER 6

Exorcism in the Age of Reason

In the eighteenth century, attitudes to exorcism divided the Catholic world. This division broadly followed a philosophical division within Catholic Christendom between adherence to a conservative interpretation of Neo-Scholastic Aristotelianism and openness to Enlightenment thought. Spain and its territories were the heartland of the conservative tradition, while France was the centre of a 'Catholic' Enlightenment that pushed the boundaries of orthodoxy. Rome, caught between the 'superstitious' practices of over-enthusiastic exorcists and the boldness of clergy prepared to deny the reality of demonic possession altogether, attempted to steer a middle course and imposed increasingly strict controls on the practice of exorcism. These, in spite of reassurances that no change of doctrine had taken place, inevitably had the consequence of pushing exorcism to the margins of Catholic life.

Erik Midelfort has described the eighteenth century as a battle between three views of exorcism: the 'magical' tradition embodied in Menghi's exorcism manuals, the moderate and restrictive position of the *Rituale Romanum*, and outright scepticism.[1] However, the primary motivation for sceptics within the Catholic community was not burgeoning 'scientific' rationalism, but rather theological objections founded on a negative view of the miraculous and political hostility to those religious orders, such as the Jesuits and Capuchins, who were most willing to make use

[1] Midelfort (2005b), p. 87.

of exorcism to promote their missionary and political agenda. The fact that negative attitudes to the miraculous amongst Catholic theologians were grounded in a conservative Augustinian theology does not diminish their status as Enlightenment thinkers. Catholic intellectuals who belonged to the continuum of 'Jansenism', such as Blaise Pascal, paradoxically combined a fideistic attitude to theology with openness to the scientific revolution. However, the narrative of elite clerical and medical debates about the nature and purpose of exorcism does not represent the whole story of Catholic exorcism in the Age of Reason. For many (perhaps most) ordinary Catholics in Europe, the exorcistic power of the priesthood remained an indispensable protection against witchcraft. As the clergy became increasingly reluctant to authorize the rite, the clamour for exorcism from the laity became intense and, on occasion, spilled over into violence.

Lay Catholic responses to exorcism cannot be ignored just because they were at odds with the theological trajectory of many of the clergy. The wildly successful healing campaign of Johann-Joseph Gassner in 1774–75 demonstrated not only that exorcism was still in demand, but also that it did not necessarily need to be associated with 'unbewitching' and end in accusations of witchcraft. Gassner, who had little interest in witchcraft, revived a form of charismatic exorcism that avoided Menghi's magicalism whilst mirroring the techniques of 'scientific' healers such as Franz Anton Mesmer (1734–1815). Mesmer coined the term 'animal magnetism', claiming that he was able to cure his patients by stroking because he transmitted an invisible vital force through his fingers. His experiments with animal magnetism often resulted in convulsive and trance-like behaviours not dissimilar to those associated with demonic possession, yet Mesmer insisted that 'animal magnetism' was a natural force, the object of scientific study rather than religious pronouncements, and distanced himself from religious healers such as Gassner.[2] The vocabulary of mesmerism appealed to science rather than religion, breaking the association between psychic phenomena and witchcraft. However, Midelfort has rightly defended the sophistication of Gassner's approach which, albeit side-lined in the priest's own lifetime, has parallels with the practice of contemporary exorcists such as Gabriele Amorth, who are similarly aware of the need to defer to a scientific discourse.

---

[2] Midelfort (2005a), pp. 18–9; see also Midelfort (2005b), p. 86.

THE LAST FLOWERING OF SPANISH EXORCISM

By the end of the reign of Charles II of Spain (1661–1700), baroque exorcism in the Iberian Peninsula had reached its high point. Exorcists made use of a variety of manuals containing elaborate rituals, the most popular of which was the *Práctica de exorcistas y ministros de la Iglesia* (1670) of Benito Remigio Noydens (1630–85).[3] Although the last edition of Noydens's manual was printed in 1711, exorcisms continued to be performed in Spain with little regard for either the prevailing climate of scepticism in other parts of Europe or the edicts of Rome. The church, or at least its representatives, was complicit in spreading the use of exorcism as a form of authorized magic.[4]

An anonymous treatise entitled *Tratado de exorcismos, muy util para los sacerdotes y ministros de la iglesia* ('A Treatise of Exorcisms, very useful for Priests and Ministers of the Church', hereafter *Tratado*),[5] written in about 1725, gives valuable insight into how the liturgical and demonological literature was actually deployed in practice in eighteenth-century Spain. The treatise can be dated from its recommendation of the work of the Franciscan Antonio Arbiol y Díez (1651–1726), whose only writings on exorcism are to be found in his *Vocacion eclesiastica examinada con las divinas escrituras*, in which he commented on the requirements for a cleric taking orders as an exorcist.[6] Furthermore, the *Tratado* misattributed Menghi's *Flagellum daemonum* to Bernard Basin,[7] which was almost certainly a deliberate mistake as the *Flagellum* was put on the Index of Prohibited Books in 1704. In addition to these works, the *Tratado* recommended the works of Noydens, Candido Brugnoli and the *Materia medica*

---

[3] Noydens, B. R., *Práctica de exorcistas y ministros de la iglesia* (Madrid, 1670).

[4] Davies (2009), p. 60. Between 1690 and 1729 four editions of Menghi's *Flagellum daemonum* and *Fustis daemonum* (individually and combined) were published, along with one edition of his *Fuga daemonum* (Midelfort (2005b), p. 83).

[5] *A Manual of Exorcism, very useful for Priests and Ministers of the Church*, trans. E. Beyersdorf and J. D. Brady (New York: Hispanic Society of America, 1975). Brady's translation of the title as *A Manual of Exorcism* is misleading; the *Tratado* was a treatise, meaning a discursive treatment of the entire process of exorcism. Manuals of exorcism contained prayers, conjurations and instructions (although an actual rite of exorcism is to be found as an appendix to the *Tratado* (pp. 91–107) along with blessings for salt, oil and holy water (pp. 111–18)).

[6] Arbiol, A., *Vocacion eclesiastica examinada con las divinas escrituras* (Zaragoza, 1725), pp. 290–7.

[7] On Basin see Baroja (1990), p. 33.

of Dioscorides, a classical work glossed and added to many times throughout the Middle Ages and the sixteenth century,[8] as well as the Italian Augustinian Filippo Picinelli's *Mondo symbolico* (1678), translated into Latin in 1687.[9] Picinelli's work was an encyclopaedia of animals, plants, metals and other natural things accompanied by their theological meanings and their use in the works of the Church Fathers, intended for use by preachers, who could draw on the book for natural analogies and metaphors. However, the author of the *Tratado* seems to have used Picinelli rather differently, as a source of magical correspondences. For instance, the *Tratado*'s suggestion that gold dust should be used in exorcisms may have derived from Picinelli's claim that gold was a symbol of purification.[10] What was a symbol for Picinelli became a powerful sacramental in the *Tratado*, illustrating the intellectual gulf that existed between the Hispanic world and much of the rest of Europe.

The *Tratado* presented exorcism as spiritual warfare, whose weapons were unshakeable faith, a clear conscience, a prayerful attitude and, above all, humility. The author repeatedly emphasized that in exorcism, God acted through the exorcist, and the success of exorcism did not depend on the exorcist's personal charisma, even if his sins might hinder it.[11] Except in exceptional circumstances, an exorcism should always take place in a church, and care should be taken to exclude servants and women from the spectacle, especially 'curious, worldly, and vain ladies'.[12] These concerns, together with the emphasis on ensuring creditable witnesses were present, suggest that exorcism was on the way to becoming a spectator sport in early eighteenth-century Spain.

The *Tratado* distinguished between *possessio* and *obsessio* in the traditional way, suggesting that the symptoms of possession included disobedience, sudden illness (including inexplicable rage, biting of hands, throwing oneself on the ground, or into fire or water), suicidal tendencies, disturbance in the presence of holy objects, hatred of spiritual things such as churches

---

[8] The Franciscan Candido Brugnoli (1607–77) was the author of the *Alexicacon* (Venice, 1714), aimed as much at physicians as at exorcists. On Brugnoli see Midelfort (2005b), pp. 83–4. It is unclear which of the many editions of *Materia medica* the author of the *Tratado* may have relied upon.

[9] Picinelli, F. (trans. A. Erath), *Mundus symbolicus in emblematum universitate* (Cologne, 1687), 2 vols.

[10] *Tratado*, p. 76; Picinelli, F., *Mondo symbolico* (Milan, 1678), vol. 2, pp. 583–5.

[11] *Tratado*, pp. 13–16.

[12] Ibid. pp. 51–2.

and the mass, blasphemy, the ability to speak and understand Latin, unusual theological knowledge and the ability to reveal secrets. Obsession, on the other hand, meant that an individual was troubled by demons but not invaded by them.[13] However, the author noted that 'in especially ignorant peasants ... the Devil rarely speaks Latin, in order to better disguise his presence and stratagems'.[14] Symptoms of possession were either cause for suspicion, conjecture or a conclusive diagnosis; the conclusive symptoms included the demoniac's ability to speak a language normally unknown to him, 'singing in ingenious ways without any special grace or miracle of God, and revealing secrets and noteworthy things which happened in foreign countries'. Such unusual knowledge was only acceptable as evidence of possession if there was no 'agreement with the devil' on the part of the demoniac in the form of magical practices. A demoniac should not be able to remember what he said under the devil's influence.[15]

The *Tratado*'s author situated himself squarely in the conservative demonological tradition when he claimed that, although the symptoms of possession often resemble natural illness, the devil deliberately simulated natural symptoms in order to conceal his wicked intentions. The principal causes of possession were personal sin on the part of the demoniac, 'too much despair or concern over losing one's worldly possessions', too much familiarity with the devil or with magicians, the effect of 'sins of fathers' or ignorance of the remedies for dealing with temptation. There is little acknowledgement here of the earlier view that a particularly holy individual might suffer possession.[16] However, the demonology of the *Tratado* was grossly physical[17]:

> Usually, before entering the body of a man, [demons] appear to him in a horrible and frightening form, at night, and in dark, obscure places. Sometimes they scare him with a horrible nightmare, and mistreat the body mercilessly when they enter. At other times they enter in the form of wind, rats, or other small animals. At other times they seem to pour a glass of very cold water down his back and ants seem to crawl over the whole body.

---

[13] Ibid. pp. 21–2.
[14] Ibid. p. 23. On the devil's reluctance to speak Latin through ordinary people see Cervantes (1994), pp. 140–141.
[15] *Tratado*, p. 24.
[16] Ibid. p. 29.
[17] Ibid. p. 30.

Furthermore, if the exorcist was unable to complete the exorcism in one session, the *Tratado* advised him that 'he may indicate a toe where the demon should stay, tying him up there, until he is given further instruction', or in the case of a noisy spirit vexing a house, the corner of a room.[18] Even after the exorcism is successful, the exorcist must take care to order the demon to a specific location, since 'demons often stay in the clothes and hair of the victim' and lie waiting to repossess them.[19] The exorcist must use only genuine relics, and avoid 'superstitious use' of objects (whatever this might mean). The exorcist was advised to know a few Hebrew and Greek words by which to conjure the devil, recalling the multitude of exotic conjurations in Menghi's works.[20] Most of all, the exorcist had to maintain control of the dialogue: 'it is very important, and worth more than all the rhetoric of Cicero, to command the Devil'. None of the doubts expressed by seventeenth-century French Jesuits about the appropriateness of demonic oaths and insulting the devil were shared by the author of the *Tratado*. The devil should not be allowed to interrupt the exorcist, who could bind the demoniac by an oath to obey the exorcist and tell the truth.[21] Indeed, the exorcist should take every opportunity to insult the devil, and pitch, brimstone and molten resin should be placed in the demoniac's presence 'so that [the devil] will see the torments that are waiting for him'. The exorcist could even spit in the demoniac's face in order to show his contempt. The author justified this on the grounds that 'the exorcist does not curse the Devil as a being out of hatred, but out of love for God against whom he is rebelling, and out of love for the human being to whom he is causing such serious pain'.[22]

However, the *Tratado*'s author did agree that the exorcist committed a mortal sin 'if he asks something through which the demon might discover someone's sin'. Likewise, it was a sin to plead with the demon rather than command it, and to show excessive curiosity. The devil was a lying spirit, and the exorcist should not believe everything he heard with perfect faith, nor should he become over-familiar with the demoniac.[23] Most stringently of all, if the demoniac was 'bound by some covenant' (i.e. bewitched), the exorcist was forbidden to identify the sorcerer as that

---

[18] Ibid. p. 36.
[19] Ibid. p. 69.
[20] Ibid. p. 45.
[21] Ibid. pp. 33–5.
[22] Ibid. pp. 41–2.
[23] Ibid. pp 37–8.

would reveal someone's sin; instead, the demon had to be compelled to reveal the location of the instrument of witchcraft. The exorcist could ask the demon which saints and angels were its greatest rivals in heaven, so that their names and prayers could be used to torment the demon still further. Asking the demon to reveal its name was essential, as it gave a clue concerning the demon's effects on the demoniac's behaviour. For instance, the demon Belial, 'without yoke', was best tormented by laying a crucifix on the demoniac's shoulders like a yoke.[24] The author of the *Tratado* upheld the use of material signs in exorcism against the objection that a spiritual being like the devil could not be punished: 'Natural actions, such as kneeling, holding the cross on one's shoulders, and other similar things can be elevated proportionately by God's power imparted to the exorcism, which has the same effect on the Devil, although he is a spirit'. Natural things and natural signs were effective *media indirecte* or *media dispositive*, meaning that 'they indirectly lead and prepare the possessed person for the expulsion of the devil'.

Exorcism could fail for a number of reasons. The *Tratado* warned that demons could not be cast out of lunatics, the blind, deaf and mute except by prayer and fasting.[25] The exorcist's lack of faith might cause failure, or God might want to exalt a different exorcist; the exorcist's power was never any greater than God chose to make it.[26] The *Tratado* contained conflicting messages on the necessity of the rite of major exorcism in every case; on the one hand, confession and communion, accompanied by the sign of the cross and devotion to the Virgin Mary, were supposed to be enough to free the demoniac.[27] On the other hand, the *Tratado* insisted that exorcism should be used even on the obsessed, and everything they eat should be blessed in case the devil used it as an opportunity to possess them.[28] The *Tratado* followed the demonologists of the sixteenth and seventeenth centuries by distinguishing sharply between the possessed and 'those who are bewitched and enchanted by the Devil'. Whilst demoniacs experienced torment from the devil *praesentialiter* ('by his presence'), the obsession of the bewitched was merely *potestative* ('by his power'). The devil 'accompanies and torments' the bewitched rather than possessing

---

[24] Ibid. pp. 40–1.
[25] Ibid. p. 43.
[26] Ibid. pp. 44–5.
[27] Ibid. pp. 63–4.
[28] Ibid. p. 77.

their bodies and subverting their wills.[29] Bewitchment, unlike possession proper, could only be accomplished through a physical instrument, and could be ended by removing and destroying it; one of the first things that the exorcist should do when called to a bewitched person was to ensure that their bedclothes were changed, since the instruments of witchcraft were often concealed there. Another form of obsession, the visits of incubi and succubi, could be combated by means of gold dust, myrrh, salt, olive wood, wax and rue.[30]

The demonology of the *Tratado* and its approach to exorcism were essentially borrowed from sixteenth- and seventeenth-century manuals, making it a somewhat anachronistic treatise, but the *Tratado* nevertheless acknowledged that some had begun to question how physical objects, cursing and spitting could be effective against the immaterial devil. Furthermore, the *Tratado* did not recommend any direct physical violence against the demoniac and warned against turning exorcisms into spectacles. Albeit in relatively small ways, an early eighteenth-century exorcism in Spain was a gentler affair than the exorcisms of the previous century. However, in spite of Suárez's metaphysical caution, an underlying faith remained that demons were beings who could occupy a space and be physically ejected. Whilst the *Tratado* did not defy the *Rituale Romanum* in any obvious way, its provisions went far beyond the rubrics of the official rite, especially in diagnosing possession and dealing with instruments of witchcraft.

THE SUPPRESSION OF EXORCISM MANUALS, 1703–10

Between 1703 and 1710, the Sacred Congregation of the Index condemned a number of exorcism manuals that went beyond the ceremonies of the *Rituale Romanum*. In the wake of high profile cases of 'mystical fraud', especially in Spain, the Roman Curia became increasingly conscious that the activities of the clergy were provoking derision in some circles, especially amongst enlightened French *philosophes*.[31] However, the authority of the Index did not necessarily extend to Spain's territories,

---

[29] Ibid. p. 73.
[30] Ibid. pp. 75–6.
[31] On the sceptical reaction to exorcism see Romeo (2003), p. 115; Quantin, J.-L., *Catholicisme Classique et les Pères de L'Eglise: un retour au sources (1669–1713)* (Paris: Institut d'Etudes Augustiniennes, 1999), pp. 474–88.

where the king retained the right to promulgate the Papal decrees he chose, and the immediate effect of Rome's action on Spain is unclear. In the first instance, it would have affected the Papal States and other Italian territories where the Pope had direct metropolitical jurisdiction. On 21 April 1704 the Index proscribed Menghi's *Flagellum*, along with Zaccaria Visconti's *Complementum artis exorcistae*. Abbot Nicolas Cuyò, secretary to the Vicar General of the Diocese of Rome, Cardinal Gaspare Carpegna (1625–1714), justified the prohibition in a letter to the Bishops of Italy on 7 July 1704[32]:

> The devil, by a clever machination, and by deceitful arts, has seduced many exorcists who have made use of the drugs of doctors, or rather the nonsense of sorcery, which deserve to be called magical rather than exorcistic; and since from all these superstitious rites growing in exorcism even to this day ... These things being brought to my most Eminent Master [i.e. Carpegna], by whose edicts and by whose penalties, at all times watches over his Vicariate of the City, he has made every effort so as to rise from the right source, and has discovered the miserable exorcists to be immersed to the depths in superstitions, and faith in the aforementioned Authors [i.e. Menghi and Visconti], and their clientele to be deceived unawares.

Carpegna, as Vicar General of Rome, was in effect Rome's diocesan bishop and acted on the Pope's behalf as Metropolitan of Italy, since the Pope was preoccupied with international political and ecclesiastical affairs. By blaming the growth of exorcistic abuses on the devil, Cuyò at once ensured that priests who made use of unauthorized exorcisms were stigmatized, and that the church continued to affirm the reality of the devil's power in the face of criticism from sceptics. Cuyò's condemnation of *medicorum pharmaca* may have been a response to the use of *materia medica* in books like the *Tratado*, which went beyond the 1614 rite. By prohibiting the use of medical formulas to combat possession, Cuyò was distancing exorcism from medicine and thereby denying, by implication, that demonic

---

[32] Quoted in Brambilla (2010), n. p. 179: *[Diabolus] callida machinatione, artibusque dolosis nonnullos exorcistas seduxit qui Medicorum Pharmaca, seu potius Pharmaceutica Deliramenta, [usi sunt] [...] quae potius magica, quam exorcistica nuncupari merentur; etenim ex istis omnes superstitiosos ritus in exorcismis usque in hac die gliscentes, [...] ad quos tollendos Eminentissimus Dominus Meus, qua edictis qua poenis, toto sui Vicariatus Urbis tempore vigilanter incubuit, elaboravitque tamquam ex proprio fonte oriri, miserosque exorcistas sub praedictorum Authorum fide, et clientula incaute decipi, et in superstitionibus ad gurgitem usque immergi compertum est.*

possession was a cause of illness. However, the separation of exorcism from medicine also made it impossible for doctors to take an interest in cases of possession and thereby suggest medical explanations for them.

Prohibition of Menghi's *Compendio dell'arte esorcistica* followed in 1707 and, finally, the Capuchin Pietro Locatelli's *Coniurationes potentissimae et efficaces* in 1710. On 14 May 1710 Cuyò sent another letter to all the archbishops and bishops of Italy, instructing them to repress uncontrolled devotion, especially among the regular clergy. Although the letter condemned French sceptics such as Jean-Baptiste Thiers it also instructed bishops that the only rite of exorcism to be used was the official Roman liturgy of 1614. For the first time, bishops were required to report exorcisms that took place under their immediate ordinary jurisdiction and depute examiners who would approve clergy for licensing as exorcists; all exorcisms by unlicensed or doubtfully licensed clergy were to cease. A second letter of 24 June 1710 condemned 'the grave disorders, which follow from the multiplicity of exorcisms, which are universally invented, and practised by persons designated to exorcize'. Bishops were to approve no secular or regular priest as an exorcist unless his piety, integrity of life and ability to make use of the *Rituale Romanum* could be demonstrated.

In Elena Brambilla's view, the background to the attack on exorcism manuals by the Congregation of the Index in the early eighteenth century lay in the eclipse of the 'Spanish party' within the Curia and the growth of the Congregation of the Index's influence during the period, under Cardinals Colloredo, Brancati di Lauria, Casanate and Slusio, who shared many of the French clergy's concerns about the purity of worship. The fact that the Index, the successor of the Inquisition and one of the Curia's most conservative bodies, was prepared to consider the possibility that medical explanations might account for some alleged possessions was a sign of the intensity of political pressure against the regular clergy. For Brambilla, Carpegna's determination to bring the regulars under control was a continuation of Popes Innocent XI's and Alexander VIII's efforts to reduce the number of enclaves outside ordinary jurisdiction. It reflected Carpegna's sympathy towards a more rigorist spirituality and preference for the secular clergy over the Jesuits and Capuchins; the Capuchins, in particular, were renowned for semi-magical conjurations.[33] However, the Holy Office's condemnation of superstitious excesses also lent weight to

---

[33] Brambilla (2010), pp. 170–9.

its condemnation of Thiers and the Gallican sceptics, and presented the official line of the church as a sober middle way between two extremes. The Spanish Inquisition, perhaps surprisingly, adopted a more extreme sceptical stance; in 1739 the Spanish Benedictine and Inquisitor Benito Feijoo wrote a treatise on demoniacs that, whilst acknowledging the reality of possession in the Gospels, concluded that all contemporary demoniacs were frauds.[34]

THE END OF EXORCISM?

From around 1740 onwards the practice of exorcism came under sustained pressure from the church, the civil authorities of most Catholic countries and the medical profession. This pressure eventually extinguished the last remnants of the magical exorcistic tradition of Girolamo Menghi in Spain and Italy, where it had survived the longest, although a Prussian visitor observed one of Menghi's exorcisms in use as late as 1781.[35] As I have argued in Chap. 5, Menghi's legacy remained alive in Catholic colonial territories. In 1730, Marie-Catherine Cadière, a novice nun who became possessed as a result of her relationship with the Jesuit Jean-Baptiste Girard, encountered no sympathy from the Parlement of Toulon and was sentenced to two years in prison for faking possession.[36]

The challenge to exorcism was not limited to self-consciously 'enlightened' regimes. On 22 June 1744 Pope Benedict XIV issued a brief to the bishops of Italy urging caution in using the rite of exorcism,[37] and in October 1745 another brief, *Sollicitudini nostrae*, was provoked by the case of Crescentia Höss (d. 1744). Höss, a Franciscan nun from Kaufbeuren in Swabia, was regularly tormented by demons and made prophetic pronouncements.[38] Benedict instructed that 'In exorcizing energumens it is above all important, that it should be distinguished before anything else,

---

[34] Levack (2013), p. 233.
[35] Cameron (2010), p. 310.
[36] Levack (2013), pp. 217–19.
[37] Brambilla (2010), p. 191.
[38] On Crescentia see Pouliot, J. C., *Vie de la Vénérable Marie-Crescence, Religieuse du Tiers Ordre de Saint-François au couvent de Kaufbeuren* (Fraserville, QC: J. E. Frenette, 1895); Miller, A. M., *Crescentia von Kaufbeuren: das Leben einer schwäbischen Mystikerin* (Augsburg : Verlag Winifried-Werk, 1968); Boespflug, F., *Dieu dans l'Art:* Sollicitudini Nostrae *de Benoît XIV et l'Affaire Crescence de Kaufbeuren* (Paris: Cerf, 1984).

whether he who asserts such a thing is genuinely obsessed by a demon'.[39] This instruction, which was quoted in the revised rite of exorcism of 1999, placed the obligation to distinguish between possession and illness at the forefront of a bishop's role in dealing with alleged cases of possession.

The case of a thirty-three-year-old woman from Cremona, who began vomiting strange objects in 1746, produced heated debate between local Jesuits, who believed that she was genuinely possessed, the Padua physician Paolo Valcarenghi who believed she was suffering from mania and proposed a naturalistic explanation, and the Augustinian Canon Giovanni Cadonici, who argued that the woman was deliberately faking her symptoms. Massimo Mazzotti has seen Cadonici's interpretation of the Cremona case as part of his long-running theological struggle against the Jesuits. Valcarenghi and Cadonici represented two distinct strands of the Catholic Enlightenment; whilst Valcarenghi diminished the role of the supernatural by expanding the sphere of natural phenomena, Cadonici advanced a purely theological argument against the false possession on the basis of a 'purified' Augustinianism.[40] Midelfort has argued that the Jansenist and anti-enthusiastic tendencies of Augustinian theology were, in reality, a more powerful force against exorcism than 'scientific' scepticism.[41]

Jansenism was a mercurial religious movement that defies easy definition; it certainly did not necessarily mean adherence to the theological views of Cornelius Jansen (1585–1638), a profound scholar of Augustine with little interest in the political issues that came to dominate the agenda of those who adopted his name. Jansenism tended to involve an intense dislike of the Jesuits and all that they stood for, hostility to the extension of Papal authority and a strong emphasis on the saving power of faith and genuine repentance rather than 'means of grace' such as sacramentals, or even the sacraments in some cases. Jansenists were associated with moral rigorism, austere liturgy, Augustinian theology and fideism, as well as Gallicanism (the belief that the French church should enjoy some independence from Papal control) and Conciliarism (belief in the supremacy of General Councils rather than Popes). Jansenists and their sympathisers were also leading figures in a revival of Catholic biblical criticism and in

---

[39] Quoted in Brambilla (2010), n. p. 191: *In exorcizandis energuminis illud potissime interest, ut ante omnia dignoscatur, an re vera obsessus sit a daemone is qui talis affirmatur.*

[40] Mazzotti, M., *The World of Maria Gaetana Agnesi, Mathematician of God* (Baltimore, MD: Johns Hopkins University Press, 2007), pp. 98–101.

[41] Midelfort (2005a), p. 7.

the world of natural philosophy, perhaps because they tended to reject the Scholastic inheritance of the past in favour of the Church Fathers and were not, therefore, burdened by Jesuit-dominated late Scholasticism.[42]

The rise of scepticism, whether from the Jansenists or natural philosophers, did not prevent the execution by beheading and burning of the subprioress of a Premonstratensian convent in Würzburg in 1749. Maria Renata Singer was accused of causing the possession of nuns in the convent by witchcraft in 1744 and, after three years of exorcisms by Jesuits, Premonstratensians and Benedictines, she finally confessed to the crime. However, the civic authorities of Würzburg proved more convinced of her guilt than the bishop's officials, who only reluctantly co-operated with the process.[43] In 1758 exorcism was prohibited entirely in the hereditary lands of Austria by a decree of the Empress Maria Theresa, who was determined to stamp out belief in vampires and regarded exorcism as just another form of pernicious superstition.[44] It was not so much that exorcism was a problem in itself, but rather the fact that it promoted belief in witchcraft and thereby destabilized society. In France, the subject of the Loudun exorcisms was still sensitive more than a century later, and in 1750 the Bishop of Poitiers ordered the Ursuline nuns of Loudun to remove a picture of Jean-Joseph Surin exorcizing Jeanne des Anges. They disobeyed, covering it up instead with a picture of Christ, but the painting was lost at the time of the French Revolution.[45]

Brambilla has argued that it was a playwright rather than a physician who first suggested that the appearance of demonic possession might arise from 'nervous illness', meaning that we might need to look to literature rather than theology for the origins of sophisticated scepticism. In Carlo Goldoni's *La finta ammalata* ('The False Invalid'), which was first performed at the Teatro di Sant'Angelo during the Venice Carnival of 1751, the old convulsionary is portrayed neither as Valcarenghi's maniac nor

---

[42] For general accounts of the Jansenists see Knox, R., *Enthusiasm: A Chapter in the History of Religion* (Oxford: Clarendon, 1950), pp. 176–230; Cragg, G. R., *The Church and the Age of Reason 1648–1789*, 2nd edn (Harmondsworth: Penguin, 1967), pp. 25–30; 193–9. On the effect of Jansenism on attitudes to the supernatural see Young (2013), pp. 56–63.

[43] Midelfort (2005a), pp. 8–9.

[44] Klueting, H., 'The Catholic Enlightenment in Austria or the Habsburg Lands' in Lehner, U. L. and Printy, M. (eds), *A Companion to the Catholic Enlightenment in Europe* (Leiden: Brill, 2010), pp. 127–64, at p. 144.

[45] De Waardt, 'Demonic Possession: An Introductory Note' in De Waardt et al. (2005), p. 26.

Cadonici's cunning fraud, but as a woman suffering from an excess of *sensibilité*, emotional sensitivity.[46] This interpretation of possession avoided the crude dichotomy of fraud and madness that had dominated sceptical discourse up to that point, and opened up the possibility that sane people in good faith, overwrought with emotion and under the influence of superstition, could come to believe themselves victims of the devil.

There is evidence of the continuing vitality of exorcism at the fringes of Counter-Reformation Europe in the form of editions of the *Rituale Romanum* produced specifically for the use of priests in Ireland and Scotland. In 1738 a *Rituale* (including the rite of exorcism) was printed at Paris, ostensibly for England, Ireland and Scotland, but in the absence of any evidence for liturgical exorcisms in England during this period, it seems probable that Irish (and perhaps Scottish) priests used the rite rather than their counterparts in England. The 1738 *Rituale* did not simply reproduce the text of the 1614 *Rituale*: the rite is entitled *De exorcizandis obsessis, vel etiam maleficiatis, a daemonio* ('Of exorcizing those obsessed, or even bewitched, by a demon'). The mention of bewitchment in the very title of the rite suggests that it was deployed in a missionary context where unbewitchment was the primary purpose of exorcism. The rite thus adhered to the letter of Rome's condemnation of malefice-focused exorcism manuals whilst clearly indicating to the priest that it was to be used in cases of witchcraft. The instructions appended to the 1614 rite are entirely omitted with the exception of *RR* 881,[47] while *RR* 900–901 (*Adjuro te serpens antique*) is entitled *Alius exorcismus* ('another exorcism'), with the implication that it is an optional addition to the rite (when it is, in fact, the central act).[48] The rite then omits everything between *RR* 903 (*Deus coeli, Deus terrae*) and the *Oratio post liberationem* (*RR* 920) with the proviso that[49]:

---

[46] Brambilla (2010), pp. 237–8; see also Rousseau, G., 'Depression's Forgotten Genealogy: Notes towards a History of Depression', *History of Psychiatry* 11 (2000), pp. 71–106, at pp. 74–5.

[47] *Ordo Baptizandi aliaeque Sacramenta administrandi ... Pro Anglia, Hibernia et Scotia* (Paris, 1738), pp. 107–8: *Sacerdos, sive alius Exorcista rite confessus, aut saltem corde peccata sua detestans; peracto, si commode fieri potest, sanctissimo Missae sacrificio, divinoque auxiliis piis precibus implorato, Superpelliceo & Stola[m] violacea[m] (cujus extrema pars ad obsessi collum circumponatur) indutus, & coram se habens obsessum ligatum (si fuerit periculum) cum, se, & astantes communiat signo Crucis, & aspergat Aqua[m] benedicta[m], & genibus flexis, aliis respondentibus, dicat Litanias ordinarias, usque ad preces exclusive.*

[48] Ibid. p. 119.

[49] Ibid. p. 123: *Praedicta omnia, quatenus opus fuerit, repeti possunt, donec Obsessus sit omnino liberates. Juvabit praeterea plurimum super Obsessum devote saepeque repetere Pater*

All of the aforesaid can, as far as may be necessary, be repeated until the obsessed person should be entirely liberated. It helps besides to repeat many times and devoutly over the obsessed the Our Father etc., similarly the Athanasian Creed, 'Whosoever would be saved' etc., similarly the seven penitential Psalms and other pious prayers and orations, for the sake of the devotion of the exorcizing priest and the people standing around.

One curious feature of these instructions is that they assume the existence of 'people standing around' (*populi circumstantis*) at a time when public exorcisms were controversial, to say the least. In addition to the rite of exorcism, the 1738 *Rituale* also included an English translation of the baptismal exorcism, suggesting that priests were encouraged either to recite the exorcism in both Latin and English or to explain it to the congregation.[50] However, since a large proportion of Catholics in Ireland and Scotland spoke Irish and Gaelic at this period the translations may have been of limited pastoral use.

The 1738 *Ritual* was followed later in the century by a version specifically for the use of missionary priests in Scotland, *Epitome Ritualis Romani in usum missionum Scotiae* (1783). The *Epitome*, unlike its predecessor, included the full instructions from the *Rituale Romanum*.[51] There was no sign that the three great adjurations could be omitted, but the *Epitome* omitted everything between *RR* 905 and *RR* 920. Unlike the *Rituale* of 1738, the *Epitome* did not even mention the additional liturgical material included in the rite, and merely suggested the repetition of the original exorcisms.[52] On the whole, however, these rituals for Ireland and Scotland displayed remarkably little effort to accommodate the realities of missionary life. Priests in eighteenth-century Ireland often operated openly, even in urban settings, with little fear of interference, but Catholicism in Scotland was largely confined to the Highlands before the nineteenth century and presented a geographically and politically challenging field of mission.[53] The appearance of the rite of exorcism in two

noster, &c. Symbolum item Sancti Athanasii. Quicumque vult, &c. Item septem Psalmos poenitentiales; aliasque pias preces & Orationes, pro devotione Sacerdotis exorcizantis, & populi circumstantis.

[50] Ibid. p. 25.

[51] *Epitome Ritualis Romani in usum missionum Scotiae* ([Edinburgh], 1783), pp. 137–43.

[52] Ibid. p. 160.

[53] On Catholicism in Scotland after the Reformation see Anson, P. F., *Underground Catholicism in Scotland* (Montrose: Standard Press, 1970).

separate editions of the *Rituale* at the height of the Enlightenment suggests that this service of the church remained very much in demand at Europe's 'Celtic fringe'.

THE RETURN OF CHARISMATIC EXORCISM

The 'Age of Reason' was also an age in which the distinction between science and magic was not entirely fixed, and perhaps we should not be so surprised that the late eighteenth century, which produced the pseudo-sciences of physiognomy and mesmerism, did not altogether discard exorcism. The second half of the century witnessed religious revival and the birth of Romanticism, which embraced popular 'superstition' as 'a necessary cultural ornament'.[54] Johann-Joseph Gassner (1727–79) was a German secular priest who came to believe he had the power to heal by casting out evil spirits. Between the summer of 1774 and the winter of 1775 he performed charismatic exorcisms on thousands of people in different parts of the Holy Roman Empire. Gassner's technique involved probative exorcisms in Latin, which he called *praecepta*, designed to force a possessing demon to manifest itself in different parts of an individual's body. Gassner did not usually deal with traditional cases of full-blown possession but rather cases of mental and physical illness caused by demons. Gassner believed that 'demons imitated nature so perfectly that only an exorcism could detect them', a feature of his ministry that, according to Midelfort, reveals Gassner's debt to the 'naturalizing' impulses of the Enlightenment.[55] At the same time, Gassner did not deny the possibility of natural illness. Once he believed a person to be possessed he passed on to *benedictiones* ('blessings'), the same euphemism for exorcisms used in the late twentieth century by Gabriele Amorth.

Gassner began his ministry in the summer of 1774 when he requested a leave of absence from the Bishop of Chur to tour Upper Swabia. So successful was he that he visited Ellwangen between November 1774 and June 1775. From there he travelled to Regensburg, enjoying the patronage of senior clergy and journeying into the Upper Palatinate, until he was banished from Regensburg by a decree of the Emperor Joseph II. Condemnation from bishops and Pope Pius VI followed, as well as a

---

[54] Cameron (2010), p. 312.
[55] Midelfort (2005a), p. 9.

denunciation from Gassner's 'rival' healer, Mesmer.[56] Mesmer, who was called to consult on Gassner, claimed that the priest was deploying animal magnetism without realizing it, and condemned the superstitious paraphernalia of his accompanying rituals.[57] Gassner's critics missed the point that Mesmer's claims were equally mysterious, yet evaded the same scrutiny as those of the exorcist because they were couched in pseudoscientific language.

The controversy concerning Gassner's exorcisms was 'one of largest and noisiest arguments of the whole German Enlightenment', and generated around 150 printed texts.[58] Foremost amongst Gassner's Catholic critics, however, was the Theatine Canon Ferdinand Sterzinger, who attacked Gassner on biblical rather than scientific grounds. Invoking the idea that Satan was chained in hell (already held by Suárez in the seventeenth century), Sterzinger questioned whether possession was possible at the present day; and, if it was, why Gassner seemed to provoke the symptoms of possession in his patients rather than responding to those described in the *Rituale*.[59] Sterzinger, along with Ludovico Antonio Muratori (1672–1750) and Scipione Maffei (1675–1755) was at the forefront of the attempt by 'Reform Catholicism' to stamp out belief in witchcraft. Midelfort has noticed the variety of authorities invoked by these critics: direct experience, church history, the *Rituale Romanum* and a literal style of biblical and Patristic exegesis independent of Scholastic tradition.[60]

Although the appeal to experience over authority was nothing new, reformists like Sterzinger realized the full potential of the cautious *Rituale Romanum* and anticipated the arguments of the twentieth-century Modernists and sceptical theologians of the post-Vatican II era. However, Euan Cameron has emphasized the gap that still existed between the 'Catholic rationalist' Sterzinger and figures closer to the centre of Enlightenment thought. Sterzinger placed the principle of authority above the principle of reason, relying on reason as an interpretative tool rather than a source of authority in its own right.[61] By contrast, Voltaire's analysis of exorcism as an import from Persian magical lore in his *Dictionnaire phi-*

---

[56] For a summary of Gassner's career see Midelfort (2005a), pp. 14–6.
[57] Midelfort (2005a), pp. 18–9.
[58] Ibid. p. 22.
[59] Ibid. pp. 95–8.
[60] On eighteenth-century Catholic Patristic criticism see Quantin (1999), pp. 74–82.
[61] Cameron (2010), pp. 293–4.

losophique (1764) lay outside the limits of what someone could reasonably believe whilst claiming to be an orthodox Catholic, since it impugned the reliability of Scripture and the historic faith of the church.[62]

On 20 April 1776 Pius VI intervened in the Gassner affair with the last eighteenth-century document on exorcism. In response to an appeal from the Bishop of Regensburg, the Pope wrote that Gassner's exorcisms were licit in and of themselves, but he condemned the public nature of Gassner's ministry and his teaching that physical illnesses were caused by the devil. Finally, the Pope declared that 'the custom of exorcisms brought in by him must be lifted and abolished completely' and restricted Gassner to performing exorcisms in private according to the prescriptions of the *Rituale Romanum*.[63] Midelfort has argued that the unique political circumstances of the Holy Roman Empire in the late eighteenth century created an environment in which Gassner's charismatic revival of exorcism could take place; central authority was weak and individual prince bishops and abbots enjoyed a degree of independence from the Emperor and from one another that ensured an uneven texture in German Catholicism. Pius VI's explicit condemnation was required finally to silence Gassner.

Exorcism on Demand

Popular religion endorsed the reality of bewitchment and possession, and ordinary people who demanded help from the church were mystified by the clergy's reluctance to get involved. In 1812 demand for exorcism in one Spanish village was so intense that female demoniacs gathered outside a priest's house with sticks and stones, threatening to kill him unless he exorcized them: 'He has the remedy in the sacristy and he doesn't want to use it because he is convinced we are not possessed, only mad!' This incident took place in the village of Tosos in Aragon, where a group of women began to convulse during the Corpus Christi procession. The priest, overwhelmed by demands for exorcism, wrote to the Bishop of Huesca, who replied that the priest should discontinue the exorcisms. Instead, he should ask the parents or husbands of the women involved 'to send them out to hard work, in such a way as not to allow them one minute of idleness'. They should also be taken to a river or stream and made to bathe fre-

---

[62] On Voltaire's argument see Cameron (2010), p. 308.
[63] Quoted in Midelfort (2005a), p. 51: *omnino inductum ab ipso hunc exorcismorum morem tollendum abolendumque.*

quently, whilst being fed on a modest diet. If they refused, the fathers and husbands should lock them up and punish them, and if they caused a commotion in church or in the street, they should be arrested and imprisoned in the public gaol and given nothing but bread and water for three or four days. The women should not be released until they agreed to behave. The bishop's advice, based on contemporary ideas about the treatment of mental illness, was the cause of more violence, and the priest fled the village.

Maria Tausiet has argued that in this, as in other cases of the period, popular anger was directed not just at the witch who was considered responsible for the possessions, but also against the church for declining to make use of its spiritual arsenal.[64] The priest's departure and the ensuing 'spiritual anarchy' in the village mirrored contemporary political events; Napoleon's government was encouraging the people to set up *juntas locales* to administer their own affairs, and traditional power structures were breaking down.[65] Eventually, a woman named Joaquina Martínez came before the court of the Archbishop of Zaragoza, accused by local people of being a witch. The clergy were divided on whether the women of Tosos really were possessed, with diagnoses ranging from deliberate trickery to madness, melancholia, hysteria and 'an overheated imagination'. None of these diagnoses necessitated exorcism, but some were more sympathetic to the women than others. Tausiet observed that the closer clergy were to the events involved, the more likely they were to be sympathetic; only officials in the Archbishop's curia with little knowledge of the case thought it was a deliberate deception.[66] Under questioning, it turned out that Joaquina had herself tried to exorcize the women, and this seems to have been what lay behind accusations that she had bewitched them. However, although Joaquina questioned the demons and applied relics to the bodies of the possessed (like a clerical exorcist), she also touched the women on their genitals.[67] Yet Joaquina, as an uneducated woman, could hardly be accused of using her position as an exorcist to abuse power. The church authorities were less interested in Joaquina's illicit exorcizing than in her moral conduct.

In early nineteenth-century Spain the clergy was divided between those who, like the Bishops of Huesca and Zaragoza, believed that victims of

---

[64] Tausiet (2005), p. 264.
[65] Ibid. p. 265.
[66] Ibid. p. 268.
[67] Ibid. p. 273.

possession could be treated like sufferers from mental illness, and the enthusiastic exorcists who practised at shrines particularly associated with deliverance from the devil.[68] The shrine of the miraculous crucifix of Calatorao at Zaragoza remained a place of pilgrimage for demoniacs until the late nineteenth century, and it was here that some of the women of Tosos sought relief. Since Calatorao lay within the jurisdiction of the Archbishop of Zaragoza, and the diocese's Synodal Laws forbade exorcism without a licence, the Church Governor of the diocese wrote to the vicar of Calatorao in 1814 expressing his disapproval of an incident in which a female demoniac removed her blouse in front of the miraculous crucifix during an exorcism; the blouse was subsequently retained at the shrine as proof of a miracle.[69] In the Tosos case it was not so much that the church was unwilling to sanction exorcism. Rather, if the church exorcized, it would be acknowledging that the women of Tosos really were possessed—and the people of Tosos were convinced that possession was the consequence of witchcraft. Consequently, an official exorcism would have constituted an endorsement of belief in witchcraft.

ROMANTIC EXORCISM

As the eighteenth century wore on, the exploration of the psychological effects of emotional and aesthetic sensitivity became an artistic preoccupation, producing Romanticism and the phenomenon of 'Gothic' literature. In E. T. A. Hoffman's novel *Die Elixire des Teufels* ('The Devil's Elixir'), for instance, the friar Medardus becomes possessed through drinking a potion given by the devil to St Anthony, but Medardus's possession represents a psychological rather than theological reality.[70] Hoffman was inspired by the English author Matthew Lewis's novel *The Monk*, in which images drawn from the religious culture of the Middle Ages stand for psychological realities.

---

[68] These included the hermitage of the Mare de Deu de la Balma in Zorita, Nuestra Señora de la Fuente de la Salud in Traiguera (both in Castellón), the collegiate church of Santa María in Cervera in Lérida, the chapel of Santa Orosia in the Cathedral of Jaca and the monastery of Cilla (both in the diocese of Huesca) and the shrine of Santo Cristo de Calatorao in Zaragoza itself (Tolosana, C. L., *Demonios y Exorcismos en los Siglos de Oro* (Madrid: Akal, 1990), p. 9).

[69] Tausiet (2005), pp. 272–3.

[70] Hoffman, E. T. A., *The Devil's Elixir* (Edinburgh: William Blackwood, 1824), vol. 1, pp. 75, 84. On literary ridicule of exorcism see Cameron (2010), pp. 301–2.

Evidence survives of two English exorcisms, one accomplished and one requested, at this period. In May 1815 a Birmingham priest, Edward Peach, was summoned to exorcize a non-Catholic woman in Worcestershire named Mrs White. Peach persevered as a storm raged overhead and conditionally baptized Mrs White, since he suspected a defective Protestant baptism might have allowed the devil's attacks against her. Peach's exorcism should be seen in the context of attacks on exorcism in Ireland by the British press. These continued throughout the 1820s, and were intended as proof that the Irish were barbarous and dangerous, thereby serving as an argument against the legal and political emancipation of Catholics in the British Isles. Rather than renouncing exorcism as a relic of the past, some Catholics in England sought to prove that performing exorcisms was adhering to the historic faith of the church, and could not therefore be dismissed as a superstitious Irish peculiarity. No evidence survives of the canonical circumstances surrounding Peach's exorcism, but it must have been authorized by the ultra-Papalist Vicar Apostolic of the Midland District, John Milner.[71]

The only surviving correspondence anywhere in a British public archive about a proposed canonical exorcism relates to a request from Thomas Moore in 1814–15 for the exorcism of his brother Peter, a series of documents of unique value in demonstrating the canonical process through which a request for exorcism might pass in the early nineteenth century. The Moores were an important Irish family who were originally Protestant, but Thomas and Peter's father George (1727–99) had converted to Catholicism on moving to Spain in the 1760s, where he was a wine and grain merchant at Alicante. In 1765 George Moore married another Irish Catholic, Catherine Killikelly, who was still living at Alicante in the early nineteenth century.[72] Thomas and Peter's brother John (1767–99) served briefly as Ireland's first republican president ('President of the Government of the Province of Connacht') during the rising of the United Irishmen in 1798.[73]

Peter suffered from recurrent mental health problems. In May 1806, his brother George (1770–1840), later noted as a historian of the Glorious Revolution,[74] first decided to try a spiritual solution, under the pretext of

---

[71] See Young (2013), pp. 223–9 for an extended discussion of this exorcism.
[72] Hone, J., *The Moores of Moore Hall* (London: Jonathan Cape, 1939), pp. 21–2.
[73] Mulloy, S., 'Moore, John (1767–99)' in *Dictionary of Irish Biography* (Cambridge: Cambridge University Press, 2009), vol. 6, pp. 646–7.
[74] Hone (1939), pp. 46–9.

a visit to the Lake District. The brothers went to stay at a lay academy at Ulverston, Lancashire, run by the Irish priest (and future Archbishop of Cashel and Emly) Patrick Everard (c. 1751–1821).[75] Here, according to Thomas, Peter underwent a kind of religious retreat that stopped short of exorcism: Peter 'went thro' … Confessions, Communions, spiritual Exercises &c.'[76] However, the brothers also seem to have visited a more conventional physician, Dr Hunter, in York, and a number of other 'mad doctors' are mentioned in the correspondence.

By 1814 Peter's mental condition had deteriorated to such an extent that Thomas dispatched a friend, James Ryan, to enquire from the Vicar Apostolic of the London District, William Poynter (1762–1827), whether an exorcism was possible. Ryan found the Bishop away from his Holborn residence but later received a reply from Poynter that set out his reservations about exorcism:

> … on the case you propose, tho' there can certainly be no doubt of the possibility of such a species of affliction as Mr Moore apprehends, yet it is absolutely necessary that the *reality* of it, in the particular case, should be evidently stated beyond a doubt, before it would be lawful for a minister of the Church to employ those means which are prescribed in our Rituals. There are so many symptoms of natural disorders which bear a resemblance to some of those which are observed in the case supposed by Mr Moore, that the judgement of medical men declaring that this is not a natural effect nor removeable by the application of natural causes or the use of natural means, would be requisite. Besides if the state of the person be not a derangement of mind, he should by prayer, by the use of the sacraments & other such spiritual means, dispose himself for the spiritual blessing of being delivered from his affliction. Without observing the precautions which the Church wisely prescribes, the power & sacred rites of the Church might & would be exposed to ridicule, especially in this Country.[77]

Poynter's response was typical of more 'liberal' bishops in eighteenth-century Europe, affirming the reality of possession and the efficacy of exorcism as articles of faith, but falling back on the strictures of the *Rituale Romanum* to ensure that the possibility of ever having to authorize an

---

[75] Peter Moore to Catherine Moore, 5 May 1806; Peter Moore to Catherine Moore, 31 May 1806, KHLC MSS U386/B12.
[76] Thomas Moore to William Poynter, 29 November 1814, KHLC MSS U386/B12.
[77] William Poynter to James Ryan, 21 November 1814, KHLC MSS U386/B12.

actual exorcism was diminished almost to nothing. There was one difference, though: Poynter's primary concern was the potential embarrassment to a Catholic minority in a Protestant nation. That this mattered more to Poynter than any other reason is shown by the fact that, in the face of a barrage of letters from Thomas Moore, Poynter prevaricated but kept returning to his fear of 'the misconstruction by Protestants & other Dissenters of the attributes which our belief attached to the mere performance of the ceremony of Exorcism'.[78]

The affair was a protracted one, and Thomas tried every expedient. He pointed out (with some justice) that Poynter's demand that the possession be verified by a physician was impossible to meet, because all physicians disbelieved in the reality of possession. Thomas subsequently approached a French priest in the hope he might be more willing to contemplate exorcism, but this priest told Thomas that the bishop's licence was still needed.[79] Thomas then decided to circumvent Poynter by approaching his Vicar General, but instead he encountered another priest, Richard Broderick, in Lincoln's Inn Fields,

> ... who on hearing our business & what we had to state in support of our anxious wish upon this subject was so kind as to offer to do every thing in his power, & intimated he did not consider any particular authority necessary ... He however expressed a desire to see my Brother for a week or two previous to his performing the ceremony in order to endeavour to bring him round to some sense of his duty to God—to which he readily agreed. My Brother in consequence was with him 3 or 4 times & promised to use prayer ... and I believe occasionally to make the sign of the Cross on the part where he feels affected.[80]

Thomas even arranged a date with Broderick for the exorcism of Peter in early January, but on the day before the planned exorcism Broderick pulled out, saying he could not do it. While Poynter was in Rome, James Ryan approached his Vicar General and tried to shame him into authorizing the exorcism, accusing him of 'pusillanimity' for fearing the Protestant response.[81] The two men tried to get hold of Broderick again but he sent them a note to the effect that, because he now believed Peter was not

---

[78] James Ryan to Thomas Moore, 25 April 1815, KHLC MSS U386/B12.
[79] Thomas Moore to William Poynter, 29 November 1814, KHLC MSS U386/B12.
[80] Thomas Moore to William Poynter, 12 January 1815, KHLC MSS U386/B12.
[81] James Ryan to Thomas Moore, 25 April 1815, KHLC MSS U386/B12.

possessed, Poynter would not oblige him to go through with the exorcism he had promised Thomas he would perform. Thomas subsequently wrote to Poynter, demanding that he find another priest willing to exorcize his brother.[82] The bishop advised him to speak to the three English priests at the chapel in Spanish Place attached to the Spanish embassy. If Thomas could persuade one of them, Poynter would grant the licence.[83]

When Thomas approached one of the priests, Joseph Francis Carpue, he made an 'involuntary gesture of ridicule' at the mention of exorcism that shut down the conversation. Thomas then moved on to a 'Mr Gandolfi' (Peter Gandolphy), reporting that:

> All I could get from him was that Exorcism had never been performed in England & if it was done in Spain I had better send my Brother thither—he said I would not obtain your Lordship's licence ... I remarked upon the proofs of possession he had required of Mr Ryan such as walking against the cieling pulling out a grate with a little finger & reading People's thoughts ... and I read him different signs stated by Thyraeus as proofs of Possession & urged his perusing that & other treaties in the British Museum ... but he said he required no reading on the subject.[84]

Gandolphy was mistaken, of course, that exorcism had never been performed on the English mission—it was a staple of missionary priests until the 1670s—but his suggestion that Thomas take his brother to Spain to be exorcized made sense, and it is puzzling that Thomas did not explore this option given his family connections with Spain; perhaps he thought Peter was not well enough to travel. Gandolphy seems to have been expressing the view that English Catholicism was somehow inherently different from Spanish Catholicism, and that exorcism was simply inappropriate in an English context. Thomas, however, responded by quoting from one of the great seventeenth-century demonologists (the Jesuit Peter Thyraeus) whose works he had read in the British Museum, a striking early instance of antiquarian interest in demonological texts underpinned by an active interest in their contents (exemplified in the twentieth century by Montague Summers). Gandolphy proposed that another priest, John Earle, who read Spanish, should consult Thyraeus' work; 'I told him it was in Latin', Thomas recorded acerbically.

---

[82] Thomas Moore to William Poynter, 25 July 1815, KHLC MSS U386/B12.
[83] William Poynter to Thomas Moore, 2 August 1815, KHLC MSS U386/B12.
[84] Thomas Moore to William Poynter, undated, KHLC MSS U386/B12.

Earle replied to Thomas that he would have nothing to do with the matter, and on 5 August Poynter curtly put an end to the whole affair: 'I request you to understand that I must decline granting a license for the purpose in question to any other clergyman'.[85] The case of Peter Moore was hardly comparable with the violent agitation of the people of Tosos in Spain, but Thomas Moore's letters ooze with passive aggression towards the bishop. Thomas was certainly a layman who expected 'exorcism on demand' from the clergy, and the correspondence demonstrates that this attitude was not confined to the popular religion of the uneducated: Thomas Moore, poring over Thyraeus in the British Museum, was clearly an educated man. The correspondence shines a unique light on what seems to have been a typical gap in views between the laity and hierarchy with respect to exorcism in the eighteenth, nineteenth and even twentieth centuries—indeed, it is not hard to imagine a similar correspondence between an exasperated lay Catholic and a cautious bishop in today's church.

Conclusion

In the eighteenth century the practice of exorcism came under concerted attack from a number of different quarters: Enlightenment rationalism, opposition to the clergy performing exorcisms, sceptical Augustinian theology and state anxiety about civil unrest. This resulted in the early years of the century in the suppression of many exorcism manuals by the Index and an increasing focus on the 1614 *Rituale* as the sole legitimate text. At the same time, however, possession panics continued in the more conservative corners of Catholic Europe and a gulf gradually opened up between a popular religion that saw exorcism as necessary and legitimate and a hierarchy of bishops extremely unwilling to countenance exorcism. Nevertheless, exceptions remained and, in England at least, support for exorcism came to be associated with extreme attachment to orthodoxy and the Pope. In the nineteenth century, it would be the rise of Ultramontanism that would bring exorcism back into the mainstream.

---

[85] William Poynter to Thomas Moore, 5 August 1815, typewritten transcription of the continuation of the correspondence held in the Archives of the Archbishop of Westminster, KHLC MSS U386/B12.

CHAPTER 7

Exorcism in an Age of Doubt: The Nineteenth and Twentieth Centuries

In the aftermath of the French Revolutionary and Napoleonic Wars, which saw Pope Pius VI deposed, Rome declared a Republic and Pope Pius VII imprisoned, the Papacy reinvented itself as the opponent of secular government and increasingly presented Catholicism as a political ideology in its own right. The overthrow of the Papal States in 1870 intensified Pius IX and Leo XIII's convictions that the Catholic church was the victim of a demonically inspired international conspiracy. Yet the basic attitude of extreme caution towards exorcism established by Pope Benedict XIV prevailed until the very end of the nineteenth century, when Leo XIII placed the fight against Satan at the centre of the church's mission. Even then, the burgeoning disciplines of psychology and psychiatry raised so many doubts concerning the reality of possession that the majority of local bishops were reluctant to authorize exorcisms, and the rite promoted by Leo XIII was an attenuated form of exorcism for a sceptical age rather than a revival of the ancient practice. Catholic biblical scholars were also critical of the continued practice of exorcism, and although the condemnation of the Modernists in 1907 temporarily silenced these voices, Vatican II gave a licence to renewed scepticism.

One narrative of the history of exorcism in the nineteenth and twentieth centuries is a story of the growing obsolescence of a practice that, while it remained part of the belief-systems of rural European Catholics and converts from animism in Africa and elsewhere, had no place in modern theology. On this reading of the evidence, cases of possession were cultural

© The Editor(s) (if applicable) and The Author(s) 2016
F. Young, *A History of Exorcism in Catholic Christianity*,
DOI 10.1007/978-3-319-29112-3_7

throwbacks, and the exorcists extreme conservatives who consciously rejected the medical and theological consensus. Although there were cases in which both exorcists and demoniacs adopted self-consciously conservative attitudes, there is also an alternative narrative that emerges from the literature of this period. In the late nineteenth century some Catholics became interested in parapsychology, the study of 'occult' phenomena as objects of scientific investigation, and thereby developed a discourse on the supernatural that avoided the twin perils of retrograde superstition and materialistic scepticism. Naturally, these authors showed an interest in exorcism, the church's traditional method of dealing with unwanted spiritual phenomena. The cultural influence of cinema and a conservative reaction to Vatican II were important factors, but only the acceptance of parapsychology by Catholic demonologists can adequately explain the revival of exorcism from the 1970s onwards, and for this reason the period up to Vatican II, in which exorcism struggled for survival against church authorities reluctant to authorize it, is critical to understanding why exorcism is once again so significant in contemporary Catholicism.

The pattern of behaviour established at Tosos in 1812, in which local people demanded exorcism and controlled the narrative of possession, persisted well into the nineteenth century. Although Maria Tausiet argued that the Spanish case 'portrayed a world in its terminal phase or, in other words, the trials and tribulations of an age that was drawing to an end', Tosos was not the last mass possession in European history.[1] At Morzine in Savoy in 1864, demands for exorcism again turned violent; demoniacs screamed insults at the local bishop for refusing to exorcize them and attacked him in the church.[2] These manifestations, far from being a sign of a world passing away, were evidence of a new tension in the nineteenth-century church between an urbane clergy keen to ingratiate themselves with the secular authorities and ordinary rural people absolutely convinced of the reality of witchcraft. Indeed, the association between possession and traditional malefic witchcraft, involving cursing or ill-wishing, was immensely powerful in many parts of Europe and endured well into the twentieth century. Civil authorities were not uniformly hostile to exorcism,[3] but in general the attitudes of both church and state were out of step with those of ordinary people.

---

[1] Tausiet (2005), p. 277.
[2] Harris (1997), pp. 472–3.
[3] State authorities intervened to arrange an exorcism of two Alsace boys in 1869; see Cristiani, L. (trans. C. Roland), *Satan in the Modern World* (London: Barrie and Rockliff, 1961), pp. 95–104; Rodewyk, A., *Possessed by Satan: The Church's Teaching on the Devil, Possession and Exorcism* (New York: Doubleday, 1975), pp. 9–11.

Indeed, some accounts of twentieth-century exorcisms are indistinguishable from early modern ones. In May 1920 a Franciscan friar at Piacenza made a woman vomit up a cursed bolus of salted pork she had eaten seven years earlier, releasing her from seven demons. During the course of the exorcism the demon Isabô declared that there were seven sorcerers in the neighbourhood.[4] Léon Cristiani, whose *Présence de Satan dans le Monde Moderne* (1959) contained numerous exorcism accounts, obtained first-hand documentation from a French priest in the Vendée, describing exorcisms of a woman between September 1950 and December 1954. These included the use of a 'remote exorcism' by a monk of Bellefontaine Abbey,[5] as well as a formal exorcism in which the woman was tied to a chair in the local church.[6] The source of the possession was a local 'magnetic healer' to whom the woman had been for help; in this case the demon was completely dominated by the will of the 'magician'. The success of exorcisms performed by Emmanuel Milingo in Italy in the 1990s, examined in Chap. 8, demonstrates that the idea of malefic witchcraft continues to play a role in popular religion in some European countries, even if the 'witches' are now therapists and 'magnetic healers'. This lends support to Harris's thesis that 'peasant cosmology' cannot be dismissed simply as a relic of a vanishing world.[7]

EXORCISTS, SAINTS AND DEMONIACS

The most famous Catholic exorcist of the nineteenth century was probably the 'Curé of Ars', Jean-Marie Vianney (1786–1859), whose process of canonization began in the 1870s. Vianney's bishop gave him unconditional permission to exorcize whenever required,[8] but in the majority of stories relating to his liberation of demoniacs he did not go this far. On one interpretation, Vianney was influenced by the prevailing reluctance to commit to formal exorcisms in the nineteenth-century church. On another,

---

[4] On the Piacenza case see Cristiani (1961), pp. 109–23.
[5] Ibid. pp. 124–36. This could only have been Leo XIII's Exorcism of Satan and the Apostate Angels.
[6] Ibid. pp. 137–55.
[7] Harris (1997), pp. 453–4. On belief in possession in nineteenth-century rural France see Devlin, J., *The Superstitious Mind: French Peasants and the Supernatural in the Nineteenth Century* (New Haven, CT: Yale University Press, 1987), pp. 120–39.
[8] Cristiani (1961), p. 32.

Vianney conformed to the model of the charismatic exorcist-saint who had no need of formal liturgical exorcisms; the demons fled at the presence of his holiness. Vianney came closest to performing an exorcism on a man named Antoine Gay (1790–1871). Vianney wrote to Cardinal de Bonald, Archbishop of Lyons, for permission to exorcize Gay and received it both from De Bonald and the Bishop of Belley, but the exorcism never took place. Vianney wanted Gay exorcized at the Marian shrine of Fourvière rather than Ars, but it is unclear why nothing happened.[9] In Cristiani's view, Gay was deliberately left unexorcized because those who examined him understood that his possession had a purpose.[10] He was a prophetic demoniac or 'demoniac-saint' in the mould of Crescentia Höss in the previous century. In the French church's fight against secularism, the possessed Antoine Gay was an asset.[11] C. J. Woollen, a British Dominican, observed in 1949 that demoniacs fell into two categories; those who were possessed because of some sin, and those who endured possession as a test from God.[12] In the case of the latter, exorcism was far from simple.

Satanists and Renegade Priests

The preoccupation with Satanism amongst supporters of exorcism in contemporary Catholicism has its roots in the nineteenth century. Although the belief that there are secret organizations dedicated to evil can be found throughout history, the perceived threat to the Catholic church from secularist and anti-clerical thought in the aftermath of the French Revolution generated an unprecedented fear that the enemies of the church were not only plotting the separation of church and state, but also the spiritual overthrow of Christendom. The enemies of Christ's church were also the worshippers of Satan, and nineteenth-century Satanism was among the 'fantastic constructions of Otherness' that Frankfurter saw as essential for defining religious identity at times of crisis.[13] Supporters of the Satanist hypothesis are generally untroubled by the absence of evidence, since a movement that hides in the shadows and deliberately

---

[9] Ibid. pp. 80–2. On Vianney's exorcism of Gay see also Rutler, G. W., *The Curé of Ars Today* (San Francisco, CA: Ignatius, 1988), pp. 174–6.
[10] Cristiani (1961), pp. 74–5.
[11] On Gay's subsequent career and prophetic pronouncements see ibid. pp. 83–91.
[12] Woollen, C. J., 'The Case for Exorcism', *New Blackfriars* 30:347 (February 1949), pp. 59–62.
[13] Frankfurter (2008), p. 118.

conceals its activities would naturally leave no tracks. For Cristiani, the obituary of the notorious occultist Aleister Crowley and the assertions of the psychic investigator Harry Price constituted sufficient evidence that Satan worship was rife in London,[14] yet Ronald Hutton has argued convincingly that rumours of British Satanism were never anything more than just that.[15]

Belief in the existence of Satanism was particularly potent in France and Italy. To this day, a strong belief in Satanist sects and systematic sacrilege persists in France, although whether sacrilege is an active form of anti-clericalism or evidence of genuine devil-worship remains hotly debated.[16] The reality of deliberate sacrilege does little to illuminate the motivations of its perpetrators. Fear of sacrilegious Satanism is distinct from, and older than, the fear of occultism (including revived 'Satanism') that began in 1960s America and spread from there to Rome, where it provoked the Congregation for the Doctrine of the Faith's condemnation of 'New Age' spirituality in 1989.[17] In Italy, Roman propaganda associated Turin with Satanism, owing to the religious toleration practised by the Piedmontese government between 1870 and 1890. Piedmont's policy of toleration was, at least in part, a strategy to antagonize the Catholic church during the campaign for the unification of Italy. Whether or not Satanism was ever practised in Turin, the city was renowned in Rome as 'the city of the devil'; Papal propaganda drew attention to the pernicious consequences of religious freedom and the supposed enormities committed by Turin's devil-worshippers.[18]

The French novelist Joris-Karl Huysmans claimed to have researched the Parisian Satanist underworld for his 1891 novel *Là-Bas* ('Down There'), in which the hero Durtal investigates the world of black magic. Debate has

[14] Cristiani (1961), pp. 179–80.

[15] Hutton, R., *The Triumph of the Moon: A History of Modern Pagan Witchcraft* (Oxford: Oxford University Press, 1999), pp. 257–61.

[16] On French Satanism see Cristiani (1961), pp. 188–98; Chave-Mahir (2011), p. 19. Hutton (1999), p. 268 argued that acts of sacrilege designed to simulate evidence of Satanic worship were stimulated by the press's promotion of the existence of Satanism.

[17] Congregation for the Doctrine of the Faith, *Letter to Bishops on Certain Aspects of Christian Meditation (Orationis Formas)* (Vatican City: Typis Polyglottis Vaticanis, 1989). On Satanist groups since the 1960s see La Fontaine, J., 'Satanism and Satanic Mythology' in De Blécourt, W., Hutton, R. and La Fontaine, J. (eds), *Witchcraft and Magic in Europe: The Twentieth Century* (London: Athlone, 1989), pp. 81–140, at pp. 94–109.

[18] Introvigne, M., 'Le Satanisme modern et contemporain en Italie', *Social Compass* 56 (2009), pp. 541–51, at pp. 541–2.

raged ever since concerning how much of Huysmans's fiction was based on fact. In the novel, Durtal's friend Des Hermies echoes Huysmans's own suspicion of exorcist priests, whom he believes are nothing but witches and magicians, following in the footsteps of Louis Gaufridy and Urbain Grandier:

> Those who celebrate these God-forsaken [black] masses conceal their feelings and declare themselves devotees of Christ, they even maintain they're defending him by fighting the possessed by means of exorcisms. But even this is a big con, it's they themselves who create or deploy the so-called 'possessed'. In this way, they're certain of a supply of subjects and accomplices, especially in convents. Every kind of murderous or sadistic excess is disguised under the ancient and pious mantle of Exorcism.[19]

However, in addition to the Satanist priest in the novel, Canon Docre, there is also a good exorcist, Dr Johannès, who is portrayed as a victim of the narrow-mindedness of church authorities. The bell-ringer of St Sulpice, Carhaix, who represents the voice of conservative Catholicism, criticizes the church for its failure to condemn Spiritualism as necromancy and for its insufficiently imaginative demonology, which does not recognize incubi and succubi.[20] Johannès exorcizes nuns who have been assaulted by incubi, incurring the anger of the Curia and the Archbishop of Paris, who accuses him of 'vile doctrines'.[21] Johannès subsequently retires to Lyons where he cures the possessed by a procedure known as 'the sacrifice to the glory of Melchisedek', and preaches the coming of the Paraclete.[22]

Huysmans modelled Johannès on the notorious laicized priest Joseph-Antoine Boullan (1824–93) who founded the 'Society for the Reparation of Souls', which practised a mixture of magic and exorcism. Boullan was imprisoned in Rome but escaped after the city fell to Italian armies in 1870. In 1875 he took over the 'Church of Carmel' founded by the visionary and mystic Eugene Vintras, a factory foreman from Tilly-sur-Seulles.[23] Boullan's magazine, *Les Annales de la Sainteté au XIXe siècle*,

---

[19] Huysmans, J.-K. (trans. B. King), *Là-Bas* (Sawtry: Dedalus, 2001), p. 75.
[20] Ibid. pp. 143–4.
[21] Huysmans (2001 [1891]), pp. 194–5.
[22] Ibid. pp. 198–9.
[23] Maxwell-Stuart, P. G., *Wizards: A History* (Stroud: Tempus, 2004), pp. 174–5. A. E. Waite in *Devil-worship in France: or, The Question of Lucifer* (London: G. Redway, 1896), p. 17 thought that Dr Johannès was based on Vintras. Jean Sempe, known as the

which Huysmans seems to have used as a source for the novel, claimed to record instances of sacrilege and exorcism. Johannès's interest in 'exorcizing' nuns under the influence of incubi was mirrored in reality by Boullan's practice of encouraging nuns to imagine sexual encounters with Christ. Huysmans, who became a devout Catholic later in life, eventually lost faith in Boullan and denounced him.[24]

The British occultist A. E. Waite (1857–1942), writing in 1896, claimed that Huysmans wrote 'under the thinnest disguise of fiction', and described him as 'the discoverer of modern Satanism'.[25] Waite acknowledged the reality of incidents of sacrilege and 'outrageous crimes' in France, and claimed that the real Canon Docre, 'leader of a "demoniac clan"', was living in Belgium.[26] However, Waite was keen to counter the misconception that his own occult organization, the Hermetic Order of the Golden Dawn, was associated with Satanism. He attacked the Catholic church for its hypocrisy, singling out Leo Meurin (1825–95), Archbishop of Port-Louis in Mauritius. Meurin, a Jesuit, was the author of *La Franc-maçonnerie: Synagogue de Satan* (1893), a virulently anti-Semitic attack on Freemasonry as a devil-worshipping cult.[27] Waite noted that, although Meurin claimed to have exposed supposed sacrilege and Satanic practices in Mauritius, the Archbishop had done nothing about this: 'The Church does not stir in the matter; it deplores and prays'.[28] Echoing Carhaix, Waite argued that if the church was really concerned about Satanism it would deploy its ancient remedies, such as exorcism. However, Meurin's anti-Semitism proved that in reality he regarded Freemasonry as a political rather than a spiritual threat.[29] Waite argued that the church reacted to 'Satanism' only when it was connected with Freemasonry or the Jews, and was apathetic when it came to genuine Satanism.[30]

Abbé Julio, was another unofficial exorcist of this period whose works remain popular (Sempe, J., *Livre Secret des Grands Exorcismes et Bénédictions* (Paris: Bussière, 1908)).

[24] On Huysmans and Boullan see Brendan King's notes on Huysmans's text (Huysmans (2001 [1891]), p. 303).

[25] Waite (1896), p. 11. On Boullan see also Cristiani (1961), pp. 185–7.

[26] Waite (1896), pp. 14–17.

[27] Meurin, L., *La Franc-maçonnerie: Synagogue de Satan* (Paris: Victor Retaux, 1893), pp. 120–1 (for the argument that Freemasons worshipped the devil).

[28] Waite (1896), pp. 84–5.

[29] Ibid. pp. 82–96.

[30] Ibid. pp. 310–12.

Leo XIII and Exorcism

Related to, but distinguishable from, the Satanic panic of the late nineteenth century was a renewed apocalypticism associated with a belief that the devil's power over the world was growing. No-one did more to encourage this strand of apocalyptic fin-de-siècle Catholicism than Pope Leo XIII (1810–1903), elected in 1878. Leo, famously dubbed 'the prisoner of the Vatican' on account of his refusal to set foot outside the Vatican and thereby recognize the sovereignty of the Kingdom of Italy over the former Papal States, was a determined opponent of state secularism. Perhaps more than any other Pope, Leo XIII is also associated with exorcism. The two principal reasons for this were his addition of an appeal to St Michael to the optional prayers after mass in 1886 and his *Exorcismus in satanam et angelos apostaticos* ('Exorcism against Satan and the Apostate Angels'), added to the *Rituale Romanum* by a decree of the Sacred Congregation of Rites on 18 May 1890.[31]

Leo's preoccupation with spiritual warfare has given rise to a number of legends that originate from two mid-twentieth-century testimonies by Domenico Pechenino and Cardinal Giovanni Nasalli Rocca di Corneliano. In 1947 Pechenino described an incident that supposedly occurred in the Vatican Palace some time before 1890[32]:

---

[31] Österreich (1930), p. 200. This exorcism did not appear in the *Rituale Romanum* as an addition to the liturgy of exorcism until 1925 (Kunzler, M., *The Church's Liturgy* (Münster: Lit Verlag, 2001), p. 317). For the text see *Rituale Romanum* (Rome: Typis Polyglottis Vaticanis, 1925), pp. 537–42.

[32] Pechenino, D., *La Settimana del Clero* (30 March 1947) quoted in P., I., 'Notae Practicae de Precibus post Missam imperatis', *Ephemerides Liturgicae* 69 (1955), pp. 54–60, at p. 58: 'Un mattino il grande Pontifice Leone XIII ... aveva celebrato la S. Messa e stava assistendo ad un'altra di ringraziamento come al solito. Ad un tratto lo si vide drizzare energicamente il capo, poi fissare intensamente qualche cosa al di sopra del capo del celebrante. Guardava fisso, senza batter palpebra, ma con un senso di terrore e di meraviglia, cambiando colore e lineamenti. Qualcosa di strano, di grande avveniva in lui. Finalmente, come rivenendo in sè, e, dando un leggero ma energico tocco di mano, si alza. Lo si vede avviarsi verso il suo studio privato. I familiari lo seguono con premura e ansiosi. 'Santo Padre!'—gli dicono sommessamente—'non si sente bene? Ha bisogna di qualcosa?'—'Niente, niente!', risponde. E si chiude dentro. Dopo una mezz'ora fa chiamare il Segretario della S. Congregazione dei Riti, e, porgendogli un foglio, gli ingiunge di farlo stampare e pervenire a tutti gli Ordinari del mondo. Che cosa conteneva? La preghiera che recitiamo al termine della Messa col populo, con la supplica a Maria e l'infocata invocazione al Principe delle milizie celesti, s. Michele'.

One morning the great Pope Leo XIII ... had celebrated mass and, as usual, was attending another mass of thanksgiving. Suddenly, he was seen to shake his head vigorously, then stare at something above the celebrant's head. With a fixed gaze, without blinking, but with a sense of terror and amazement, the colour and the lines of his face changed. Something strange and great was happening in him. Finally, as though returning to himself, and giving a light but energetic tap of the hand, he rose. He was seen to go towards his private office. His retinue followed anxiously and solicitously: 'Holy Father', they said in a low voice, 'are you not feeling well? Do you need anything?' He answered: 'Nothing, nothing'. And he shut himself in. After about half an hour he called for the Secretary of the Sacred Congregation of Rites and, handing him a sheet of paper, ordered him to print it and send it to all the ordinaries of the world. What did it contain? The prayer that we recite at the end of mass with the people, with the supplication to Mary and the fervent invocation to the Prince of the heavenly host, St Michael.

'I. P.', the author of the article in *Ephemerides Liturgicae* that reported this reminiscence, believed that Pechenino was confusing the prayer to St Michael at the end of the mass, which was authorized in 1886, with the exorcism published in 1890. Cardinal Rocca di Corneliano reported another version of the story, supposedly derived from Rinaldo Angeli, a 'familiar prelate of the Pontiff', who claimed that the Pope had a vision of demons congregating against the city of Rome, and composed the prayer to St Michael there and then, reciting it frequently in St Peter's Basilica. The Pope personally wrote the exorcism against Satan and the apostate angels and frequently recited it; he also recommended that bishops and priests should read these exorcisms often in their dioceses and parishes.[33]

The new Exorcism of Leo XIII began with extracts taken from Psalms 67 and 34, followed by a lengthy petition addressed to St Michael and then the exorcism itself, which began with a series of ten conjurations[34]:

[33] 'Notae Practicae' (1955), pp. 58–9.
[34] *Rituale Romanum* (1925), pp. 539–41: *Exorcizamus te, omnis immundus spiritus, omnis satanica potestas, omnis incursio infernalis adversarii, omnis legio, omnis congregatio et secta diabolica, in nomine et virtute Domini Nostri Jesu Christi ... Non ultra audeas, serpens callidissime, decipere humanum genus, Dei Ecclesiam persequi, ac Dei electos excutere et cribrare sicut triticum. Imperat tibi Deus altissimus, cui in magna tua superbia te similem haberi adhuc praesumis ... Imperat tibi Deus Pater; imperat tibi Deus Filius; imperat tibi Deus Spiritus Sanctus. Imperat tibi majestas Christi, aeternum Dei Verbum, caro factum ... Imperat tibi sacramentum Crucis, omniumque christianae fidei Mysteriorum virtus. Imperat tibi excelsa Dei Genitrix Virgo Maria, quae superbissimum caput tuum a primo instanti immaculatae suae conceptionis in sua humilitate contrivit. Imperat tibi fides sanctorum Apostolorum Petri et Pauli, et ceterorum Apostolorum. Imperat tibi Martyrum sanguis, ac pia Sanctorum et Sanctarum omnium intercessio.*

We exorcize you, every unclean spirit, every Satanic power, every incursion of the infernal adversary, every legion, every diabolical sect and gathering, in the name and by the virtue of our Lord Jesus Christ ... May you not dare further, most clever serpent, to deceive the human race, to persecute the Church of God, to thresh and sift God's elect like wheat. God the highest commands you, to whom in your great pride you still presume to be taken as alike ... God the Father commands you, God the Son commands you, God the Holy Spirit commands you. The majesty of Christ, the eternal Word of God made flesh commands you ... The sacrament of the Cross commands you, and the power of all the Mysteries of the Christian faith. The exalted Mother of God, the Virgin Mary commands you, who crushed your most proud head in humility at the first moment of her Immaculate Conception. The faith of the holy Apostles Peter and Paul, and of the other Apostles commands you. The blood of the Martyrs commands you, and the intercession of all the pious saints.

The exorcism proceeded to an adjuration[35]:

Therefore, accursed dragon and every diabolical legion, we adjure you by the living God, by the true God, by the holy God ... cease to deceive human creatures and offer them to drink the poison of eternal damnation. Stop harming the Church and casting her freedom into snares. Depart, Satan, inventor and master of every falsehood, enemy of human salvation. Yield to Christ, in whom you have found none of your works; yield to the one, holy, catholic and apostolic Church, whom Christ himself acquired by his blood. Humble yourself beneath the powerful hand of God; tremble and flee at our invocation of the holy and terrible name of Jesus, who shakes hell, to whom the Virtues of the heavens and the Powers and Dominions are subject; whom the Cherubim and Seraphim praise with tireless voices, saying: holy, holy, holy Lord God of hosts.

---

[35] *Ergo, draco maledicte et omnis legio diabolica, adjuramus te per Deum vivum, per Deum verum, per Deum sanctum ... cessa decipere humanas creaturas, eisque aeternae perditionis venenum propinare: desine Ecclesiae nocere, et ejus libertati laqueos injicere. Vade, satana, inventor et magister omnis fallaciae, hostis humanae salutis. Da locum Christo, in quo nihil invenisti de operibus tuis; da locum Ecclesiae uni, sanctae, catholicae, et apostolicae, quam Christus ipse acquisivit sanguine suo. Humiliare sub potenti manu Dei; contremisce et effuge, invocato a nobis sancto et terribili nomine Jesu, quem inferi tremunt, cui Virtutes caelorum et Potestates et Dominationes subjectae sunt; quem Cherubim et Seraphim indefessis vocibus laudant, dicentes: Sanctus, Sanctus, Sanctus Dominus Deus Sabaoth.*

Parts of this exorcism are clearly derived from the *Rituale Romanum* (*RR* 896, 900–901, 904), but Leo's liturgy has certain distinctive features. It is in the first person plural, (*exorcizamus* rather than *exorcizo*), suggesting that it was intended as a collective act of the whole church. The phrase 'every diabolical sect and gathering' (*omnis congregatio et secta diabolica*) is distinctive to the exorcism, and recalls Leo's belief in organized Satanism. The exorcism also makes an explicit reference to the dogma of the Immaculate Conception and commands Satan to stop harming the church, both nineteenth-century preoccupations. Indeed, the most striking feature of the exorcism is that it was not intended to exorcize a specific person or object. It was, instead, a 'general exorcism' directed against the powers of darkness, for which there was no obvious liturgical precedent. Woollen explained that Leo's exorcism did not contain the danger to the exorcist present in the major exorcism and could be used privately by priests and by the laity, thereby recruiting them to the struggle against Satan.[36] The exorcism could also be used remotely. As such, it was an acknowledgement that the rite of major exorcism was not fit for purpose, and furnished an alternative to ensure that Catholics continued to confront the devil.

Leo believed that he was aware of a demonic influence, invisible and insidious, directed against the church, and the use of the term 'apostate angels' rather than 'demons' calls to mind the apostasy of which Leo considered secular Europe guilty. However, although Leo showed an impressive command of the language of exorcism from the *Rituale Romanum*, recombining elements of the ancient liturgy in new and creative ways, his 'general exorcism' was a theological and liturgical innovation. For the first time, exorcism was being deployed against the devil as the enemy of the institutional church rather than as the enemy of God and humankind.

The Theological Challenge

As Pechenino acknowledged, an important component of Leo XIII's personal struggle against the powers of darkness was his campaign against 'international masonry'. However, the church's opposition to Freemasonry would also produce the greatest embarrassment of Leo's pontificate. In his encyclical *Humani generis* (1884) Leo denounced

---

[36] Woollen (1949), p. 62. There is little evidence that exorcism was thought to be risky before the Earling exorcism of 1928.

Freemasonry as the ideology at the root of all attempts to separate church and state. It was an organized alternative to Christianity and indirectly (or even directly) Satanic. An anti-clerical French author, Léo Taxil (1854–1907), declared himself to have been converted by *Humani generis* and, under the pseudonym of 'Docteur Bataille', wrote *Le Diable au XIXe siècle* (1892) to expose 'Palladism', a form of Satanism supposedly practised by Freemasons. Taxil's book introduced Diana Vaughan, an ex-Satanist who described her experiences and later wrote two books 'in her own right'. Taxil's work was well received by the church and he even obtained an audience with Leo, who supposedly praised Vaughan's writings. On 19 April 1897 Taxil publicly announced that his 'conversion' was fake, that Vaughan was a fiction and that he had deliberately written his book to exploit the credulity of the Catholic church and mock its opposition to Freemasonry.[37]

In 1909 the British priest and Modernist theologian George Tyrell (1861–1909) condemned Leo's credulity and the tendency of Catholics to personify evil in the shape of Freemasons and Jews. Tyrell included a rejection of the theology of exorcism:

> A host of mental, moral and physical evils, which science now deals with, not to speak of storms, plagues and other destructive phenomena of nature, have, till quite recent times, been ascribed to the Devil by the Church, and treated by prayer and exorcism. Even so modern a Pope as Leo XIII accepted the fables of Leo Taxil and his mythical Diana Vaughan, and exorcised Rome daily; and the prevailing mind of uncritical Catholics is still quick to explain all the evils of the time by the Devil and his human agents—Jews, Freemasons, Protestants and Modernists.[38]

John Ratté has argued that, rather than opposing traditional Catholic demonology, Tyrell believed that the 'pessimistic' stage in which believers thought of themselves as beset by the devil was just one in the evolution of religion; the mistake of Catholic theologians was to uphold a fossilized

---

[37] On Diana Vaughan and the Taxil hoax see Closson, M., '*Le Diable au XIXe siècle* de Léo Taxil: ou les "mille et un nuits" de la démonologie' in Lavocat, F., Kapitaniak, P. and Closson, M. (eds), *Fictions du Diable: Démonologie et Littérature de Saint Augustin à Léo Taxil* (Paris: Droz, 2007), pp. 313–32, at pp. 326–7; Ziegler, R., *Satanism, Magic and Mysticism in Fin-de-siècle France* (Basingstoke: Palgrave Macmillan, 2012), pp. 50–73.

[38] Tyrell, G., *Christianity at the Crossroads* (London: Longmans, Green and Co., 1909), pp. 71–2.

theology.[39] The American Modernist William L. Sullivan (1872–1935), a Paulist priest who converted to Unitarianism in 1911, did not so much condemn exorcism as assume its redundancy, using exorcism as an example to argue that the church had been influenced by, and now defended, pagan superstition[40]:

> When we see Christianity born to the inheritance of this universal religious conception, when we find the Gospels attributing sickness to devils, St. Paul declaring that the very air is full of them, and early Christianity setting up a body of ministers to expel them, shall we be so stubborn as to say that Christianity was uninfluenced by extraneous ideas? The world of devils, the swarming myriads of them have disappeared. We now call in not the exorcist but the physician to an epileptic ... The once busy exorcists in the church, have now absolutely nothing to do. In other words, we have grown away from a New Testament notion which we perceive was sprung from superstition and pre-Christian paganism.

Although the Modernists had been officially silenced or ejected from the Catholic church by 1910, their criticism of practices such as exorcism as superstitious and 'medieval' continued to carry weight in popular perceptions of Catholicism. The most notable instance of an 'anti-Modernist reaction' in the field of demonology was Alexis Lépicier's *Le Monde Invisible* (1921), which obtained a personal endorsement from Pope Benedict XV.[41] Although only a small portion of Lépicier's work was devoted to exorcism, Lépicier insisted on the necessity of imperative rather than deprecative exorcisms and the distinction between exorcism and prayer—an issue that would become controversial with the publication of the revised rite of exorcism in 1999.[42]

The 1917 Code of Canon Law reiterated the *Rituale Romanum*'s instructions that major exorcisms could only be carried out by a minister specifically licensed to do so by his local ordinary, and emphasized that such a priest should be characterized by piety, prudence and integrity of life. Furthermore, the Code re-echoed Benedict XIV's insistence that

---

[39] Ratté, J., *Three Modernists: Alfred Loisy, George Tyrrell, William L. Sullivan* (London: Sheed and Ward, 1968), pp. 229–30.

[40] Sullivan, W. L., *Letters to His Holiness Pope Pius X* (Chicago, IL: Open Court, 1910), pp. 109–10.

[41] Lépicier, A. H. M., *The Unseen World: An Exposition of Catholic Theology in Reference to Modern Spiritism* (London: Sheed and Ward, 1929), pp. ix–x.

[42] Ibid. pp. 248–53.

'a diligent and prudent investigation' should be carried out to decide if a person was genuinely possessed (Canon 1151). For the first time, the Code formally restricted exorcism to priests, preventing deacons and seminarians in minor orders from performing them, yet it also explicitly permitted exorcisms of non-Catholics (Canon 1152). The Code clarified the relationship between major and minor exorcisms, stating that 'The ministers of the exorcisms that occur in baptism and in consecrations and benedictions are the same who are legitimate ministers of those same sacred rites' (Canon 1153). In other words, any priest or deacon could perform a 'minor exorcism', such as the exorcism of holy water and its apotropaic use, without episcopal permission.[43]

THE MEDICAL CHALLENGE

Modern medicine's challenge to the ideas of possession and exorcism took its most extreme form between 1860 and 1863, when French doctors employed the military to impose their diagnosis of 'hysteria-demonopathy' on demoniacs in the Savoyard village of Morzine. The outbreak of possessions began in 1857 with visions of the Virgin Mary similar to those which occurred around Lourdes in the years after Bernadette Soubirous's original vision of the 'Immaculate Conception'. The parish priest, the Abbé Favre, willingly exorcized the young women and girls of Morzine until he was ordered to desist by French authorities concerned by this outbreak of superstition. A Paris physician, Adolphe Constans, brought in the army to deal with the unruly demoniacs and, by a mixture of incarceration, expulsion and, later, cultural education, forced the possessions underground or over the border into Switzerland.[44]

In 1884 Dr Gabriel Legué published *Urbain Grandier et les Possédées de Loudun*, an early attempt to reinterpret the famous Loudun possessions in terms of late nineteenth-century understandings of mental illness. In 1887 another physician, Jean-Martin Charcot, a doctor at the Salpêtrière (Paris's principal hospital for the insane), extended Legué's attempt at 'historical diagnosis' by arguing that the symptoms of his patients resembled those depicted in artistic representations of demonic possession

---

[43] *Codex Iuris Canonici* (ed. P. Gasparri) (Rome: Typis Polyglottis Vaticanis, 1963), pp. 385–6.
[44] Harris (1997), pp. 451–2.

throughout history.[45] While Charcot was by no means the first to suggest that 'possession' was mental illness, he was the first to systematically apply historical diagnosis to past cases of possession, a vogue that culminated in Aldous Huxley's *The Devils of Loudun* (1952), yet another treatment of the Ursuline nuns. In the late 1930s Joseph de Tonquédec, exorcist for the Archdiocese of Paris, initiated a debate in the French church concerning the appropriateness of exorcism that resulted in French bishops becoming very reluctant to authorize the rite.[46] De Tonquédec, who served as an exorcist for almost fifty years, was not convinced that he ever came across a genuine case of possession. Indeed, De Tonquédec was prepared to confess that he frequently made the mistake of exorcizing the sick early on in his ministry, and in these cases the impressive rituals of exorcism called up 'a diabolical mythomania in word and deed in a psyche already weak'.[47]

As the disciplines of psychiatry and psychology began to produce physiological explanations for mental pathologies, Catholic theologians were confronted with the dilemma of how to distinguish demonic possession from natural illness, and indeed from a possessing demon deliberately simulating the symptoms of natural illness. The French Catholic neurologist Jean Lhermitte, whilst accepting the possibility of demonic possession, categorized pseudo-possessions as epileptic attacks, psychoneuroses or hysteria; indeed, the only true possessions he referred to were those in

---

[45] Charcot, J.-M. and Richer, P., *Les Démoniaques dans l'Art* (Paris: Delahaye et Lecrosnier, 1887). On Charcot see Céard, J., 'Démonologie et Démonopathies au temps du Charcot', *Histoire des Sciences Médicales* 28 (1994), pp. 337–43; Ferber, S., 'Charcot's Demons: Retrospective Medicine and Historical Diagnosis in the Writings of the Salpêtrière School' in Gijswijt-Hofstra, M., Marland, H. and De Waardt, H. (eds), *Illness and Healing Alternatives in Western Europe* (London: Routledge, 1997), pp. 120–40; Levack (2013), pp. 127–9. On exorcism and psychology in the nineteenth century see Vandermeersch, P., 'The Victory of Psychiatry over Demonology: The Origin of the Nineteenth-Century Myth', *History of Psychiatry* 2 (1991), pp. 351–63; Guillemain, H., *Diriger les Consciences, Guérir les Âmes: Une Histoire comparée des Pratiques Thérapeutiques et Religieuses (1830–1939)* (Paris: La Découverte, 2006).

[46] On the debate in the French church see De Tonquédec, J., *Les Maladies Nerveuses ou Mentales et les Manifestations Diaboliques* (Paris: Beauchesne, 1938); Chave-Mahir (2011), pp. 18–9.

[47] De Tonquédec, J., 'Some Aspects of Satan's Activity in this World' in *Satan* (New York: Sheed and Ward, 1951), pp. 40–51; see also Maquart, F. X. and De Tonquédec, J., 'Exorcism'; Sheed, F. J. (ed.), *Soundings in Satanism* (Mowbrays: London, 1972), pp. 72–91. On De Tonquédec see Kelly (1968), pp. 93–4.

the Gospels.[48] In effect, therefore, Lhermitte side-stepped the diagnostic problem by adopting a *de facto* cessationist approach to possession similar to that of some eighteenth-century theologians.[49]

The development of psychiatry as a scientific discipline had little effect on the liturgy, although in the 1952 edition of the 1614 *Rituale Romanum* the mention of 'black bile' in the instructions for exorcists was changed to 'some disease, especially those caused by psychic factors'. Furthermore, the phrase 'the signs of a possessing demon are …' was weakened to 'the signs of a possessing demon can be …'.[50] Yet as late as 1949, Woollen argued that schizophrenia was psychiatry's label for possession rather than an alternative interpretation of the phenomenon. The growth of 'schizophrenia' diagnoses did not demonstrate that it was different from possession, but rather that the devil's power over the world was growing.[51] However, since exorcism remained the responsibility of diocesan bishops, the easiest response to the doubts thrown up by psychology and psychiatry was to withhold permission for exorcisms.

Beyond Europe

European missionaries imported their ideas about exorcism into other continents in the twentieth century, yet the influence was by no means one-way, and exorcists struggled to come to terms with local cultural expectations. One particularly well-publicized case of a 'colonial exorcism' took place in early twentieth-century South Africa. In July 1906 a sixteen-year-old Zulu girl living at the St Michael Mission Station at Umzinto, near Durban in South Africa, told her confessor that she had made a pact with the devil. Clara Germana Cele (1890–1913), known as Germana, displayed some of the symptoms of possession, speaking in an alternate, demonic voice that demonstrated knowledge of hidden things. However, at other times Germana was normal, and continued to confess and receive communion throughout her possession. The Rector of the mission,

---

[48] Lhermitte, J. (trans. P. J. Hepbourne-Scott), *Diabolical Possession: True and False* (London, 1963), pp. 72–88; Lhermitte, J., 'Pseudo-Possession' in Sheed, F. J. (ed.), *Soundings in Satanism* (London: Mowbrays, 1972), pp. 12–35.

[49] On demonological debates in twentieth-century France see Cristiani (1961), pp. 156–7; Guillemain, H., 'Déments ou Démons? L'exorcisme face au sciences psychiques', *Revue d'Histoire de l'Eglise en France* 87 (2001), pp. 439–71.

[50] Balducci (1959), p. 391; Kelly (1968), p. 84.

[51] Woollen (1949), p. 61.

Fr Mansuet, wrote to the Vicar Apostolic asking for permission to begin an exorcism. However, as the Bishop was absent at the time, permission was given by the Vicar General, and the exorcism took place in September 1906. Mansuet was assisted by another priest, Hörner Erasmus, and the exorcism took place in the mission chapel from early morning until noon, then from three o'clock until late into the night. Three priests, three monks, 14 nuns and 150 of the mission station's inhabitants were present.

The demonic voice speaking through Germana claimed that it would make the demoniac levitate as a sign of its departure, which supposedly took place at ten o'clock the next morning. Germana showed no further signs of demonic possession, but shortly afterwards she made a second pact with the devil and was possessed again. Henri Delalle, the Vicar Apostolic of Natal who had been absent when permission for the first exorcism was given, was sceptical and visited the mission station along with another priest named Delagues who did believe in its reality. Delalle was present for the second exorcism which began on 24 April 1907 and, like the first, lasted for two days. Delalle wanted to stop the exorcism, but Germana herself insisted it should carry on. When the priests stopped she became uncontrollable, and Delalle permitted it to continue for this reason.[52]

By the time of Germana's second exorcism the Umzinto possessions were spreading; a second girl at the mission station, Monica Moletshe, was also possessed. Monica said she had made a pact with the devil in March 1907; when Delalle visited her in April, he concluded that she was either ill or obsessed rather than possessed, but just as he was about to leave he agreed to stay and recite Leo XIII's prayer to St Michael. At this point Monica showed what Delalle considered to be genuine signs of possession—'The Devil is here,' the Bishop declared, 'but he is a very strong one, I'm not sure I can drive him out'.[53] In addition to Germana and Monica, a third girl at Umzinto named Engelberta was also possessed at this time.[54]

All of the girls at the mission station were Christian converts, and Germana had apparently been sexually abused by a female witch doctor earlier in life. The precise cultural context of the Umzinto exorcisms is difficult to reconstruct, but it is quite evident that Germana's attitude to spirit

---

[52] Rodewyk (1975), pp. 120–7. On the Umzinto possessions see also Cristiani (1961), pp. 106–7.
[53] Rodewyk (1975), pp. 127–33.
[54] Ibid. pp. 133–4.

possession was dramatically different from that of her European exorcists. On two occasions she willingly made a pact with the devil, suggesting that she viewed the spiritual world as a community of spirits with whom she could make beneficial agreements rather than a struggle between good and evil. The cultural chasm between Germana's understanding of exorcism and that of her exorcists made it difficult to reconcile her behaviour with that of European demoniacs throughout the centuries, and perhaps contributed to Bishop Delalle's incredulity. The theological categories of possession and obsession broke down when confronted by the experiences of participants in an animistic culture with 'a fluid pantheon of ghosts and harmful spirits'.[55] Delalle's suspicions may also have been aroused by the relatively short duration of Germana's exorcism (a day and a half). Again, the clergy assumed that exorcism was a bitter struggle against the devil. Within Germana's animistic culture, it may have been closer to a ritual whereby allegiance to one spirit was replaced by allegiance to another.

Robert Hugh Benson, a British priest and convert from Anglicanism, recreated a fictional exorcism resembling the Umzinto case in his *Mirror of Shalott* (1907), a collection of tales in which a French priest, Fr Meuron (perhaps named after Archbishop Meurin), recounts what happened to him as a young priest on an island in the Lesser Antilles. Meuron notes that 'exorcism … is a matter with which we who live in Europe are not familiar in these days', because in Europe 'the sacrifices offered and the prayers poured out have a faculty of holding Satan in check and preventing his more formidable manifestations'. The Caribbean, by contrast, was 'a stronghold of darkness'. Meuron is portrayed as a student of Charcot who dismisses the symptoms of a possessed woman as a combination of epilepsy and suggestion, but is convinced of the reality of the demonic when, following the successful exorcism by another priest, a plate of meat in the room instantly corrupts. Benson clearly had little knowledge of the rite of exorcism, which he erroneously claimed appeared neither in the *Ritual* nor the *Pontifical*.[56] However, Benson's story reveals dramatically how encounters between Catholic missionaries and native peoples conscious of the reality of a spiritual world challenged European scientific

---

[55] On the introduction of demonology into non-European societies see Frankfurter (2008), pp. 31–7.

[56] Benson, R. H., *A Mirror of Shalott* in *The Supernatural Stories of Monsignor Robert H. Benson* (Landisville, PA: Coachwhip Publications, 2010), pp. 129–38.

orthodoxy and created a double standard in which exorcism was appropriate for the 'savage' world, but not for Europe.

Catholic immigrant communities brought their own ideas of possession and exorcism with them to America. A dramatic exorcism at Earling, Iowa conducted between August and December 1928 by a Capuchin, Theophilus Riesinger, was first reported in a German pamphlet before being translated into English and reprinted numerous times up to the twenty-first century. Riesinger, who was conducting a mission in the parish, asked the local priest for permission to exorcize Anna Ecklund, a woman whom he believed to be possessed. The priest's reported reaction suggests that exorcism was Riesinger's speciality: 'You have already dispossessed the devil in a number of such cases!' Riesinger had, in fact, exorcized the woman once before in June 1912,[57] and Bishop Thomas Drumm of Des Moines had entrusted Riesinger with the case in advance of his arrival.[58] By initiating the exorcism himself, determining where it should take place and acting as a sort of travelling exorcist, Riesinger's ministry in the twentieth-century American Midwest was a striking continuation of that of seventeenth-century Capuchins.

The Earling exorcism was characterized by extensive dialogue between the exorcist and the possessing demons that went far beyond the rubrics of the *Rituale Romanum*, along with extreme violence directed towards the exorcist. Bishop Drumm even warned the parish priest that he could expect to face personal danger in the exorcism and that the devil might take revenge.[59] Neither violence nor the apocalyptic prophecies that featured prominently in the Earling case were common in reported European exorcisms from the same period.[60] Ecklund was possessed by Judas Iscariot as well as her own father, Jacob. She was first possessed in 1908 through the agency of her aunt Mina, who was her father's mistress, 'known among the people as a witch'.[61] However, the principal cause of her possession was not traditional malefic witchcraft but a curse she received from her father, presented by Carl Vogl as a consequence of her father's sexual sins.[62] Vogl's account of the Earling exorcism belongs to the genre of sensational pious

---

[57] Vogl, C. (trans. C. Kapsner), *Begone Satan! A Soul-Stirring Account of Diabolical Possession* (Hong Kong: Catholic Truth Society, 1970 [first published 1935]), p. 47.
[58] Ibid. pp. 5, 9.
[59] Ibid. p. 7.
[60] For the apocalyptic prophecies of the coming of Antichrist see ibid. pp. 40–1.
[61] Ibid. p. 47.
[62] Ibid. pp. 19–20.

literature, demonstrated by his frequent references to Theresa Neumann and Anne Catherine Emmerich, visionaries whose popular writings did not enjoy the church's official approbation. The popular nature of Vogl's narrative may explain the emphasis on the gross physicality and violence of the possession, yet the same themes of violence recurred in the diary of the Mount Rainier exorcism between 7 March and 19 April 1949, which was produced for internal consumption only.[63] However, the Jesuits involved in the Mount Rainier exorcism were aware of the Earling case, which by the mid-twentieth century set the pattern for the 'American exorcism'.[64]

A thirteen-year-old boy from the Mount Rainier area of Washington DC, called 'Robbie Mannheim' by Thomas Allen and 'Roland Doe' in other accounts (here I refer to him by the initial R) manifested signs of possession accompanied by pronounced paranormal phenomena such as telekinesis after playing with a Ouija board given to him by his aunt Harriet.[65] R's family were Lutheran, but after receiving little help from the Lutheran minister or psychiatrists, they sought the help of E. Albert Hughes, a local parish priest. Hughes was authorized by Patrick O'Boyle, Archbishop of Washington, to carry out the exorcism himself, although in Allen's view he was unprepared for the task. Hughes may have been influenced by Vogl's view that the devil cannot reveal during an exorcism what the priest has confessed,[66] but he did not anticipate the violence of the demoniac, which apparently left him seriously injured after an abortive attempt to exorcize R in hospital.[67]

R's family subsequently moved to St Louis, Missouri in an effort to distance the boy from the site of the disturbances, but problems continued and the family made contact with local Jesuits. William S. Bowdern (1897–1983), a Jesuit who taught at St Louis University, approached the Archbishop of St Louis, Joseph Ritter, for authorization of an exorcism on 14 March 1949. Allen portrayed Ritter as reluctant to do so on account of his liberal theological leanings, and interpreted his decision to appoint Bowdern as the exorcist as an indication of his reluctance to seek help from another diocese. No actual evidence survives of Ritter's reaction, however, and all we know for certain is that he enjoined Bowdern and the other

---

[63] For the text of the diary, see Allen (2000), pp. 243–91.
[64] Ibid. pp. 82–4.
[65] For an alternative to Allen's account see Kelly, H. A., *The Devil, Demonology and Witchcraft*, 2nd edn (Eugene, OR: Wipf and Stock, 2004), pp. 94–100.
[66] Vogl (1970 [1935]), pp. 31–2; Allen (2000), p. 33.
[67] On Hughes's first exorcism see Allen (2000), pp. 35–8.

Jesuits to absolute secrecy.[68] However, the case was publicized, apparently by the Lutheran minister whom R's family first approached, prompting a press release from the Archdiocese of Washington that further fanned public interest. The case's notoriety and significance in American culture derives from the fact that it caught the attention of the young William Peter Blatty.[69] Years later, in 1971, Blatty changed the gender of the protagonist but used the events of the exorcism as the basis for his novel *The Exorcist*, which in turn became a globally successful film in 1973.

From a historical point of view the interest of the Mount Rainier exorcism lies not in the spectacular paranormal events that are supposed to have accompanied the possession of the boy, but the interpretation of events by the priests and R's family. The influence of Spiritualism in America was evident in the prominent role played by a Ouija board as the source of the possession. The Mount Rainier possession set the cultural pattern for possessions in the late twentieth and twenty-first centuries, which are often supposed to follow the possessed individual 'meddling with the occult', rather than traditional bewitchments. Just before the Jesuit exorcisms that finally freed R, his family turned to the Ouija board themselves, wondering whether it was the ghost of Aunt Harriet that was plaguing R in an effort to reveal the location of money hidden before her death.[70] The evocation of ghosts and the dead in relation to possession was nothing new in itself, but in a twentieth-century context, especially when linked with a Ouija board, it is clear that the influence of Spiritualism (with its tendency to interpret all spirits as spirits of the dead) was at play.

Perhaps the most strikingly 'modern' feature of the Mount Rainier exorcism was its denouement. In a vision, R saw:

> …a very beautiful man, with flowing wavy hair that blew in the breeze. He wore a white robe that fitted close to his body. The material gave the impression of scales. Only the upper half of the body of this man was visible to R. In his right hand he held up a wavy and fiery sword in front of him. With his left hand he pointed down to a pit or cave.[71]

The figure was immediately recognizable as St Michael, whom Leo XIII had invoked against the powers of darkness and who also played a promi-

---

[68] Ibid. pp. 86–90.
[69] Ibid. pp. 216–20.
[70] Allen (2000), pp. 72–5.
[71] Ibid. p. 289.

nent role in the Earling exorcism.[72] The Earling and Mount Rainier exorcisms shared other similarities: in both cases the identity of the possessing entity ultimately emerged as the devil himself. The role of the prayer to St Michael in the Earling exorcism and the prominent appearance of St Michael in R's vision suggests that the development of the idea of 'diabolical' as opposed to demonic possession should be located in the context of late nineteenth-century apocalypticism and Leo XIII's emphasis on a cosmic battle waged between St Michael and Satan, played out in the history of nations. The Earling demoniac introduced a political dimension to the exorcism when she referred to the Mexican Revolution as evidence of the devil's activity in the world.[73] The exorcism of R in 1949 was the first 'modern exorcism', in the sense that it followed a pattern established by late nineteenth-century demonological preoccupations and set the agenda both for subsequent exorcisms and global cultural perception of the rite.

Animal Magnetism, Spiritualism and the Rise of Parapsychology

The story of theological and medical ridicule of exorcism in the nineteenth and twentieth centuries is balanced by another development within Catholicism that was to have far-reaching consequences: the endorsement of parapsychology by some Catholic theologians. The engagement of Catholicism with parapsychology can be divided into three distinct stages. In the nineteenth century, the church was faced with the challenge of responding to mesmerists, who claimed that animal magnetism was a natural, morally neutral force. By 1900 mesmerism had declined in significance to be replaced by Spiritualism, which the church grappled with until the 1940s. After the Second World War the focus shifted to distinguishing genuine possession from parapsychological phenomena such as telepathy and telekinesis, whose reality many Catholic theologians accepted. The Austrian Cistercian Alois Wiesinger, the British Jesuit Herbert Thurston and the Italian priest Corrado Balducci, amongst others,[74] expanded the terms of the debate on demonology by introducing a third alternative. It was not simply a case of whether possession was demonic or

[72] Vogl (1970 [1935]), pp. 24, 43.
[73] Ibid. p. 27.
[74] Corrado Balducci listed these theologians in 'Parapsychology and Diabolic Possession', *International Journal of Parapsychology* 8 (1966), pp. 193–212, at p. 203.

psychological; a possessed person might be the victim of the occult powers of their own psyche. Yet as soon as it was admitted that the psyche was capable of occult powers such as telekinesis, the proposition that malevolent spiritual beings existed and possessed the same power was no longer absurd. Acceptance of parapsychology ensured that the exorcism debate was no longer a simple matter of 'superstition versus science'.

Spiritualism, which emerged in America in the 1840s and rapidly crossed the Atlantic, claimed that communication with the dead was not only possible, but a natural ability of certain individuals. The new faith represented a significant challenge not only to the Catholic doctrine of the afterlife but also to Catholic demonology. For the Spiritualists, there were no evil spirits but only misguided souls. Nevertheless, Jenny Hazelgrove, who has analysed a series of pamphlets issued by the Catholic Truth Society in Britain against Spiritualism, has argued that Spiritualism was 'heavily influenced by a Christian repertoire of signs with a Catholic bias'.[75] One of the earliest articles in a British Catholic periodical to deal with Spiritualism (in August 1893) did so from a sympathetic standpoint: the author, Mrs Whitehead, described how her spiritualistic experiences had convinced her of the errors of Protestantism and led to her conversion to Catholicism.[76] Other British Catholics were less sympathetic, however. In 1908 Alexander Miller (1867–1914), a priest of the 'Oblates of St Charles' founded by Cardinal Manning at St Mary of the Angels, Bayswater, published a series of anti-Spiritualist sermons in which he argued that involvement in Spiritualism led to possession.

Miller recalled 'a serious case of real possession in this parish' which involved a non-Catholic medium who was warned by a Catholic friend to stay away from Spiritualism. When 'the evil manifested itself' she summoned a Catholic priest (presumably Miller himself), but went into 'paroxysms of frenzy and violence' when Miller and the Catholic friend prayed with her. The woman was delivered 'by the power of prayer'; at no point did Miller request an exorcism or perform one himself. Miller's willingness to identify possession and lunacy may explain why: 'I feel no difficulty in agreeing that these cases of possession amount to lunacy, but it is lunacy

---

[75] Hazelgrove, J., *Spiritualism and British Society between the Wars* (Manchester: Manchester University Press, 2000), p. 53.
[76] [Whitehead, A. E.], 'A Convert through Spiritualism', *The Month* (August 1893), reprinted in Thurston, H., *The Church and Spiritualism* (Milwaukee, WI: Bruce Publishing Co., 1933), pp. 368–84.

arising from the fact that the spirits have responded to the invitation given to them in Spiritualism'. In other words, the woman was really driven mad by the spirits rather than possessed by them, so exorcism was inappropriate.

At some point before 1903 a wealthy Australian businessman came to London for a surgical operation; staff at a Catholic nursing home observed that he regularly conversed with a spirit. They advised him to meet with 'a Catholic gentleman who had had a considerable experience of Spiritualism', who in turn suggested that the Australian should meet with the Archbishop of Westminster, Cardinal Vaughan.

> No sooner was the visitor shown into the presence of the Cardinal than his control seemed to be moved with rage, which vented itself upon the body of the unfortunate man ... another personality, entirely strange to himself—coarse, violent, demoniacal—took possession of him. His whole appearance was altered; he seemed to shrink to a withered old man; his face indicated a frenzy of rage, his eyes started from his head, and he literally foamed at the mouth, and there came from him a torrent of foul, disgusting, and obscene language, of terribly blasphemous insults to God and of coarse abuse of religion, church, and priesthood.

After this 'paroxysm', the Cardinal 'spoke very seriously of the danger he was in' to the Australian, whom he instructed to say prayers to St Joseph and St Michael. Vaughan saw the man once more before his spirit control told him to return to Australia.[77] The Archbishop's involvement in this second case suggests that Vaughan may have been contemplating performing an exorcism, but the view espoused by Miller that possession was nothing more than a form of madness produced by spirits precluded the need for it. Whether Vaughan shared Miller's view it is impossible to know.

The urgency with which Catholics engaged in polemic against Spiritualism in the early twentieth century was at least partly due to the similarity of certain Spiritualist beliefs and practices to Catholicism.[78] The Roman Curia was slow in identifying Spiritualism as a potential danger,[79]

---

[77] Miller, A. V., *Sermons on Modern Spiritualism* (London: Kegan Paul, 1908), pp. 132–8.

[78] Hazelgrove (2000), p. 60. The Californian medium Carl Wickland spoke of 'obsession' by misguided souls (Wickland, C. A., *Thirty Years among the Dead* (Los Angeles, CA: Wolfer, 1924), p. 21). On Wickland's use of exorcistic terminology see Hazelgrove (2000), pp. 66–8.

[79] See Young, F., 'The Dangers of Spiritualism: The Roman Catholic Church's Campaign against Spiritualism during and after the First World War', *Paranormal Review* 71 (June 2014), pp. 18–20.

and the high tide of the church's campaign against Spiritualism in Britain and America came in the years after the First World War, when the Catholic convert John Godfrey Raupert (1858–1929), a former Anglican priest and member of the British Society for Psychical Research, was sent on a lecture tour of America by Pope Pius X. Raupert showed an interest in exorcism, relating the story of the Umzinto possessions and describing the prayers of exorcism and the diagnostic criteria of the *Rituale Romanum* for the benefit of readers to whom the idea of exorcism was entirely unfamiliar.[80] Raupert combined anti-Spiritualist and anti-Modernist polemic, condemning the 'false idea' that the New Testament did not distinguish between physical illness and possession.[81]

Whilst in America, Raupert wrote an article condemning the use of Ouija boards, warning that 'while it was an easy thing for [the user] to *open* the mental door by which the mind could be invaded, it was a difficult, if not an impossible thing, to *shut* that door and to expel the invader'.[82] He described the effects of demonic possession as well as dramatic events that occurred during exorcisms, such as a demon who lifted a man out a chair and threw him violently to the floor, telling the exorcists that they had no chance of dislodging him.[83] It is probable that Raupert's campaign publicized the dangers of Ouija boards in America and thereby influenced the Mount Rainier case.

Others went further than Raupert. Montague Summers, an eccentric former Anglican who claimed to be a Catholic cleric, included a chapter on possession and exorcism in his *History of Witchcraft* (1926), an eclectic and sensational but still well-researched work. Summers included an English translation of the entire rite of exorcism,[84] and insisted that Spiritualists ran the danger of diabolic possession although he was not able to provide evidence that exorcism had been successfully used to free possessed

---

[80] Raupert, J. G., *Christ and the Powers of Darkness* (London: Heath, Cranton and Ouseley, 1914), pp. 83–96.

[81] Ibid. pp. 128–9.

[82] Raupert, J. G., 'The Truth about the Ouija Board', *American Ecclesiastical Review* (November 1918), pp. 463–78, at p. 475; see also Raupert, J. G., *The New Black Magic and the Truth about the Ouija Board* (New York: Devin-Adair, 1919), pp. 205–34. On Raupert see Hazelgrove (2000), pp. 136–7.

[83] Hazelgrove (2000), p. 133.

[84] Summers, M., *A History of Witchcraft and Demonology* (London: Kegan Paul, 1926), pp. 211–19.

Spiritualists.[85] The British Jesuit Herbert Thurston (1856–1939) deviated from the standard view expressed in anti-Spiritualist Catholic pamphlets and embraced the possibility of parapsychology. Thurston had been at school with Britain's leading Spiritualist, the author Sir Arthur Conan Doyle, at the Jesuit-run Stonyhurst College. After Doyle's conversion to Spiritualism, Thurston carried on a public correspondence with him on the subject.[86] Thurston did not hesitate to endorse the church's condemnation of all Spiritualism, simply on the grounds that its dangers were unknown.

In the late 1950s Alois Wiesinger suggested that the understanding of unknown languages and knowledge of distant things could no longer be regarded as diagnostic of possession, since these existed as parapsychological phenomena in the absence of any demonic influence.[87] Corrado Balducci (1923–2008) picked up the theme of parapsychology in his book *Gli Indemoniati* ('The Demoniacs', 1959), although Balducci's concern was not, like earlier authors, to combat Spiritualism, but rather to provide diagnostic criteria to distinguish genuine demonic possession from psychic activity as well as mental illness. Balducci avoided any assertion that parapsychological phenomena would always accompany exorcism, but he did believe that an aversion to sacred things was diagnostic of possession.[88] Both Thurston and Wiesinger argued that phenomena previously attributed to evil spirits, such as telekinesis, were the natural result of activity of the human soul, as yet not understood.[89]

In an article published in 1966, Balducci argued that through the centuries, purely natural parapsychological phenomena had been taken as signs of demonic possession, and individuals who were merely psychic had been taken as demonically possessed. However, parapsychological manifestations were natural 'and therefore totally and essentially different' from effects caused by demons.[90] Parapsychology, Balducci argued,

---

[85] Ibid. pp. 250–69.
[86] Thurston. H., *The Church and Spiritualism* (Milwaukee, WI: Bruce Publishing Co., 1933), p. 21. On this correspondence see Kollar, R., 'Spiritualism and Religion: Sir Arthur Conan Doyle's Critique of Christianity and a Roman Catholic Response', *Recusant History* 24 (1999), pp. 397–413.
[87] Wiesinger, A. (trans. B. Battershaw), *Occult Phenomena in the Light of Theology* (London: Burns and Oates, 1957), pp. 253–5.
[88] Balducci (1959), pp. 324–5, 393–425.
[89] Thurston (1933), pp. 143–66; Wiesinger (1955), pp. 170–2.
[90] Balducci (1966), p. 193.

made possible a 'science of the occult'. One defining diagnostic feature of demonic possession was the abhorrence of sacred objects shown by demoniacs; the same was not true of psychics capable of causing effects like telekinesis, whether willingly or unwillingly.[91] Balducci recommended that diagnosis of demoniacs should be divided into two phases: a 'Phase of Observation' in which the exorcist should look for signs of possession, distinct from natural parapsychological phenomena, and a 'Phase of Evaluation' in which a decision should be made concerning the likelihood of a demonic component. This included a holistic 'sense of the presence of evil', which might be confirmed by experiences that the demoniac had undergone in the past or events that took place in his or her vicinity.[92]

Like Wiesinger, Balducci stressed that demonic possession was not always accompanied by parapsychological phenomena, and therefore it was a mistake to take these as diagnostic of possession.[93] Balducci, like many churchmen after him, regarded parapsychology as a genuine science, and noted that the church could not possibly be opposed to advances towards the truth about nature. The church did not condemn Spiritualism because Spiritualists believed in parapsychology, but because they committed doctrinal errors by claiming to be able to communicate with the dead.[94] By embracing the insights of parapsychology, Balducci sought to demonstrate the church's openness to the modern world while endorsing traditional teaching on the reality of Satan. Balducci's views were by no means in the theological mainstream in the 1950s and '60s, but his influence on Gabriele Amorth ensured that Balducci's thought played a key role in the revival of exorcism in the late twentieth century.

[91] Ibid. pp. 195–7.
[92] Ibid. pp. 198–200.
[93] Ibid. p. 202.
[94] Ibid. pp. 203–5.

CHAPTER 8

The Return of Exorcism

The debate about the relationship between possession and mental illness that dominated discussion of the appropriateness of exorcism in the first half of the twentieth century has receded into the background in the twenty-first century to be replaced by new concerns. Sceptical voices speaking openly against the ministry of exorcism are now marginal within global Catholicism, although a large number of Catholics, laity and clergy alike, have no interest in or experience of the subject. In spite of the resurgence of exorcism, a gap remains between clerical discourse and the expectations of lay Catholics, many of whom are more concerned with curses, haunted houses and witchcraft than with demonic possession in the true sense. Prominent contemporary exorcists such as Gabriele Amorth and José Antonio Fortea have inherited the interest shown in parapsychology by Wiesinger, Thurston and Balducci, yet their emphasis on the dangers of the occult and Satanic worship is something new. Furthermore, a gulf has opened between approaches to exorcism that acknowledge the reality of malefic witchcraft, such as the practice of Amorth and Fortea, and an 'official demonology' that denies the reality of witchcraft and curses.

In the aftermath of Vatican II, Catholic approaches to exorcism developed in line with the different political reactions to the Council. For some, the supposedly 'liberalizing' trend of the Council was an indication that certain ancient features of Christian belief, such as demonology, should be downgraded or discarded altogether. This approach represented a return to the critical, Modernist theology of the late nineteenth and early twentieth centuries. Some traditionalists reacted in the opposite direction, channelling their ideological, theological and political opposition to the Council into a renewed emphasis on ancient Catholic practices, including exorcism. A third tendency took the form of a revival of charismatic exorcism (described as 'deliverance' or 'prayer of liberation') as a charism or spiritual gift. Catholic deliverance ministry remains controversial, partly because it seems to owe as much to Pentecostalism as it does to the ancient tradition of Catholic exorcism. Nevertheless, deliverance ministry is now itself part of a burgeoning Catholic tradition and cannot simply be dismissed as an alien intrusion.

This chapter largely restricts its examination of exorcism in the late twentieth and twenty-first centuries to Europe and North America, on the grounds that a survey of everything that could be considered contemporary 'Catholic exorcism' would require a book-length study in its own right. However, exorcism (and especially charismatic exorcism) in Africa, South America and the Indian Subcontinent has been treated elsewhere, primarily by scholars working within the field of anthropology.[1] A study of exorcism in Europe and North America must not lose sight of the fact that, in many other parts of the world, possession and exorcism have never ceased to be part of Catholic life. On a global scale, the 'revival' of exorcism is a local phenomenon.

VATICAN II AND EXORCISM

Vatican II marked a dramatic shift in the church's engagement with contemporary society. The intentions and legacy of the Council are still intensely debated by church historians, but at the very least, the conciliar decrees embodied a change of tone, rejecting much of the political legacies of Popes Pius IX and Leo XIII. The Council endorsed religious liberty and disavowed the statements of previous Popes concerning the Jews.

---

[1] Stirrat (1977); Lantenari, V., 'From Africa into Italy: The Exorcistic-Therapeutic Cult of Emmanuel Milingo' in Clarke, P. B. (ed.), *New Trends and Developments in African Religions* (Westport, CT: Greenwood Press, 1998), pp. 263–82; Kapferer (1991); Deliège, R., 'La Possession Démoniaque chez les Intouchables catholiques de l'Inde du Sud', *Archives de Sciences Sociales des Religions* 79 (1992), pp. 115–34; Ter Haar, G., *Spirit of Africa: The Healing Ministry of Archbishop Milingo of Zambia* (London: C. Hurst and Co., 1992); Stirrat (1992); Chesnut, R. A., 'A Preferential Option for the Spirit: The Catholic Charismatic Renewal in South America's New Religious Economy', *Latin American Politics and Society* 45 (2003), pp. 55–85, at pp. 71–2.

Thus, while the church's condemnation of Freemasonry remained, the Vatican implicitly withdrew from nineteenth-century 'conspiracy theories' about the collaboration of Jews, Freemasons and secularists in creating a Satanic world order. In reaction to the Council's agenda, some traditionalist Catholics suspicious or dismissive of Vatican II continue to place a great deal of emphasis on these supposed Satanic conspiracies.[2] Exorcism was never mentioned during the sessions of the Council, and more significant than the decrees of the Council itself for the history of exorcism was the freedom granted to theologians in the aftermath of Vatican II.

Nicolotti has argued that Vatican II coincided with a tendency towards 'minimising demonology' and an emphasis on the difficulty of believing in the devil as anything more than a symbol of evil.[3] Gratsch, writing in the *New Catholic Encyclopedia* (1967), insisted that 'Today the Church maintains its traditional attitude toward exorcism', yet his definition of exorcism fell short of expressing that 'traditional attitude': 'Exorcism is nothing more than a prayer to God (sometimes made publicly in the name of the Church, sometimes made privately) to restrain the power of demons over men and things'.[4] The view that exorcism is essentially prayer would later influence the revision of the rite of exorcism. Dallen argued that 'The Church ... is reluctant to admit a supernatural possession in particular cases', on the grounds that 'Both modern biblical scholarship and current psychological theory and practice are inclined to admit a supernatural explanation only when a natural explanation has been proved impossible'.[5] In Dallen's view, the abolition of the minor order of exorcist in 1972 was a 'practical indication' of this reluctance.

On 26 June 1975 the Sacred Congregation for Divine Worship's document 'Christian Faith and Demonology' summarized a typical attitude to exorcism in the post-Vatican II era[6]:

---

[2] See, for instance, the continued anti-Semitic statements of Bishop Richard Williamson of the canonically irregular Society of St Pius X ('British Bishop fined for Holocaust Denial on TV', *The Guardian*, 27 October 2009, p. 10).

[3] Nicolotti (2011), p. 25. On this theological development see Cini Tassinario, A., *Il Diavolo secondo l'Insegnamento recente della Chiesa*, Studia Antoniana 28 (Rome: Pontificium Athenaeum Antonianum, 1984).

[4] Gratsch, E. J., 'Exorcism' in *New Catholic Encyclopedia* (2003 [1967]), vol. 5, p. 551.

[5] Dallen, J., 'Exorcism: Liturgy' in *New Catholic Encyclopedia* (2003 [1967]), vol. 5, p. 553.

[6] 'Christian Faith and Demonology' in *Vatican Council II, Volume 2: More Post-Conciliar Documents*, ed. A. Flannery (Dublin: Dominican Press, 1982), pp. 456–85, at p. 473.

The special ministry of the exorcist, though not totally abolished, has in our time been reduced to a remotely possible service which may be rendered only at the request of the bishop; in fact, there is now no rite for the conferring of this ministry. Such an attitude to exorcism evidently does not mean that priests no longer have the power to exorcize or that they may no longer use it. Since, however, the Church no longer makes exorcism a special ministry, it no longer attributes to exorcisms the important role they had in the early centuries of its life.

Although the Congregation insisted that the relegation of exorcism involved 'no lessening or revision of the traditional faith', it is clear that the description of exorcism as 'a remotely possible service' was aimed at directing the practice of bishops when confronted with requests for exorcism. Furthermore, the suggestion that exorcisms were once important in the life of the church carried the implication that Christianity had outgrown this practice. Both Dallen and the Congregation for Divine Worship regarded the abolition of the minor order of exorcist as significant for the future of exorcism. Yet as Kelly has argued, the order of exorcist originated as a means of conferring the power to exorcize catechumens, a task later amalgamated with that of the baptizing priest. Consequently, abolition of the minor order of exorcist need not have implied that any downgrading of the exorcism of demoniacs was intended.

The Council's emphasis on a return to scriptural sources precipitated the reform of exorcistic rites in baptism, which removed 'a demonology in certain cases much more developed ... not consonant with the sobriety of the biblical tradition'.[7] In Nicolotti's view, the weakening and dilution of references to the devil in the revised rites of Christian initiation had the effect of 'renouncing completely the dramatic and realistic force of the ancient imperative exorcisms'. Furthermore, the development of the historical study of the liturgy as a separate discipline, and the unwillingness of liturgists to address demonological questions, meant that scholars neglected exorcism. However, Balthasar Fischer did produce a study of baptismal exorcism in the mid-1970s and Elmar Bartsch addressed the issue of the exorcism of inanimate objects as part of the Roman ritual.[8]

[7] Nicolotti (2011), p. 26.
[8] Fischer, B., 'Baptismal Exorcism in the Catholic Baptismal Rites after Vatican II', *Studia Liturgica* 10 (1974), pp. 48–55; Bartsch (1967). On the changing role of exorcism in baptismal liturgies see Duggan, R. D., 'Conversion in the *Ordo initiationis christianae adultorum*', *Ephemerides Liturgicae* 96 (1982), pp. 57–83, 209–52; Kelly (1985), pp. 262–6.

THE RETURN OF EXORCISM 213

The 1960s and early 1970s represented a nadir in the practice of exorcism, when exorcisms were rarer, perhaps, than they had been at any time since the eighteenth century. Few formal studies of the decline of exorcism were conducted, however, with the exception of a 1973 investigation by Bernard Chaput in Quebec's 'Cantons de l'Est' (Eastern Townships). Chaput found that of 111 parish priests who responded to his survey, not one practised exorcism. Chaput concluded that 'belief in demonic possession was on its way to disappearing', because Satan himself had disappeared from Catholic belief.[9] In 1969 the Swiss Jesuit theologian Herbert Haag (1915–2001) published *Abscheid vom Teufel* ('Goodbye to the Devil'), an influential rejection of literal belief in the devil as a spiritual personality.[10] Haag's work captured the prevailing theological mood of the post-Conciliar era; literal belief in the devil was a relic of the past that the church had outgrown. In the English-speaking world, opposition to the continued practice of exorcism was led by two American Jesuits, Henry Ansgar Kelly and Juan B. Cortés. Kelly and Cortés shared the view that theologians had systematically misunderstood the New Testament, which makes a distinction between 'unclean spirits' and Satan, whose function is to tempt and test. The unclean spirits are not necessarily under Satan's dominion, and are better understood as 'Spirit-parasites', personifications of physical and mental illnesses rather than evil spiritual personalities. Christian mythology furnished the connection between 'unclean spirits' and the fallen angels, which was nowhere spelled out in the Bible. It followed, therefore, that no-one could be possessed by the devil or a fallen angel.[11]

American and German Jesuits led the attack against exorcism in the 1960s, but it was also a German Jesuit who led the defence. Adolf Rodewyk (1894–1989) began practising as an exorcist in Trier during the Second World War. He recommended in his 1963 *Dämonische Bessesenheit in der Sicht des* Rituale romanum ('Demonic Possession in the Light of the *Rituale Romanum*') that the exorcist should make use of silent 'probative exorcisms', prayers whispered in the presence of the suspected demoniac that were likely to produce preternatural phenomena or a response

---

[9] Chaput, B., 'Réflexion sur l'Etude des Religions populaires et l'Histoire: l'exemple de la possession démonique dans les Cantons de l'Est' in Désilets, A. and Laperrière, G. (eds), *Recherche et Religions Populaires: un colloque international 1973* (Montreal, QC: Bellarmin, 1976), pp. 143–62, at p. 148.
[10] Kelly (2006), p. 321.
[11] Kelly (1968), pp. 69, 98. See also Kelly (2006), pp. 303–4.

from the demon, an approach subsequently endorsed by Amorth.[12] Kelly was critical of Rodewyk's approach, noting that in the light of Rodewyk's acceptance of parapsychological phenomena, such as telepathy, a person's awareness of secret 'probative exorcisms' did not prove possession.[13] Kelly was scathing of Rodewyk's acceptance of 'many of the more implausible hagiographical tales of possession',[14] a reference to Rodewyk's *Dämonische Besessenheit heute* (1966), translated in 1975 as *Possessed by Satan*. In addition to being the most influential book on exorcism until the publication of Amorth's *Un Esorcista Raconta* ('An Exorcist tells his Story', 1990), *Possessed by Satan* drew on Rodewyk's extensive collections of documentation relating to twentieth-century exorcisms.

Rodewyk's book provoked considerable controversy amongst German Jesuits.[15] J. Sudbrack argued that 'a direct crystallization of Satan's direct causality is almost impossible to recognize'. Rather incongruously, Rodewyk shared the writing of the article on 'Possession' in the *Lexikon für Theologie und Kirche* (1957–68) with Karl Rahner, renowned for his revisionist approach to theology. However, Rahner, unlike Sudbrack, was prepared to admit that genuine possession existed and could, in theory, be distinguished from natural illness by preternatural manifestations.[16] Kelly went further than either Sudbrack or Rahner in his criticism of exorcists, aimed primarily at Rodewyk[17]:

> The modern advocates of the reality of possession, who are for the most part Roman Catholic theologians, have added to the simple character of the unclean spirits of the gospel ... concepts evolved out of obsolete and, for the most part, abandoned mythologies and philosophies, which transformed them into fallen angels and pure spirits. The resulting hypothesis of possession, therefore, has very little connection either with scripture or with the observable world, and its claim to be taken seriously must be received with skepticism.

Although he acknowledged that imperative commands to mentally ill individuals who believed themselves to be possessed might have the

---

[12] Amorth (1999), p. 69.
[13] Kelly (1968), p. 88.
[14] Ibid. p. 90.
[15] On the Rodewyk controversy see Haag, H., *Teufelsglaube* (Tübingen: Katzmann, 1974), pp. 396–403.
[16] Kelly (1968), pp. 91–2.
[17] Ibid. p. 91.

psychological effect of a 'counter-suggestion', Kelly's final conclusion was that exorcism should be banished completely[18]:

> Until ... the theory of demonic possession can make a more respectable case for itself, the exorcist seems as much out of place in a sickroom or mental asylum as a witchdoctor. For while the latter could no doubt effect the same kind of cures on patients of certain conditioned mentalities as exorcists have done in the past, a safer and more enlightened method would be to attempt to disabuse the victims of their fixations of possession by normal therapeutic methods.

In a general audience of 15 November 1972, perhaps in response to the publicity surrounding Haag's scepticism, Pope Paul VI reiterated the church's traditional teaching on the devil: 'Evil is not only a deficiency, but an efficient force, a living essence, spiritual, perverted and perverting; a terrible reality, mysterious and terrifying.'[19] However, Paul VI avoided any mention of possession and exorcism, emphasizing the influence of the devil on the character of human individuals and societies. He noted that discernment of the action of the devil 'demands much caution, even if signs of the devil seem to be obvious'. Paul VI reaffirmed the teaching of the Fourth Lateran Council on the devil as a fallen angel and called for more theological study. At the very least, the address served to remind Catholic theologians that belief in the devil remained part of the deposit of faith.

Kelly has continued to argue against the idea of demonic possession, most recently drawing attention to the unimpressive nature of those wonders supposedly performed by the devil through the possessed[20]:

> If the Devil is regarded as the direct cause of the pathological symptoms manifested by suspected Demoniacs, it does not say much either for his intelligence or for his priorities. Even in the rare cases where the suggested criteria of the *Roman Ritual* seem to be met (a person using Diabolical force or knowing uncanny things), the wonders performed are usually not very wonderful or impressive.

---

[18] Ibid. p. 95.
[19] Pope Paul VI, General Audience of 15 November 1972. Retrieved from the world wide web, 3 October 2012, http://www.vatican.va/holy_father/paul_vi/audiences/1972/documents/hf_p-vi_aud_19721115_it.html: 'Il male non è più soltanto una deficienza, ma un'efficienza, un essere vivo, spirituale, pervertito e pervertitore. Terribile realtà. Misteriosa e paurosa'.
[20] Kelly (2006), pp. 306–7.

Although Kelly acknowledged that 'a theoretical explanation for the paltriness of Demoniacal wonders might be that Satan can only do what God tells him or allows him to do', it is clear that Kelly was not satisfied by this answer. Already, by the mid-1970s, Rodewyk's work, combined with the influence of literature and cinema, was beginning to turn back the tide of sceptical indifference to exorcism. In 1974 the German newspaper *Der Spiegel* reported that the Jesuit Karl Patzelt successfully exorcized a young couple and their two-year-old son in San Francisco. Accusations of priestly violence also resurfaced; in 1973 *Time* magazine reported that Annette Hasler, a twelve-year-old girl from a small Swiss village was beaten to death in an exorcism conducted by a priest and supported by her parents.[21]

THE KLINGENBURG CASE

In 1968 Kelly expressed his desire that, with the advent of 'scientific methods of investigation and recording', future exorcisms would be corroborated by this kind of evidence, without the need for observers.[22] In the case of Anneliese Michel (1952–76), a young Bavarian woman who died after months of exorcism, his wish was fulfilled. Because Anneliese's exorcists were the defendants in a criminal trial, the records of the exorcisms performed on Anneliese, including audio tapes, were made available to the court and the general public. Felicitas Goodman's account of the exorcism, whilst by no means impartial, is nevertheless the most detailed, since she gained access to the main participants as well as the documents and tapes in the late 1970s.

The exorcism of Anneliese Michel was arguably the most politically significant of the twentieth century, focusing the conflict between religious and secular outlooks in post-war West Germany and revealing troubling divisions within German Catholicism. This exorcism is riddled with paradoxes. At the time of the trial the German media portrayed it as a throwback to a conservative Bavarian religious culture, but the influences at play were not necessarily so straightforward. Ernst Alt, who was responsible for the recordings of the exorcism sessions, was a young priest with an active interest in parapsychology.[23] Anneliese was hostile to the reforms

---

[21] Dégh, L., 'Foreword' in Goodman (1988), p. xiii.
[22] Kelly (1968), p. 90.
[23] Ibid. p. 45.

of Vatican II, especially the reception of communion in the hand,[24] but she was also interested in an unauthorized pilgrimage site, San Damiano near Piacenza, and the burgeoning cult of the Capuchin friar and alleged stigmatic Padre Pio. Furthermore, neither Anneliese nor her family were reluctant to involve psychiatrists and other medical professionals, and one of the disputed points in the criminal trial concerned whether or not one of the doctors had recommended that Anneliese's parents consult a Jesuit. The court case, which called upon Rodewyk as a witness, breathed real and disturbing life into an issue that had hitherto been an academic dispute between theologians.

Quite early on in the case a family friend of the Michels made contact with Rodewyk, but in view of his advanced age he declined to visit the family, and put Anneliese in touch with another Jesuit.[25] In September 1974 a local priest, Ernst Alt, wrote to the Bishop of Würzburg, Josef Stangl, requesting permission to conduct an exorcism. Stangl was not convinced by Alt's initial request and instructed him to continue observing but not to recite the rite of exorcism.[26] On 1 July 1975, however, Alt found Anneliese in considerable distress and recited a probative exorcism.[27] Finally, at the beginning of August, Alt managed to obtain permission from Stangl to recite 'the small exorcism', which Goodman interpreted as a German excerpt from the *Rituale Romanum*.[28] However, Karl Roth's record of the exorcism shows that it was Leo XIII's Exorcism against Satan and the Apostate Angels, which any priest could recite even without episcopal approval. Stangl, in spite of considerable pressure from Alt, Roth and Anneliese's parents and friends, was resisting the authorization of major exorcism. Rodewyk finally visited Anneliese in September 1975,[29] and composed an 'expert opinion' that he presented to Roth and Alt, arguing strongly in favour of genuine possession. By this time, like the demoniacs of Tosos and Morzine, Anneliese herself was demanding to be exorcized.[30] The priests discussed taking Anneliese to Italy for an exorcism but rejected this idea, and agreed that Stangl should be formally approached to authorize an exorcism conducted by the Salvatorian priest

---

[24] Ibid. pp. 63, 67.
[25] Goodman (1988), p. 41.
[26] Ibid. p. 66.
[27] Ibid. p. 73.
[28] Ibid. p. 80.
[29] Ibid. pp. 85–6.
[30] Ibid. p. 87.

Arnold Renz. Alt wrote to Stangl, enclosing a copy of Rodewyk's opinion 'unintelligible to third parties' (in Latin?). On 16 September, Stangl made the fateful decision to allow Renz to proceed with an exorcism under Canon 1151,[31] and on 24 September the exorcists got to work.[32]

The demons possessing Anneliese named themselves as Judas, Lucifer, Nero, Cain, Adolf Hitler and an evil priest, Fleischmann. Anneliese's exorcists assumed that human souls could possess just like demons. Hitler's appearance was particularly apposite; shortly after the Second World War, the Benedictine Aloïs Mager asserted that Hitler was 'the medium of Satan',[33] and Cristiani described Germany's enthusiastic embrace of Nazism, along with Russian and Chinese Communism, as 'collective possession'.[34] The case of Anneliese Michel gave literal expression to postwar Germany's metaphorical exorcism of Hitler. However, the possession also contained an element of witchcraft. The demons revealed that a neighbour cursed Anneliese as an unborn child, and the ghost of the priest Fleischmann came to torment Alt in his parish house.[35] Renz exceeded the prescriptions of the *Rituale*, asking numerous questions beyond the names of the demons and the hour of their departure, and interrogating them in multiple languages.[36] By October Anneliese was receiving regular messages from the Virgin Mary, and turning into a 'prophetic demoniac', in the belief that God wanted her to complete the mission of a local woman venerated for her holiness, Barbara Weigand.[37] The messages suggested that Anneliese was divinely, as well as demonically, possessed, while the demons declared their approval for liturgical innovations.[38]

The exorcisms continued into the summer of 1976, apparently driven by Anneliese's own requests.[39] Both she and the exorcists had come to interpret her possession as a 'penance possession': Anneliese was accepting the punishment of demonic possession for the sins of others. Renz claimed

---

[31] Ibid. pp. 88–90.

[32] For an account of what occurred during the exorcism sessions see Goodman (1988), pp. 94–131.

[33] Mager, A., *Satan* (Paris: Desclée, 1948), p. 639.

[34] Cristiani (1961), p. 161. On Communism as demonic possession and infestation see pp. 165–72. On the theory of 'collective possession' see also Woollen (1949), p. 61.

[35] Goodman (1988), pp. 98, 108.

[36] Ibid. p. 101.

[37] Ibid. pp. 112–21.

[38] Ibid. p. 142.

[39] Ibid. p. 167.

that this interpretation derived from Rodewyk, who told him that a penance possession was particularly difficult for an exorcist to deal with.[40] However, Anneliese's death on 1 July 1976, apparently of malnutrition, put a stop to the exorcisms. Her parents and the exorcists were charged with causing her death by negligence. The Diocese of Würzburg gave no support to the defendants, since Bishop Stangl became embroiled in a dispute with his own officials about the exorcisms.[41] The court considered indicting Rodewyk, who had been closely involved (though never as an exorcist); eventually he was called as a witness only. However, the prosecution case went beyond proving the negligence of the defendants and drew on the testimony of a psychoanalyst who pronounced the defendants' belief in possession and exorcism abnormal.[42] Psychiatrists who examined Renz during the course of the trial found him psychologically normal, but were puzzled that he was 'incapable of critical evaluation' when it came to the subject of exorcism, attributing this to a small calcification of the brain.[43] In 1979, with the intention of avoiding similar cases, the German Bishops' Conference set up a commission to investigate exorcism; the commission was intended to report back to the Sacred Congregation of Rites with a view to informing future reform of the rite.[44]

THE REVIVAL OF EXORCISM

The publication of William Blatty's novel *The Exorcist* in 1971 and the release of William Friedkin's film of the same title in 1973 marked a watershed in twentieth-century attitudes to exorcism. The film's 'realistic' portrayal of a case of possession transcended mere entertainment, and caused Catholics and non-Catholics alike to take the possibility of demonic possession (and therefore exorcism) seriously.[45] The interest in

[40] Ibid. p. 172.
[41] Ibid. pp. 182–3.
[42] Ibid. pp. 190–4.
[43] Ibid. p. 92.
[44] Kunzler (2001), p. 317.
[45] On the influence of *The Exorcist* (book and film) see Claggett, T. D., *William Friedkin: Films of Aberration, Obsession and Reality* (Jefferson, NC: MacFarland and Co., 1990), pp. 388–420; Blatty, W. P., *Before* The Exorcist: *William Peter Blatty's own story of taking the novel to film* (Eye: ScreenPress Books, 1998); Heller-Nicholas, A., '"The Power of Christ Compels You": Moral Spectacle and *The Exorcist* Universe' in Hansen, H. (ed.), *Roman Catholicism in Fantastic Film: Essays on Belief, Spectacle and Imagery* (Jefferson, NC: MacFarland and Co., 2011), pp. 65–80.

exorcism generated by the film necessitated the appointment of new diocesan exorcists,[46] although the office of diocesan exorcist pre-dated the 1970s in major dioceses. In the 1980s the idea that Satanist groups were abusing children emerged in America, based on cases in which children undergoing psychotherapy claimed to 'remember' participation in Satanic rituals. The 'Satanic Ritual Abuse' panic quickly spread to Europe, resulting in numerous trials and convictions that were later deemed unsound on the grounds of the questioning methods used by psychotherapists, social workers and law-enforcement agencies.[47] The credibility of tales of organized Satanic abuse was bolstered by the real existence of self-proclaimed Satanists such as Anton LaVey's Church of Satan, founded in 1966.[48] Taken together, Friedkin's film and the Satanic Abuse Panic provided the ideal environment for the flourishing of exorcism.

The Irish-born ex-Jesuit Malachi Martin (1921–99) was one the most prominent proponents of exorcism as a weapon in a war against global Satanic conspiracy. His *Hostage to the Devil* (1976) was a dramatic description of the stages of traditional exorcism, in which he accepted that phenomena very like those depicted in Blatty's book were possible, and even likely. Although Martin insisted that no exorcism should be conducted without the authority of the church, his demonological beliefs became a political platform for an attack on Vatican II. Martin recounted how a priest who adopted the post-Conciliar liturgy was subsequently possessed.[49] He claimed (without evidence) that as a consequence of Catholic bishops' hostility to exorcism in America, an 'exorcism underground' had

---

[46] Kelly (2006), p. 320.

[47] On the Satanic abuse panic see La Fontaine (1989), pp. 115–38; Frankfurter (2008), pp. 2–3.

[48] Ferber has argued that contemporary debates about child sexual abuse even informed scholars of early modern exorcism, who speculated that child sexual abuse may have led to the self-identification by teenage girls and young women of themselves as witches (Ferber, S., 'The Abuse of History? Identity Politics, Disordered Identity and the "Really Real" in French Cases of Demonic Possession' in Tarbin, S. and Broomhall, S. (eds), *Women, Identities and Communities in Early Modern Europe* (Farnham: Ashgate, 2008), pp. 29–44, at pp. 32–9). For the scholarship in question see Walker, A. M. and Dickerman, E. H., 'Magdeleine des Aymards: Demonism or Child Abuse in Early Modern France?', *Psychohistory Review* 24 (1996a), pp. 239–64; Walker, A. M. and Dickerman, E. H., 'The Haunted Girl: Possession, Witchcraft and Healing in Sixteenth Century Louviers', *Proceedings of the Annual Meeting of the Western Society for French History* 23 (1996b), pp. 207–18.

[49] Martin, M., *Hostage to the Devil*, 2nd edn (San Francisco, CA: Harper, 1992). pp. 83–171.

emerged, in which '800 to 1300 major Exorcisms' were performed each year.[50]

Martin's reliability has rightly been questioned,[51] yet *Hostage to the Devil* was widely read and served to inform popular perceptions of Catholic exorcism. The psychologist Scott Peck was inspired by Martin to assist in exorcisms and dedicated his own book on the subject to the former Jesuit.[52] Furthermore, Martin dissociated exorcism from its formal authorization by a diocesan bishop and influenced non-denominational lay exorcists, such as Ed and Loraine Warren, who adopted a pluralistic view of the efficacy of exorcisms by non-Catholics, yet made use of the full panoply of traditional Catholic demonology in their dramatic exorcisms.[53] Martin initiated a process by means of which, in America at least, 'sacramental-style' exorcism has become a spiritual commodity, a 'service industry' that need not have any formal connection to the Catholic church.

Belief in organized Satanism suffuses Amorth's commentary on exorcism in *Un Esorcista raconta* (1990), a book which went through twelve Italian editions before it was translated as *An Exorcist tells his Story* in 1999. As Amorth himself noted in the preface to the tenth edition, the transformative effect on the church of the international media coverage he received was remarkable, and extended well beyond Italy.[54] In 1998 the Archbishop of Mechelin-Brussels received no less than 900 requests for exorcisms.[55] However, it seems unlikely that the impact of Amorth's book would have been as great if *The Exorcist* and Satanic abuse mythology had not already made the public receptive to the idea of exorcism and spiritual evil. One controversial feature of Amorth's book was his emphasis on the evil effects of curses and witchcraft, defined in the broadest possible terms as any treatment or therapy invoking a power other than God. Since Amorth defined witchcraft as the worship of Satan, practitioners of alternative therapies were witches and Satanists according to Amorth's logic.[56] Satanism, for Amorth, represents a distinct religion.[57]

---

[50] Ibid. p. xviii.
[51] Collins (2009), pp. 154–60.
[52] Peck, M. S., *People of the Lie* (New York: Touchstone, 1985). See also Collins (2009), pp. 166–70.
[53] Collins (2009), pp. 160–6.
[54] Amorth (1999), p. 17.
[55] De Waardt (2005), p. 27.
[56] On curses and witchcraft see Amorth (1999), pp. 129–52.
[57] Ibid. pp. 29–30.

His theory of witchcraft included a distinctively Italian (or at least southern European) emphasis on curses and physical instruments of witchcraft, and Benedict Groeschel, in his preface to the American edition, noted Amorth's use of 'theological concepts alien to our [i.e. American readers'] way of thinking'.[58] Although the idea of a curse as a source of possession was part of the plot of *The Exorcist*, mediation of curses through physical objects does not seem to have found a place in American popular religion.

For Jeremy Davies, exorcist of England's Archdiocese of Westminster, the role of the occult is just as important as it is for Amorth as a source of demonic influence. However, Davies is more cautious in making links with Satanic worship; he mentions neither Satanism nor witchcraft in his published introduction to exorcism, although he has insisted to me that Satanic groups do exist. Davies argues that occult practices develop a 'sixth sense' in humans, morally neutral in itself but a potential 'channel for the demonic'. Davies's opposition to alternative therapies is based on the idea that auto-suggestion diminishes our relationship to reality rather than the certainty that they represent Satanic worship: 'The infinitely precious power given to man which enables him to put his faith in the truth, in Christ, is sinfully wasted when it is misdirected to unrealities by auto-suggestion'.[59]

The revival of exorcism is not merely the transmission of an Italian cultural phenomenon; Davies's nuanced approach demonstrates that the phenomenon largely initiated by Amorth can be adapted for the Anglo-Saxon world. However, Amorth's determination to set the demonological agenda for exorcism rather than responding to the beliefs of his 'patients' (except insofar as he recognizes the reality of witchcraft and curses) meant that he refused to acknowledge the possibility of ghosts: 'The souls of the dead who are present during séances or the souls of the dead who are present in living bodies to torture them are none other than demons'.[60] Amorth's position is in contrast to Davies, who notes that 'Where there are signs of objective evil, the cause is usually a demonic spirit—or possibly a damned human spirit, in which case it should be treated in the same way as a demon'.[61] Davies's openness to the possibility of spirits of

---

[58] Ibid. p. 7.
[59] Davies, J., *Exorcism from a Catholic Perspective* (London: Catholic Truth Society, 2009), pp. 17–19.
[60] Amorth (1999), p. 30.
[61] Davies (2009), p. 46.

the dead behaving like demons is in line with the attitudes of Thurston and Wiesinger earlier in the twentieth century, but Amorth adopted an extremely sceptical stance towards ghosts traceable to earlier demonological traditions. However, the relative insignificance of belief in ghosts in Italian popular religion, compared with the prevalence of belief in ghosts in Britain even amongst people of no faith, may also go some way towards explaining the differences in approach between Amorth and Davies on this issue.

A further controversial stance adopted by Amorth is his insistence that 'An unnecessary exorcism never harmed anyone'. If the exorcist is in doubt, he should exorcize. Furthermore, Amorth insists that, whilst questioning of the suspected demoniac and his or her relatives before an exorcism is valuable, 'only through the exorcism itself can we determine with certainty whether there is a satanic influence'.[62] The signs of demonic influence set out in the *Rituale Romanum* emerge only during the course of an exorcism. In this respect, Amorth follows Rodewyk's belief that 'probative exorcisms' are required to detect demonic influence, yet his attitude runs contrary to the *Praenotanda* of the 1999 rite. On the other hand, Amorth is supportive of the idea of exorcists collaborating with specialists in mental illness, on the grounds that this has always been the church's practice.[63]

Amorth's emphasis on Satanism and the reality of curses and witchcraft separates him from earlier twentieth-century Catholic writers on exorcism, notably those theologians who showed an interest in parapsychology: Thurston, Wiesinger and Balducci. Indeed, Amorth himself acknowledges that, whilst Balducci's writings on demonology are useful, his practical advice on exorcism is without value because he was not a practising exorcist.[64] Although they do not reject the existence of morally neutral parapsychological phenomena, both Amorth and Davies are more cautious than their predecessors. Davies, for instance, suggests that poltergeist phenomena can be demonic in origin.[65]

Florence Chave-Mahir has described Amorth and the members of his International Association of Exorcists as 'clerical extremists', in contrast to the French bishops, who have approached the subject of exorcism

---

[62] Amorth (1999), pp. 44–5.
[63] Ibid. p. 47.
[64] Ibid. p. 15.
[65] Davies (2009), pp. 45–6.

with 'prudence and attentive listening'.[66] However, the French church's coolness towards exorcisms is exceptional, and Chave-Mahir's comments highlight the cultural gulf that exists between the practice of Catholicism in France and some other European countries. Amorth's International Association was founded in 1992 with seven exorcists, three French, two American and two British (including Davies). Shortly after the Association's first formal meeting in 1994, an International Association of Deliverance was formed by a Bavarian priest, Martin Ramoser, to assist the participation of the laity in fighting evil.[67]

Amorth may have courted controversy by his reluctance to make use of the 1999 rite, but his belief in witchcraft and curses is not alien to ordinary Italian Catholics, even those who are less than devout, and this emphasis may be seen as a creative accommodation of local concerns rather than a sign of extremism. James Collins, comparing Amorth with charismatic Catholics, has noted that his 'ministry of exorcism is ... enthusiastic although it is a form of enthusiasm mitigated somewhat by his involvement with the hierarchy of the Church'.[68] 'Enthusiastic' elements of Amorth's ministry include his adaptation of the rite of exorcism to make reference to the Virgin Mary and his insistence on delivering people from curses. Amorth emphasizes the difficulty of exorcism and the importance of experience: 'To assign such a task to a priest is like demanding that someone perform surgery after reading a textbook on the subject'. Collins has argued that both 'sacramental exorcism' and charismatic evangelical 'deliverance ministries' emerged as a major force only in the last three decades of the twentieth century. Prior to that point, 'stifling institutionalisation' largely prevented the use of the 'innately enthusiastic' rite of exorcism.[69]

Exorcism and the Charismatic Renewal

Bill Ellis associated the appearance of charismatic Catholics with a conservative backlash against the reforms of Vatican II.[70] However, Ellis concentrated his attention on the writings of Malachi Martin and the 'Bayside

[66] Chave-Mahir (2011), p. 20.
[67] Jeremy Davies, pers. comm. 27 June 2013.
[68] Collins (2009), pp. 170–5.
[69] Ibid. pp. 152–3.
[70] Ellis, B., *Raising the Devil: Satanism, New Religions, and the Media* (Lexington, KY: University Press of Kentucky, 2000), pp. 109–12.

Prophecies' of Veronica Lueken in California, which condemned changes to the liturgy between 1971 and 1977 and prophesied Satanic conspiracies. These entirely negative responses to Vatican II were not typical of the Renewal, in which many progressive tendencies are also discernible—not least a willingness to import ideas from Protestant groups. This importation began in August 1967 when an American Dominican, Francis MacNutt (b. 1925), came to believe that he had experienced 'baptism in the Holy Spirit'. Barbara Shlemon, a Catholic nurse, encouraged him to listen to tapes of sermons by the Pentecostal evangelist Derek Prince (1915–2003).[71] In 1974 MacNutt published an influential book on Christian healing, in which he argued that charismatic deliverance was equivalent to a 'minor exorcism' and did not, therefore, require the permission of a diocesan bishop.[72] In 1980 MacNutt was laicized but remained a Catholic. In a later book, he argued that 'possession' is extremely rare, thus demonstrating that there was little need for formal exorcism, and claimed that any attempt to perform exorcism without empowerment by the Holy Spirit was likely to fail.[73] MacNutt emphasized the importance of experience over demonological theory in motivating him to begin a ministry of exorcism.[74]

Although MacNutt's approach deviated from the official norms of the church, there is little to suggest that he wallowed in the sensational, and his ministry retained a distinctively Catholic character. He advocated the use of consecrated (i.e. exorcized) water, oil and salt.[75] Without confining exorcism to the clergy, he recommended that only those who had received a 'calling' to exorcism should attempt it; furthermore, all exorcisms should be carried out in private.[76] In Collins's view, in the 1970s MacNutt 'viewed deliverance as a necessary evil' and in his 'simplistic spiritual methodology' was 'careful to avoid speculation'.[77] By the 1990s, however, MacNutt's demonology had become more elaborate and incorporated many of the ideas current in charismatic evangelical theology, including 'ancestral spirits' passed on by the sins of ancestors and an acceptance of the reality

---

[71] On Prince see Collins (2009), pp. 44–53.
[72] MacNutt, F., *Healing*, 2nd edn (Bantam: New York, 1997), p. 189.
[73] MacNutt, F., *Deliverance from Evil Spirits* (Grand Rapids, MN: Chosen, 1995), pp. 67–72, 274.
[74] Ibid. p. 15.
[75] Ibid. pp. 241–7.
[76] Ibid. pp. 198–205.
[77] Collins (2009), p. 59.

of Satanic Ritual Abuse.[78] Collins has observed that, although MacNutt did not share the 'immanent eschatology' characteristic of many Christian charismatic healers, his appeals to experience rather than authority and his tendency 'to perceive spiritual causes for even the most trivial of events' render him an 'enthusiast' under Ronald Knox's definition of the term.[79]

Another American Catholic charismatic, the Franciscan Michael Scanlan (b. 1931), argued that exorcism should be practised within a stable community setting, resulting in what Collins has described as a 'comparatively sober approach' to the subject. Like MacNutt, Scanlan argued that charismatic deliverance amounted to minor exorcism; however, unlike MacNutt he viewed the manifestation of a demonic personality as an indication that a case was beyond his expertise, and recommended that anyone suffering from true possession should be sent to an approved expert.[80] In Collins's view, Scanlan placed a low value on demonic manifestations and, almost uniquely, 'views [demonic manifestations] as largely unnecessary human responses to the beneficial internal spiritual benefits of deliverance'.[81] Scanlan's approach is 'a gentle and informed mystical form of deliverance firmly focused on a mature and genuine compassion'.

The most controversial of all charismatic Catholic exorcists was Emmanuel Milingo (b. 1939), Archbishop of Lusaka in Zambia 1969–83, the creator of an 'exorcism cult' in his native country that combined Catholicism with elements of local animistic religion. Milingo performed public exorcisms attended by large crowds throughout the 1970s, and at a conference in Ann Arbor, Michigan in 1976, Milingo developed contacts in the Catholic Charismatic Renewal who supported his cause. However, facing opposition from European missionary clergy in Zambia, he was called to Rome to explain himself to Pope John Paul II. The Pope forbade Milingo from returning to Zambia, but he continued to act as an exorcist in Italy, without the permission of local ordinaries.

Milingo's blend of faith healing, charismatic exorcism, invective against the devil and promotion of belief in sorcery and witchcraft proved immensely popular amongst Italian Catholics, suggesting that the difference between the underlying religious cultures of Italy and Zambia was

---

[78] Ibid. pp. 61–2.
[79] Ibid. p. 63. For Knox's definition see Knox (1950), p. 1.
[80] Scanlan, M. and Cirner, R., *Deliverance from Evil Spirits* (Cincinatti, OH: Servant, 1980), p. 69.
[81] Collins (2009), p. 84.

slight.[82] Milingo tapped into a combination of popular Catholicism and suspicion of the Catholic hierarchy, accusing high-ranking figures in the church of Satanism, until the Archbishop's exorcisms in Milan in 1996 finally led the Vatican to curtail his activities.[83] Nevertheless, Milingo continued to conduct exorcisms in churches until he broke with the Catholic church altogether, marrying a South Korean woman in a ceremony conducted by the leader of the Unification Church, Sun Myung Moon. The significance of Milingo's 'exorcism cult' lay in the fact that he was able to transmit ideas of exorcism from an African cultural context to a European one, thus accomplishing the opposite of what the French clergy at Umzinto attempted in 1906: the imposition of European assumptions about exorcism on Africa.

The popularity of the term 'deliverance' among charismatic Catholics owes something to the fact that it is not, like 'exorcism', associated with violence in the popular imagination. However, whilst neither MacNutt nor Scanlan ever advocated physical restraint of victims of possession, not all charismatic exorcists have been averse to violence. In 1993, the defence counsel for John Reichenbach, an Australian non-denominational lay-exorcist accused of causing the death of Joan Vollmer during an exorcism, brought in John Shanley, a charismatic Catholic priest, as an expert witness. Shanley, from a rural parish in Victoria, claimed that he was called upon to perform exorcisms seven or eight times a week, although he was not a diocesan exorcist. He believed that the swollen state of Joan Vollmer's body was a sign of possession, since he had seen a possessed priest whose 'belly used to blow up so big that the inside of his navel was turning inside out and his head was blowing out'. Shanley believed the possession was a result of 'Satan's ritual abuse' and refused to condemn the violence used against Vollmer; he claimed that violence against the possessed was analogous to the slapping of hysterics. When asked whether he would have done the same to a possessed person, Shanley said 'he might have waited until he got her back "to reasonableness" before deciding what to do next'.[84] Shanley's expert testimony, with its emphasis on the gross physicality of possession, had more in common with Malachi

---

[82] Lantenari (1988), pp. 264–6.

[83] Malcolm, T., 'Vatican limits Faith Healer', *National Catholic Reporter*, 12 April 1996, p. 21.

[84] Ferber, S. and Howe, A., 'The Man who Mistook his Wife for a Devil: Exorcism, Expertise and Secularisation in a Late Twentieth-Century Australian Criminal Court' in De Waardt et al. (2005), pp. 281–92, at p. 285.

Martin's melodramatic descriptions of exorcism than with the charismatic approaches of Scanlan and MacNutt.

The Renewal, including its emphasis on the demonic activity that rises up to oppose it, received the endorsement of the Belgian Cardinal Léon-Joseph Suenens (1904–96) and even Cardinal Joseph Ratzinger, later Pope Benedict XVI.[85] In 1983, Ratzinger noted that 'a new, concrete awareness of the Powers of Darkness and their cunning, which threaten man, is growing in the context of the Renewal'.[86] However, Ratzinger was critical of the 'prayer of deliverance from the devil' that subsequently became 'an integral part of the life of some charismatic groups', on the grounds that 'mere personal experience unrelated to the faith of the Church remains blind'.[87] Prayer of deliverance, commendable in itself, had evolved to resemble a rite of exorcism, yet unlike the church's official rite of Major Exorcism, prayer of deliverance was often conducted by the laity or by priests without the permission of their local ordinary. Furthermore, charismatic groups did not follow the diagnostic criteria for possession set out in the *Rituale Romanum*. Most concerning of all for Ratzinger, they based their decision to carry out prayers of deliverance on their personal experiences of the demonic, thus creating the conditions for the 'isolation of experience' that, in Ratzinger's view, led to religious fundamentalism. He insisted that 'Ambiguity is a distinctive feature of the demonic phenomenon'.[88]

Ratzinger described Suenens's book on Catholic deliverance ministry, *Renewal and the Powers of Darkness* (1983), as both a 'highway code' for charismatics and a 'safety line' for groups which had fallen into inappropriate practices. The Congregation for the Doctrine of the Faith, of which Ratzinger was then Prefect, issued an official comment on the growth of deliverance ministry, the written response *Inde ab aliquot annis* (29 September 1985). This document set out the norms for exorcism under the terms of the 1983 Code of Canon Law and added[89]:

---

[85] On Suenens see Collins (2009), pp. 80–2.
[86] Ratzinger in Suenens (1983), p. ix.
[87] Ibid. p. x.
[88] Ibid. p. ix.
[89] Ratzinger, J., *Inde ab aliquot annis* (29 September 1985), retrieved from the world wide web on 10 October 2012, http://www.vatican.va/roman_curia/congregations/cfaith/documents/rc_con_cfaith_doc_19850924_exorcism_en.html: *Ex hisce praescriptionibus sequitur ut christifidelibus etiam non liceat adhibere formulam exorcismi contra satanam et angelos apostaticos, excerptam ex illa quae publici iuris facta est iussu summi pontificis Leonis XIII, ac multo minus adhibere textum integrum huius exorcismi.*

From these prescriptions it follows that it is not permitted for the Christian laity to administer the formula of exorcism against Satan and the apostate angels, excerpted from that which was made law by order of the Supreme Pontiff Leo XIII, and much less to administer the entire text of this exorcism.

Ratzinger instructed that 'Those who take care of this matter by the duty of authority ought to moderate those gatherings, in which prayers are administered in order to obtain liberation, in the course of which demons are directly addressed and an attempt is made to know their identities'.[90] The church's strategy in dealing with the potential abuses that might arise from deliverance ministry was to differentiate it clearly—perhaps more clearly than was possible—from sacramental exorcism, and to place charismatic groups under clerical direction. Nevertheless, it is significant that the liturgical scholar Achille Triacca drew attention to the renewed importance of the Holy Spirit in the 1999 rite,[91] and this is evidence that the contribution of charismatic Catholics to the revival of exorcism has not gone unnoticed.

David Kiely and Christina McKenna's collection of exorcism accounts from Ireland, *The Dark Sacrament* (2007), gives some indication of the changing face of exorcism in a twenty-first-century European Catholic culture. None of the 'exorcisms' described by the priests who spoke to Kiely and McKenna featured the use of Major Exorcism on a possessed person, and the majority concerned exorcisms of haunted houses. In 2003, a priest attempted to free a house in the Dingle Peninsula from a troublesome spirit by celebrating mass in the house, sprinkling the rooms with holy water, and advising that an image of the Virgin Mary should be prominently displayed.[92] When this failed, a second priest performed 'a more elaborate ritual', following the mass with long prayers in every room and blessing with holy water and incense. He also anointed the members of the family affected by the disturbances with oil of chrism.[93] The second exorcist, called 'Father Ignatius' by the authors, considered that the

---

[90] *Ii qui debita potestate carent conventus moderentur, in quibus ad liberationem obtinendam precationes adhibentur, quarum decursu daemones directe interpellantur et eorum identitas cognoscere studetur.*

[91] Triacca, A. M., 'Spirito Santo ed Esorcismo: in margine al recente Rituale', *Ephemerides Liturgicae* 114 (2000), pp. 241–69.

[92] Kiely, D. M. and McKenna, C., *The Dark Sacrament: Exorcism in Modern Ireland* (Dublin: Gill and MacMillan, 2006), pp. 95–7.

[93] Ibid. pp. 102–3.

cause of the phenomena was 'generalised evil' brought about by the fact that incest and child abuse had been perpetrated in the house many years earlier.[94]

A priest used a similar procedure to exorcize the house of a woman who, having used a Ouija board, found herself tormented by an 'entity'.[95] In October 2004 'Father Ignatius' made use of the help of another priest and a Carmelite nun to exorcize the house of a woman who had experimented with out-of-body experiences and 'astral voyaging', but the essential content of the 'exorcism', mass followed by blessings, was the same.[96] In only one case did 'Father Ignatius' consider a man to be possessed, but in this case it was the man's neighbour who alerted the priest, and the supposed demoniac could not be exorcized without his consent.[97] In this case, however, it was the man's unnaturally evil and apparently motiveless behaviour that led to the priest's diagnosis rather than the usual symptoms of possession.

THE REFORM OF THE LITURGY

The evolution of the revision of the rite of exorcism has been described in detail by Manfred Hauke, who traced its origins to a 'liturgy for liberation from evil' drafted by the German Bishops' Conference in 1983.[98] A draft of the ritual was circulated for experimental use in 1990,[99] although some commentators were surprised that the ritual affirmed the personal nature of evil. One of the first signs of renewed attention to the rite of exorcism after Vatican II was to be found in the revised Code of Canon Law (1983), which simplified, but did not substantially alter, the Canons of 1917. Exorcism was dealt with in Canon 1172: 'No-one is legitimately able to offer exorcism to the obsessed, unless he shall have obtained from the ordinary of the particular place an express licence; this licence may be conceded by the ordinary of the place only to a priest distinguished by piety,

---

[94] Ibid. pp. 104–6.
[95] Ibid. pp. 130–6.
[96] Ibid. pp. 355–64.
[97] Ibid. pp. 201–44.
[98] Hauke, M., 'The Theological Battle over the Rite of Exorcism, "Cinderella" of the new *Rituale Romanum*', *Antiphon* 10 (2006), pp. 32–69, at p. 36.
[99] Ibid. p. 41.

knowledge, prudence and integrity of life'.[100] Canon 1172 guaranteed the continued existence of exorcism as part of the church's life, but received clarification in the *Praenotanda* to the revised rite of 1999. These define the minister of exorcism as *sacerdos* rather than *presbyter* (thus permitting a bishop to exorcize), insist that a priest must have special preparation for the office, and enjoin that the exorcist should usually (*plerumque*) be appointed by a diocesan bishop and exercise the ministry under his direction.[101]

The publication of Vatican II's rite of exorcism, *De Exorcismis et Supplicationibus Quibusdam* ('Of Exorcisms and certain Supplications', hereafter *DESQ*) was announced on 22 November 1998 by Cardinal Medina Estévez, Prefect of the Congregation of Divine Worship.[102] The first edition of the Latin text was published on 26 January 1999, supplanting the 1614 rite after 385 years.[103] The ritual itself is prefaced by a theological *Prooemium*, which expounds the origins of evil and the nature of evil spirits, but places particular emphasis on the victory of Christ[104]:

> The victory of the Son of God dissolves the work of all these unclean, worthless, and seducing spirits ... Christ, by the paschal mystery of his death and resurrection has torn us from the servitude of the devil and of sin, overthrowing their rule and freeing all things from evil contagions. But when the harmful and contrary action of the Devil affects persons, things, places, and appears in a diverse way, the Church, always conscious that 'the days

---

[100] *The Code of Canon Law Annotated*, ed. E. Caparros, M. Thériault and J. Thom, 2nd edn (Montreal, QC: Wilson and Lafleur, 2004), pp. 911–12: *Nemo exorcismos in obsessos proferre legitime potest, nisi ab Ordinario loci peculiarem et expressam licentiam obtinuerit. Haec licentia ab Ordinario loci concedatur tantummodo presbytero pietate, scientia, prudentia ac vitae integritate praedito.*

[101] Huels, J., 'Other Acts of Divine Worship' in *New Commentary on the Code of Canon Law* (Mahwah, NJ: Paulist Press, 2000), pp. 1400–23, at p. 1405.

[102] For the text of the decree see *DESQ*, pp. 3–4.

[103] On the structure of the 1999 rite see Pistoia, A., 'Riti e Preghiere di Esorcismo: Problemi de Traduzione', *Ephemerides Liturgicae* 114 (2000), pp. 227–40, at pp. 233–6; Van Slyke (2006), pp. 70–116.

[104] *DESQ*, pp. 5–6: *Opera horum omnium spirituum immundorum, nequam, seductorum victoria Filii Dei dissolvit ... Christus per suum paschale mysterium mortis ac resurrectionis nos 'a servitute diaboli et peccati eripuit', eorum imperium evertens, omnia a contagiis malignis liberans. Cum autem noxia atque contraria action Diaboli et daemonum afficiat personas, res, loca et appareat diverso modo, Ecclesia, semper conscia quod 'dies mali sunt', oravit et orat, ut ab insidiis diaboli homines liberentur.* On the terminology used in the *Prooemium* see Pistoia (2000), pp. 229–32.

are evil', prayed and prays, that men might be delivered from the deceits of the devil.

The first seven of the *Praenotanda* preceding the ritual are theological, affirming traditional Catholic demonology with reference to the decrees of Vatican II and the *Catechism of the Catholic Church*.[105] The *Praenotanda* then set out a brief history of exorcism and the distinction between simple (i.e. baptismal) exorcism and Major Exorcism.[106] The *Praenotanda* follow the *Rituale Romanum* in stipulating that the exorcist should be 'endowed with piety, knowledge, prudence and integrity of life', but add that he should be 'specifically prepared for this ministry (*munus*)'. The cautions of the *Rituale* are expanded to make specific reference to the danger of mistaking mental illness (*morbo ... ex psychicis*) for possession, and the exorcist is warned against exorcizing those who believe themselves to be bewitched:

> Let [the exorcist] rightly distinguish a case of diabolic attack from the false opinion, by which certain people, even the faithful, think themselves to be the object of witchcraft, bad luck or a curse, which have been brought upon them by themselves, their relatives or their goods. He should not deny spiritual help to these people, but he ought not to administer exorcism.

The *Praenotanda* explicitly quote Benedict XIV's brief *Sollicitudini nostrae* (1745) yet retain the symptoms of possession from the *Rituale*: the ability to understand languages unknown to the demoniac, make known secrets or things happening far away and unnatural strength, as well as aversion to sacred things.[107] However, the exorcist is expected to consult experts in psychiatric medicine 'who have a sense of spiritual things' (*qui sensum habeant rerum spiritalium*). The *Rituale*'s warning against public exorcisms is updated to include the instruction that 'no space may be given to any of the social media of communication while the exorcism is being performed, even before the exorcism is performed and, when it is completed, the exorcist and those present, preserving their duty of discretion, may not give notice of it'.[108]

---

[105] *DESQ*, pp. 7–9.
[106] *DESQ*, pp. 9–11.
[107] *DESQ*, p. 12.
[108] *DESQ*, pp. 12–13: *Mediis communicationis socialis omnibus, dum peragitur exorcismus, nullo modo spatium detur, etiam antequam exorcismus peragatur, et, eo peracto, exorcista et praesentes eius notitiam ne divulgent, debitam discretionem servantes.*

The final *Praenotanda* concern the practicalities of the administration of the rite, lawful additions to the rite, and the adaptation of the text by national episcopal conferences. The latter permit vernacular translations of the rite, as well as the adaptation of rites and gestures 'attentive to the culture and genius of the people' (*attenta cultura et genio ... populi*) with the consent of the Holy See. Most importantly, the *Praenotanda* permit bishops' conferences to add a 'pastoral directive' to the rite, 'by which exorcists may not only understand more profoundly the doctrine of the *Praenotanda* and learn more fully the meaning of the rites, but even [find] documents gathered from approved authors concerning the way of acting, speaking, questioning, and exercising judgement'.[109] The pastoral directive is an opportunity for bishops' conferences to add their interpretation to the *Praenotanda*.

The rite begins with a deprecative prayer and proceeds to an optional blessing of holy water (*DESQ* 41–3). The sprinkling of holy water on the demoniac is made an official part of the liturgy (*DESQ* 44), followed by a litany of the saints (*DESQ* 46), which is not part of the *Rituale*. The first component of the 1999 rite substantially lifted from 1614 is the short prayer *Deus, cui proprium est misereri semper* ('God, whose nature it is always to have mercy ...'). The only Psalm to form part of the standard liturgy of Major Exorcism is Psalm 90 (*DESQ* 50), which does appear in the *Rituale Romanum*, while the only reading from scripture is John 1:1–14 (*DESQ* 52).

The 1999 rite departs significantly from its predecessor by including a renewal of baptismal promises, which may consist either of the recitation of the Nicene Creed or a more formal question and answer model (*DESQ* 54–6). Since the Creed forms part of the 1614 liturgy, it would seem that the authors of the 1999 rite interpreted its presence as reminding the demoniac and others assembled of their baptism. The authors' belief that the rite of exorcism derived from the rite of baptism is shown by the addition of an optional exsufflation (*DESQ* 59) in which the priest blows on the demoniac, a component that was never part of the 1614 rite and its Gelasian antecedents. Furthermore, according to the *Praenotanda*, 'special attention should be given to those gestures and rites which have their first place and meaning from those that are administered at the time

---

[109] *DESQ*, pp. 15–16: ... *quo exorcistae non solum doctrinam Praenotandorum profundius intellegant et significationem rituum plenius addiscant, sed etiam documenta de modo agenda, loquendi, interrogandi, iudicandi ex probatis auctoribus colligantur.*

of purification during the catechumenate. Such are the sign of the cross, the imposition of hands, the exsufflation and aspersion with holy water'.[110]

The obligatory deprecative formula of exorcism (*DESQ* 61) preserves a link with the ancient prayer *Deus conditor*, although it deviates substantially from the older text. To this prayer of exorcism the priest may join an imperative exorcism, the first of which (*DESQ* 62) preserves the threefold adjuration of Satan from the Gelasian Sacramentary. However, the new adjurations all command Satan to acknowledge (*agnosce*) the power of God by leaving the demoniac, and the element of conjuration (*per factorem tuum*, etc.) is entirely absent. A form of the old prayer *Deus caeli, Deus terrae* is retained as an alternative form of deprecative exorcism (*DESQ* 81), to be read in addition to *DESQ* 61, but the alternative imperative formula (*DESQ* 84) is the most traditional of all. Based fairly closely on *RR* 896, this formula retains the conjurations (*per Deum vivum, per Deum verum*), the threefold declaration *ipse tibi imperat* and the final *recede ergo*. However, this formula contains only a single adjuration and fails to preserve the ancient triple adjuration (Table 8.1).

In addition to the rite of Major Exorcism, *DESQ* also contains a series of psalms and prayers (psalm collects) that may be interspersed with the rite (*DESQ* 67–80),[111] as well as an appendix containing an exorcism for places and things (*DESQ* A1–A11) whose principal component (*DESQ* A10) is clearly based on Leo XIII's Exorcism of Satan and the Apostate Angels. Broadly speaking, the 1999 rite retains the structure and the principal components of the rite of 1614. The most striking omission from the 1999 rite is the *Praecipio tibi* (*RR* 887) and this, combined with the absence of conjurations from all but one of the alternative formulas of exorcism (*DESQ* 84) suggests a prejudice against conjurations on the part of the authors. The authors of the 1999 rite attempted to 'revive' the relationship between exorcism and baptism by including an optional exsufflation and renewal of baptismal vows, yet (as I have shown in Chap. 2) the idea that the rite of exorcism of demoniacs originated as a baptismal rite is erroneous. However, in countries where Catholicism co-exists with

---

[110] *DESQ*, p. 13: *attentio specialis praebeatur gestibus ac ritibus illis, qui primum habent locum ac sensum, ex eo quod adhibentur tempore purificationis in itinere catechumenali. Tales sunt signum crucis, manuum imposition, exsufflatio et aspersio aquae benedictae.*

[111] On the Psalms and Psalm collects of *DESQ* see Ward, A., 'The Psalm Collects of the New Rite of Exorcism', *Ephemerides Liturgicae* 114 (2000), pp. 270–301.

Table 8.1 Comparison of the 1614 and 1999 rites of exorcism

RR	DESQ
885: O God, to whom it is proper always to have mercy and spare us, receive our prayer, so that the pity of your loving kindness may mercifully release this your servant whom the shackles of sins have bound.	47: O God, to whom it is proper always to have mercy and spare us, receive our prayer, so that the pity of your loving kindness may mercifully release this your servant N., whom the shackles of diabolical power bind.
911: Psalm 90	50. Psalm 90
909: Nicene Creed	55: Nicene Creed
894: Behold the cross of the Lord : flee, hostile powers.	58: Behold the cross of the Lord : flee, hostile powers.
898: O God the creator and defender of the human race, who have made man in your own image, regard this your servant …	61: O God the creator and defender of the human race, regard this your servant N., whom you have made man in your own image …
900: I adjure you, ancient serpent, by the judge of the living and the dead …	62: … I adjure you, Satan, enemy of human salvation …
900: I adjure you again, not by my infirmity ….	62: I adjure you, Satan, prince of this world …
901: I adjure you, therefore, worthless dragon …	62: I adjure you, Satan, deceiver of the human race …
901: Draw back now from man, therefore, having been adjured in the name of him who formed him …	62: Draw back, therefore, Satan, in the name of the Father, and of the Son, and of the Holy Spirit …
903: God of heaven, God of earth …	81 (alternative formula): God of heaven, God of earth …
896: I exorcize you, most unclean spirit …	82 (alternative formula): I exorcize you, old enemy of man …
904: Go out, therefore, impious one … give place to the Holy Spirit …	82 (alternative formula): Go out from him, unclean spirit, give place to the Holy Spirit …
896: I exorcize you, most unclean spirit …	84 (alternative formula): I exorcize you by the living and true God, by the holy God, most unclean spirit …
901: Therefore I adjure you, worthless dragon …	84 (alternative formula): I adjure you, accursed dragon …
907: Magnificat	63: Magnificat

animistic cultures, exsufflation is a particularly powerful ritual act and this consideration may have weighed heavily with the authors of the rite.

Alessandro Pistoia has drawn attention to the linguistic problems posed by a rite of exorcism for global application. On the one hand, the authors were compelled to seek an 'irenic' language to refer to possession that did not trespass on the territory of psychology and psychiatry, yet on the other hand, they were constrained to draw on existing liturgical and biblical vocabulary. Furthermore, the rite had to be accessible to societies in which manifestations of the demonic are taken more seriously than they are in most parts of the West.[112] Pistoia considered it important that the rite should not 'domesticate' exorcism by assimilating it to the 'materialist-hedonist' presuppositions of Western society. The language of exorcism had to elevate the minds of all participants to the mystery of salvation rather than offering an alternative form of psychotherapy. Furthermore, the use of liturgical language by Satanists to present an inverted Christian message (Pistoia gave the example of the 'black mass') made it all the more important that the language of exorcism 'should speak clearly and with force the specific, unique and unmistakeable meaning of God's intervention, mediated by the Church, in the situation of the spiritual and physical prison in which the obsessed person finds himself'.[113] Pistoia situated himself firmly in the mainstream of twenty-first-century Catholic commentary on exorcism, by assuming that involvement in the occult is the most likely cause of possession and/or obsession.

In 2000 Amorth caused controversy by claiming in an interview with an Italian magazine that the new rite of exorcism was ineffective. He criticized its focus on deprecative rather than imperative exorcisms and its condemnation of exorcisms of bewitched and cursed individuals.[114] Fortea, who included a Spanish translation of the deprecative formula in his *Manual del Exorcista* (2008), nevertheless insisted that 'If an exorcism does not have conjuration, there would be no real exorcism. The defining and specific feature of exorcism is conjuration'.[115] However, Davies has justified the approach of the new rite on the grounds that both deprecative and imperative exorcisms are needed[116]:

> A deprecative exorcism is a prayer that qualifies as an exorcism because it is a certain kind of prayer ... The exorcist, in the name of Christ, brings the evil

---

[112] Pistoia (2000), p. 237.

[113] Ibid. pp. 238–9.

[114] Hauke (2006), pp. 40–1. On Amorth's response to the new rite see also Bartocci, G. and Eligi, A., 'L'Antinomie entre Thaumaturgie religieuse et Thérapies médicales: le cas "Catholicisme et Psychiatrie" en Italie', *L'Evolution Psychiatrique* 73 (2008), pp. 53–67.

[115] Fortea (2008), p. 164: 'Si en un exorcismo no hubiera conjuración, no habría verdadero exorcismo. El rasgo definitorio y específico del exorcismo es la conjuración'.

[116] Davies (2009), pp. 39–40.

spirit before God to be judged. An imperative exorcism expresses our faith in Christ's promise to be with his Church until the end ... A deprecative exorcism expresses our total dependence on God and on his will. These two kinds of exorcism balance each other and so important is this balance that the Rite forbids, in a Major Exorcism, one kind to be used without the other.

Davies defends the reform of the rite of exorcism on the grounds that exponents of the 1614 rite, such as Malachi Martin, tended to place the emphasis on a personal battle between the exorcist and Satan, 'rather than on prayer to the Holy Spirit for discernment of the blockage, the deception behind which the demons was protected'. The new rite facilitates a form of exorcism that relies 'on faith in the Holy Spirit and the word of God, working through prayer and love and kindness to reveal the truth and set captives free'.[117]

The latitude given to bishops' conferences to add a 'pastoral directive' to the rite of exorcism was used by the Bishops' Conference of France to further restrict the practice of exorcism by insisting that exorcists acquire a thorough understanding of psychiatric illnesses before proceeding. This document, prepared by the National Service for Pastoral and Sacramental Liturgy of the Bishops' Conference of France, accompanied the vernacular translation of the 1999 rite.[118] At the time of writing, an English translation of *DESQ* has yet to be published. In Brian Levack's view, the new rite of exorcism 'represented an effort to reduce rather than expand the number of exorcisms'.[119] This may be true, but a reduction in the number of exorcisms is certainly not what has happened.

A Revival in Full Swing

Since the publication of Amorth's book in 1990, exorcism has experienced an impressive revival in Europe. Consciousness of exorcism in popular culture is such that so-called 'Cathsploitation' films about exorcism now constitute a sub-genre of horror.[120] The sympathetic attitude to religious rituals

---

[117] Jeremy Davies, pers. comm. 27 June 2013.
[118] *L'Exorcisme dans l'Eglise Catholique* (Paris: Desclée-Mame, 2006).
[119] Levack (2013), p. 243.
[120] On exorcism in film see Nadeau, B., 'The Devil in Pictures; The Vatican is steadfast in its defense of exorcism', *Newsweek International*, 24 October 2005, p. 70; McNary, D., '"Rite" time to purge demons', *Variety*, 18 October 2010, p. 11; Wilkes, G. C., 'The Rite,' *Journal of Religion and Film* 15 (2011), Article 13.

now adopted by some secular psychologists has weakened the polarization that once existed between exorcism and psychiatry. The Belgian psychoanalyst Antoine Vergote (1921–2013), a pupil of Lacan, argued that the interpretation of possession and obsession as psychological phenomena need not diminish the significance of the ancient rites of the church.[121] Even the Catholic church in France, whose hierarchy has traditionally been hostile to exorcism, makes provision for people seeking exorcism in Paris through the Accueil St Irenée.[122] Responses remain mixed, however; in February 2006 Pierre Boz, the Archimandrite of the Melkite Catholic Church in France, invited the historian of medieval exorcism Florence Chave-Mahir to speak on the subject of 'The return of Satan' on Radio Notre-Dame. Chave-Mahir interpreted the resurgence of interest in exorcism in terms of immigration, rejecting the possibility of a latent demand for exorcism among native French Catholics and associating superstition with France's West African community.[123] The evidence of Archbishop Milingo's success in northern Italy, not to mention the vitality of belief in possession in rural France in the 1950s, count against this potentially divisive view.

Demand for exorcism in the twenty-first century is such that in 2005, the Regina Apostolorum University in Rome began a course for diocesan exorcists directed by the Legionaries of Christ.[124] The course, whose existence reflects the post-Vatican II disruption of exorcistic training highlighted by Amorth, attracted considerable media attention.[125] By 2008, a centre dedicated to exorcism was operating in Poland,[126] and in November 2010 a conference was organized specifically for American

---

[121] Vergote, A., 'Exorcisme et prières de délivrance, le point de vue de la psychologie religieuse', *La Maison-Dieu*, 183/184 (1990), pp. 123–37; idem, 'Anthropologie du diable: l'homme séduit et en proie aux puissances ténébreuses' in *Figures du Démoniaque hier et aujourd'hui* (Université de St Louis: Brussels, 1992), pp. 83–108.

[122] Chave-Mahir (2011), n. p. 22.

[123] Ibid. n. p. 19.

[124] Ibid. n. p. 20.

[125] 'College Course gives the Details on getting the Devil out', *The Washington Post*, 23 October 2005; Bollag, B., 'A Course Guides Students through the Legal, Medical, and Pastoral Aspects of Demonic Possession', *The Chronicle of Higher Education* 52 (2 June 2006), p. 8; 'Ritual of dealing with Demons undergoes a Revival', *The Washington Post*, 2 November 2008; McBrien, R., 'Conference on Exorcism will make your head spin', *National Catholic Reporter*, 9 July 2010, p. 21. On these training courses see Levack (2013), pp. 243–4.

[126] Delaney, S., 'Ritual of dealing with demons undergoes a revival', *The Washington Post*, 2 November 2008.

bishops. R. Scott Appleby, a Professor of History at the University of Notre Dame, claimed that the bishops were so keen to promote exorcism because it was something distinctive that only the church could offer.[127] Kelly, however, has been critical of exorcism-focused courses and conferences on the grounds that 'Such environments also tend to foster belief in Satan worship ... Christians who strongly believe in the active malevolence of Satan in the World find it easy to believe that *other people* worship the Devil, usually in connection with the practice of Diabolical Sorcery/witchcraft'.[128]

José Antonio Fortea, a Spanish priest and exorcist of the Diocese of Alcalá de Henares (which includes Madrid), has even revived the early modern genre of the exorcism manual for the twenty-first century. Fortea's *Summa Daemoniaca* (2008) self-consciously imitates the style and structure of seventeenth-century Spanish exorcism manuals, using the Scholastic 'question and answer' form.[129] Fortea's association with the Opus Dei-controlled University of Navarre, which revives the teaching methods of a Counter-Reformation seminary, partly explains the ease with which a literary form extinct in Spain for two centuries could re-emerge. Fortea's treatise goes beyond reliance on authority and argument and draws on the testimony of exorcists, including Amorth. For instance, Fortea does not hesitate to name and describe specific demons and their roles.[130] Like Amorth, Fortea is a believer in the possibility of demonic pacts,[131] and acknowledges the perceived challenge of witchcraft.[132] At the same time, however, he is critical of exorcists who place great emphasis on the form of ritual used to break curses and witchcraft, condemns the use of insults against demons,[133] and insists that faith and the name of Jesus are the only weapons required.[134] Fortea rejects belief in incubi and

---

[127] McBrien, R., 'Conference on exorcism will make your head spin', *National Catholic Reporter*, 9 July 2010, p. 21; 'Exorcism is on the Rise', *First Things*, 1 January 2011, pp. 68–9.
[128] Kelly (2006), p. 320.
[129] Fortea, J.-A., *Summa Daemoniaca: Tratado de Demonología y Manual de Exorcistas* (Madrid: Palmyra, 2008), p. 11.
[130] Ibid. p. 29.
[131] Ibid. p. 52.
[132] Ibid. pp. 61–7.
[133] Ibid. pp. 104–5.
[134] Ibid. p. 65.

succubi,[135] and his cautiously orthodox work is certainly not a revival of Menghi's magical exorcisms.

Fortea's *Manual del Exorcista*, the first contemporary example of the genre and the first to be based on the 1999 revision of the rite, analyses the nature and diagnosis of possession, including psychiatric aspects.[136] Fortea argues that possession may be caused by an offering of a child to Satan by its mother, as well as the Satanic pact, involvement in Satanism or Spiritualism and witchcraft.[137] Following Rodewyk, he recommends a short Latin probative exorcism.[138] Fortea adopts a rigorously classificatory approach to demons,[139] and differs from Amorth by insisting that 'the souls of the damned are able to possess exactly the same as a demon'.[140] Furthermore, Fortea does not believe that an exorcist is required in every diocese, considering it sufficient that an archdiocese provide support to the dioceses under the archbishop's metropolitan jurisdiction.[141] Whilst prohibiting the laity speaking during exorcisms, Fortea allows their presence and recommends that they pray the rosary.[142]

In addition to his examination of possession, Fortea provides a comprehensive classification of other kinds of demonic activity,[143] and offers suggestions for 'prayers of liberation' for those oppressed rather than possessed.[144] Fortea's demonological treatise is supplemented by a series of cases taken from his own experience,[145] a commentary on Canon Law with respect to exorcism and even a brief history of Christian exorcism.[146] The very existence of a manual of exorcism in the twenty-first century may scandalize some Catholics, but Fortea generally follows the *Praenotanda* of the 1999 rite and adopts a moderately sceptical approach to some disputed questions not covered by the rite. An exception is his approach to witchcraft, where his experience as an exorcist outweighs the 1999 rite's

---

[135] Ibid. pp. 202–4.
[136] Ibid. pp. 141–50.
[137] Ibid. pp. 154–5.
[138] Ibid. p. 154.
[139] Ibid. pp. 28–30, 160.
[140] Ibid. p. 161: 'las almas de los condenados pueden poseer exactamente igual que un demonio'.
[141] Ibid. p. 165.
[142] Ibid. pp. 181–2.
[143] Ibid. pp. 191–5.
[144] Ibid. pp. 195–200.
[145] Ibid. pp. 205–43.
[146] Ibid. pp. 248–54.

implicit condemnation of belief in witchcraft and curses. Nevertheless, Fortea is not nearly as outspoken a critic of the church as Amorth.

Conclusion

There is no reason to believe that the late twentieth-century revival of exorcism sparked in popular culture by William Blatty and in the church by Gabriele Amorth will end any time soon. In spite of his perception as 'liberal' by some conservative Catholics, Pope Francis has proved strongly supportive of exorcism. On 3 July 2014 the Vatican's newspaper, *L'Osservatore Romano*, reported that the Congregation of the Clergy had approved the International Association of Exorcists as a pontifical entity, and in November 2014 the Bishops of the United States passed a proposed English translation of the rite to the Congregation for Divine Worship. Some in the church see exorcism as a missionary opportunity—and history shows this has always been the case—yet in a 'postmodern' world, ancient practices are often valued for their perceived authenticity, and for some, questions about the 'reality' of possession seem to be of secondary importance to the potential psychological benefits of ritual. However, there remains a considerable body of priests and laity in Europe and America (not to mention a probable majority of Catholics in the rest of the world) for whom the devil and his activity in the world is very real, and for whom exorcism remains a viable remedy in its own right. Indeed, the threats to the survival of the practice of exorcism that once existed—religious change, liturgical reform, pressure from governments and medical professionals—seem to have receded as exorcism becomes one among many options in a religious marketplace. The increasing influence of bishops from Africa, South America and Asia within the global Catholic church, together with the need to compete with proselytizing Pentecostalism, make it highly unlikely that the sceptical caution of the European bishops' conferences with regard to exorcism will prevail. The exorcists, it would seem, are here to stay.

BIBLIOGRAPHY

MANUSCRIPTS

Cambridge, Cambridge University Library, MS Add. 3544
Cambridge, Corpus Christi College, Parker Library MS 146
London, British Library, MS Add. 8289
London, British Library, MS Add. 57337
London, British Library, MS Add. 34652
London, British Library, MS Cotton Caligula E XI
London, British Library, MS Harley 585
London, British Library, MS Royal 2 A II
London, British Library, MS Royal 2 A XX
London, British Library, MS Sloane 3846
Maidstone, Kent History and Library Centre, MSS U386/B12

PRIMARY SOURCES

Amorth, G. 1999. *An exorcist tells his story*. San Francisco: Ignatius Press.
Amorth, G. 2002. *An exorcist: More stories*. San Francisco: Ignatius Press.
Amorth, G. 2011. *Exorcisme et Psychiatrie*. Rocher: Monaco.
Andrieu, M. (ed.) 1931–1961. *Les Ordines Romani du Haut Moyen Âge*, 5 vols. Louvain: Spicilegium Sacrum Lovaniense.
Aquinas, Thomas. 1963. *S. Thomae Aquinatis Summa theologiae*, ed. P. Caramello, 3 vols. Turin: Marietti.
Aquinas, Thomas. 2001. In *The De malo of Thomas Aquinas*, ed. B. Davies. Oxford: Oxford University Press.
Arbiol, A. 1725. *Vocacion eclesiastica examinada con las divina escrituras*. Zaragoza.

Baddely, R. 1622. *The boy of Bilson: Or, a true discovery of the late notorious impostures of certaine Romish priests*. London.
Baglio, M. 2009. *The rite: The making of a modern exorcist*. London: Simon and Schuster.
Balducci, C. 1959. *Gli Indemoniati*. Rome: Coletti.
Balducci, C. 1966. Parapsychology and diabolic possession. *International Journal of Parapsychology* 8: 193–212.
Balducci, C. 1990. *The Devil: Alive and Active in Our World*. Trans. J. Aumann. New York: Alba House.
Benson, R.H. 2010. *The supernatural stories of monsignor Robert H. Benson*. Landisville: Coachwhip Publications.
Beyersdorf, E., and J.D. Brady (Trans.) 1975. *A manual of exorcism, very useful for priests and ministers of the church*. New York: Hispanic Society of America.
Bonaventure. 1882–1902. *Opera omnia*, 10 vols. Rome: Quaracchi.
Bontier, P., and J. Le Verrier (eds.). 1872. *The Canarian*. London: Hakluyt Society.
Bradshaw, P.F., M.E. Johnson, and L.E. Phillips (eds.). 2002. *The apostolic tradition: A commentary*. Minneapolis: Fortress Press.
Brewer, J., J. Gairdner, and R. Brodie (eds.) 1892–1932. *Letters and papers, foreign and domestic, of the reign of Henry VIII*, 35 vols. London: HMSO.
Brugnoli, C. 1714. *Alexicacon, hoc est de maleficiis, ac morbis maleficis cognoscendis*. Venice.
Bullarum diplomatum et privilegiorum sanctorum Romanorum Pontificium Taurinensis editio, 24 vols. Turin: A. Vecco, 1863.
Caparros, E., M. Thériault, and J. Thom (eds.). 2004. *The code of canon law annotated*, vol. 2. Montreal: Wilson and Lafleur.
Charcot, J.-M., and P. Richer. 1887. *Les Démoniaques dans l'Art*. Paris: Delahaye et Lecrosnier.
Chertsey, A. (trans.) 1502. *The Ordynarye of Crystyanyte or of Cristen Men*. London.
Congregation of the Doctrine of the Faith. Christian faith and demonology. In *Vatican Council II, volume 2: More post-conciliar documents*, ed. A. Flannery, 456–485. Dublin: Dominican Press, 1982.
Cini Tassinario, A. 1984. *Il Diavolo secondo l'Insegnamento recente della Chiesa*, Studia Antoniana 28. Rome: Pontificium Athenaeum Antonianum.
Cockayne, T.O. 1864–1866. *Leechdoms, Wortcunning and Starcraft of early England*, 3 Vols. London: Longman, Roberts and Green.
Congregation for the Doctrine of the Faith. 1989. *Letter to Bishops on certain aspects of Christian meditation (Orationis Formas)*. Vatican City: Typis Polyglottis Vaticanis.
Corpus Christianorum Continuatio Mediaevalis, 316 vols. Turnhout: Brepols, 1966–2014.
Corpus Christianorum Series Latina, 201 vols. Turnhout: Brepols, 1953–2014.
Corpus Scriptorum Ecclesiasticorum Latinorum, 99 vols. Salzburg: University of Salzburg, 1866–2011.
Cronin, H.S. 1907. The twelve conclusions of the Lollards. *English Historical Review* 22: 292–304.
Congregation for Divine Worship. *De Exorcismis et Supplicationibus Quibusdam*, 2nd edn. Vatican City: Typis Vaticanis, 2004.
Davies, J. 2009. *Exorcism from a Catholic perspective*. London: Catholic Truth Society.
de Adam, Salimbene. 1966. *Cronica*, ed. G. Scalia, 2 vols. Bari: Laterza.
De Lempèrière, J., and P. Maignart. 1644. *Response a l'Examen de la Possession des Religieuses de Louviers*. Rouen.

De Ocampo, B. 1907. Account of the province of Vilcapampa and a narrative of the execution of the Inca Tupac Amaru. In *History of the Incas and the execution of the Inca Tupac Amaru*, ed. C. Markham. Cambridge: Hakluyt Society.
Deshusses, J. (ed.). 1992. *Le Sacramentaire Gregorien: ses principales formes d'après les plus anciens manuscrits*, 3rd ed. Fribourg: Editions Universitaires.
Digby, K. 1658. *A Late Discourse ... Touching the Cure of Wounds by the Powder of Sympathy*. Trans. R. White. London.
Doble, G.H. (ed.). 1937. *Pontificale Lanaletense: (Bibliothèque de la ville de Rouen A. 27. cat. 368.) A Pontifical formerly in use at St. Germans, Cornwall*. London: Harrison and Sons.
Dumas, A. (ed.). 1981. *Liber sacramentorum Gellonensis, textus*, CCSL 159, 159A, 2 vols. Turnhout: Brepols.
Epitome Ritualis Romani in usum Missionum Scotiae. Edinburgh, 1783.
Erasmus. 1965. *The Colloquies of Erasmus*. Trans. C.R. Thompson. Chicago: University of Chicago Press.
Eriugena, John Scotus. 1996–2010. *Periphyseon*, CCCM, 5 vols. 161–165. Turnhout: Brepols.
Fontaine, J. (ed.). 2006. *Scriptores Christianae*, 510. Paris: Cerf.
Foreman, P. 2015. *The Cambridge Book of Magic: A Tudor Necromancer's Manual*. Trans. F. Young. Texts in Early Modern Magic: Cambridge.
Fortea, J.-A. 2008. *Summa Daemoniaca: Tratado de Demonología y Manual de Exorcistas*. Madrid: Palmyra.
Franz, A. 1909. *Die Kirchlichen Benediktionen im Mittelalter*, 2 vols. Freiburg-im-Breslau: Herdersche Verlagshandlung.
Gamber, K. (ed.). 1973. *Sacramentarium Gelasianum mixtum von Saint-Amand*. Regensburg: Pustet.
Gasparri, P. (ed.). 1963. *Codex Iuris Canonici*. Rome: Typis Polyglottis Vaticanis.
Gavilán, R. 1621. *Historia del celebre santuario de Nuestra Señora de Copacabana*. Lima.
Gee, J. 1624. *New shreds of the old snare, containing the apparitions of two new female ghosts*. London.
Gerald of Wales. 1978. *The Journey Through Wales and the Description of Wales*. Trans. L. Thorpe. Harmondsworth: Penguin.
Gervase of Tilbury. 2002. *Otia imperialia: Recreation for an emperor*, ed. S.E. Banks and J.W. Binns. Oxford: Oxford University Press.
Hallett, N. (ed.). 2007. *Witchcraft, exorcism and the politics of possession in a seventeenth-century convent: How Sister Ursula was once bewitched and Sister Margaret twice*. Aldershot: Ashgate.
Harsnett, S. 1603. *A declaration of egregious popish impostures*. London.
Hernaman, I. 1924. *Spiritualism and the child*. London: Catholic Truth Society.
Hilary of Poitiers. 1891. *Tractatus super Psalmos*, CSEL, ed. A. Zingerle, 22. Vienna: F. Tempsky.
Hippolytus of Rome. 1946. *La Tradition Apostolique*, ed. B. Botte. Paris: Cerf.
Hoffman, E.T.A. 1824. *The devil's elixir*, 2 vols. Edinburgh: William Blackwood.
Institoris, H. 2009. *The Hammer of Witches: A Complete Translation of the Malleus Maleficarum*. Trans. C.S. Mackay. Cambridge: Cambridge University Press.
Isidore of Seville. 1989. *Sancti Isidori Episcopi Hispalensis De ecclesiasticis officiis*, CCSL, ed. M. Lawson, 113. Turnhout: Brepols.

Kelke, W.H. 1869. 'Master John Schorne', *Records of Buckinghamshire* 2: 60–74.
Kellam, L. (ed.) 1610. *Manuale sacerdotum ... iuxta usum insignis ecclesiae Sarisburiensis*. Douai.
Kellam, L. (ed.), *Sacra institutio baptizandi ... iuxta usum insignis ecclesiae Sarisburiensis*.
Klaes, M. (ed.). 1993. *Vita Sanctae Hildegardis*, CCCM 126. Turnhout: Brepols.
Krusch, B. (ed.). 1969. *Scriptores rerum merovingicarum*. Hanover: Hahn.
Lagarde, P.A. (ed.). 1862. *Constitutiones apostolorum*. London: Williams and Norgate.
Las Casas, B. 1967. *Apologética Historia*, ed. E. O'Gorman. Mexico City: Universidad Nacional Autónoma de México.
Lavater, L. 1659. *De spectris, lemuribus et magnis insolitis fragoribus*. Leiden.
Lépicier, A.H.M. 1929. *The unseen world: An exposition of Catholic theology in reference to modern spiritism*. London: Sheed and Ward.
Lough, J., and D.E.L. Crane. 1986. Thomas Killigrew and the possessed Nuns of Loudun: The text of a letter of 1635. *Durham University Journal* 78: 259–268.
Lowe, E.A. 1926. The Vatican MS of the Gelasian Sacramentary and its supplement at Paris. *Journal of Theological Studies* 27: 357–373.
Marsh, R. 2007. *The beetle*. Wordsworth: Ware.
Menghi, G. 1578. *Flagellum daemonum, seu exorcismi terribiles, potentissimi et efficaces*. Bologna.
Menghi, G. 1605. *Compendio dell'arte essorcistica*. Venice.
Meurin, L. 1893. *La Franc-maçonnerie: Synagogue de Satan*. Paris: Victor Rétaux.
Michaelis, S. (trans. W. B.). 1613. *The admirable history of the possession and conversion of a penitent woman*. London.
Migne, J.-P. (ed.). 1844–1864. *Patrologia Latina*, 221 vols. Paris.
Migne, J.-P. (ed.). 1857–1866. *Patrologia Graeca*, 161 vols. Paris.
Miller, A.V. 1908. *Sermons on modern spiritualism*. London: Kegan Paul.
Mohlberg, C., et al. 1960. *Liber sacramentorum romanae aecclesiae ordinis anni circuli*. Rome: Rerum Ecclesiasticarum Documenta.
Munier, C., and C. De Clerq (eds.). 1963. *Concilia Galliae*. Turnhout: Brepols.
Nangle, E. 1665. *From Cloandaragh the first of April in the year of our Lord God 1665*. (n.p.)
Nicastor, N. 1554. *The doctrine of the masse booke*. Wittenberg.
Nicetas of Remesiana. 1964. *Instructio ad Competentes: frühchristliche Katechesen aus Dacien*, ed. K. Gamber. Regensburg: F. Pustet.
Nider, J. 1517. *Formicarius*. Strasbourg.
O'Neill, H.V. 1947. *Spiritualism as spiritualists have written of it*. London: Burnes, Oates and Washbourne.
Ogden, M.S. (ed.). 1938. *The 'Liber de Diversis Medicinis' in the Thornton Manuscript (MS. Lincoln Cathedral A.5.2.)*. London: Early English Text Society.
Ordo baptizandi aliaeque sacramenta administrandi ... pro Anglia, Hibernia et Scotia. Paris, 1738.
Paulinus of Nola. 1975. *The Poems of St. Paulinus of Nola*. Trans. P. G. Walsh. New York: Newman Press.
Petrus Cantor. 1954. *Summa de sacramentis*, ed. J.-A. Dugauquier. Lille: Löwen.
Picinelli, F. 1680. *Mondo symbolico*, 2 vols. Milan.
Picinelli, F. 1687. *Mundus symbolicus in emblematum universitate*. Trans. A. Erath, 2 vols. Cologne.
Powicke, F.M., and C. R. Cheney (eds.). 1964. *Councils and synods with other documents relating to the English Church: II A.D. 1205–1313*, 2 vols. Clarendon: Oxford.

Prinz, O. (ed.). 1960. *Egeria, Itinerarium Egeriae*. Heidelberg: Carl Winter.
Rackham, O. (ed.). 2007. *Transitus Beati Fursei*. East Harling: Fursey Pilgrims.
Raupert, J.G. 1914. *Christ and the powers of darkness*. London: Heath, Cranton and Ouseley.
Raupert, J.G. 1918. The truth about the ouija board. *American Ecclesiastical Review* (November): 463–478.
Raupert, J.G. 1919. *The new black magic and the truth about the ouija board*. New York: Devin-Adair.
Rituale Romanum. Rome: Typis Polyglottis Vaticanis, 1925.
Rituale Romanum: ordo baptismi parvulorum, 2nd edn. Vatican City: Libreria Editrice Vaticana, 1973.
Rituale Romanum: ordo initiationis Christianae adultorum, 2nd edn. Vatican City: Libreria Editrice Vaticana, 1974.
Santori, G.A. 1584. *Rituale sacramentorum Romanum Gregorii XIII Pont. Max. iussu editum* Rome.
Schwartz, E. (ed.). 1935. *Acta Conciliorum Oecumenicorum. Concilium Oecumenicum Chalcedonense*. Berlin: De Gruyter.
Sempe, J. 1908. *Livre Secret des Grands Exorcismes et Bénédictions*. Paris: Bussière.
Sodi, M., and J.J. Flores Arcas (eds.). 2004. *Rituale Romanum editio princeps (1614)*. Vatican City: Libreria Editrice Vaticana.
Sparrow Simpson, W. 1870. 'Master John Schorne', *Records of Buckinghamshire* 3: 354–69.
Stampa, P.A. 1608. *Fuga satanae* in *thesaurus exorcismorum*. 1193–1272. Cologne.
Suárez, F. 1856. *Opera omnia*. 28 vols. Paris: Vivès.
Sullivan, W.L. 1910. *Letters to His Holiness Pope Pius X*. Chicago: Open Court.
Summers, M. 1926. *A history of Witchcraft and Demonology*. London: Kegan Paul.
Surin, J.-J. 1990. *Triomphe de l'Amour Divine sur les Puissances de l'Enfer*, ed. M. De Certeau. Grenoble: J. Millon.
Tacchi Venturi, P. 1911–1913. *Opere Storichi del Padre Matteo Ricci S. J.* 2 vols. Macerata: Giorgetti.
Thiers, J.-B. 1697. *Traité des superstitions*, 2nd edn, 2 vols. Paris.
Thiesinger, T. 1934. *The earling possession case: An exposition of the exorcism of "Mary", a demoniac* (n.p.).
Thomas of Cantimpré. 1627. *Bonum universale de apibus*. Douai.
Thyraeus, P. 1594. *De demoniacis liber unus*. Cologne.
Thyraeus, P. 1604. *Daemoniaci cum locis infestis et terriculamentis nocturnis*. Cologne.
Véritable relation des justes procédures observées au fait de la possession des Ursulines à Loudun et au procès de Grandier. Paris, 1634.
Vogl, C. 1970. *Begone Satan! A Soul-Stirring Account of Diabolical Possession*, 2nd edn. Trans. C. Kapsner. Hong Kong: Catholic Truth Society.
Waite, A.E. 1896. *Devil-worship in France: Or, The question of Lucifer*. London: G. Redway.
Warren, F.E. (ed.). 1883. *The Leofric Missal, as used in the Cathedral of Exeter*. Oxford: Clarendon.
White, C. (trans.). 1998. *Early Christian lives*. London: Penguin.
Whitelock, D., M. Brett, and C.N.L. Brooke (eds.). 1981. *Councils and synods with other documents relating to the English Church: I A.D. 871–1204*, 2 vols. Clarendon: Oxford.
William of Auxerre. 1964. *Summa aurea*, ed. P. Pigouchet. Frankfurt-am-Main: Minerva.
Williams, J. (ed.). 1930. *Life in the Middle Ages*, 3rd edn. Cambridge: Cambridge University Press.

Wilmart, A. (ed.). 1971. *Auteurs spirituels et textes dévots du moyen âge latin*. Paris: Etudes Augustiniennes.
Wyclif, J. 1913. *Johannis Wyclif opera minora*, ed. J. Loserth. Wyclif Society: London.
Yvelin, P. 1643. *Examen de la possession des religieuses à Louviers*. Paris.
Yvelin, P. 1643. *Apologie pour l'autheur de l'examen de la possession des religieuses de Louviers*. Paris.

Unpublished PhD Thesis

O'Neill, M.R. 1981. Discerning superstition: Popular errors and orthodox response in late sixteenth-century Italy. Unpublished PhD thesis, Stanford University, California, USA.

Newspapers and Periodicals

British Bishop fined for Holocaust Denial on TV, *The Guardian* (27 October 2009): 10.
College course gives the details on getting the Devil out, *The Washington Post* (23 October 2005).
Delaney, S. 2008. Ritual of dealing with demons undergoes a revival, *The Washington Post* (2 November).
Exorcism is on the rise, *First Things* (1 January 2011): 68–69.
McBrien, Richard. 2010. Conference on exorcism will make your head spin, *National Catholic Reporter* (9 July): 21.
McNary, D. 2010. "Rite" time to purge demons, *Variety* (18 October): 11.
Nadeau, B. 2005. The Devil in pictures; the Vatican is steadfast in its defense of exorcism, *Newsweek International* (24 October): 70.
On the powers of exorcism, &c. pretended to be conferred on the clergy of the Church of Rome, *John Bull* 40(4 October 1824): 325–326.
Priest arrested in alleged exorcism, *National Catholic Reporter* (1 September 2000): 5.
Ritual of dealing with demons undergoes a revival, *The Washington Post* (2 November).
Whitehead, A.E. 1893. A convert through spiritualism, *The Month* (August). Reprinted in Thurston, H. 1933. *The church and spiritualism*, 368–384. Milwaukee: Bruce Publishing Co.
Wilkes, G.C., The rite, *Journal of Religion and Film* 15(2011): Article 13.

Secondary Sources

Allen, T.B. 2000. *Possessed: The true story of an exorcism*, 2nd edn. Lincoln: iUniverse.
Allison, A.F., and D.M. Rogers (eds.). 1956. *A catalogue of Catholic books in English printed abroad or secretly in England 1558–1640*, 2 vols. Bognor Regis: Arundel Press.
Almond, P.C. 2004. *Demonic possession and exorcism in early modern England: Contemporary texts and their cultural contexts*. Cambridge: Cambridge University Press.
Amirav, H. 2011. The application of magical formulas of invocation in Christian contexts. In *Demons and the devil in ancient and mediaeval Christianity*, ed. N. Vos and W. Otten, 117–127. Leiden: Brill.

Anson, P.F. 1970. *Underground Catholicism in Scotland*. Montrose: Standard Press.
Backus, I. 1994. *Le Miracle de Laon: le deraisonnable, le raisonnable, l'apocalyptique et le politique dans les recits du Miracle de Laon, 1566–1578*. Paris: J. Vrin.
Baker, R. 1975. *Binding the devil: Exorcism past and present*. London: Random House.
Barbierato, F. 2002. Magical literature and the Venice inquisition from the sixteenth to the eighteenth centuries. In *Magia, Alchimia, Scienza dal '400 al '700; l'influsso di Ermete Trismegisto*, ed. C. Gilly and C. Van Heertum, 159–175. Florence: Centro Di.
Baroja, J.C. 1990. Witchcraft and Catholic theology. In *Early modern European witchcraft: Centres and peripheries*, ed. B. Ankarloo and G. Henningsen, 19–43. Oxford: Oxford University Press.
Bartelink, G. 2011. Denominations of the devil and demons in the *Missale Gothicum*. In *Demons and the devil in ancient and mediaeval Christianity*, ed. N. Vos and W. Otten, 195–209. Leiden: Brill.
Bartocci, G., and A. Eligi. 2008. L'Antinomie entre Thaumaturgie religieuse et Thérapies médicales: le cas "Catholicisme et Psychiatrie" en Italie. *L'Evolution Psychiatique* 73: 53–67.
Bartsch, E. 1967. *Die Sachbeschwörungen der römischen Liturgie: eine liturgiegeschichtliche und liturgietheologische Studie*. Aschendorff: Münster.
Bastiaensen, A.A.R. 2011. Exorcism: Tackling the devil by word of mouth. In *Demons and the devil in ancient and mediaeval Christianity*, ed. N. Vos and W. Otten, 129–144. Leiden: Brill.
Behar, R. 1987. Sex and sin, witchcraft and the devil in late-colonial Mexico. *American Ethnologist* 14: 34–54.
Bell, R., and D. Weinstein. 1982. *Saints and society: Christendom, 1000–1700*. Chicago: University of Chicago Press.
Binterim, A.J. 1979. *Über die Besessenen (Energumenen) und ihre Behandlung in der alten Kirche*. Munich: Arbeitsgemeinschaft für Religions.
Blackwell, J. 2000. German narratives of women's divine and demonic possession and supernatural visions 1555–1800: A bibliography. *Women in German Yearbook* 16: 241–257.
Blair, J. 2005. *The church in Anglo-Saxon society*. Oxford: Oxford University Press.
Blatty, W.P. 1998. *Before the exorcist: William Peter Blatty's own story of taking the novel to film*. Eye: ScreenPress Books.
Boddy, J. 1994. Spirit possession revisited: Beyond instrumentality. *Annual Review of Anthropology* 23: 407–434.
Boespflug, F. 1984. *Dieu dans l'Art: Sollicitudini Nostrae de Benoît XIV et l'Affaire Crescence de Kaufbeuren*. Paris: Cerf.
Boglioni, P., and G. Boudreau. 2007. "Du tems de la cadi": possessions diaboliques et exorcismes populaires en Acadie au début du XIXe siècle'. *Revue d'Histoire de l'Amerique Française* 60: 487–515.
Boureau, A. 2006. *Satan the heretic: The birth of demonology in the medieval west*. Trans. T. L. Fagan. Chicago: University of Chicago Press.
Brakke, D. 2006. *Demons and the making of the monk: Spiritual combat in early Christianity*. Cambridge, MA: Harvard University Press.
Brambilla, E. 2010. *Corpi Invasi e Viaggi dell'Anima: santita, possessione, esorcismo dalla teologia barocca alla medicina illuminista*. Rome: Viella.

Brown, T. 1961. Examples of post-reformation Folklore in Devon. *Folklore* 72: 388–399.
Brown, P. 1978. *The making of late antiquity*. Cambridge, MA: Harvard University Press.
Brown, P. 1981. *The cult of the saints: Its rise and function in Latin Christianity*. Chicago: University of Chicago Press.
Brucker, G. 1963. Sorcery in renaissance florence. *Studies in the Renaissance* 10: 7–23.
Butler, E.M. 1949. *Ritual magic*. Cambridge: Cambridge University Press.
Butler, S.M. 2007. Cultures of suicide? Suicide verdicts and the "community" in thirteenth- and fourteenth-century England. *The Historian* 69: 427–449.
Bynum, C.W. 1982. *Jesus as mother: Studies in the spirituality of the High Middle Ages*. Berkeley: University of California Press.
Caciola, N. 1996. Wraiths revenants and ritual in medieval culture. *Past and Present* 152: 3–45.
Caciola, N. 2000. Mystics demoniacs and the physiology of spirit possession in medieval Europe. *Comparative Studies in Society and History* 42: 268–306.
Caciola, N. 2003. *Discerning spirits: Divine and demonic possession in the Middle Ages*. Ithaca: Cornell University Press.
Cameron, E. 2010. *Enchanted Europe: Superstition, reason, and religion, 1250–1750*. Oxford: Oxford University Press.
Carmona, M. 1988. *Le Diable de Loudun*. Paris: Fayard.
Carrin-Bouez, M. (ed.). 1999. *Managing distress: Possession and therapeutic cults in South Asia*. New Delhi: Manohar.
Carver, M. 2003. *The cross goes north: Processes of conversion in northern Europe, 300–1300*. York: York Medieval Press.
Ceard, J. 1994. Démonologie et Démonopathies au temps du Charcot. *Histoire des Sciences Médicales* 28: 337–343.
Cervantes, F. 1994. *The devil in the New World: The impact of diabolism in New Spain*. New Haven: Yale University Press.
Chadwick, H. 2007. Origen. In *The Cambridge history of later Greek and early mediaeval theology*, 7th ed, ed. A.H. Armstrong, 182–194. Cambridge: Cambridge University Press.
Chaput, B. 1976. Réflexion sur l'Etude des Religions populaires et l'Histoire: l'exemple de la possession démonique dans les Cantons de l'Est. In *Recherche et Religions Populaires: un colloque international 1973*, ed. A. Désilets and G. Laperrière, 143–162. Montreal: Bellarmin.
Chardonnens, L.S. 2007. *Anglo-Saxon prognostics, 900–1100: Study and texts*. Brill: Leiden.
Chave-Mahir, F. 2011. *L'Exorcisme des Possédés dans l'Eglise d'Occident (Xe–XIVe siècle)*. Turnhout: Brepols.
Chène, C. 1995. *Juger les Vers: Exorcismes et Procès d'Animaux dans le Diocèse de Lausanne (XVe–XVIe s.)*. Lausanne: Université de Lausanne.
Chesnut, R.A. 2003. A preferential option for the spirit: The Catholic Charismatic Renewal in South America's new religious economy. *Latin American Politics and Society* 45: 55–85.
Chesters, T. 2011. *Ghost stories in late Renaissance France*. Oxford: Oxford University Press.
Chohan, S.S. 2004. The exorcist: Personification of human wickedness or upholder of religious duties? In *This thing of darkness: Perspectives on evil and human wickedness*, ed. R.P. Hamilton and M.S. Breen, 103–114. Amsterdam: Rodopi.

Claggett, T.D. 1990. *William Friedkin: Films of aberration, obsession and reality*. Jefferson: MacFarland and Co.
Clark, S. 1997. *Thinking with demons: The idea of witchcraft in early modern Europe*. Oxford: Clarendon.
Clark, S. 2002. Protestant witchcraft, Catholic witchcraft. In *The witchcraft reader*, ed. D. Oldridge, 165–177. London: Routledge.
Clark, S. 2007. Magic and witchcraft. In *Finding Europe: Discourses on margins, communities, images ca. 13th–ca. 18th centuries*, ed. A. Molho, D.R. Curto, and N. Koniordos, 115–130. Oxford: Berghahn Books.
Clarke, B. 1975. *Mental disorder in earlier Britain: Exploratory studies*. Cardiff: University of Wales Press.
Closson, M. 2007. 'Le Diable au XIXe siècle de Léo Taxil: ou les "mille et un nuits" de la démonologie'. In *Fictions du Diable: Démonologie et Littérature de Saint Augustin à Léo Taxil*, ed. F. Lavocat, P. Kapitaniak, and M. Closson, 313–332. Paris: Droz.
Collins, J.M. 2009. *Exorcism and deliverance ministry in the twentieth century: An analysis of the practice and theology of exorcism in modern western Christianity*. Bletchley: Paternoster.
Colmcille, Fr. 1955. Three unpublished Cistercian documents. *Journal of the County Louth Archaeological Society* 13: 252–278.
Cornwell, J. 1991. *Powers of darkness, powers of light: Travels in search of the miraculous and demonic*. London: Penguin.
Cortés, J.B., and F. Gatti. 1975. *The case against possessions and exorcisms: A historical, biblical and psychological analysis of demons, devils and demoniacs*. New York: Vantage.
Cox, J.D. 2007. *Seeming knowledge: Shakespeare and skeptical faith*. Waco: Baylor University Press.
Cragg, G.R. 1967. *The church and the age of reason 1648–1789*, 2nd ed. Harmondsworth: Penguin.
Cristiani, L. 1961. *Satan in the Modern World*. Trans. C. Roland. London: Barrie and Rockliff.
Crouzet, D. 1996. A woman and the devil: Possession and exorcism in sixteenth-century France. In *Changing identities in early modern France*, ed. M. Wolfe, 191–215. Durham: Duke University Press.
Cuneo, M.W. 2002. *American exorcism: Expelling demons in the land of plenty*, 2nd ed. London: Bantam.
Dall'Olio, G. 2012. The devil of inquisitors, demoniacs and exorcists in counter-reformation Italy. In *The devil in society in pre-modern Europe*, ed. P. Dendle and R. Raiswell, 511–536. Toronto: Centre for Reformation and Renaissance Studies.
Davies, O. 1999. *Witchcraft, magic and culture 1736–1951*. Manchester: Manchester University Press.
Davies, O. 2007a. *The haunted: A social history of ghosts*. Palgrave MacMillan: Basingstoke.
Davies, O. 2007b. *Popular magic: Cunning folk in English history*, 2nd ed. London: Hambledon Continuum.
Davies, O. 2009. *Grimoires: A history of magic books*. Oxford: Oxford University Press.
De Certeau, M. 1975. *L'Ecriture de l'Histoire*. Paris: Gallimard.
De Certeau, M. 1980. *La Possession de Loudun*, 2nd ed. Paris: Archives Gallimard Juliard.

De Certeau, M. 1990. *Les Aventures de Jean-Joseph Surin*. Grenoble: Jérôme Millon.

De Mello e Souza, L. 2003. *The Devil and the Land of the Holy Cross: Witchcraft, Slavery, and Popular Religion in Colonial Brazil*. Trans. D. Grosklaus Whitty. Austin: University of Texas Press.

De Waardt, H. 2009. Jesuits propaganda and faith healing in the Dutch Republic. *History* 94: 344–359.

De Waardt, H., and W. De Blécourt. 1991. "It is no sin to put an evil person to death", judicial proceedings concerning witchcraft during the reign of Duke Charles of Gelderland. In *Witchcraft in the Netherlands from the fourteenth to the twentieth century*, ed. M. Gijswijt-Hofstra and W. Frijhoff, 66–78. Rotterdam: Universitaire Pers.

Dean, R.J. 1999. *Anglo-Norman literature: A guide to texts and manuscripts*. London: Anglo-Norman Texts Society.

DeConick, A.D. 2011. *Holy misogyny: Why the sex and gender conflicts in the early church still matter*. London: Continuum.

Deliège, R. 1992. La Possession Démoniaque chez les Intouchables catholiques de l'Inde du Sud. *Archives de Sciences Sociales des Religions* 79: 115–134.

Devlin, J. 1987. *The superstitious mind: French peasants and the supernatural in the nineteenth century*. New Haven: Yale University Press.

Dölger, F.J. 1909. *Der Exorzismus im altchristlichen Taufritual*. Paderborn: F. Schöningh.

Donaldson, C. 1980. *Martin of tours: Parish priest, mystic and exorcist*. London: Routledge and Kegan Paul.

Dondelinger-Mandy, P. 1990. Le Rituel des Exorcismes dans le *Rituale Romanum* de 1614. *Le Maison-Dieu* 183/184: 99–121.

Duffy, E. 1992. *The stripping of the altars*. New Haven: Yale University Press.

Duggan, R.D. 1982. Conversion in the *Ordo initiationis christianae adultorum*, *Ephemerides Liturgicae* 96(1982): 57–83, 209–252.

Ebon, M. 1975. *Exorcism: Past and present*. London: Cassell.

Ebright, M., and R. Hendricks. 2006. *The witches of Abiquiu: The governor, the priest, the Genizaro Indians, and the devil*. Albuquerque: University of New Mexico Press.

Elliott, D. 1999. *Fallen bodies: Pollution, sexuality and demonology in the high Middle Ages*. Philadelphia: University of Pennsylvania Press.

Ericson, G. 1977. The enigmatic metamorphosis: From divine possession to demonic possession. *Journal of Popular Culture* 11: 656–681.

Favret-Saada, J. 1977. *Les Mots, la Mort, les Sorts*. Paris: Gallimard.

Ferber, S. 1997. Charcot's demons: Retrospective medicine and historical diagnosis in the writings of the Salpêtrière school. In *Illness and healing alternatives in Western Europe*, ed. M. Gijswijt-Hofstra, H. Marland, and H. De Waardt, 120–140. London: Routledge.

Ferber, S. 2004. *Demonic possession and exorcism in early modern France*. London: Routledge.

Ferber, S., and A. Howe. 2005. The man who mistook his wife for a devil: Exorcism, expertise and secularisation in a late twentieth-century Australian criminal court. In *Dämonische Besessenheit: zur Interpretation eines kulturhistorischen Phänomens*, ed. H. De Waardt, J.M. Schmidt, H.C.E. Midelfort, and D.R. Bauer, 281–292. Bielefeld: Verlag für Regionalgeschichte.

Finlay, A. 1999. *Demons! The devil, possession and exorcism*. London: Blandford.

Finucane, R. 1977. *Miracles and pilgrims: Popular beliefs in medieval England.* London: Dent.
Fischer, B. 1974. Baptismal exorcism in the Catholic baptismal rites after Vatican II. *Studia Liturgica* 10: 48–55.
Fisher, J.D.C. 1965. *Christian initiation: Baptism in the medieval west: A study in the disintegration of the primitive rite of initiation.* London: SPCK.
Forget, J. 1903–1950. Exorcisme. In *Dictionnaire de Théologie Catholique*, ed. A. Vacant et al., vol. 5:2, 1762–1780. Paris: Letouzey et Ané.
Forsyth, N. 1987. *The old enemy: Satan and the combat myth.* Princeton: Princeton University Press.
Frankfurter, D. 2008. *Evil incarnate: Rumors of satanic conspiracy and satanic abuse in history.* Princeton: Princeton University Press.
Frankfurter, D. 2010. Where the spirits dwell: Possession Christianization and saints' shrines in late antiquity. *Harvard Theological Review* 103: 27–46.
Freeman, T.S. 2000. Demons, deviance and defiance: John Darrell and the politics of exorcism in late Elizabethan England. In *Conformity and orthodoxy in the English Church, c. 1560–1660*, ed. P. Lake and M. Questier, 34–63. Woodbridge: Boydell.
Gentilcore, D. 1992. *From Bishop to witch: The system of the sacred in early modern Terra d'Otranto.* Manchester: Manchester University Press.
Gentilcore, D. 1998. *Healers and healing in early modern Italy.* Manchester: Manchester University Press.
Gibson, M. 2006. *Possession, puritanism and print: Darrell, Harsnett, Shakespeare and the Elizabethan exorcism controversy.* London: Pickering and Chatto.
Gillespie, R. 1997. *Devoted people: Belief and religion in early modern Ireland.* Manchester: Manchester University Press.
Goddu, A. 1980. The failure of exorcism in the Middle Ages. In *Soziale Ordnungen im Selbstverständnis des Mittelalters*, ed. A. Zimmerman, 540–557. Berlin: Walter de Gruyter.
Goodman, F.D. 1988. *How about demons? Possession and exorcism in the modern world.* Bloomington: Indiana University Press.
Goodman, F.D. 2005. *The exorcism of Anneliese Michel*, 2nd ed. Eugene: Resource Publications.
Gratsch, E.J. 2003. Exorcism. In *The New Catholic encyclopedia*, vol. 5, 2nd ed, 551–553. Washington, DC: Catholic University of America.
Green, T. 2008. *Inquisition: The reign of fear*, 2nd ed. London: Pan MacMillan.
Guillemain, H. 2001. Déments ou Démons? L'exorcisme face au sciences psychiques. *Revue d'Histoire de l'Eglise en France* 87: 439–471.
Guillemain, H. 2006. *Diriger les Consciences, Guérir les Âmes: Une Histoire comparée des Pratiques Therapeutiques et Religieuses (1830–1939).* Paris: La Découverte.
Haag, H. 1974. *Teufelsglaube.* Tübingen: Katzmann.
Hall, A. 2007. *Elves in Anglo-Saxon England: Matters of belief, health, gender and identity.* Woodbridge: Boydell.
Hanlon, G., and G. Snow. 1988. Exorcisme et Cosmologie Tridentine: trois cas agenais en 1619. *Revue de la Bibliothèque Nationale* 28: 12–27.
Harline, C. 1994. *The burdens of Sister Margaret.* New York: Doubleday.

Harris, R. 1997. Possession on the borders: The "Mal de Morzine" in nineteenth-century France. *Journal of Modern History* 69: 451–478.
Hauke, M. 2006. The theological battle over the rite of exorcism, "Cinderella" of the new *Rituale Romanum*. *Antiphon* 10: 32–69.
Hazelgrove, J. 2000. *Spiritualism and British society between the wars*. Manchester: Manchester University Press.
Heller-Nicholas, A. 2011. "The power of Christ Compels you": Moral spectacle and *The Exorcist* universe. In *Roman Catholicism in fantastic film: Essays on belief, spectacle and imagery*, ed. H. Hansen, 65–80. Jefferson: MacFarland and Co.
Hemming, J. 1993. *The conquest of the Incas*, 2nd ed. London: Pan MacMillan.
Henningsen, G. 1980. *The witches' advocate: Basque witchcraft and the Spanish Inquisition (1609–1614)*. Reno: University of Nevada Press.
Henningsen, G. 1990. "The ladies from outside": An archaic pattern of the witches' sabbath. In *Early modern European witchcraft: Centres and peripheries*, ed. B. Ankarloo and G. Henningsen, 191–215. Oxford: Oxford University Press.
Hole, C. 1940. *English folklore*. London: Batsford.
Hone, J. 1939. *The Moores of Moore hall*. London: Jonathan Cape.
Hoyt, O. 1978. *Exorcism*. London: F. Watts.
Hübener, G. 1935. Beowulf and Germanic exorcism. *Review of English Studies* 11: 163–181.
Hubert, O. 2000. *Sur la Terre comme au Ciel: La Gestion des Rites par l'Eglise Catholique du Québec (fin XVIIe–mi-XIXe siècle)*. Quebec City: Les Presses de L'Université Laval.
Huels, J. 2000. Other acts of divine worship. In *New commentary on the Code of Canon Law*, 1400–1423. Mahwah: Paulist Press.
Hughes, J. 1988. *Pastors and visionaries: Religion and secular life in late medieval Yorkshire*. Boydell: Woodbridge.
Hutton, R. 1999. *The triumph of the moon: A history of modern pagan witchcraft*. Oxford: Oxford University Press.
Introvigne, M. 2009. Le Satanisme modern et contemporain en Italie. *Social Compass* 56: 541–551.
Johnson, T., et al. 2005. Besessenheit, Heiligkeit und Jesuitspiritualität. In *Dämonische Besessenheit: zur Interpretation eines kulturhistorischen Phänomens*, ed. H. De Waardt, J.M. Schmidt, H.C.E. Midelfort, and D.R. Bauer, 234–247. Bielefeld: Verlag für Regionalgeschichte.
Johnstone, N. 2006. *The devil and demonism in early modern England*. Cambridge: Cambridge University Press.
Jones, P., and N. Pennick. 1995. *A history of pagan Europe*. London: Routledge.
Kahlos, M. 2015. The early church. In *The Cambridge history of magic and witchcraft in the west*, ed. D.J. Collins, 148–182. Cambridge: Cambridge University Press.
Kallendorf, H. 2003. *Exorcism and its texts: Subjectivity in early modern literature of England and Spain*. Toronto: University of Toronto Press.
Kallendorf, H. 2005. The rhetoric of exorcism. *Rhetorica* 23: 209–237.
Kapferer, B. 1991. *A celebration of demons: Exorcism and the aesthetics of healing in Sri Lanka*. Providence: Berg.
Kaplan, B.J. 1996. Possessed by the devil: A very public dispute in Utrecht. *Renaissance Quarterly* 49: 738–759.

Kaptchuk, T.J., C.E. Kerr, and A. Zanger. 2004. The art of medicine: Placebo controls, exorcisms, and the devil. *The Lancet* 374: 1234–1235.
Keck, D. 1998. *Angels and angelology in the Middle Ages*. Oxford: Oxford University Press.
Kelly, H.A. 1968. *Towards the death of Satan: The growth and decline of Christian demonology*. London: Geoffrey Chapman.
Kelly, H.A. 1985. *The devil at baptism: Ritual, theology and drama*. Ithaca: Cornell University Press.
Kelly, H.A. 2004. *The devil, demonology and witchcraft*, 2nd ed. Eugene: Wipf and Stock.
Kelly, H.A. 2006. *Satan: A biography*. Cambridge: Cambridge University Press.
Kieckhefer, R. 1976. *European witch trials: Their foundation in popular and learned culture, 1300–1500*. Berkeley: University of California Press.
Kieckhefer, R. 1990. *Magic in the Middle Ages*. Cambridge: Cambridge University Press.
Kieckhefer, R. 1997. *Forbidden rites: A necromancer's manual of the fifteenth century*. Stroud: Sutton.
Kiely, D.M., and C. McKenna. 2006. *The dark sacrament: Exorcism in modern Ireland*. Dublin: Gill and MacMillan.
Klaassen, F. 2013. *The transformations of magic: Illicit learned magic in the later Middle Ages and renaissance*. University Park: Pennsylvania State University Press.
Klueting, H. 2010. The Catholic enlightenment in Austria or the Habsburg Lands. In *A companion to the Catholic enlightenment in Europe*, ed. U.L. Lehner and M. Printy, 127–164. Leiden: Brill.
Knox, R. 1950. *Enthusiasm: A chapter in the history of religion*. Oxford: Clarendon.
Kollar, R. 1999. Spiritualism and religion: Sir Arthur Conan Doyle's critique of Christianity and a Roman Catholic response. *Recusant History* 24: 397–413.
Kunzler, M. 2001. *The Church's liturgy*. Münster: Lit Verlag.
La Fontaine, J. 1989. Satanism and satanic mythology. In *Witchcraft and magic in Europe: The twentieth century*, ed. W. De Blécourt, R. Hutton, and J. La Fontaine, 81–140. London: Athlone.
Lahaire, M. 1991. *La Folie au Moyen Age, XIe–XIIIe siècles*. Paris: Léopard d'Or.
Lantenari, V. 1998. From Africa into Italy: The exorcistic-therapeutic cult of Emmanuel Milingo. In *New trends and developments in African religions*, ed. P.B. Clarke, 263–282. Westport: Greenwood Press.
Leather, E.M. 1912. *The Folk-lore of Herefordshire*. Hereford: Jakeman and Carver.
Lecouturier, Y. 2012. *Sorciers, Sorcières et Possédés en Normandie: procès en sorcellerie du Moyen Âge au XVIIIe siècle*. Rennes: Ouest-France.
Lederer, D. 2005. Exorzieren ohne Lizenz.... In *Dämonische Besessenheit: zur Interpretation eines kulturhistorischen Phänomens*, ed. H. De Waardt, J.M. Schmidt, H.C.E. Midelfort, and D.R. Bauer, 213–231. Bielefeld: Verlag für Regionalgeschichte.
Lederer, D. 2006. *Madness, religion and the state in early modern Europe: A Bavarian Beacon*. Cambridge: Cambridge University Press.
Leeper, E.A. 1990. From Alexandria to Rome: The Valentinian connection to the incorporation of exorcism as a prebaptismal rite. *Vigiliae Christianae* 44: 6–24.
Levack, B. 2013. *The devil within: Possession and exorcism in the Christian west*, 240–253. New Haven: Yale University Press.
Levi, G. 1988. *Inheriting power: The story of an exorcist*. Chicago: University of Chicago Press.

Lhermitte, J. 1972. Pseudo-possession. In *Soundings in Satanism*, ed. F.J. Sheed, 12–35. London: Mowbrays.
Loisy, A. 1920. *Les Actes des Apôtres*. Paris: E. Nourry.
Lunn-Rockliffe, S. 2012. Visualizing the demonic: The Gadarene exorcism in early Christian art and literature. In *The devil in society in pre-modern Europe*, ed. R. Raiswell and P. Dendle, 439–458. Toronto: Centre for Reformation and Renaissance Studies.
MacCormack, S. 1998. *Religion in the Andes: Vision and imagination in early colonial Peru*. Princeton: Princeton University Press.
MacCormack, S. 2007. *On the wings of time: Rome, the Incas, Spain, and Peru*. Princeton: NJ Princeton University Press.
Machielsen, J. 2015. *Martin Delrio: Demonology and scholarship in the counter-reformation*. Oxford: British Academy.
MacMullen, R. 1984. *Christianizing the Roman Empire (A.D. 100–400)*. New Haven: Yale University Press.
MacNutt, F. 1995. *Deliverance from evil spirits*. Grand Rapids: Chosen.
MacNutt, F. 1997. *Healing*, 2nd ed. New York: Bantam.
Macy, G. 1996. Was there a "the church" in the Middle Ages? In *Unity and diversity in the church*, ed. R. Swanson, 107–116. Cambridge: Cambridge University Press.
Mager, A. 1948. *Satan*. Paris: Desclée.
Maggi, A. 2001. *Satan's rhetoric: A study of renaissance demonology*. Chicago: University of Chicago Press.
Maggi, A. 2006. *In the company of demons: Unnatural beings, love, and identity in the Italian Renaissance*. Chicago: University of Chicago Press.
Mandouze, A. 1986. *Histoire des Saints et de la Sainteté chrétienne*, vol. 2. Paris: Hachette.
Maquart, F.X., and J. de Tonquédec. 1972. Exorcism. In *Soundings in Satanism*, ed. F.J. Sheed, 72–91. London: Mowbrays.
Marin, J.M. 2007. A Jesuit Mystic's Feminine Melancholia: Jean-Joseph Surin SJ (1600–1665). *Journal of Men, Masculinities and Spirituality* 1: 65–76.
Marshman, M. 1999. Exorcism as empowerment: A new idiom. *Journal of Religious History* 23: 265–281.
Martin, A.L. 1988. *The Jesuit mind: The mentality of an elite in early modern France*. Ithaca: Cornell University Press.
Martin, M. 1992. *Hostage to the devil*, 2nd ed. San Francisco: Harper.
Maxwell-Stuart, P.G. 2004. *Wizards: A history*. Stroud: Tempus.
Mazzotti, M. 2007. *The world of Maria Gaetana Agnesi, mathematician of God*. Baltimore: Johns Hopkins University Press.
Menegon, E. 2010. *Ancestors, virgins and friars: Christianity as a local religion in late imperial China*. Cambridge, MA: Harvard-Yenching Institute.
Messadié, G. 1996. *The History of the Devil*. Trans. M. Romano. London: Newleaf.
Metzger, N. 2012. Incubus as an illness: Taming the demonic by medical means in late antiquity and beyond. In *The devil in society in pre-modern Europe*, ed. R. Raiswell and P. Dendle, 483–510. Toronto: Centre for Reformation and Renaissance Studies.
Midelfort, H.C.E. 2005a. *Exorcism and enlightenment: Johann Joseph Gassner and the demons of eighteenth-century Germany*. New Haven: Yale University Press.
Midelfort, H.C.E. 2005b. Natur und Besessenheit: Natürliche Erklärungen für Besessenheit von der Melancholie bis Magnetismus'. In *Dämonische Besessenheit: zur Interpretation eines kulturhistorischen Phänomens*, ed. H. De Waardt, J.M. Schmidt, H.C.E. Midelfort, and D.R. Bauer, 73–87. Bielefeld: Verlag für Regionalgeschichte.

Miller, A.M. 1968. *Crescentia von Kaufbeuren: das Leben einer schwäbischen Mystikerin*. Augsburg: Verlag Winifried-Werk.
Mills, K. 2013. Demonios within and without: Hieronymites and the devil in the early modern Hispanic world. In *Angels, demons and the new world*, ed. F. Cervantes and A. Redden, 40–68. Cambridge: Cambridge University Press.
Monter, E.W. 1976. *Witchcraft in France and Switzerland: The borderlands during the Reformation*. Ithaca: Cornell University Press.
Muchembled, R. 2003. *A History of the Devil from the Middle Ages to the Present*. Trans. J. Birrell. Cambridge: Polity Press.
Mulloy, S. 2009. Moore, John (1767–99). In *Dictionary of Irish biography*, vol. 6, 646–647. Cambridge: Cambridge University Press.
Mungello, D.E. 1994. *The Chinese rites controversy: Its history and meaning*. Nettetal: Steyler Verlag.
Newman, B. 1998. Possessed by the spirit: Devout women, demoniacs and the apostolic life in the thirteenth century. *Speculum* 73: 733–770.
Nichols, B., and A. MacGregor (eds.). 2003. *Deliver us from evil: Medieval blessings and exorcisms of the Latin West*. Durham: Ushaw College Library.
Nicolotti, A. 2011. *Esorcismo Cristiano e Possessione Diabolica tra II e III Secolo*. Turnhout: Brepols.
Nischan, B. 1987. The exorcism controversy and baptism in the late reformation. *Sixteenth Century Journal* 18: 31–52.
Nugent, C. 1983. *Masks of Satan: The demonic in history*. London: Sheed and Ward.
O'Grady, J. 1989. *The Prince of darkness: The devil in history, religion and the human psyche*. Longmead: Element Books.
O'Hara, T. 1997. A vision of hell in early modern Ireland. *Archivium Hibernicum* 51: 87–99.
Oldridge, D. 2010. *The devil in Tudor and Stuart England*, 3rd ed. Stroud: History Press.
Österreich, T.K. 1930. *Possession, demoniacal and other, among primitive races, in antiquity, the Middle Ages, and modern times*. New York: Routledge and Kegan Paul.
Otten, W. 2011. Overshadowing or foreshadowing return: The role of demons in Eriugena's *Periphyseon*. In *Demons and the devil in ancient and Mediaeval Christianity*, ed. N. Vos and W. Otten, 211–230. Leiden: Brill.
P., I. 1955. Notae Practicae de Precibus post Missam imperatis, *Ephemerides Liturgicae* 69(1955): 54–60.
Pagels, E. 1996. *The origin of Satan*. London: Allen Lane.
Pearl, J.L. 1983. French Catholic demonologists and their enemies in the late sixteenth and early seventeenth centuries. *Church History* 52: 457–467.
Pearl, J.L. 1985. Demons and politics in France, 1560–1630. *Historical Reflections* 12: 241–251.
Pearl, J.L. 1989. "A school for the rebel soul": Politics and demonic possession in France. *Historical Reflections* 16: 286–306.
Pearl, J. 1999. *The crime of crimes: Demonology and politics in France, 1560–1620*. Waterloo: Wilfrid Laurier University Press.
Peck, M.S. 1985. *People of the lie*. New York: Touchstone.
Petersen, A.K. 2003. The notion of demon: Open questions to a diffuse concept. In *Die Dämonen: die Dämonologie der israelitisch-jüdischen und frühchristlichen Literatur im Kontext ihrer Umwelt (Demons: The demonology of Israelite-Jewish and early Christian literature in context of their environment)*, ed. A. Lange and H. Lichtenberger, 23–41. Tübingen: Mohr Siebeck.

Pistoia, A. 2000. Riti e Preghiere di Esorcismo: Problemi de Traduzione. *Ephemerides Liturgicae* 114: 227–240.
Po-chia Hsia, R. 2005. *The world of Catholic renewal, 1540–1770*. Cambridge: Cambridge University Press.
Porterfield, A. 2005. *Healing in the history of Christianity*. Oxford: Oxford University Press.
Pouliot, J.C. 1895. *Vie de la Vénérable Marie-Crescence, Religieuse du Tiers Ordre de Saint-François au couvent de Kaufbeuren*. Fraserville: J. E. Frenette.
Probst, F. 1872. *Sakramente und Sakramentalien in den drei ersten christlichen jahrhunderten*. Tübingen: H. Laupp'schen.
Probst, F. 2008. *Besessenheit, Zauberei und ihre Heilmittel: Dokumentation und Untersuchungen von Exorcismushandbüchern des Girolamo Menghi (1523–1609) und des Maximilian von Eynatten (1574/75–1631)*. Münster: Aschendorff.
Quantin, J.-L. 1999. *Catholicisme Classique et les Pères de L'Eglise: un retour au sources (1669–1713)*. Paris: Institut d'Etudes Augustiniennes.
Quay, P. 1981. Angels and demons: The teaching of IV Lateran. *Theological Studies* 42: 20–45.
Raiswell, R. 2012. Introduction: Conceptualising the devil in society. In *The devil in society in pre-modern Europe*, ed. R. Raiswell and R. Dendle, 23–68. Toronto: Centre for Reformation and Renaissance Studies.
Raiswell, R., and P. Dendle. 2008. Demon possession in Anglo-Saxon and early modern England: Continuity and evolution in social context. *Journal of British Studies* 47: 738–767.
Raiswell, R., and P. Dendle. 2012. Epilogue: Inscribing the devil in cultural contexts. In *The devil in society in pre-modern Europe*, ed. R. Raiswell and P. Dendle, 537–551. Toronto: Centre for Reformation and Renaissance Studies.
Ratté, J. 1968. *Three modernists: Alfred Loisy, George Tyrrell, William L. Sullivan*. London: Sheed and Ward.
Rex, R. 2004. Wentworth, Jane [Anne; *called* the Maid of Ipswich] (*c*.1503–1572?). In *The Oxford dictionary of national biography*, vol. 58, 127–128. Oxford: Oxford University Press.
Rodewyk, A. 1975. *Possessed by Satan: The church's teaching on the devil, possession and exorcism*. New York: Doubleday.
Romeo, G. 2003. *Inquisitori, Esorcisti e Streghe nell'Italia della Controriforma*. Florence: Sansoni.
Roper, L. 1994. *Oedipus and the devil: Witchcraft, sexuality and religion in early modern Europe*. London: Routledge.
Ross, A. 2001. *Folklore of Wales*. Stroud: Tempus.
Rousseau, G. 2000. Depression's forgotten genealogy: Notes towards a history of depression. *History of Psychiatry* 11: 71–106.
Rowell, S.C. 1994. *Lithuania ascending: A Pagan Empire within east-central Europe, 1295–1345*. Cambridge: Cambridge University Press.
Russell, J.B. 1977. *The devil: Perceptions of evil from antiquity to primitive Christianity*. Ithaca: Cornell University Press.
Russell, J.B. 1984. *Lucifer: The devil in the middle ages*. Ithaca: Cornell University Press.
Russell, J.B. 1986. *Mephistopheles: The devil in the modern world*. Ithaca: Cornell University Press.

Rutler, G.W. 1988. *The Curé of Ars today*. San Francisco: Ignatius.
Sangha, L. 2012. *Angels and belief in England, 1480–1700*. London: Pickering and Chatto.
Scala, M. 2012. *Der Exorzismus in der Katholischen Kirche: Ein liturgisches Ritual zwischen Film, Mythos und Realität*. Hamburg: F. Pustet.
Scanlan, M., and R. Cirner. 1980. *Deliverance from evil spirits*. Cincinnati: Servant.
Segelberg, E. 1964. The Benedictio Olei in the Apostolic Tradition of Hippolytus. *Oriens Christianas* 48: 268–281.
Seitz, J. 2011. *Witchcraft and inquisition in early modern Venice*. Cambridge: Cambridge University Press.
Silverblatt, I.M. 1987. *Moon, sun and witches: Gender ideologies and class in Inca and colonial Peru*. Princeton: Princeton University Press.
Simmons, M. 1974. *Witchcraft in the Southwest: Spanish and Indian supernaturalism on the Rio Grande*. Flagstaff: Northland Press.
Simpson, J. 2003. Repentant soul or walking corpse: Debatable apparitions in Medieval England. *Folklore* 114: 389–402.
Skemer, D.C. 2006. *Binding words: Textual amulets in the Middle Ages*. University Park: Pennsylvania State University Press.
Sluhovsky, M. 1996. A divine apparition or demonic possession? Female agency and church authority in demonic possession in sixteenth-century France. *Sixteenth Century Journal* 27: 1039–1055.
Sluhovsky, M. 2007. *Believe not every spirit: Possession, mysticism and discernment in early modern Catholicism*. Chicago: University of Chicago Press.
Smith, J.Z. 1978. Towards interpreting demonic powers in hellenistic and Roman antiquity. *Aufstieg und Niedergang der römischen Welt* 2.16.1, 425–439. Berlin: De Gruyter.
Soergel, P.M. 1993. *Wondrous in his saints: Counter-reformation propaganda in Bavaria*, 99–158. Berkeley: University of California Press.
Solomon, R.M. 1994. *Living in two worlds: Pastoral responses to possession in Singapore*. Frankfurt-am-Main: P. Lang.
Sorensen, E. 2002. *Possession and exorcism in the New Testament and early Christianity*. Mohr Siebeck: Tübingen.
Spencer, W.D. 1989. *Mysterium and mystery: The clerical crime novel*. Ann Arbor: UMI Research Press.
Stirrat, R.L. 1977. Demonic possession in Roman Catholic Sri Lanka. *Journal of Anthropological Research* 33: 133–157.
Stirrat, R.L. 1992. *Power and religiosity in a post-colonial setting: Sinhala Catholics in contemporary Sri Lanka*. Cambridge: Cambridge University Press.
Suenens, L.-J. 1983. *Renewal and the powers of darkness*. London: Darton, Longmann and Todd.
Tausiet, M. 2005. The possessed of Tosos (1812–1814): Witchcraft and popular justice during the Spanish revolution. In *Dämonische Besessenheit: zur Interpretation eines kulturhistorischen Phänomens*, ed. H. De Waardt, J.M. Schmidt, H.C.E. Midelfort, and D.R. Bauer, 263–280. Bielefeld: Verlag für Regionalgeschichte.
Ter Haar, G. 1992. *Spirit of Africa: The healing ministry of Archbishop Milingo of Zambia*. London: C. Hurst and Co.
Teyssèdre, B. 1991. *Il Diavolo e l'Inferno ai tempi di Gesù*. Genoa: ECIG.
Teyssèdre, B. 1992. *Nascita del Diavolo*. Genoa: ECIG.

Thomas, K. 1991. *Religion and the decline of magic*, 4th ed. London: Penguin.
Thorndike, L. 1923–1958. *A history of magic and experimental science*, 8 vols. New York: Columbia University Press.
Thurston, H. 1920. *A sober condemnation of spiritualism*. London: Catholic Truth Society.
Thurston, H. 1933. *The church and spiritualism*. Milwaukee: Bruce Publishing Co.
Thurston, H. 1953. *Ghosts and poltergeists*, ed. J. H. Crehan. London: Burns and Oates.
Tolosana, C.L. 1990. *Demonios y Exorcismos en los Siglos de Oro*. Madrid: Akal.
Tonquédec de, J. 1938. *Les Maladies Nerveuses ou Mentales et les Manifestations Diaboliques*. Paris: Beauchesne.
Tonquédec de, J. 1951. Some aspects of Satan's activity in this world. In *Satan*, 40–51. New York: Sheed and Ward.
Triacca, A.M. 1987. Esorcismo: un sacramentale discusso. *Ecclesia Orans* 4: 285–300.
Triacca, A.M. 2000. Spirito Santo ed Esorcismo: in margine al recente Rituale. *Ephemerides Liturgicae* 114: 241–269.
Twelftree, G.H. 2007. *In the name of Jesus: Exorcism among the early Christians*. Grand Rapids: Baker Academic.
Tyrell, G. 1909. *Christianity at the crossroads*. London: Longmans, Green and Co.
Van Arsdall, A. 2002. *Medieval herbal remedies: The Old English herbarium and Anglo-Saxon medicine*. London: Routledge.
Van Slyke, D.G. 2006. The ancestry and theology of the rite of major exorcism. *Antiphon* 10: 70–116.
Vandermeersch, P. 1991. The victory of psychiatry over demonology: The origin of the nineteenth-century myth. *History of Psychiatry* 2: 351–363.
Vecchio, A. 1954. *Intervista col Diavole*. Modena: Edizione Paoline.
Venard, M. 1980. Le Démon controversiste. In *La Controverse Religieuse (XVIe–XIXe siècles): Actes du Ier Colloque Jean Boisset*, vol. 2, ed. M. Péronnet, 45–60. Montpellier: Université Paul Valery.
Vergote, A. 1990. Exorcisme et prières de déliverance, le point de vue de la psychologie religieuse. *La Maison-Dieu* 183: 123–137.
Vergote, A. 1992. Anthropologie du diable: l'homme séduit et en proie aux puissances ténébreuses. In *Figures du Démoniaque hier et aujourd'hui*, 83–108. Brussels: Université de St Louis.
Vising, J. 1923. *Anglo-Norman language and literature*. Oxford: Oxford University Press.
Vos, N. 2011. Demons without and within: The representation of demons, the saint, and the soul in early Christian lives, letters and sayings. In *Demons and the devil in ancient and mediaeval Christianity*, ed. N. Vos and W. Otten, 159–182. Leiden: Brill.
Walker, D.P. 1981. *Unclean spirits: Possession and exorcism in France and England in the late sixteenth and early seventeenth centuries*. London: Scolar.
Walker, D.P. 1982. Demonic possession used as propaganda in the later sixteenth century. In *Scienze, credenze occulte, livelli di cultura*, ed. G. Garfagnini, 237–248. Florence: Leo S. Olschki.
Walker, A.M., and E.H. Dickerman. 1991. "A woman under the influence": A case of alleged possession in sixteenth-century France. *Sixteenth Century Journal* 22: 535–554.
Walker, A.M., and E.H. Dickerman. 1996a. Magdeleine des Aymards: Demonism or child abuse in early modern France? *Psychohistory Review* 24: 239–264.
Walker, A.M., and E.H. Dickerman. 1996b. The haunted girl: Possession, witchcraft and healing in sixteenth century Louviers. *Proceedings of the Annual Meeting of the Western Society for French History* 23: 207–218.

Walsham, A. 2003. Miracles and the counter-reformation mission to England. *The Historical Journal* 46: 779–815.
Ward, A. 2000. The Psalm collects of the new rite of exorcism. *Ephemerides Liturgicae* 114: 270–301.
Watkins, C.S. 2002. Sin, penance and purgatory in the Anglo-Norman realm: The evidence of visions and ghost stories. *Past and Present* 175: 3–33.
Watkins, C.S. 2007. *History and the supernatural in medieval England*. Cambridge: Cambridge University Press.
Watt, J.R. 2009. *The scourge of demons: Possession, lust and witchcraft in a seventeenth-century Italian convent*. Woodbridge: Boydell and Brewer.
Weber, H. 1983. L'Exorcisme à la fin du XVIe siècle: Instrument de la Contre Réforme et Spectacle Baroque. *Nouvelle Revue du Seizième Siècle* 1: 79–101.
Weber, A. 1990. Between ecstasy and exorcism: Religious negotiation in sixteenth-century Spain. *Journal of Medieval and Renaissance Studies* 23: 221–234.
Weber, D.J. 2001. Conquistadores of the spirit. In *Colonial America: Essays in politics and social development*, ed. S.N. Katz, J.M. Murrin, and D. Greenberg. New York: McGraw Hill.
Weber, A. 2005. The inquisitor, the flesh, and the devil: Alumbradismo and demon possession. In *Dämonische Besessenheit: zur Interpretation eines kulturhistorischen Phänomens*, ed. H. De Waardt, J.M. Schmidt, H.C.E. Midelfort, and D.R. Bauer, 177–189. Bielefeld: Verlag für Regionalgeschichte.
Wickland, C.A. 1924. *Thirty years among the dead*. Los Angeles: Wolfer.
Wieland, F. 1897. *Die genetische Entwicklung der sog Ordines Minores in den drei erstern Jahrhunderten*. Rome: Herder.
Wiesinger, A. 1957. *Occult Phenomena in the Light of Theology*. Trans. B. Battershaw. London: Burns and Oates.
Wingens, M. 2005. Political change and demon possession in the south of the Dutch Republic: The confrontation of a Protestant Bailiff and a Catholic priest in 1650. In *Dämonische Besessenheit: zur Interpretation eines kulturhistorischen Phänomens*, ed. H. De Waardt, J.M. Schmidt, H.C.E. Midelfort, and D.R. Bauer, 249–262. Bielefeld: Verlag für Regionalgeschichte.
Woollen, C.J. 1949. The case for exorcism, *New Blackfriars* 30:347 (February): 59–62.
Young, F. 2009. Catholic exorcism in early modern England: Polemic, propaganda and folklore. *Recusant History* 29: 487–507.
Young, F. 2013. *English catholics and the supernatural, 1553–1829*. Farnham: Ashgate.
Young, F. 2014. The dangers of spiritualism: The Roman Catholic church's campaign against spiritualism during and after the First World War. *Paranormal Review* 71: 18–20.
Zhang Qiong. 1999. About God, demons and miracles: The Jesuit discourse on the supernatural in late Ming China. *Early Science and Medicine* 4: 1–36.
Ziegler, R. 2012. *Satanism, magic and mysticism in Fin-de-siècle France*. Basingstoke: Palgrave MacMillan.
Zupanov, I.G. 2007. Goan Brahmins in the land of promise: Missionaries, spies and gentiles in seventeenth- and eighteenth-century Sri Lanka. In *Re-exploring the links: History and constructed histories between Portugal and Sri Lanka*, ed. J. Flores, 171–210. Wiesbaden: Harrassowitz Verlag.

INDEX

A

Abelard, Peter, 67
acolytes, 31, 34, 35, 144
Acosta, José de, 144
adjuration, 18–19, 27, 35, 37, 39–40, 46–8, 49–51, 53, 70–1, 75, 83–7, 92, 94, 102, 103, 119, 127, 134, 141, 169, 190, 234, 235
Ælfric of Eynsham, 87–8
Africa, exorcism in, 154, 181, 196–8, 210, 226–7, 238, 241
Alcuin, 37, 38, 89
Alexander VI, Pope, 142
Alexander VIII, Pope, 164
Alt, Ernst, exorcist, 216–18
alumbradismo, 113
St Amand Sacramentary, 52
Amantini, Candido, exorcist, 13
Ambrose of Milan, 38–9
Ambrosian rite, 129
America, United States of, exorcism in, 12, 13, 20, 185, 199–203, 205, 210, 213, 216, 220–1, 222, 224–6, 238–9, 241. *See also* Ecklund, Anna; Florida; Mexico, exorcism in; Mount Rainier exorcism
Amorth, Gabriele, exorcist, 13, 156, 170, 207, 210, 214, 221–4, 236–41
amulets, 75, 111, 141. *See also* apotropaic practices
Anges, Jeanne des, demoniac, 123–4, 167
Angeli, Rinaldo, 189
angels, 18, 20, 22, 48, 57, 67, 70, 72–3, 75, 87, 150, 161. *See also* Michael, Archangel; Raphael, Archangel
angels, apostate. *See* demons
Anglo-Saxon England, exorcism in, 80–8
animals, exorcism of, 69–70, 75, 91, 102, 104, 108, 135, 145, 151
animism. *See* indigenous religion
anointing. *See* oil, consecrated
Anthony of Padua, 75
Anthony of the Desert, 54, 174
anthropology, 3, 12, 15, 16, 210
Antichrist, 115, 199n

anti-clericalism, 184, 185, 192
anti-Semitism, 187, 211n
apocalypticism, 2, 6, 67, 92, 101n, 107, 108n, 138, 142, 188, 199n, 202
apotropaic practices, 15, 16, 31n, 38, 65, 75, 91, 110, 111, 134, 194. *See also* amulets
Aquinas, Thomas, 70–3
Arbiol y Díez, Antonio, demonologist, 157
Aretius. *See* Marti, Benedikt
Arianism, 54
Aristotelianism, 70, 72, 108, 125, 155. *See also* Scholasticism
Arriaga, José Pablo de, 144
art, portrayals of exorcism in, 43–4, 194–5
Ashmole, Elias, 76
Aubry, Nicole, demoniac, 105–6
Augustine of Canterbury, 80
Augustine of Hippo, 28, 31n, 32–3, 37, 40, 42, 73, 108, 114, 134
Augustinianism, 57–8, 72, 95, 138, 156, 166. *See also* Jansenism
Augustinians (religious order), 88, 143–5, 148, 158, 166, 179
Australia, 121, 204, 227
Avicebron, 72
Aztecs, 143

B

Balducci, Corrado, 21, 202, 206–7, 209, 223
baptism, 6, 29, 39, 43, 52, 69, 79, 84, 87, 116, 175, 233, 234
  exorcism in, 4n, 7, 17, 28, 30–8, 40, 41, 44–5, 48–9, 50–3, 63–5, 70–2, 84–5, 89–90, 95, 96, 102, 103, 105n, 134, 141, 169, 194, 212, 232

  see also Effeta; exsufflation; *Ordo Romanus XI*; *Traditio apostolica*
Barré, Pierre, exorcist, 121–2, 123
Basin, Bernard, 157
Bede, 81–2
Belgium, exorcism in, 187, 221, 238
Bellefontaine Abbey, 183
Benedict XIV, Pope, 165–6, 181, 232
Benedict XV, Pope, 193
Benedict XVI, Pope, 13, 228
Benedictines, 96, 165, 167, 218
Benson, Robert Hugh, 198
Binterim, Anton Joseph, 6
bishops, authority of, 5, 31, 41, 44–5, 106, 119–20, 122, 154, 163–4, 165–7, 170, 172–4, 176–9, 183–4, 195–7, 199, 200, 212, 217, 219, 221, 223–4, 225, 231, 233, 237, 240
black mass, 186, 236
blasphemy, 104, 129, 149, 159, 204
Blatty, William Peter, 201, 219, 220, 241
blessing, 39, 80, 86, 88, 91, 93, 95, 96, 111, 115, 116, 140, 141, 151, 157n, 161, 170, 229, 230, 233
body parts, exorcism of, 56, 73, 86, 91–2, 170
Bonaventure, 72, 73
books of exorcism. *See* manuals of exorcism
Boullan, Joseph-Antoine, exorcist, 186–7
Bowdern, William S, exorcist, 200
Boz, Pierre, Bishop, 238
Brazil, exorcism in, 150–1
bread, exorcized, 6, 31, 88, 95n
British Museum, 178–9
Broderick, Richard, exorcist, 177
Brossier, Marthe, demoniac, 106, 125

Browne, Steven, exorcist, 135
Brugnoli, Candido, demonologist, 149, 157, 158n1
Buddhism, 131, 139, 141
Bury St Edmunds, Abbot of, 96
Byzantine Christianity, 38, 39, 43

C
Cadière, Marie-Catherine, demoniac, 165
Cadonici, Giovanni, 166, 168
Calatorao, shrine of, 174
Calvinism, 95, 106
Canada, exorcism in, 151–3, 213
Canary Islands, 142
Canisius, Peter, exorcist, 105
Canon Law, vii, 5, 6, 12, 30, 90, 101, 116, 117, 175
    Code of 1917, 193–4, 218
    Code of 1983, 228, 230–1, 240
    see also bishops, authority of
Cantor, Petrus, 64, 71
Capuchins, 122–3, 155, 164, 199, 217
Carmelites, 122, 123n, 135, 148, 150, 151, 230
Carpegna, Gaspare, Cardinal, 163–4
Cassian, John, 53–4
Castañega, Martín de, 104
Castellani, Alberto, 116
Catechism of the Catholic Church, 232
catechists, 139
catechumens. *See* baptism
catechumens, oil of. *See* oil, consecrated
Cathars, 3, 66
Cele, Clara Germana, demoniac, 196–8
Chalcedon, Council of, 19
Charcot, Jean-Martin, 194–5, 198
charismatic exorcism, 2, 6, 13, 17, 18, 40–1, 62, 100, 117, 156, 158, 170, 172, 184, 226, 228

Charismatic Renewal, Catholic, 224, 225, 229
Charlemagne, Emperor, 56
Charles II, King of Spain, 157
Charles IX, King of France, 105, 106
Chertsey, Andrew, 95
China, exorcism in, 138–41
chrism, oil of. *See* oil, consecrated
Cistercians, 66, 135, 202
cinema, 1, 7n, 121, 182, 201, 216, 219
Ciruelo, Pedro, 104
Clement XI, Pope, 139, 141
Cnut, King of England, 87
Commands. *See* imperative exorcism
Communism, 218
Conan Doyle, Arthur, 206
conjuration, 16, 18, 76, 102–3, 108, 113, 120, 145, 148, 157n, 160, 164, 189, 234, 236n. *See also* magic
Conquistadors, 132, 141, 143
Constans, Adolphe, 194
Cordoba, Pedro de, 145
Cornelius, Pope, 31
Cortés, Hernán, 143
Cotrau, Rosalie, demoniac, 152–3
Council of Carthage (398), 44, 53, 104
Counter-Reformation, 6, 7, 23, 44, 100, 102, 107, 112, 114, 118, 121, 131–3, 137, 153, 168, 239
Cremona, Italy, 166
Cristiani, Leon, 183
cross, sign of, 16, 31, 35, 46, 68, 90, 119, 122, 161, 177, 234
Crowley, Aleister, 185
crucifix, 140, 146, 161, 174
Cuyò, Nicolas, 163
Cuthbert of Lindisfarne, 81
Cyprian of Carthage, 31, 38, 42

D

Daoism, 131, 139–1
Davies, Jeremy, exorcist, viii, 12, 222–4, 236–7
deacons, 30, 31, 44, 45, 74, 194
Dee, John, 76
Delalle, Henri, Bishop, 197–8
Delrio, Martin, demonologist, 23, 115
demoniacs, 1, 5, 6, 10, 12, 14, 16, 20–2, 23–5, 26, 28, 40–1, 43, 45, 48, 51–2, 53–6, 61–2, 64–6, 68, 73–5, 77, 78, 81, 82, 84, 85, 87–90, 93, 94, 96, 97, 102, 107, 108, 109n, 110, 112–14, 117–20, 122–4, 125, 128, 135, 138, 146, 148, 149, 151, 160–2, 165, 172, 174, 182–4, 194, 198, 200, 202, 210, 213, 215, 217, 218, 223, 230, 233, 234
  diagnosis of (signs), 79, 205, 232
  preternatural abilities of, 159, 197
  see also possession
demonology, 3, 8, 10–11, 13, 22–3, 29, 36, 54, 57, 58, 62, 63, 66, 70, 72–3, 78, 104, 110, 113, 114, 120, 123, 141, 157, 159, 161, 162, 178, 182, 186, 192, 193, 196n, 198n, 202, 203, 209, 211, 212, 220–3, 225, 232, 240. *See also* sin demons
demons, 5, 15, 16, 18, 19, 21–3, 29, 30, 32, 37, 39, 41, 42, 46, 53, 55, 57–9, 62, 65–8, 70–4, 71n, 77–81, 84, 85n, 87–90, 93, 95, 101, 103, 108, 110, 111n, 112, 114, 115, 117, 118, 122, 123, 123n, 125, 126, 128, 129, 144, 159–62, 165, 170, 173, 183, 184, 189, 191, 199, 206, 211, 218, 222, 223, 229, 237, 239, 240
deliverance ministry, 4n, 110, 210, 224–9. *See also* charismatic exorcism

Demandolx de la Palud, Madeleine, demoniac, 120
deprecative exorcism, 58, 110, 111, 118, 193, 233–4, 236–7
Devil, the. *See* Satan
Dioscorides, 158
Divine Worship, Sacred Congregation for. *See* Rites, Sacred Congregation of
Doctrine of the Faith, Sacred Congregation of. *See* Holy Office
Dölger, Franz Joseph, 7, 30
Dominicans, 68, 100, 104, 112–13, 120–1, 132, 133, 138–41, 143, 145, 148–50, 184, 225. *See also* Aquinas, Thomas
Donatism, 30
Doucet, Anne, demoniac, 153
drama
  exorcism as, 5, 30, 32, 34, 55, 100, 212
  portrayal of exorcism in, 167–8
Drumm, Thomas, Bishop of Des Moines, 199
Duns Scotus, John, 72
Dutch Republic. *See* Netherlands, exorcism in

E

EASTERN ORTHODOXY. *See* Byzantine Christianity
Ecklund, Anna, demoniac, 199
Effeta, 38
Egeria, 31
Elizabeth I, Queen of England, 133
elves, 83
Emmerich, Anne Catherine, 200
energumens. *See* demoniacs; possession
England, exorcism in, 11, 14, 63, 70, 75–7, 80–97, 132–5, 137, 138, 142, 152, 168, 175–9, 204–6, 222

Enlightenment, Catholic, 155, 156, 162, 165, 166, 170, 171, 179
epilepsy, 14, 64n, 193, 195, 198
Erasmus, Desiderius, 103–4
Erasmus, Hörner, exorcist, 197
Eriugena, John Scotus, 57–9
eschatology. *See* apocalypticism
Estévez, Medina, Cardinal, 231
etymology, 18–19
eucharist, 6, 79, 86–8, 93, 103, 105–6, 117, 118, 135, 139–41, 145, 146, 153, 159, 189, 229, 230
Eudes, Jean, 124
Eusebius of Caesarea, 18, 31
Everard, Patrick, Archbishop of Cashel and Emly, 176
exorcism, definitions of, 5, 13–22
The Exorcist (novel and film), 1, 6, 121, 201, 219, 221, 222. *See also* Mount Rainier exorcism
exorcist, order of, 7, 30–1, 40, 44, 65, 87, 93n, 117, 157
  abolition, 211–12
exsufflation, 31, 33, 37, 233–5

F
fairies, 24
fasting, 42, 78, 84, 86, 118, 133, 140, 161
Feijoo, Benito, 165
Florence, Italy, 76
Florida, 145
Folklore, 24, 83, 89, 90, 94, 152
Fortea, José Antonio, exorcist, 13, 209, 236, 239–41
Foulow, Richard, exorcist, 135
France, exorcism in, 2, 77, 99–100, 105–6, 125–30, 155, 167, 183n, 185–7, 196n, 223–4, 237, 238

Francis, Pope, 241
Francis of Assisi, 67
Franciscans, 72–3, 79, 100, 107–9, 112, 122, 132, 145–6, 147–9, 157, 158n, 165, 183, 226. *See also* Capuchins
Freemasonry, 3, 187, 191–2, 211. *See also* Leo XIII, Pope
Frey, Bernhard, 114–15
Frideswide of Oxford, 82–3
Friedkin, William, 1, 121, 219, 220
Fuente, Alonso de la, 113
functionalism, 22–3, 25

G
Gallicanism, 165, 166
Gandolphy, Peter, 178
García, Marcos, 143
Gassner, Johann-Joseph, exorcist, 2, 12, 156, 170–2
Gay, Antoine, demoniac, 184
Gaufridy, Louis, 117, 120, 186
Gavilán, Ramos, 145
Gelasian Sacramentary, 7n, 34, 37, 38n, 39, 45, 50, 52, 56, 57, 65, 83–6, 101, 116, 233, 234
Gellone Sacramentary, 45, 48–53, 56, 58, 85n, 91
Gennadius of Marseilles, 43
gender, 3, 24–5
Gerasene demoniac, 21, 43, 48, 81, 114
Germany, exorcism in, 2, 68–9, 105, 109n, 153, 170–2, 213–14, 216–19, 230
ghosts, 85n, 90, 96, 105, 121, 140, 198, 201, 218, 222, 223. *See also* houses, haunted
gods, pagan. *See* paganism
gold, 75, 158, 162
Golden Dawn, Hermetic Order of, 187

Goldoni, Carlo, 167
Gómez de Cervantes, Francisco Javier, Archbishop of Mexico, 149
Grandier, Urbain, 121–4, 128, 186, 194
Gregorian Sacramentary, 44
Gregory of the Great, Pope, 142
Gregory XIII, Pope, 116
grimoires. *See* magic
Groeschel, Benedict, 222

H
Haag, Herbert, 213, 215
hagiography, 9, 25, 63, 65, 66, 78, 214. *See also* saints
Hands, Everard, 20n
Hasler, Annette, demoniac, 216
healing, 8, 11, 28, 40, 55, 56, 77, 78, 83, 89, 120, 135n, 141, 144, 151, 156, 170, 171, 183, 225, 226
Henri IV, King of France, 125
Henry VI, King of England, 93, 94
herbs, 69, 90, 108, 151
heresy, as cause of possession, 3, 38, 62, 64, 66, 101, 106, 107, 120
Hidalgo, Alonso, 147
Hilary of Poitiers, 42
Hildegard of Bingen, exorcist, 62, 78
Hippolytus of Rome, 30
Hispaniola, 132
Hitler, Adolf, 218
Hoffman, E. T. A., 174
Holy Office (Roman Inquisition), 112, 150, 157, 162–4, 179, 185, 228
Hospicius of Piedmont, exorcist, 78
Höss, Crescentia, demoniac, 165, 184
Houbraken, Joannes, exorcist, 138
houses, haunted, 100, 111–12, 139–40, 141, 151, 160, 172, 209, 218, 229–30. *See also* ghosts

Hughes, E. Albert, exorcist, 200
Huguenots, 100, 105, 106, 122
Huxley, Aldous, 121, 195
Huysmans, Joris-Karl, 185–7
hypnosis. *See* mesmerism
hysteria, 121, 173, 194, 195, 227

I
Icha, Juana, demoniac, 144–5
iconoclasm, 143–4
idolatry. *See* iconoclasm; indigenous religion; paganism
Immaculate Conception, 190, 191, 194
imperative exorcism, 18, 37, 46, 47, 72, 110, 118, 127, 154, 193, 212, 214, 234, 236–7
Incas, 143–5
incense. *See* suffumigation
incubation, 88, 90
incubi and succubi, 68, 81, 108, 149, 162, 186, 187, 239–40
Index, Sacred Congregation of the. *See* Holy Office
indigenous religion, 131, 132, 143–5, 146, 147, 151, 153, 181, 198, 226, 235
Innocent I, Pope, 44
Innocent III, Pope, 66
Innocent XI, Pope, 164
Inquisition
   Mexican, 11, 146–50
   Peruvian, 11, 144
   Portuguese, 11, 102, 150
   Roman (*see* Holy Office)
   Spanish, 11, 102, 112–13, 165
insanity. *See* mental illness
Institoris, Heinrich, demonologist. *See* Kramer, Heinrich
International Association of Exorcists (IAE), viii, 223–4, 241
Ipswich, England, 96

Ireland, exorcism in, 39, 135–7, 168–9, 175, 229–30
Isidore of Seville, 42, 73
Islam, 140, 142

J
Jansenism, 138, 156, 166–7
Japan
Jerome, 54n, 79, 132
Jerusalem, 31
Jesuits, 13, 100, 105, 107, 112–16, 121, 124, 126–8, 132, 133, 138–9, 140–1, 144, 147, 148, 150, 151, 155, 160, 164–7, 178, 187, 200–1, 202, 206, 213–14, 216, 217, 220
Jesús María, Manuel de, 148
Joachim of Fiore, 66
John XXII, Pope, 66
John the Deacon, 33, 38
John Paul II, Pope, 13, 226
Joseph II, Emperor, 170
Judaism, 4, 72, 187, 192, 210–11. *See also* anti-Semitism
Judas Iscariot, 199, 218
Julio, Abbé, exorcist, 186n

K
Kellam, Laurence, 134
Killigrew, Thomas, 121, 123
Knox, Ronald, 226
Kramer, Heinrich, demonologist, 68–9, 104, 121

L
Lacnunga Manuscript, 84, 91
Lactantius, 27–8, 42,
laity, 1, 12, 108, 156, 179, 191, 209, 224, 228, 229, 240, 241

languages, demonic, 75, 76, 79, 117, 122, 159, 204, 206, 218, 232
Laon, miracle of, 105–6, 107
lapidaries, 92
Las Casas, Bartolomé de, 143, 145
Lateran Council (1215), 66, 215
Laurac, France, 99–100
Lavater, Ludwig, 111–12
LaVey, Anton, 220
legal language, 18, 47, 55
Legionaries of Christ, 238
Legué, Gabriel, 194
Leo the Great, Pope, 33, 42
Leo XIII, Pope, 2, 3, 181, 192, 197, 201, 202, 210
  exorcism of, 7n, 181, 183n, 188–91, 217, 229, 234
Lépicier, Alexis, demonologist, 193
Lewis, Matthew, 174
Lhermitte, Jean, 195–6
liturgy. *See* rites of exorcism
Locatelli, Pietro, 164
Lollards, 92–3, 95
Lopez, Luís, exorcist, 150
Los Reyes, Juana de, demoniac, 148–9
Loudun, possessions of, 23, 107, 121–4, 125–7, 129, 130, 167, 194–5
Louviers, possessions of, 129–30
Loyola, Ignatius, 115, 132
Lueken, Veronica, 225
Luo Wenzao, Gregorio, exorcist, 139
Lutheranism, 104, 200, 201
Lyndwood, William, 90

M
MacNutt, Francis, 225–6, 227, 228
Macumba, 151
Maffei, Scipione, 171
Mager, Aloïs, 218

magic, vii, 16–19, 28, 29, 41, 62, 71, 73–7, 79, 85, 87, 90, 91, 99n, 100, 101, 103, 104, 107–9, 117, 118, 120, 124, 128, 130, 133, 141, 150–1, 152, 155–9, 163–5, 170, 171, 185–6, 240
 as target of exorcism, 63–4, 66, 96, 115, 135, 183
 see also witchcraft
magnetic healing. *See* mesmerism
major exorcism, rite of. *See* exorcism, rites of
Malleus maleficarum, 64, 68, 104, 113–14
manuals of exorcism, 10, 11, 24, 44, 53, 66, 67, 77, 79, 95, 103, 107, 108, 149, 155, 157–62, 236, 239–40
 suppression, 162–5, 168, 179
Maria Theresa, Empress, 671
Marti, Benedikt, theologian, 104
Martin of Tours, 53, 54, 56, 75
Martin, Malachi, exorcist, 220–1, 224, 228, 237
Martínez, Joaquina, exorcist, 173
Mary, Virgin, 76, 79, 96, 112, 136, 142, 143, 161, 184, 189, 190, 194, 218, 224, 229
mass. *See* eucharist
Matos, Bento de, 139–40
Maximus the Confessor, 58
medicine, 3, 12, 14, 61, 63, 82, 92, 106, 125, 150, 156, 163–4, 165, 176, 182, 194–6, 202, 217, 232, 241. *See also* healing; mental illness; St Bartholomew's Hospital
mediumship, 89, 139, 140, 203, 204n, 218. *See also* prophecy; Spiritualism
Meilyr of Caerleon, demoniac, 88–9
Mejía, Francisca, demoniac, 148
Menghi, Girolamo, exorcist, 23, 103, 107–9, 112, 115, 116, 119, 123, 136, 144, 146–8, 155–7, 160, 163–5, 240

mental illness, 3, 8, 14, 21n, 77, 79, 84, 87, 88, 114, 121, 170, 173–6, 192, 194–6, 206, 209, 213–15, 223, 232. *See also* hysteria
mesmerism, 156, 170–1, 202
Meurin, Leo, Archbishop of Port-Louis, 187, 198
Mexican Revolution, 202
Mexico, exorcism in, 132, 143, 146–50. *See also* Aztecs; Inquisition, Mexican
Michael, Archangel, 25, 67, 188, 189, 197, 201–2, 204
Michaelis, Sébastien, demonologist, 120
Michel, Anneliese, demoniac, 12, 216–19
Milingo, Emmanuel, Archbishop of Lusaka, 183, 226–7, 238,
Miller, Alexander, 203–4
Milner, John, Bishop, 175
minor exorcism, rites of. *See* baptism, exorcism in
modernism (theology), 171, 181, 192–3, 205, 209
Moletshe, Monica, demoniac, 197
monasticism, 53–4, 62, 135
Mongols, 142
Moore, Peter, demoniac, 175–9
Morzine, France, possessions of, 182, 194, 217
Motte, Pierre de la, 105
Mount Rainier exorcism, 12–13, 200–2, 205
Murano Gospel, 43
Muratori, Ludovico Antonio, 171
music, 92

N

Nangle, Edmond, 136–7
Nantes, Edict of, 122
Nautonier, Guillaume de, 99–100

Nazaré, Luís de, exorcist, 150–1
Netherlands, exorcism in, 11, 132–3, 137–8, 153
Neumann, Theresa, 200
New France. See Canada, exorcism in
New Mexico. See Mexico, exorcism in
Nicastor, Nicholas, 95n
Nicetas of Remesiana, 34
Nicetius of Trier, 54
Nicuesa, Hilario, 119
Nider, Johannes, demonologist, 68
Nola, Italy, 20, 54
nomina ignota. See magic
Nova Scotia. See Canada, exorcism in
Noydens, Benito Remigio, demonologist, 157
nuns, 68, 82, 120–4, 128, 130, 165, 167, 186, 187, 195, 197, 230

O
O'Boyle, Patrick, Archbishop of Washington DC, 200
objects
  exorcism of, 15, 20, 30, 38–9, 75, 93, 95–6, 102, 104, 111, 191, 212, 222
  use of, in exorcism, 17, 28, 160, 162
Obry, Nicole. See Aubry, Nicole
occultism, 103, 182, 185, 187, 201, 203, 207, 209, 222, 236
Ockham, William of, 72–3
oil, consecrated, 28, 30, 31, 38, 53, 78, 82, 116, 157n, 225, 229
Old Catholics, 138
Optatus of Mileve, 32
Opus Dei (organisation), 239
Ordo Romanus XI, 34–7, 45, 48–51, 116
Original Sin, 32
Ortiz, Diego, exorcist, 143–4
Ouija board, 200, 201, 205, 230

P
pacts, demonic, 81, 99, 100, 107, 113, 128, 145, 150, 196–8, 239, 240. See also witchcraft
paganism, 3, 25, 29, 30, 37, 53, 55, 63, 80, 84–5, 91, 96, 142, 145, 193. See also indigenous religion
Palladism. See Satanism
Papal Schism, 66
Papal States, 163, 181, 185, 188
parapsychology, 8, 182, 200–3, 206–7, 209, 214, 216, 223
Paris, 64, 72, 106, 125, 168, 185–6, 194–5, 238
Pascal, Blaise, 156
Patzelt, Karl, exorcist, 216
Paul VI, Pope, 215
Peach, Edward, exorcist, 175
Pecham, John, Archbishop of Canterbury, 89, 134
Pechenino, Domenico, 188–9, 191
Peck, Scott, 221
Pelagianism, 32
Pentecostalism, 13, 210, 225, 241
Peru, exorcism in. See Incas; Inquisition, Peruvian
Phillip II, King of Spain, 113
Piacenza, Italy, 183, 217
Picinelli, Filippo, 158
Piedmont, Kingdom of, 185
Pio of Pietrelcina, 217
Pius VI, Pope, 170, 172, 181
Pius VII, Pope, 181
Pius IX, Pope, 181, 210
Pius X, Pope, 205
Pizarro, Francisco, 143
Pizarro, María, demoniac, 150
Polidori, Valerio, 109
pontifical (book), 48, 63, 64, 67, 74, 77, 84–6, 88, 91, 92, 198
popular religion, 75, 91, 92, 100, 103, 170, 172, 179, 183, 200, 222, 223, 227

Portillo, Jerónimo Ruiz de, exorcist, 150
possession
  demonic, vii, 2, 6, 10, 12, 14–16, 19, 20, 22–5, 27–9, 32, 37, 42–5, 53–5, 58, 61, 63, 65, 67–8, 70, 73, 74, 77–80, 82, 84, 88–91, 96, 100–2, 104, 106, 107, 109, 110, 115–22, 124–6, 128, 129, 136, 140, 145–9, 153, 155, 156, 158–68, 170–4, 176–9, 181, 182, 184, 186, 194–8, 200–4, 205–7, 209, 211, 213–15, 217, 219, 222, 225–30, 235–6, 241
  divine, 20
  obsession, 19–20, 110, 112, 114, 119, 159, 161, 162, 169, 197, 198, 204n, 230, 236, 238, 240
Poynter, William, Bishop, 176–7, 179
prayer. *See* deprecative exorcism
Price, Harry, 185
priests, as ministers of exorcism, 1, 6, 16, 17, 19, 31, 44, 61, 65, 70–1, 74, 80–2, 84, 87, 127, 133–5, 163, 164, 169, 189, 191, 193–4, 212, 238
Prince, Derek, 225
printing, 62, 76, 95, 102–3
Probst, Ferdinand, 6
prophecy, 20, 68, 75, 89, 122, 165, 184, 199, 218, 224–5
Protestantism, 4, 6, 11, 18, 76, 95n, 100, 102–6, 111, 122, 123, 131–3, 135–8, 153, 175, 177, 192, 203, 225. *See also* Calvinism; Huguenots; Lutheranism; Pentecostalism; Reformation
psalms, 112, 119, 169, 189, 233, 234
Pseudo-Ambrose, 13, 42
Pseudo-Dionysius, 67, 72
psychiatry. *See* mental illness
psychology, 6, 12, 21, 22, 71, 77, 78, 149, 174, 181, 195, 196, 203, 211, 215, 219, 221, 236, 238, 241
purgatory, 103, 109. *See also* ghosts

Q
Qing dynasty. *See* China, exorcism in
Quebec. *See* Canada, exorcism in
Querétaro, New Mexico, possessions of, 148–50
questioning, of demons, 77, 79, 90, 106, 122, 127–9, 173, 218, 223

R
Rahner, Karl, 214
Ramoser, Martin, exorcist, 224
Raphael, Archangel, 93
Ratzinger, Joseph. *See* Benedict XVI, Pope
Raupert, John Godfrey, 205
recusancy, 133
Reformation. *See* Protestantism
Reichenbach, John, exorcist, 227
relics, 6, 17, 65, 67, 81, 90, 100, 115, 135–6, 148, 160, 173
Renz, Arnold, exorcist, 218–19
revenants. *See* ghosts
rhetoric, exorcism as, 9, 36, 48, 79, 160
Ricci, Matteo, 132, 138, 139
Riccio, Victorio, 140
Riesinger, Theophilus, exorcist, 199–200
rites of exorcism
  of, 1614 (*see Rituale Romanum* (1614))
  of, 1999 23, 119, 154, 166, 193, 223–4, 229, 231–7, 240
  see also baptism, exorcism in
Rites, Sacred Congregation of, 188, 189, 211, 219

Ritter, Joseph, Archbishop of St Louis, 200
Rituale Romanum (1614), 49–51, 101, 102, 110, 112, 114, 116–20, 122, 127, 129, 134, 151, 155, 162, 164, 168–70, 171, 172, 176, 179, 188, 191, 193, 196, 199, 205, 213, 217, 218, 223, 228, 232, 233
Rocca di Corneliano, Giovanni Nasalli, Cardinal, 188–9
Rodewyk, Adolf, exorcist, 213, 216–19, 223, 240
Romanticism, 170, 174
rosary, 240
Roth, Karl, exorcist, 217

S
sacraments, 6–7, 38, 64, 92, 95, 116–17, 126
sacramentals, 6–7, 17, 64–5, 68–9, 74, 100, 104, 115, 126, 127n, 135, 158, 221, 224, 229
saints, 6, 18, 23, 29, 43, 53–6, 62, 63, 65, 67–9, 75, 77, 78, 81, 93–5, 96, 103, 112, 115–16, 133, 161, 183–4, 233
  demoniac, 25, 107, 183–4, 218
  shrines of, 17, 29, 54–5, 62, 67, 82–3, 90, 94–5, 96–7, 109n, 174, 184
  see also hagiography; relics
St Bartholomew's Hospital, London, 88, 94
St Peter's Basilica, Rome, 102–3, 189
Saldaña, Josefa de, demoniac, 149
salt, 28, 30, 31, 33, 34, 38, 82, 85, 91, 92, 93n, 95n, 111, 146, 153, 157n, 162, 225
Samarini, Francesco, 116
San Pedro, González de, 140

Santori, Giulio Antonio, Cardinal, 101, 116, 120, 134
Sarmiento, Pablo, 148
Sarum rite, 64n, 93, 134
Satan, 1, 5, 6, 11, 13–15, 23–5, 29, 30, 32–3, 34–7, 42–3, 44, 46–9, 50, 52–4, 56, 58, 59, 61–73, 75, 76, 78, 79, 83–9, 93, 94, 97, 102, 107, 109–11, 113, 115, 117, 125, 128–30, 134, 136, 137, 141, 143–6, 159–61, 163, 168, 171, 172, 174, 175, 181, 188–92, 196–200, 202, 207, 211–18, 226, 228, 229, 231–2, 234, 235, 237–41
Satan and the Apostate Angels, Exorcism of. *See* Leo XIII, exorcism of
Satanic abuse, 1, 220, 221, 226
Satanism, 3, 102, 114, 115, 117, 119, 121, 129, 131, 143, 146, 184–6, 187, 188, 191, 192, 209, 211, 220–2, 223, 225, 227, 236, 239, 240. *See also* witchcraft
Scanlan, Michael, 226–8
scepticism, 13, 130, 133, 138, 148, 153, 155, 157, 163–5, 166–8, 171, 179, 181, 182, 197, 209, 215, 216, 223, 240, 241
Scholasticism, 70, 114, 125–6, 128, 155, 167, 171, 239
Schorne, John, exorcist, 93–4
Scotland, exorcism in, 90, 132, 168–9
Second Vatican Council. *See* Vatican II
secularism, 3, 181, 184, 188, 191, 211, 216
Sempe, Jean. *See* Julio, Abbé
Sepúlveda, Juan Ginés de, 144
sexual intercourse, 61, 82, 102, 113, 121, 144–5, 149, 187, 199
sexual abuse, 108n, 120, 150–1, 197, 220n
  see also Satanic abuse
shamans, 68

Shanley, John, exorcist, 227
Sigewize, demoniac, 62, 78
Sigogne, Jean Mandé, 152–3
sin, 30, 66, 77, 87, 88, 106, 107, 158, 218
  ancestral, 45, 159, 199, 225
  see also Original Sin
sin demons, 22, 27, 30, 33, 35, 40, 42, 48, 50, 55, 79–81, 84, 190, 213, 214, 231
Singer, Maria Renata, 167
Sixtus V, Pope, 112
Slavery, 132, 143, 150, 151
Society for Psychical Research (SPR), 205
Spain, exorcism in, 112–16, 157–62, 165, 172–4, 182, 239–41. See also Inquisition, Spanish
Spiritualism, 186, 201–7, 240
Sri Lanka, exorcism in, 139, 141
Stampa, Pietro Antonio, demonologist, 109–11
Stangl, Josef, Bishop of Würzburg, 217–19
Sterzinger, Ferdinand, 171
stole (vestment), 111, 140, 146
storms, exorcism of, 147, 151
Stowe Missal, 39
Suárez, Francisco, 114–15, 126, 162, 171
Suenens, Léon-Joseph, Cardinal, 228
suffumigations, 108, 111, 115, 144
Sullivan, William L., 193
Summers, Montague, demonologist, 178, 205
Surin, Jean-Joseph, exorcist, 121, 124, 167
Switzerland, exorcism in, 69–70, 85n, 194, 216

T
Taxil, Léo, 192
telekinesis, 200, 202, 203, 206, 207
telepathy, 202, 214

Theatines, 119, 171
Thiers, Jean-Baptiste, 164–5
Thurston, Herbert, 202, 206, 209, 223
Thyraeus, Peter, demonologist, 107, 112, 115, 140, 178, 179
Titu Cusi, Inca, 144
Toledo, Juan José, exorcist, 146
Tonquédec, Joseph de, exorcist, 195
toothache, 61, 91, 92
torture, 27, 55, 129, 222
Tosos, Spain, possessions of, 172–4, 179, 182, 217
Traditio apostolica, 30–1, 40
Trent, Council of, 3, 100, 106, 116, 119, 120, 133
Trujillo, María, demoniac, 146
Tupac Amaru, Inca, 144
Turnout, William, 79–80
Tydi, exorcist, 81
Tyrell, George, 192

U
Ultramontanism, 175, 179
unclean spirits. *See* sin demons
Unification Church ('Moonies'), 227
Umbanda, 151
Umzinto, possessions of, 196–8

V
Valcarenghi, Paolo, 166, 167
Valentinus, 30
Vallées, Marie des, 124
Valverde, Vincente de, 143
Van de Velde, Jason, 125
Van Neercassel, Johannes, Bishop, 138
Varo, Francisco, 140
Vaughan, Diana. *See* Taxil, Léo Vaughan, Herbert, Cardinal Archbishop of Westminster, 204
Vergote, Antoine, 238
Vianney, Jean-Marie, exorcist, 183–4

Victricius of Rouen, 55
violence, in exorcism, 28, 41, 42, 78, 136, 145, 156, 162, 173, 182, 199, 200, 203–5, 216, 227. *See also* torture
Vintras, Eugene, 186
Visconti, Zaccaria, 110, 163
Vogl, Carl, 199–200
Vollmer, Joan, demoniac, 227
Voltaire, 171–2
vomiting, 118, 135, 148, 151, 166, 183
Voragine, Jacques de, 9
Vosmeer, Sasbout, Bishop, 138

W

Waite, Arthur Edward, 187
Warren, Ed and Loraine, exorcists, 221
water
   holy, 28, 30, 31, 36, 38–9, 68, 75, 80, 81, 83n, 84–5, 86–7, 88, 91–3, 95, 96, 111, 115, 125, 140, 146, 153, 157n, 194, 225, 229, 233, 234
   ordeal by, 86–7
Weigand, Barbara, 218
Wentworth, Jane, demoniac, 96

Wieland, Franz, 7
Wiesinger, Alois, 202, 206, 207, 209, 223
William of Auxerre, 65
witchcraft, vii, 2, 3, 9, 11, 20, 63–6, 76n, 77, 78, 96, 101, 102, 106, 107, 109–11, 112–14, 115, 118, 120–1, 124, 128, 130, 131, 133, 145–6, 148–51, 153, 156, 160–2, 167, 168, 171–4, 182, 183, 186, 197, 199, 201, 209, 218, 220n, 221–4, 226, 232, 236, 239–1
   indigenous religion defined as, 145–6
   instruments of (*maleficalia*), 15, 110–11, 118, 145, 161, 162, 222
   see also pacts, demonic; Satanism
women. *See* gender
worms, 39, 69
Wyclif, John, 92, 93n

X

Xavier, Francis, 115–16

Y

Yvelin, Pierre, 129

GPSR Compliance

The European Union's (EU) General Product Safety Regulation (GPSR) is a set of rules that requires consumer products to be safe and our obligations to ensure this.

If you have any concerns about our products, you can contact us on

ProductSafety@springernature.com

In case Publisher is established outside the EU, the EU authorized representative is:

Springer Nature Customer Service Center GmbH
Europaplatz 3
69115 Heidelberg, Germany

www.ingramcontent.com/pod-product-compliance
Ingram Content Group UK Ltd.
Pitfield, Milton Keynes, MK11 3LW, UK
UKHW022236230426
12048UKWH00018BA/1294